Big Data Analytics (Database Management Systems)

Big Data Analytics (Database Management Systems)

Edited by **Conor Suarez**

WILLFORD **P**RESS

New York

Published by Willford Press,
118-35 Queens Blvd., Suite 400,
Forest Hills, NY 11375, USA
www.willfordpress.com

Big Data Analytics (Database Management Systems)
Edited by Conor Suarez

International Standard Book Number: 978-1-68285-180-7 (Hardback)

Printed in the United States of America.

Contents

Preface

Big data is a broad term that defines the structured or unstructured data sets. It is a challenging field which includes analysis, transfer and visualization of data. This book presents in-depth description of various dimensions of big data analysis like complexity and variability. It elucidates the handling and storing of data through database management systems. It examines the challenges involved in big data analysis including data mining tools and techniques. Students and professionals engaged in this field will find this book beneficial.

This book is a comprehensive compilation of works of different researchers from varied parts of the world. It includes valuable experiences of the researchers with the sole objective of providing the readers (learners) with a proper knowledge of the concerned field. This book will be beneficial in evoking inspiration and enhancing the knowledge of the interested readers.

In the end, I would like to extend my heartiest thanks to the authors who worked with great determination on their chapters. I also appreciate the publisher's support in the course of the book. I would also like to deeply acknowledge my family who stood by me as a source of inspiration during the project.

Editor

A big data methodology for categorising technical support requests using Hadoop and Mahout

Arantxa Duque Barrachina[1] and Aisling O'Driscoll[2*]

* Correspondence:
aisling.odriscoll@cit.ie
[2]Department of Computing, Cork
Institute of Technology, Cork, Ireland
Full list of author information is
available at the end of the article

Abstract

Technical Support call centres frequently receive several thousand customer queries on a daily basis. Traditionally, such organisations discard data related to customer enquiries within a relatively short period of time due to limited storage capacity. However, in recent years, the value of retaining and analysing this information has become clear, enabling call centres to identify customer patterns, improve first call resolution and maximise daily closure rates. This paper proposes a Proof of Concept (PoC) end to end solution that utilises the Hadoop programming model, extended ecosystem and the Mahout Big Data Analytics library for categorising similar support calls for large technical support data sets. The proposed solution is evaluated on a VMware technical support dataset.

Keywords: Big data analytics; Distributed clustering; Parallelised programming; Hadoop; HBase; Hive; Mahout; Support call center

Introduction

In recent years, there has been an unprecedented increase in the quantity and variety of data generated worldwide. According to the IDC's Digital Universe study, the world's information is doubling every two years and is predicted to reach 40ZB by 2020 (Digital Universe Study (on behalf of EMC Corporation) [1]). This increase in data, often referred to as a "data tsunami", is driven by the proliferation of social media along with an increase in mobile and networked devices (the Internet of Things), finance and online retail as well as advances in the physical and life sciences sectors. As evidence of this, the online microblogging service Twitter, processes approximately 12 TB of data per day, while Facebook receives more than five hundred million likes per day (McKinsey Global Institute [2]). In addition, the Cisco Internet Business Solutions Group (IBSG) predicts that there will be 25 billion devices connected to the Internet by 2015 and 50 billion by 2020 (Cisco Internet Business Solutions Group (IBSG) [3]). Such vast datasets are commonly referred to as "Big Data". Big Data is characterised not only by its volume, but by a rich mix of data types and formats (variety) and it's time sensitive nature which marks a deviation from traditional batch processing (velocity) (Karmasphere [4]). These characteristics are commonly referred to as the 3 V's.

Traditional distributed systems and databases are no longer suitable to effectively capture, store, manage and analyse this data and exhibit limited scalability. Furthermore, relational databases support structured data by imposing a strict schema; however, data growth is currently driven by unstructured data by a factor of 20:1 (Karmasphere [5]). Finally, data warehouses are no longer able to process whole datasets due to their massive size; hence the information stored in these solutions is no longer statistically representative of the data from which it was extracted, making the data analytics performed on it less reliable. Big Data requires new architectures designed for scalability, resilience and efficient parallel processing.

As a result, big data processing and management (capturing and storing big data) has gained significant attention in recent years e.g. the MapReduce paradigm. However it is now recognised that it is necessary to further develop platforms that can harness these technologies in order to gain meaningful insight and to make more informed business decisions. The implementation of data analytics on such datasets is commonly referred to as *big data analytics*. Data mining and machine learning techniques are currently used across a wide range of industries to aid organisations in optimising their business, reduce risks and increase profitability. Sectors employing these techniques include retailers, banking institutions and insurance companies as well as health related fields (Huang et al. [6]; Lavrac et al. [7]). In the current marketplace big data analytics has become a business requirement for many organisations looking to gain a competitive advantage as evidenced by IBM's 2011 Global CIO study that places business intelligence and analytics as the main focus for CIOs over the next five years, on top of virtualisation and cloud computing (IBM [8]).

Importantly, this has further been recognised in the technical support space of leading technology multinationals, as call centres have begun to explore the application of data analytics as a way to streamline the business and gain insight regarding customer's expectations, a necessity in an industry challenged by economic pressures and increased competition (Aberdeen Group [9]). Thus this paper;s contributions are two-fold:

- An end to end proof of concept solution based entirely on open source components is described that can be used to process and analyse large technical support datasets to categorise similar technical support calls and identify likely resolutions. The proposed solution utilises the Hadoop distributed data processing platform, extended ecosystem and parallelised clustering techniques using the Mahout library. It is envisaged that if such a solution was deployed in commercial environments with large technical support datasets, updated on a daily basis, it would expedite case resolution and accuracy to maximise daily closure rates by providing similar case resolutions to staff when a new technical support case is received. If achieved, the reduction of resolution time would also ultimately aid technical support teams to increase customer satisfaction and prevent churn. Furthermore this solution could also be used to identify the most problematic product features and highlight staff knowledge gaps leading to more directed staff training programmes.
- Secondly an evaluation of the performance and accuracy of parallelised clustering algorithms for analysing a distributed data set is conducted using a real-world technical support dataset.

The rest of this paper is organised as follows: Section II describes the algorithms and technologies underpinning the proposed architecture along with related work in this

Section III outlines the architecture and implementation of the proposed technical support analytics platform. Section V details the performance evaluation and analysis of the proposed solution with Section VI outlining final conclusions.

Background & literature review

A brief overview of the constituent technologies is now provided. The need for efficient, scale out solutions to support partial component failures and provide data consistency motivated the development of the *Google File System (GFS)* (Ghemawat et al. [10]) and the *MapReduce* (Dean & Ghemawat [11]) paradigm in the early 2000s. The premise behind the Google File System and MapReduce is to distribute data across the commodity servers such that computation of data is performed where the data is stored. This approach eliminates the need to transfer the data over the network to be processed. Furthermore, methods for ensuring the resilience of the cluster and load balancing of processing were specified. GFS and MapReduce form the basis for the *Apache Hadoop* project, comprising two main architectural components: the *Hadoop Distributed File System (HDFS)* and *Hadoop MapReduce* (Apache Hadoop [12]). HDFS (Shvachko et al. [13]) is the distributed storage component of Hadoop with participating nodes following a master/slave architecture. All files stored in HDFS are split into blocks which are replicated and distributed across different slave nodes on the cluster known as *data nodes*, with a master node, called the *name node*, maintaining metadata e.g. blocks comprising a file, where in the cluster these blocks are located and so on. MapReduce (Bhandarkar [14]) is the distributed compute component of Hadoop. MapReduce jobs are controlled by a software daemon known as the *JobTracker*. A job is a full MapReduce program, including a complete execution of Map and Reduce tasks over a dataset. The MapReduce paradigm also relies on a master/slave architecture. The *JobTracker* runs on the master node and assigns *Map* and *Reduce* tasks to the slave nodes in the cluster. The slave nodes run another software daemon called the *Task-Tracker* that is responsible for actually instantiating the Map or Reduce tasks and reporting the progress back to the JobTracker.

The extended Hadoop ecosystem includes a growing list of solutions that integrate or expand Hadoop's capabilities. *Mahout* is an open source machine learning library built on top of Hadoop to provide distributed analytics capabilities (Apache Mahout [15]). Mahout incorporates a wide range of data mining techniques including collaborative filtering, classification and clustering algorithms. Of relevance to this paper, Mahout supports a wide variety of clustering algorithms including: k-means, canopy clustering, fuzzy k-means, Dirichlet Clustering and Latent Dirichlet Allocation. *HBase* is a distributed column-oriented database that resides on top of Hadoop's Distributed File System, providing real-time read/write random-access to very large datasets (Apache Hbase [16]). Additionally, *Hive* defines a simple SQL-like query language, called HiveQL, to abstract the complexity of writing MapReduce jobs from users. Hive transforms HiveQL queries into MapReduce jobs for execution on a cluster (Apache Hive [17]).

While research associated with machine learning algorithms is well established, research on big data analytics and large scale distributed machine learning is very much in its infancy with libraries such as Mahout still undergoing considerable development. However some initial experimentation has been undertaken in this area.

Esteves et. al studied the use of Mahout k-means clustering on a 1.1GB data set of TCP dumps from an airforce LAN, while examining clustering scalability and quality (Esteves et al. [18]). The authors subsequently evaluated the applications of k-means and fuzzy c-means clustering on an 11GB Wikipedia dataset with respect to clustering algorithm and system performance (Esteves & Rong [19]). However in contrast to this work, the authors of this paper consider a 32GB dataset, the impact of five clustering algorithms and, most importantly, provide a complete end to end solution including data pre-processing, daily upload of new data, real-time access and a user interface by using the extended Hadoop ecosystem. Ericson et.al use the 1987 Reuters dataset, one of the most widely used text categorisation data sets containing approximately 21,578 documents, to evaluate clustering algorithms over Hadoop but also over their own runtime environment, Granules (Ericson & Palliekara [20]). While the performance of four clustering algorithms was evaluated, the primary evaluation concentrated on the underlying runtime environment and unlike the proposed architecture, a complete end to end solution was not provided as a clean data set was used.

In contrast, the end to end framework presented in this paper successfully integrates Hadoop and Mahout to provide a fully functional end to end solution that addresses a real world problem, facilitating the streamlining of call centre operations and evaluating multiple clustering algorithms in terms of timeliness and accuracy.

Research design and methodology

The proposed solution provides an end to end solution for conducting large scale analysis of technical support data using the open source Hadoop platform, components of the Hadoop Extended Ecosystem such as HBase and Hive and clustering algorithms from the extended Mahout library. Figure 1 illustrates the architecture of the proposed analytics solution.

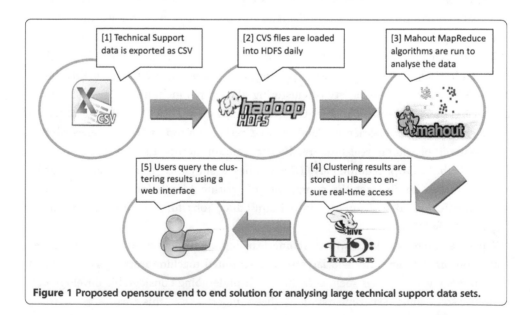

Figure 1 Proposed opensource end to end solution for analysing large technical support data sets.

Data pre processing

To allow technical support data to be processed by Mahout, it must be uploaded to HDFS and converted in text vectors. The VMware technical support data under consideration in this paper is stored in the cloud Software as a Service (SaaS) application, Salesforce, a popular Customer Relationship Management (CRM) service. Thus a Hadoop job is devised to convert the technical support data exported from Salesforce in CSV format into Hadoop *SequenceFile* format. A Hadoop Sequence File is a flat file data structure consisting of binary key/value pairs. Hadoop mappers employ an *InputReader* to parse input keys and values, which the *mapper* task subsequently processes before outputting another set of keys and values. As the default Hadoop *InputReader* is the *TextInputFormat* where every line of text represents a record, this is not applicable for CSV format as technical support calls span multiple lines. Thus a custom *input record reader* and *partitioner* were required in the proposed solution. This custom *input record reader* accumulates text from the input file until it reaches a specified end of record marker. As the *mapper* requires a key and value, the *value* is the resultant text from the *input record reader*, including the support call identifier and support call description. The *key* is set to the position in the file of that record i.e. the byte offset. The *mapper* extracts the support call identifier (passed to the *reducer* as the key) and the support call description (passed to *reducer* as the value). Finally, the *reducer* receives

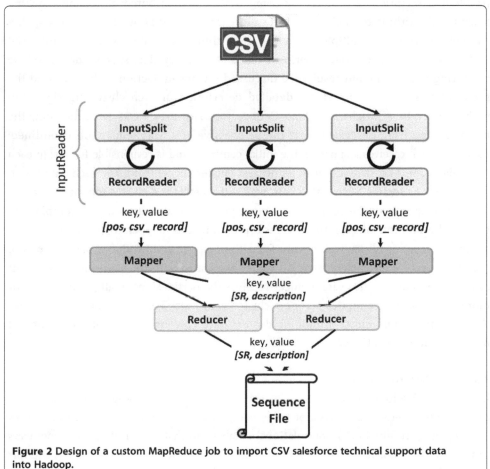

Figure 2 Design of a custom MapReduce job to import CSV salesforce technical support data into Hadoop.

these key/value pairs and writes them into a Hadoop *SequenceFile* format so they can be further processed using Mahout. Figure 2 illustrates this process by displaying the anatomy of the custom developed MapReduce job, illustrating input and output keys and values. SR represents the Service/Support Request.

Automated periodic refresh of new technical support data

As technical support data sets will be updated daily with new solutions derived, a mechanism to automatically update the technical support data from which the clustered results are derived to ensure accurate output is required. Given the nature of the data, it is sufficient to perform such a procedure on a daily basis. To avoid uploading the entire technical support data set on a daily basis, a cron job can be scheduled to automatically backup the changes that occurred over the preceding 24 hours. It is proposed that a separate Hadoop job is responsible for uploading the CSV files containing the details of the support requests received that day into HDFS.

Parallelised clustering

In order for data to be processed by the Mahout clustering algorithms, it must first be converted to vector format. Technical support data stored in HDFS is converted into vectors using Mahout's existing command line for subsequent clustering analysis. Importantly, the challenge of identifying related support calls based on their problem description is resolved by using Mahout's distributed clustering machine learning algorithms to analyse the data set, thereby identifying support calls with a similar description. Multiple clustering algorithms are evaluated in the proposed system with respect to system performance and accuracy. The specific details of the clustering evaluation and results are discussed further in Section V. It is beyond the scope of this paper to provide a detailed description of each clustering algorithm with respect to a parallelized Map Reduce job. However to as an indication, the k-means algorithm described from the perspective of a MapReduce job is outlined: Each map task receives a subset of the initial centroids and is responsible for assign each input data-point i.e. text vector to its nearest cluster i.e. centroid. For each data point, the mapper generates a key/value pair, where the key is the cluster identifier and the value corresponds to the coordinates of that point. The algorithm uses a combiner to reduce the amount of data to be transferred from the mapper to the reducer. The combiner receives all key/value pairs from the mapper and produces partial sums of the input vectors for each cluster. All values associated with the same cluster are sent to the same reducer, thus each reducer receives the partial sums of all points of one or more clusters and computes the new cluster centroids. The driver program iterates over the points and clusters until all clusters have converged or until the maximum number of iterations has been reached.

Real-time platform access

Importantly, Hadoop does not provide real-time access and is designed for batch processing. Thus, once the analysis phase is completed, a Hadoop MapReduce job stores the clustering results into a non-relational database so that technical support engineers can query the information in real-time. The information stored includes the support call number, the cluster identifier and the probability of that support call belonging to a given cluster. Given its native integration with Hadoop, HBase has been chosen for this purpose. When an engineer requests the support calls related to a particular case, the cluster to which such a case should belong is identified in HBase, with all support calls within that cluster sorted based on their cluster membership probability. An ordered list containing the support call identifier and its associated cluster membership probability is returned to the technical support engineer. The support calls displayed at the top of such list are more likely to contain similar problems to the specified unresolved technical support case and as a result are more likely to share the same resolution. Figure 3 illustrates this step in the solution by displaying the anatomy of the custom developed MapReduce job, illustrating input and output keys and values.

User query of results

Finally, it should be noted that directly querying HBase to obtain similar support calls is not user friendly and is technically complex requiring the development of a MapReduce job. To overcome this, HBase has been integrated with Hive. Such an approach allows technical support engineers to obtain similar support calls from a web-based interface that generates HiveQL to query the clustering results derived from Mahout. It can be envisaged

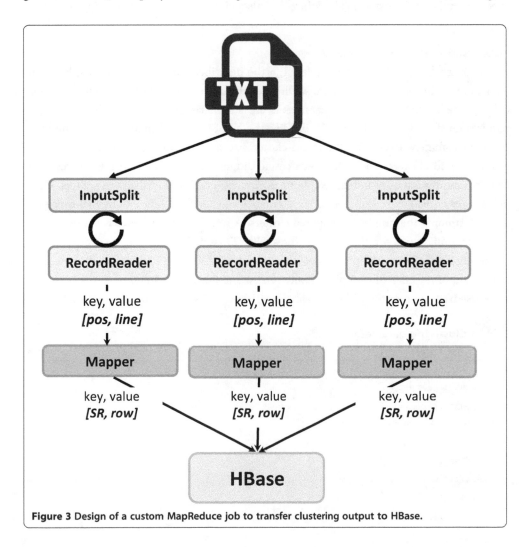

Figure 3 Design of a custom MapReduce job to transfer clustering output to HBase.

that this proof of concept web interface could be easily enhanced for integration with existing BI tools and to provide advanced technical support dashboards.

This section has outlined an end to end, open source proof of concept solution to transform, process, analyse and identify resolutions to similar technical support calls given an open case. A VMware technical support dataset is now analysed using five of Mahout's distributed clustering algorithms. The output from each of these algorithms outlining the impact of the nuances of each clustering algorithm as well as their performance is now discussed.

Results and discussion

The implemented solution outlined in the previous Section is now evaluated using a real-world VMware technical support data set of approximately 0.032 TB. This is based on an average call size of 60 KB from 4 main call centres, with an estimated 1900 calls per week. The four node Hadoop cluster is based on commodity hardware with each node following the same configuration: 8GB RAM; 2 TB hard drive; 4 MB Cache; 1 CPU Intel Core i7; 2 cores at 2.20 GHz; Onboard 100Mbps LAN; Linux CentOS with Hadoop v0.20 and Mahout v0.5.The evaluation is discussed with respect to the processing performance of the specific parallelized clustering algorithms and also with respect to the clustering accuracy.

Parallelised clustering performance

Five clustering algorithms are considered in the described evaluation: k-means, k-means with canopy clustering, fuzzy k-means, Dirichlet allocation and Latent Dirichlet Allocation (LDA). The employed clustering parameters are summarised in Table 1. The number of required clusters, k, was estimated by dividing the number of total support calls in the sample, approximately 10,000, by the target cluster size of 250 support calls, resulting in an estimate of 40 clusters. The well-known cosine distance is used as distance measures such as Euclidean distance are influenced by the document length rather than the content. Canopy clustering was next explored as an alternative method of creating the initial centroids and determining the number of required clusters. A well-known challenge is the derivation of meaningful values for the distance thresholds $T1$ and $T2$. Multiple executions of the clustering algorithm found that values of 1.0 and 1.4 for $T1$ and $T2$ respectively generated a meaningful number of canopies of between 20 and 50, with resultant canopy centroids were used as an input for the k-means algorithm. The fuzzy k-means *fuzziness factor*

Table 1 Clustering parameters

Parameter	Value
k (k-means)	40
$T1$ (Canopy clustering)	1.0
$T2$ (Canopy clustering)	1.4
Fuzziness Factor (Fuzzy-kmeans)	1.05
Dirichlet Clusters	50
Max Dirichlet Iterations	10
LDA Clusters	50
Words in Corpus	12886
Max LDA Iterations	30

Table 2 Mahout algorithms and their execution times

Algorithm	Mahout command	Fixed clusters	Partial membership	Execution Time (ms)
K-means	kmeans	Y	N	61096
Canopy	canopy	Y	N	121178
K-means	kmeans			
Fuzzy k-means	fkmeans	Y	Y	644471
Dirichlet	dirichlet	N	Y	15011080
LDA	lda	Y	Y	3373535

determines the degree of overlap between the generated clusters and analysis of the evaluated data set found that a value of 1.05 generated well-defined and differentiated clusters. To provide consistency with canopy clustering, Dirichlet clustering also specified 50 clusters with 50 topics also specified for LDA.

Table 2 summarises the characteristics of the clustering algorithms available in Mahout and their incurred execution times on the 4 node cluster. The simplicity and scalability of the k-means and canopy clustering algorithm result in very low execution times of approximately 1 minute and 2 minutes respectively. More complex clustering techniques such as fuzzy k-means and in particular Dirichlet clustering and Latent Dirichlet Allocation incur significantly higher execution times of over 10 minutes, approximately 4 hours and 56 minutes respectively. The execution delays experienced by the LDA clustering algorithm are dependent on the number of words in the corpus. LDA calculations are CPU intensive when performed on large datasets such as the support calls under study. The CPU utilisation of the slave nodes of the Hadoop cluster was analysed using the 'top' command (measures CPU utilisation, process statistics and memory utilisation) while running the LDA algorithm. Hadoop slave nodes showed an average CPU utilisation of

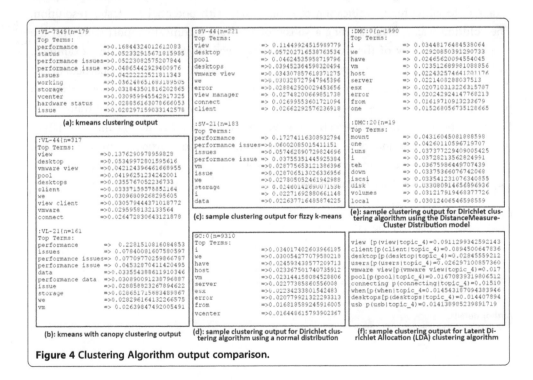

Figure 4 Clustering Algorithm output comparison.

99.2% during this period. Thus it can be determined that k-means or fuzzy k-means offers better performance and scalability with comparable clustering results as discussed in the next section.

The output of the clustering algorithms is now examined as well as the accuracy of the clusters.. Figure 4 shows the output of all considered clustering algorithms for clusters including support calls related to "performance" issues. It can be noted that the results are quite similar for k-means, k-means with a pre-processing step using canopy clustering and fuzzy k-means. The number of support calls included in the clusters are comparable using all techniques. The output of the probabilistic clustering algorithms is the most applicable but given the prohibitive delays incurred with Dirichlet, the output of the LDA clustering algorithm is deemed the most appropriate with the relevant generated topics problems matched with those frequently encountered by VMware customers. However, it can be noted that current clustering output has limitations. The relevance of the output is limited. This problem is not related to the proposed system so much as the method used to generate the text vectors. At present, Mahout only supports TF or TF-IDF weighting (Owen et al. [21]). Although TD-IDF weighting was used to convert the support calls descriptions into vectors, stop words still appeared in the clustering results. While not currently supported in Mahout, more advanced techniques exist to transform text documents into vectors is required. As described in (Soucy & Mineau [22]), supervised weighting methods such as *Gain Ratio* based on statistical confidence intervals could be used to improve the quality of the text vectors and, as a consequence, the clustering results. Furthermore it is necessary to consider collocation.

Conclusions

The research presented in this paper presents a complete open source solution for processing and categorisation of similar service calls within large technical supports data sets to allow for identification of similar calls with potential for faster resolution. The solution was evaluated using a subset of VMware technical support data with the output and accuracy of the five commonly employed clustering algorithms examined. Although, this paper discusses the analysis of VMware support data in particular, the described techniques and procedures are generally applicable to other organisations providing similar services, thereby providing a proof of concept Industry framework. Future work will examine alternative text vectorisation methods to TD and TD-IDF to further improve the quality of the clustering results and to consider word collocation. Additionally, orchestration tools such as Oozie could be considered to automate the steps required to identify related support calls.

Competing interests
The authors declare that they have no competing interests.

Authors' contributions
ADB designed the study, developed the methodology, implemented the system, performed the analysis and evaluation and wrote the manuscript. AOD supervised the project. Both authors read and approved the final manuscript.

Author details
[1]VMware, Inc, Cork, Ireland. [2]Department of Computing, Cork Institute of Technology, Cork, Ireland.

References

1. Digital Universe Study (on behalf of EMC Corporation) (2012) Big Data, Bigger Digital Shadows, and Biggest Growth in the Far East. In: http://idcdocserv.com/1414
2. McKinsey Global Institute (2011) Big data: The next frontier for innovation, competition, and productivity. In: http://www.mckinsey.com/insights/business_technology/big_data_the_next_frontier_for_innovation
3. Cisco Internet Business Solutions Group (IBSG) (2011) The Internet of Things: How the Next Evolution of the Internet is Changing Everything. In: http://www.cisco.com/web/about/ac79/docs/innov/IoT_IBSG_0411FINAL.pdf
4. Karmasphere (2011) Deriving Intelligence from Big Data in Hadoop: A Big Data Analytics Primer.
5. Karmasphere (2011) Understanding the Elements of Big Data: More than a Hadoop Distribution.
6. Huang DW, Sherman BT, Lempicki RA (2009) Systematic and integrative analysis of large gene lists using DAVID Bioinformatics Resources. Nat Protoc 4(1):44–57
7. Lavrac N, Keravnou E, Zupan B (2000) Intelligent data analysis in medicine. In: Encyclopaedia of Computer Science and Technology, vol 42. pp 113–157
8. IBM (2011) The Essential CIO. In: http://www-935.ibm.com/services/uk/cio/pdf/CIE03073-GBEN-01.pdf
9. Aberdeen Group (2010) Unlocking Business Intelligence in the Contract Center.
10. Ghemawat S, Gobioff H, Leung S (2003) The Google File System. In: SOSP '03 Proceedings of the 19th ACM symposium on Operating Systems Principles., vol 6. ACM, pp 10-10. http://dl.acm.org/citation.cfm?id=945450.
11. Dean J, Ghemawat S (2004) MapReduce: Simplified Data Processing on Large Clusters. OSDI' 04 Proceedings of the 6th symposium on Operating System Design and Implementation, San Francisco, CA Vol 6. pp 10-10. http://dl.acm.org/citation.cfm?id=1251264.
12. Apache Hadoop (2012), http://hadoop.apache.org/
13. Shvachko K, Kuang H, Radia S, Chansler R (2010) The Hadoop Distributed File System. In: IEEE 26th Symposium on Mass Storage Systems and Technologies (MSST' 10). ACM pp 1–10. http://dl.acm.org/citation.cfm?id=1914427.
14. Bhandarkar M (2010) MapReduce programming with apache Hadoop. In: IEEE 24th International Symposium on Parallel & Distributed Processing (IPDPS' 10)
15. Apache Mahout (2012), https://mahout.apache.org/
16. Apache Hbase (2012), http://hbase.apache.org/
17. Apache Hive (2012), http://hive.apache.org/
18. Esteves RM, Pais R, Rong C (2011) K-means Clustering in the Cloud – A Mahout Test. In: IEEE International Conference on Advanced Information Networking and Applications (WAINA '11). IEEE pp 514–519. http://www.ieeeexplore.us/xpl/articleDetails.jsp?tp=&arnumber=6133195&queryText%3Desteves+clustering+wikipedia.
19. Esteves RM, Rong C (2011) Using Mahout for Clustering Wikipedia's Latest Articles: A Comparison between K-means and Fuzzy C-means in the Cloud. In: IEEE Third International Conference on Cloud Computing Technology and Science (CloudCom '11). IEEE pp 565–569. http://www.ieeeexplore.us/xpl/articleDetails.jsp?tp=&arnumber=5763553&queryText%3Desteves+K-means+Clustering+in+the+Cloud+%E2%80%93+A+Mahout+Test.
20. Ericson K, Pallickara S (2012) On the Performance of High Dimensional Data Clustering and Classification Algorithms. Elsevier Future Generation Computer Systems, Available from: http://dl.acm.org/citation.cfm?id=2435540
21. Owen S, Anil R, Dunning T, Friedman E, Manning Publications (2012) Mahout in action. Chapter 8. Shelter Island, N.Y, pp 130–144
22. Soucy P, Mineau GW (2005) Beyond TFIIDF Weighting for Text Categorization in the Vector Space Model. In: Proceedings of the 19th International Joint Conference on Artificial Intelligence (IJCAI '05). ACM pp 1130–1135. http://dl.acm.org/citation.cfm?id=1642474.

Cultivating a research agenda for data science

Chris A Mattmann[1,2]

Correspondence:
chris.a.mattmann@nasa.gov
[1] Jet Propulsion Laboratory,
California Institute of Technology,
4800 Oak Grove Drive M/S 171-264,
91109 Pasadena, USA
[2] Computer Science Department,
University of Southern California,
941 W. 37th Place, 90089 Los
Angeles, USA

Abstract

I describe a research agenda for data science based on a decade of research and operational work in data-intensive systems at NASA, the University of Southern California, and in the context of open source work at the Apache Software Foundation. My vision is predicated on understanding the architecture for grid computing; on flexible and automated approaches for selecting data movement technologies and on their use in data systems; on the recent emergence of cloud computing for processing and storage, and on the unobtrusive and automated integration of scientific algorithms into data systems. Advancements in each of these areas are a core need, and they will fundamentally improve our understanding of data science, and big data. This paper identifies and highlights my own personal experience and opinion growing into a data scientist.

Keywords: Data dissemination; Open source; Science algorithm integration; Data science; Software architecture; Big data

Findings

Over the last decade I have been primarily engaged in research associated with NASA's Jet Propulsion Laboratory (JPL), the University of Southern California and the Apache Software Foundation. The research has explored the fundamentally changing paradigm of data-intensive systems and its emerging frontier of *Big Data* and *Data Science*, and on how software architecture and software reuse can assist in bridging the boundary in science from a previously silo'ed and independent nature to one that is increasingly more collaborative, and multi-disciplinary. This research has been applied in the development and delivery of ground data systems software for a number of national scale projects including the next generation of NASA's Earth science missions (OCO/OCO-2, NPP Sounder PEATE, SMAP, etc.); the National Cancer Institute's Early Detection Research Network (EDRN), NSF funded activities in geosciences, and radio astronomy, and also in the recent context of DARPA's BigData initiative called XDATA.

This paper identifies and highlights my own personal experience growing into a *data scientist*. I begin by describing a nexus of training in grid computing and software architecture inspired through work on the Apache Object Oriented Data Technology (OODT) project. A need to compare OODT with similar grid technologies led to precise and specific architectural analyses of grid software and an effort to more completely describe the architecture of grid computing based on a study of nearly twenty topical grid technologies over the last decade. This analysis identified gaps in the grid computing realm, specifically in the areas of data management, and in cataloging and archiving. Grid computing systems required stronger support for file and metadata management, for workflow processing and for resource management. Furthermore grid systems needed stronger approaches for automated ingestion, for remote content acquisition and for science algorithm integration, *unobtrusively* and *rapidly*. I describe the contributions made in these areas, and the influence that the web search engine community and open source community had on my specific contributions. Cloud computing and its benefits for processing and storage are described in the context of my experience studying data movement and in comparing science processing approaches. I identify the importance of open source communities and of open source foundations including the Apache Software Foundation as well.

Drawing upon the above background, I close with my vision for data science, in the form of four specific areas where fundamental and advanced research must be conducted. The areas are: (1) Rapid Algorithm Integration; (2) Intelligent Data Movement; (3) Use of Clod Computing; and (4) Use of Open Source as a mechanism to bringing the new architectures and contributions to the masses. These areas are influenced by my personal experience and this provenance is highlighted in the conclusion of the paper.

Apache OODT: a data science learning environment

My work has focused on the nexus between software architecture and grid computing, with an eye towards empirically evaluating data movement technologies and developing approaches for rapidly and automatically assessing their suitability for scientific data dissemination scenarios [1-3] in the context of the Apache OODT project [4]. Apache OODT is an open source, data-grid middleware used across many scientific domains, such as astronomy, climate science, snow hydrology, planetary science, defense and intelligence systems, cancer research, and computer modeling, simulation and visualization. The framework itself contains over 10 years of work and 100+ FTEs of investment and holds the distinction as NASA's *first ever* project to be stewarded at the open source Apache Software Foundation. Apache is a 501(c)(3) non-profit focused on developing world-class software for no charge to the public and is home to the some of the most prolific and well-known software technologies including the Apache HTTPD web-server that powers the majority share (53%) of the Internet; as well as emerging *Big Data* technologies that I have helped to pioneer including Apache Nutch, Apache Hadoop, Apache Tika, and Apache Lucene/Solr. I am currently a member of Apache's *Board of Directors* for the 2013-14 term. My experience at Apache and within OODT has influenced research agenda item (4) Use of Open Source, described later in the *Looking towards the future* section of the paper.

Drawing inspiration from the grid

While studying grid computing and data-intensive systems including OODT, I found that little software engineering and architecture research work was performed to characterize the architectural properties of grid computing, besides the initial pioneering work by Kesselman and Foster to define the grid's *anatomy* [5], and *physiology* [6], respectively. Namely, the grid's reference requirements, its detailed physical architecture and mapping to implementation technologies was missing – especially considering that so many technologies (including OODT) claimed to be a "grid" technology. So, I undertook several studies to develop automated approaches for discerning the grid's reference architecture and requirements, and its detailed as-implemented architecture as evidenced from code, requirements, free-text documentation, and other information from over 20+ topical open source software systems claiming to be a grid. The initial study I published in 2005 [7] at the *Component-based Software Engineering* conference represented early work only focusing on 5 of the eventual 20 technologies and only on the approach for automatically recovering a grid's architecture – four years later I expanded the work [8] and actually identified a new grid reference architecture, demonstrating how the as-recovered architectures of grid technologies better mapped to it when compared with the original grid's anatomy and physiology. An expanded version of this work is currently under review with *J. Grid Computing*. Our work in identifying a more descriptive grid architecture strong suggests that current architectures and software may not be appropriate and that new architectural approaches and paradigms will be needed in the Big Data domain.

I took the knowledge and research products from studying grid computing systems and better defining their architecture and applied this to the design of several national scale systems across scientific domains. In particular, from 2005-2009, I led the development of NASA's Orbiting Carbon Observatory (OCO) ground data system, as well as the National Polar Orbiter Earth System Satellite (NPOESS) Preparatory Project (NPP) and its Sounder data Product Evaluation and Testbed Element (PEATE), two next generation data systems that took NASA into the realm of *Big Data*. The prior NASA Earth science missions that I had worked on (QuickSCAT/Seawinds) had a database catalog and archive that grew to 10 gigabytes after ten years of operations/extended mission – OCO's catalog and archive would eclipse 150+ terabytes within the *first three months of operations*. QuickSCAT/Seawinds regularly processed in the order of tens of jobs per day – OCO and NPP PEATE would eclipse tens of *thousands* of jobs per day. The application of OODT to these science data systems and the specific architectural description of grid computing derived from the study of grid technologies has influenced research agenda item (3) to better understand cloud computing; and also agenda item (4) the use of open source software to construct these data systems described later in the *Looking towards the future* section of the paper.

Flexible cataloging and archiving

The requirements and shift in paradigm for OCO and NPP PEATE led me to lead a large refactoring and modernization of the Apache OODT data processing subsystem called CAS (for "Catalog and Archive System"). The OODT CAS, under my leadership, underwent a series of changes.

First, I separated the CAS from a monolithic component that handled both aspects of file and metadata management, and split that component into its constituent functionalities – a *File Manager* component to handle ingestion; data movement, and cataloging/archiving of files and metadata – and a *Workflow Manager* component to model data and control flow; tasks, their execution and lifecycle, and workflow metadata. In large part the efforts to refactor the Workflow Manager component were based on the pioneering research by Dr. Raj Buyya, and his Taxonomy of Workflow Management Systems for Grid Computing [9]. Taking the refactoring a step further, and also expanding on my research into the Ganglia and Gexec resource management, monitoring and execution systems [10], I went ahead and expanded the CAS to also include a *Resource Manager* component, separate from the Workflow Manager, whose job was to model the requirements for job execution (e g , requires X% CPU, or requires Y disk space; or Z programming language, e.g., IDL/Python/etc., to run), and also the current monitored status (load, CPU, etc.) of the hardware and computing resources for the job to run on.

I published the results of this initial refactoring at the IEEE Space Mission Challenges for Information Technology conference with my co-authors that included computer scientists, and experts in chemistry and spectroscopy, and in climate science [11]. This particular experience has helped to influence research agenda item (1) rapid and unobtrusive science algorithm integration described later in the *Looking towards the future* section of the paper.

Drawing on the web search experience

In addition to the above initial refactoring, I also drew from my experience helping to develop Apache Nutch [12], a large-scale, distributed search engine, the predecessor to Apache Hadoop, the current industry standard Big Data technology. While developing Nutch, I contributed to (at the time, and still one of the largest and most widely used) web crawler/fetchers that existed.

Drawing upon this experience for Nutch and improving upon it, I modeled a new CAS component for OODT based upon the Nutch fetcher system – the new component was called Push Pul [13], and its responsibility was to negotiate the myriad web and other protocols for acquiring remote content available both on the web, from FTP servers, and from other data servers accessible from a URL protocol scheme. Different from Nutch, I designed Push Pull to separate its remote content acquisition functionality from the actual ingestion and crawling process. This was in direct response to real world experience and also drawing upon my software architecture experience and research when I realized that remote content acquisition is a large enough and complex enough functionality to warrant its own separate stack of services.

Separating remote content acquisition from actual ingestion was also a realization of my PhD dissertation work wherein which I demonstrated that data movement and acquisition technologies experience largely different qualities of service depending on data dissemination scenarios – so by separating Push Pull as its own component, we could isolate a major potential bottleneck in a data-intensive and grid software system, allowing it to evolve independent, and be improved independently of local ingestion. So, with Push Pull in hand, I also drew from Nutch and my experience building the Apache Tika [14] content detection and analysis framework to construct the CAS crawler, an automated ingestion, file detection and classification technology that works in concert with Push Pull to ingest remote and local content. During this time I also co-wrote a full book on Apache Tika published by Manning and one that I use to teach CSCI 572. Search Engines and Information Retrieval at USC.

The work in this area especially in remote content acquisition has helped to bring the importance of research agenda item (2) intelligent data movement and the need for a better understanding of existing remote content acquisition systems and data delivery methods described later in the *Looking towards the future* section of the paper.

Computing the same way the scientists do

The other major research contribution I delivered based on the OODT CAS was the development of a software framework for rapid science algorithm integration. The new system, called "CAS PGE" [15] codifies a single step in the overall scientific process as a workflow task and leverages Apache OODT, Apache Tika, Apache Solr and other Big Data software systems that I have helped to principally construct.

CAS-PGE uses these software to stage file input and metadata; to allow for automatically selected and optimal data movement services; to seamlessly execute IDL, Matlab, Python, R and other custom scientific codes; to perform automatic metadata and text extraction from the scientific algorithm outputs; and finally to capture of workflow provenance and metadata as produced by the algorithm.

The CAS-PGE framework has proven to be an effective encapsulation for not just the scientific step in an investigation, but also for unobtrusively integrating algorithms into large scale production workflow and Big Data systems, without having to rewrite the algorithm. This is a key insight that I developed from this work to help reduce cost and risk in scientific software and to preserve the stewardship of the algorithms in the scientific communities where they are developed. This experience has heavily influenced research agenda item (1) the rapid and unobtrusive integration of science algorithms described later in the *Looking towards the future* section of the paper.

Harnessing the cloud

I am also interested in cloud computing, and in its use for processing and storage within software systems. I have led several studies since 2010 to investigate: (1) cloud computing as a platform for data movement, and storage [16]; (2) cloud computing as a platform for scientific processing [17]; and (3) a hybrid combination of public and private cloud resources for storage, processing and for platform virtualization [18]

The contributions from these studies involved the identification of when, and where to leverage cloud in a software system's architecture; a comparison model for cloud versus local storage and processing resources, and a set of insights for delivering cloud-based virtual machines with data system software to the Earth science community. These and other contributions were disseminated at the 2011 International Conference on Software Engineering SECLOUD (Software Engineering for Cloud Computing) workshop that I chaired [19]. Experience in this area has suggested research agenda item (3) a better understanding of the implications of cloud computing for storage and processing described later in the *Looking towards the future* section of the paper.

Keeping the door open

Experience working throughout many life, physical, natural, Earth and planetary scientific domains has increased my interest in collaboration both in terms of science but also software – making it *open source* and its nexus within software reuse, and software engineering. I have led and published several topical studies exploring open source as a framework for enabling scientific collaboration, and as a framework for software reuse, including the cover feature [20] of the IEEE IT Professional magazine's special issue on NASA's contributions to IT, as well as a study published [21] exploring the role of open source in NASA's program called ESDIS, for Earth Science Data and Information System, the program under which the Earth science Distributed Active Archive Centers (DAACs) are housed; and a study of open source in the National Cancer Institute's Early Detection

Research Network (EDRN) program [22] which includes over 40+ institutions all performing cancer biomarker research for early stage detection, a program funded for over 10+ years by the NCI.

I have also chaired several open source topical meetings of relevance exploring its connection to science including the Apache in Space! (OODT) track in 2011 at ApacheCon, and the Apache in Science track at the 2013 meeting, as well as several organized open source meetings at the American Geophysical Union (AGU) Fall meeting for the past three years, and at the Earth Science Information Partners (ESIP) Foundation meetings during that same time. I am also one of the lead organizers of the Open Source Summit [23], a meeting that originally began with only NASA participation and has grown to include over 12 government agencies including NASA, NSF, NIH/NCI, NLM, DARPA, DOD, the State Department, the Census Bureau and other agencies.

My primary research contribution in this area is an identification of a classification and comparison framework for open source software based on nine dimensions of importance including licensing; community-structure (open, closed, etc.); redistribution strategy; attribution strategy and more. The work in this area has influenced research agenda item (4) the understanding and application of open source in Big Data and in data science described next in the *Looking towards the future* section of the paper.

Looking towards the future

Based on the above research history and background, I published an article in *Nature* magazine in January 2013 [24] identifying the four thrusts of my research vision for *Data Science* and *Big Data*. The four main areas of advancement that I plan to investigate over the next decade are:

Rapid science algorithm integration Researchers need to do a better job at rapidly and unobtrusively integrating scientific algorithms into Big Data production systems and workflow systems. The current state of the art is to tell a scientist to rewrite her algorithm in Map Reduce in order to make it faster, or to integrate it into a data system – this takes away from the scientific stewardship of the algorithm and transfers it to the software engineering team, who may lack the necessary background and training to maintain that algorithm, and furthermore, largely computer scientists are not trained in scientific programming environments like Matlab, R, Python, IDL, etc. Scientific Workflow Systems can help here [25], and also current efforts for DARPA XDATA, NASA's RCMES project, and for NSF EarthCube will provide an evaluation environment for future work in this area.

Intelligent data movement At a recent Hadoop Summit meeting, I recall the VP of Amazon Web Services explaining to an audience member what the best way to send 10+ terabytes of data to Amazon would be in order to process it on EC2. The VP made some joke about "Well, you know how Amazon is *really great* at shipping things to *you* – in this case, you ship things to us, that is, *your data*". This is very much still the state of the art and practice for data movement – shipping "data bricks" around. This is an extremely cost effective and viable option, however the decisions and rationale and scientific reasons as to *why* data movement selections be them electronic (GridFTP, bbFTP, HTTP, REST, etc.) or hardware ("brick") based are made are largely undocumented, not reproducible and an art form. In other words, the selection of a data movement technology *does matter*, can affect all sorts of functional properties in a Big Data system, and ultimately is a key portion of the architecture yet as a field we do not have good reasons as to why particular data movement technologies are chosen, and others ignored. This is an exciting future area of research, since it both continues my PhD work, and also has practical applications for technology transfer e.g., into Amazon, the open source community, NASA Earth Science missions, the SKA project, etc., as well as very fruitful domains for evaluation in industry, climate science, astronomy and future and current Big Data projects.

Appropriate use of cloud computing for storage/processing To develop effective architectural and software engineering techniques for cloud computing services to both assess their cost, and also the suitability of their processing and storage components, researchers need to perform an assessment of cloud computing vendors and providers and their integration capabilities, processing and storage capabilities. Further, studies attempting to discern the canonical software components and services for the cloud are timely and needed. Understanding cloud providers that are both reusable, and that fulfill software architecture requirements, and ultimately the requirements of the Big Data system is an important step in this process. This research and software engineering understanding of the cloud is an area that will have large applicability and technology transfer potential.

Harnessing the power of open source in software development for science Identifying the methods and the approach in which open source foundations, legal frameworks, and licenses affect software development, and scientific collaboration is an important near-term research study that is required. We currently lack strong empirical research and data that identifies the most appropriate and inappropriate software ecosystems for housing software components. Methods must be developed to track the evolution of software components at these foundations, and to identify the role of emerging distributed versus centralized configuration management (e.g., Git versus Subversion) at these foundations. Strategies that employ social scientists to investigate the community implications of open source, and the effectiveness of open source as a software engineering development process and architectural strategy are in need of development.

Conclusion

I am committed to the above four areas of research and see them as both necessary and exciting if we are to advance the fields of Big Data and data science. I plan to attack the above research areas with a multi-disciplinary eye and to make a contribution in software architecture, design, reuse, and open source. I am excited to pursue these topics and am confident that the results of the pursuit will have a potential for tremendous impact in science and industry and the broader community.

Competing interests
The author declare that he/she has no competing interests.

Acknowledgements
Effort supported by NSF awards PLR-1348450, ICER-1343800, ACS-1125798, and GEO-1229036 and GEO-1343583. Effort also partially supported by the Jet Propulsion Laboratory, managed by the California Institute of Technology under a contract with the National Aeronautics and Space Administration.

References

1. Mattmann C, Crichton D, Hughes JS, Kelly S, Hardman S, Joyner R, Ramirez P (2006) A classification and evaluation of data movement technologies for the delivery of highly voluminous scientific data products. In: Proceedings of the NASA/IEEE Conference on Mass Storage Systems and Technologies (MSST2006). IEEE Computer Society, Maryland, pp 131–135
2. Mattmann C, Crichton D, Hart A, Kelly S, Hughes JS (2010) Experiments with storage and preservation of nasas planetary data via the cloud. IEEE IT Prof Spec Theme Cloud Comput 12(5): 28–35
3. Crichton D, Mattmann C, Cinquini L, Braverman A, Waliser D, Hart A, Goodale C, Lean P, Kim J (2012) Sharing satellite observations with the climate modeling community: software and architecture. IEEE Softw 29(5): 63–71
4. Mattmann C, Crichton DJ, Medvidovic N, Hughes S (2006) A software architecture-based framework for highly distributed and data intensive scientific applications. In: ICSE. IEEE Computer Society, Shanghai, China, pp 721–730
5. Foster IT, Kesselman C, Tuecke S (2001) The anatomy of the grid: Enabling scalable virtual organizations. IJHPCA 15(3): 200–222
6. Foster I, Kesselman C, Nick JM, Tuecke S (2002) The physiology of the grid: an open grid services architecture for distributed systems integration. Open grid service infrastructure WG, Global grid forum. http://www.globus.org/research/papers/ogsa.pdf.
7. Mattmann C, Medvidovic N, Ramirez PM, Jakobac V (2005) Unlocking the grid. In: Heineman GT, Crnkovic I, Schmidt HW, Stafford JA, Szyperski CA, Wallnau KC (eds) CBSE. Lecture notes in computer science, vol. 3489. Springer, St. Louis, MO, pp 322–336
8. Mattmann C, Garcia J, Krka I, Popescu D, Medvidovic N (2009) The anatomy and physiology of the grid revisited In: WICSA/ECSA. IEEE/IFIP, London, UK
9. Yu J, Buyya R (2005) A taxonomy of workflow management systems for grid computing. J Grid Comput 3(3–4): 171–200
10. Massie ML, Chun BN, Culler DE (2004) The ganglia distributed monitoring system: design, implementation, and experience. Parallel Comput 30(7): 817–840
11. Mattmann C, Freeborn D, Crichton D, Foster B, Hart A, Woollard D, Hardman S, Ramirez P, Kelly S, Chang AY, Miller CE (2009) A reusable process control system framework for the orbiting carbon observatory and npp sounder peate missions. In: 3rd IEEE Intl' Conference on Space Mission Challenges for Information Technology (SMC-IT 2009). IEEE Computer Society, Pasadena, CA, pp 165–172
12. Cafarella M, Cutting D (2004) Nutch, building open source search. ACM Queue 2(2): 54–61
13. Kang Y, Kung SH, Jang H-J (2013) Simulation process support for climate data analysis In: Proceedings of the 2013 ACM Cloud and Autonomic Computing Conference. ACM, Vietri sul Mare, Italy, p 29
14. Mattmann C, Zitting J (2011) Tika in action. Manning Publications Co., NY, USA
15. Mattmann CA, Crichton DJ, Hart AF, Goodale C, Hughes JS, Kelly S, Cinquini L, Painter TH, Lazio J, Waliser D, Medvidovic N, Kim J, Lean P (2011) Architecting data-intensive software systems. In: Handbook of Data Intensive Computing. Springer, pp 25–57. http://www.springer.com/computer/database+management+%26+information+retrieval/book/978-1-4614-1414-8
16. Mattmann CA, Crichton DJ, Hart AF, Kelly SC, Hughes JS (2010) Experiments with storage and preservation of nasa's planetary data via the cloud. IT Prof 12(5): 28–35
17. Kwoun O-i, Cuddy D, Leung K, Callahan P, Crichton D, Mattmann CA, Freeborn D (2010) A science data system approach for the desdyni mission. In: Radar Conference, 2010 IEEE. IEEE, Arlington, VA, pp 1265–1269
18. Mattmann CA, Waliser D, Kim J, Goodale C, Hart A, Ramirez P, Crichton D, Zimdars P, Boustani M, Lee K, Loikith P, Whitehall K, Jack C, Hewitson B (2013) Cloud computing and virtualization within the regional climate model and evaluation system. Earth Sci Inf: 1–12
19. Mattmann CA, Medvidovic N, Mohan T, O'Malley O (2011) Workshop on software engineering for cloud computing: (secloud 2011). In: Software Engineering (ICSE), 2011 33rd International Conference On. IEEE, Honolulu, HI, pp 1196–1197
20. Mattmann CA, Crichton DJ, Hart AF, Kelly SC, Goodale CE, Ramirez P, Hughes JS, Downs RR, Lindsay F (2012) Understanding open source software at nasa. IT Prof 14(2): 29–35
21. Mattmann CA, Downs RR, Ramirez PM, Goodale C, Hart AF (2012) Developing an open source strategy for nasa earth science data systems. In: Information Reuse and Integration (IRI), 2012 IEEE 13th International Conference On. IEEE, Las Vegas, NV, pp 687–693
22. Hart AF, Verma R, Mattmann CA, Crichton DJ, Kelly S, Kincaid H, Hughes S, Ramirez P, Goodale C, Anton K, Colbert M, Downs RR, Patriotis C, Srivastava S (2012) Developing an open source, reusable platform for distributed collaborative information management in the early detection research network. In: Information Reuse and Integration (IRI), 2012 IEEE 13th International Conference On. IEEE, Las Vegas, NV, pp 263–270
23. Open Source Summit 3.0: Communities. http://ossummit.org/. Accessed 3 March 2014
24. Mattmann CA (2013) Computing: A vision for data science. Nature 493(7433): 473–475
25. Woollard D, Medvidovic N, Gil Y, Mattmann C (2008) Scientific software as workflows: From discovery to distribution. IEEE Softw 25(4): 37–43

3

Airline new customer tier level forecasting for real-time resource allocation of a miles program

Jose Berengueres[1][*] and Dmitry Efimov[2]

* Correspondence: jose@uaeu.ac.ae
[1]UAE University, 17551 Al Ain, Abu Dhabi, UAE
Full list of author information is available at the end of the article

Abstract

This is a case study on an airline's miles program resource optimization. The airline had a large miles loyalty program but was not taking advantage of recent data mining techniques. As an example, to predict whether in the coming month(s), a new passenger would become a privileged frequent flyer or not, a linear extrapolation of the miles earned during the past months was used. This information was then used in CRM interactions between the airline and the passenger. The correlation of extrapolation with whether a new user would attain a privileged miles status was 39% when one month of data was used to make a prediction. In contrast, when GBM and other blending techniques were used, a correlation of 70% was achieved. This corresponded to a prediction accuracy of 87% with less than 3% false positives. The accuracy reached 97% if three months of data instead of one were used. An application that ranks users according to their probability to become part of privileged miles-tier was proposed. The application performs real time allocation of limited resources such as available upgrades on a given flight. Moreover, the airline can assign now those resources to the passengers with the highest revenue potential thus increasing the perceived value of the program at no extra cost.

Keywords: Airline; Customer equity; Customer profitability; Life time value; Loyalty program; Frequent flyer; FFP; Miles program; Churn; Data mining

Background

Previously, several works have addressed the issue of optimizing operations of the airline industry. In 2003, a model that predicts no-show ratio with the purpose of optimizing overbooking practice claimed to increase revenues by 0.4% to 3.2% [1]. More recently, in 2013, Alaska Airlines in cooperation with G.E and Kaggle Inc., launched a $250,000 prize competition with the aim of optimizing costs by modifying flight plans [2]. However, there are very little works on miles programs or frequent flier programs that focus on enhancing their value. One example is [3] from Taiwan, but they focused on segmenting customers by extracting decision-rules from questionnaires. Using a *Rough Set Approach* they report classification accuracies of 95%. [4] focused on segmenting users according to return flight and length of stays using a k-means algorithm. A few other works such as [5], focused on predicting the future value of passengers (Customer Equity). They attempt to predict the top 20% most valuable customers. Using SAS software they report false positive and false negative rate of 13% and 55% respectively. None of them have applied this knowledge to increase the value-proposition of miles programs. All this in spite the fact that some of these programs have become more valuable than the airline that started them. Such is the case of Aeroplan, a spin off of the miles programs started by Toronto based Air Canada. Air Canada is as of today valued at \$500 M whereas Aeroplan is valued at \$2bn, four times more [6]. Given this it is surprising that so many works focus in ticket or "revenue management" [7] but few focus on their miles programs. In this case study we report the experience gained when we analyzed the data of an airline's miles program. We show how by applying modern data mining techniques it is possible to create value for both: (1) the owner of the program and (2) future high-value passengers.

The data of the miles program was provided by Etihad Airlines and was 1.2GBytes in size when zip compressed. It contained three tables of anonymized data from year 2008 to 2012, corresponding to about 1.8 million unique passengers. The tables contain the typical air miles program data such as:

1. Age and demographics.
2. Loyalty program purchases etc.
3. Flight activity, miles earned etc.

Case Description

Objective

After co-examining the opportunities that the data offered with the airline we decided to focus on high-value passengers with the objective to: predict and discriminate which of the new passengers who enroll the miles program will be high-value customers before it is obvious to a human expert.

Rationale

Business justification:

1. So that potential high-value customers are identified in order to gain their loyalty sooner.
2. So that limited resources such as upgrades are optimally allocated to passengers with potential to become high-value.
3. To enhance customer profiling.

Current method: linear extrapolation

The miles program was using three main tiers to classify customer by value. Ordered form less to more value these are: basic, silver, gold. The airline was using the following method to predict future tier status: a passenger flight activity is observed on a monthly basis then, a linear extrapolation on how much they will fly in the coming month(s) is performed (Figure 1). This information was then used in interactions with customers.

Definition of the target variable

After some discussion we decided that we are interested in transitions from basic to silver or gold. After a user flights for first time with the airline, their activity is observed for D days, (Figure 2). At the same time we mark each user with 1 or 0 depending on

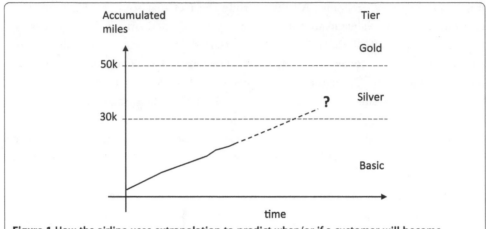

Figure 1 How the airline uses extrapolation to predict when/or if a customer will become high-value customer. Y-axis, accumulated miles earned by a given customer. X-axis, time. Dashed-line prediction.

whether they will attain Silver or greater tier status within S additional days after day D. We will later refer to this binary variable as *silver_attain*, and to this model as D/S model. Then past behavior of customers is feed into the model. The model is described further in the text.

Identifying future high value customers

When a new customer joins the program, (and D days have passed since then) the model can be used to make a prediction about the likelihood that they will become Silver in the near or far future. Figure 2 and Table 1 show examples. For business

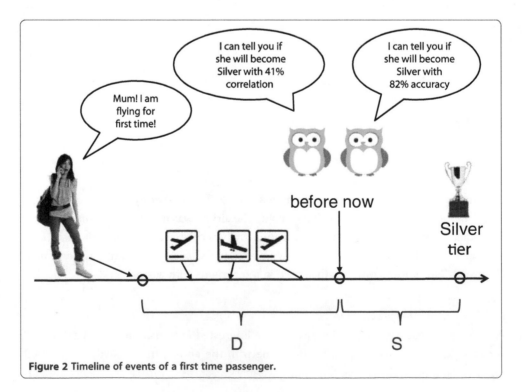

Figure 2 Timeline of events of a first time passenger.

Table 1 Miles program dataset

Dataset	Fields	Rows	Cols
Passengers	Id, Date_of_birth, Nationality, City, State, Country, Interest_1, Interest_2, Interest_3, Interest_4, Interest_5, Tier	1.8 M	12
Flights	Id, Company, Activity_date, Origin, Destination, Class_code, Flt_number, Definition, Miles, Points,	12 M	10
Activity (not used)	Id, Definition, Issue_date, Miles, Redeposited_points, Flight_date, Class_code, Origin, Destination, Flight_number, ret_flight_date, Ret _flight_number, Ret_class_code, Ret_origin, Ret_destination, Product_code, Cash_before_premium	1.6 M	17

purposes we equate Silver tier status with high-value customer. However, this hypothesis was not validated in the scope of the project.

Previous to model construction we performed two actions:

1) Cleaning of the data.
2) Feature extraction.

Cleaning

Initially, we had three tables: *Passengers*, *Flights* and *Activity*. *Activity*, which contains data related to miles transactions, was not used because it did not help improve results. The Airline suggested that this might be due to incompleteness of data. For example, by Airline policy all monetary transactions were unavailable to us and had been removed from datasets. Table 1 shows the list of fields for each table. First we removed two outlier cases for passengers whose future tier prediction is straightforward or has little merit:

1) Passengers who fly less than one return trip in six years.
2) Passengers with very high activity (number of flights greater than 500).

Additionally, before the data was handed over to us, the airline anonymized the id field. The id had been replaced by an alphanumeric hash code of length 32 characters long. We changed these cumbersome hash ids into integer numerical values to increase the performance. Big datasets made it very difficult for R Language to operate with hash ids during feature engineering.

Feature extraction

The system works in the following way: For each passenger a vector is constructed considering data pertaining to the D period only. For example, if $D = 15$ days, then the flights and data we would consider to build the aforementioned vector are any flights between start_date and start_date + D, where start_date is the first flight date of a new passenger. Note that start_date varies for every passenger. Now for each passenger we construct a vector that depends on three variables:

1) The passenger data in the Tables.
2) *start_date*.
3) Length of D.

Each component of the vector is called a "feature". The length of the vector is 634 features. The vector is equivalent to a digital fingerprint for each passenger considered in a given period. Some features are straightforward to calculate and others require complex calculations. Following we explain how each feature was calculated. We have divided the features in three groups: metric, categorical and cluster features.

Group 1 - Metric features

A metric feature is data that is already in numerical format. For example, age of a customer.

Group 2 - Categorical features

A categorical feature is a text variable, the content of which can only belong to a finite group of choices. The column "City" is such an example. The main problem with categorical variables is that they must be converted to numbers somehow. Since a computer does not understand "city names" per se, there are different ways to operate with such variables. One way is to encode code each name (aka level or category) of each categorical variable into a binary feature. Therefore, we opted for an interpretation of categorical variables using the dummy variable method as follows:

Let N be the total number of values for a given categorical variable, then we create N new "dummy" features. If a given record has value = i^{th} level, then the ith dummy feature equals 1, otherwise 0.

Unfortunately, this transformation restricts range of algorithms that are effective: algorithms based on metrical approach such as SVM [8] yield poor results in such cases.

One of such features is: *"city"* (Cities to where the passenger has flown during D, from the table flights). Following, we explain an example on how the categorical *city* variable was processed. Each city to where the airline flies is represented as a feature in the vector. If the given passenger did not fly even once to the given city during D, then the feature is set to 0, if it flew one or more times it is set to 1. The same process is performed for Class tickets letters. The categorical variables that are exploded to binary format using the dummy method are:

1) Passenger Nationality.
2) City of Passenger's address.
3) State of Passenger's address.
4) Country of Passenger's address.
5) Passenger's Company (Employer).
6) Flight Origin (Airport).
7) Flight Destination (Airport).
8) Ticket Class Code (Economy E, F, K...).

Note that the absolute order of the features must be always the same for all passengers. However, the chosen ordering is arbitrary and does not affect performance. We chose to use alphabetical order. Table 2 shows an example of how city was converted from categorical to binary.

Table 2 Example of conversion from categorical to binary for a given passenger

Feature label	Example value
City_1 (Amsterdam)	0
City_2 (Barcelona)	1
...	...
City_323 (Zagreb)	1
Class_code_1 ("A")	0
Class_code_2 ("B")	1
Class_code_3	1
Class_code_45 ("Z")	0

Group 3. Cluster features

Once all categorical features are converted to binary ones, even if their quantity has increased, it is possible to apply clustering algorithms to identify groups of passengers with similar associated "vectors". In this case, we applied the tried and proven k-means algorithms with different number of clusters (2, 3, 5, 7, 10, 15, and 20) to classify all passengers in clusters. The k denotes the number of clusters. So for example is k = 3 it means there are 3 clusters (A, B, C). Every passenger vector will be assigned to the "closest" cluster center as defined by Euclidean distance in n-dimensions, where n is the number of features of the vectors. At this point a cluster label ("A", "B" or "C") is assigned to each passenger vector. Then as before we use the dummy variable method to explode cluster labels into binary features. This was done in the following way: For each passenger all previous features (of Tables 3 and 2) are put in vector form. Then, if we are considering 100 passengers, and data of say 354 flights that satisfy the condition of belonging in the D period, then we produce 100 vectors. This is input into a k-means algorithm for k = 3. k denotes de number of clusters into which the vectors will be classified. The algorithm will attempt to classify each of the 100 vectors into k = 3 clusters, A or B or C. Using the dummy variable method we generate three new variables: *Cluster_k3_A,* Cluster_k3_B, Cluster_k3_C. These 3 variables will become new additional features instead of a categorical feature that says ("A", "B" or "C"). Then if a vector (passenger) belongs to "A", its Cluster_k3_A feature is set to 1 and 0 otherwise, conversely, if the vector belongs to "B" then only Cluster_k3_B is set to 1, and so on. This process is repeated for k = 2, 5, 7, 10, 15, 20. Table 4, shows the features and

Table 3 Metric features

Feature label	Example
Age_of_passenger	43 (years)
Sum of miles	25500 (miles)
Average miles	2300
Interest_1	0 or 1
Interest_2	0 or 1
Interest_3	0 or 1
Interest_4	0 or 1
Interest_5	0 or 1

(1 = customer marked as interested in Interest_1 in the website when he registers).

Table 4 Example of creation of 60 cluster features by the dummy method

k	Example of K-means output (*categorical*)	Label of the new binary features	Binary value
2	"B"	Cluster_k2_A	0
		Cluster_k2_B	1
3	"A"	Cluster_k3_A	1
		Cluster_k3_B	0
		Cluster_k3_C	0
5	"C"	Cluster_k5_A	0
		Cluster_k5_B	0
		Cluster_k5_C	1
		Cluster_k5_D	0
		Cluster_k5_E	0
7	"C"	Cluster_k7_A	0
		Cluster_k7_B	0
		Cluster_k7_C	1
		Cluster_k7_D	0
		Cluster_k7_E	0
		Cluster_k7_F	0
		Cluster_k7_G	0
10	"A"	Cluster_k10_A	1
		…	…
		Cluster_k10_K	0
20	"A"	Cluster_k20_A	1
		…	…
		Cluster_k20_T	0

an example where a passenger vector has been classified into cluster "B" for k = 2, cluster "A" for k = 3 etc...

After all this process, for each passenger vector, we add these binary cluster features to the corresponding passenger vector. Table 5 shows an example. At this point it should be clear the label assigned to each feature is irrelevant. The order of the features is also irrelevant, only maintaining a consistent ordering of features in the vectors is important. Naturally, the more training vectors available, the more accurate the predictions can be. We used 50,000 vector examples to train the model. A benefit of feeding clustered features to a model is that it could help to find high order relationships between similar data points. We use a GBM model that accounts for up to 5-degree relations.

Target variable

Once the vectors for each passenger are generated we need to define the target variable. This is the variable that we want to predict. In our case, the variable is 1 if the user became Silver tier during the S period as shown in Figure 2 and 0 otherwise. To generate training

Table 5 Example of feature vectors generated per each passenger

Passenger Id	Example vector
1	(43, 13.54, …, 0, 0, 12, 0, …, 0, 1, 1, 0, 0, 0, …, 0, 0, 0)
2	(26, 2.9, …, 0, 0, 12, 0, …, 0, 1, 1, 0, 0, 0, …, 0, 0, 0)

examples we use samples from past years and check what happened to them. This set of vectors and associated target variables constitutes a training set. Table 6 shows an example of passenger vectors from Table 5 with the corresponding target variable.

Now, we can consider all this vectors as a matrix, where rows are passengers, columns are features, and the last column is the target variable. We will use such a matrix to train a mathematical model with the purpose of predicting the target variable in new passengers. Once the model is trained, to predict if a passenger will attain silver status in a given time frame S (in the future) we only need to generate its feature vector by observing the passenger for a period of time D since their first flight. Once the vector is generated (naturally, without target variable) we can input it into the model and the model will output a number. There are no restrictions on when to ask a model for a prediction as long as the data for the given S period is available.

Model

The high nonlinearity of the features (meaning low correlation between target variable and features) restricts the number of algorithms we can use to predict with high accuracy. We chose to blend two algorithms, which were in our opinion the most appropriate for this dataset: the GBM (Generalized Boosting Machine package) and GLM (Generalized Linear Model, glm in R). Both models are trained with the same target variable: *silver_attain*, and try minimize the binomial deviance (Log Loss) of prediction error. While, we chose GLM and GBM because they produce different models, GLM can be considered as non-parametric version of GBM.

GBM

The aforementioned training matrix was used to train a GBM model in R Language. This is convenient because an implementation of GBM is available as an open source library in R, so we don't need to code it from scratch. GBM has various parameters that can affect the performance of the model. For example, the number of trees (size) is one of them and usually the most important. Manual grid search was performed to determine the optimal parameter values. 75% of the data was used to train a model and 25% was used to test the prediction. The optimal GBM parameters were:

1) distribution = "bernoulli",
2) n.trees = 2000,
3) shrinkage = 0.01,
4) interaction.depth = 0.5,
5) bag.fraction = 0.5,
6) train.fraction = 0.1,
7) n.minobsinnode = 10.

Table 6 Example of feature vectors and target variables

Passenger Id	Feature vector	Target variable
1	(43, 13.54, …, 0, 0, 12, 0, …, 0, 1, 1, 0, 0, 0, …, 0, 0, 0)	0 (he did not achieve silver status during S period)
2	(26, 2.9, …, 0, 0, 12, 0, …, 0, 1, 1, 0, 0, 0, …, 0, 0, 0)	1 (yes he did)

A good description of the GBM implementation we used can be found in [9]. It works as follows: the training matrix is used to train the model with the aforementioned parameters. After, some minutes we have a trained model. Now to make a new prediction on a passenger vector or a number of passenger vectors, we input it in the model and the model will return a number from 0 to 1 for each passenger vector. 0 means that the model predicts 0% chance for that passenger to attain silver tier status within the S period of time. A 1 means that the model is the most confident the silver tier will be attained. Training the model takes about 1 hour, but asking the model to predict what will happen to 10,000 passengers takes just seconds.

GLM

The other algorithm used is GLM. GLM stands for General Linear Model. As before we used the implementation in R Language provided by [10]. GLM is just a simple logistic regression where we optimize binomial deviance, where *Error = silver_attain – prediction.* Default parameters where used except for family which was set to "binomial".

Blending with grid search

Combining predictions is known to improve accuracy if certain conditions are met [11]. In general, the less correlation between the individual predictors, the higher the gain in accuracy. A way that usually lowers cross-correlation is to combine models of different "nature". We chose to combine a decision tree based algorithm (GBM) and regression based one (GLM). For a 3/3 model the relative gain in accuracy due to blending was 3%. The final prediction was constructed as a linear combination of the output of the two. Grid search was used to find which linear combination was optimal on the training set. The optimal combination was 90% of the GBM prediction plus 10% of the GLM prediction.

Loss function

A natural way to estimate the error in problems where the target variable is binary is the use of Precision and Recall so we can account for the number of false positives and false negatives. However, one of the exceptional properties of the target variable (*silver_attain*) was the huge number of 0's and small number of 1's. This is hardly surprising: after all, by design, only a small percentage of the total passengers are supposed to attain a privileged tier. Another interesting fact is that the airline desired to determine future silver and gold passengers with highest possible accuracy; this is, a low false positive rate (mistakes). However, since the penalty cost for false negatives is not high, the acceptable precision level can be lower. These two observations enabled us to modify the usual definition of Precision and Accuracy in the following way:

$$P = \frac{N_0}{N_0 + N_1} \qquad A = \frac{N_0}{N_0 + N_2} \tag{1}$$

where P is precision, A is accuracy, N_0 is a number of true positives or users predicted to become silver and that later indeed became silver, N_1 is the number of false positives or users predicted to become silver but who did not indeed become silver after S days and N_2 is the number of false negatives or number of users predicted to not become silver and who indeed became silver. In the next section we will show the calculated error for the normal Precision and Recall and the calculated error according to chosen loss functions (Eq. 1).

Discussion and evaluation

It takes about 18 hours on a laptop to clean the data and construct the features. To build a D/S model takes about 1 hour per each D/S combination. Once a model is pre-calculated, making a prediction for one single passenger takes less than 350 ms (similar to a Google search).

Compared performance

Figure 3, Tables 7 and 8 compare key performance indicators of predictive power between the previous model used by the airline (monthly extrapolation) and the D/S model. The columns P and A of Table 7 were calculated according to Eq. 1. Table 8 shows actual numbers on one particular example for D/S = 3/3 months respectively. Table 8 also shows why the calculation of Precision and Accuracy in the usual way is not suitable to assess model performance on the given dataset because of huge number of 0's. A trade-off between Accuracy, Precision, D and S clearly exists. These parameters can be adjusted to suit various forecasting needs. Additionally, Table 7 data shows that accuracy is, roughly speaking, inversely proportional to the length of S. This is, the longer the S time span the lower A and P will be. This came a bit of a surprise to us as we expected that the averaging effects of longer S time span would to facilitate prediction, but in fact the opposite is true: shorter more limited time spans lead to more accurate predictions. On the other hand, as is the case with weather forecasts, it is easier to predict events that are close in the future than those that are farther away.

Confirmation of no data leakage

However, due to the spectacular high accuracy rates obtained, the airline showed a healthy concern that the prediction might be wrong due to data leakage. Data leakage happens when some data from the training set somehow contains information about what wants to be predicted (*target_variable*). The only way to proof 100% that there is

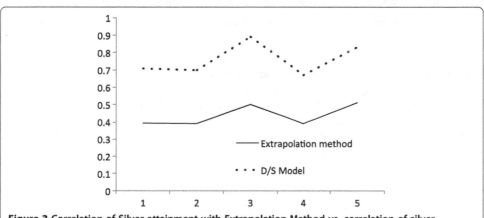

Figure 3 Correlation of Silver attainment with Extrapolation Method vs. correlation of silver attainment with D/S model for five different D/S cases as defined in Table 7.

Table 7 Comparison of prediction power of extrapolation vs. D/S model

	Question asked D months after 1st flight: will they become *Silver* within S months?			
Case	D	S	Extrapolation of miles Rx[1]	D/S Model Rx[2] P[3] A[4]
0	0.5	3	0.39	0.60 81% 31%
1	1	1	0.39	0.71 87% 53%
2	1	2	0.39	0.70 89% 48%
3	3	1	0.50	0.89 97% 82%[5]
4	3	3	0.39	0.67 95% 46%
5	6	3	0.51	0.83 96% 69%

Notes. [1]To compare predictive power between two models we use correlation as a proxy. Rx = correlation of accumulated miles with binary variable silver_attain. [2]correlation of the Model's prediction with binary variable silver_attain. [3]P = Precision, of all users who were predicted to become Silver, How many of them did indeed become silver? [4]A = Accuracy: Of all users who will become silver how many did we not miss? 5: See Table 8 for details on case 3.

no data leakage is to do predictions in the future (about data that does not exist at the time of the prediction). To address this valid concern the model was used to predict what the passengers would do in the future.

To this end on February 28th 2013 we where asked to predict what existing customers would do in the future in two weeks and 3 months in the future respectively. In particular, the company asked us to predict two questions:

1) Which of the 49572 customers that had enrolled during the last quarter of 2012 would attain silver in the first 30 days of 2013, this is a D = 3/S = 1 model and

2) Which of the 7890 customers that had enrolled during the last two weeks of December 2012 would attain silver during the first 90 days of 2013 a D = 0.5/S = 3 model.

The data we previously had, contained information from mid 2006 but only until December 2012. So there was no possible data leakage. We made predictions but then instead of handing over all the predictions for all the passengers, we ordered the predictions by confidence from high to low, then we cutoff the predictions at confidence 0.91 and 0.48 (there was a low number of high confidence predictions in the second case), this was about 600 and 200 passengers, respectively. We sent two lists to the Airline in mid-March 23rd. Three months later, on June 9th the company sent a list with the corresponding tiers and attainment dates for each customer. The accuracy was

Table 8 Precision and accuracy of silver attainment

Will a user become Silver in 1 month?			Stats	
Predicted (With 3 months of data)	What really happened	Is the prediction correct?	Numbers by case	Percent of total
No	No	Yes	54752	97.09
Yes	Yes	Yes	1309	2.32
No	Yes	No	293	0.52
Yes	No	No	37	0.07
		Total	56391	100

Notes: Prediction performed for each passenger with 3 month of data since 1st flight at time point: end of the three months. Precision = 2.75%. Accuracy = 81.71%.

100% with no false positives for both models. After this proof the company was convinced about the validity of the model and asked us to provide code to integrate it with his existing CRM system.

How can this knowledge help to create value? Let's consider a flight from ADX to TYO. There are only five available seats in business class. Let's assume that these five seats can be used to upgrade five lucky passengers. Of the 150 passengers expected to board the flight, lets assume that 20 are eligible for upgrade. The model will take less than one second to rank all the 150 passengers by probability of becoming Silver. Most importantly, it will also rank the 20 candidates. Figure 4 shows an example app. With this ranking at hand, we can now rationally allocate the five upgrades to the five customers most likely to become Silver rather than to customers with a zero probability of becoming Silver.

Discussion

By translating passenger data from "Airline" timeline to a timeline relative to each passenger first flight, we have shown that a D/S model yields high accuracies. Furthermore, taking advantage of recently made available data mining libraries [9,10] we outperformed simple extrapolation models and previous works [5]. False positive rates are less than 3%. The causes of a false positive have not been investigated in the scope of this project, but can be due to either/or a combination of: (1) the predictive nature of the data is not unlimited. (2) The predictive power of the model can be improved. However, the most interesting result is that

Passenger Name	Tier Status	Probability they will become Silver in X months
Wolfgang Amadeus Motzart	Basic	⇧ 0.99
Ludvig Van Beetoven	Basic	⇧ 0.97
Giuseppe Verdi	Basic	⇧ 0.89
Jean-Michel Jarre	Basic	⇧ 0.77
Yasuharu Konishi	Basic	⇧ 0.77
Maki Nomiya	Basic	⇨ 0.45
Teresa Teng	Basic	⇨ 0.42
Carl Philip Emanuel Bach	Basic	⇨ 0.41
Enric Granados	Basic	⇩ 0.00
Leonard Bernstein	Basic	⇩ 0.00
Carl Loewe	Basic	⇩ 0.00
Johan Strauss	Basic	⇩ 0.00
Isaac Albeniz	Basic	⇩ 0.00
George Gerschwin	Basic	⇩ 0.00
John Lenon	Basic	⇩ 0.00
John Williams	Basic	⇩ 0.00

Figure 4 Example of ranking application for real-time resource allocation of business seat upgrades.

the perceived value of a miles program can be increased dramatically to the very customers that matter most to the airline: the ones with high likelihood of becoming Silver.

In our experience with previous data mining projects, rather than fine tune models, the most effective way to improve accuracy is to add new features which are as uncorrelated as possible with existing features. A good place to look for potential candidates are features derived from different data sources other than the Airline CRM database, for example publicly available social media data.

Competing interests
We do not have any competing interest. We do not work for any airline or have a commercial relationship with any airline or any financial interest.

Authors' contributions
JB developed de business logic and DE carried out the data modelling. All authors read and approved the final manuscript.

Acknowledgments
Sajat Kamal for the Aeroplan insights. Dr. Barry Green and Roy Kinnear showing themselves to be greater than their prejudices and letting us modelling the data.

Author details
[1]UAE University, 17551 Al Ain, Abu Dhabi, UAE. [2]Moscow State University, Leninskie gori 1, 117234, Moscow.

References
1. Lawrence RD, Hong SJ, Cherrier J (2003) Passenger-based predictive modeling of airline no-show rates. Proceedings of the ninth SIGKDD international conference on Knowledge discovery and data mining. pp 397–406
2. Alaska Airlines GE Flight Quest data mining challenge 2013, http://www.gequest.com/c/flight
3. Liou JJH, Tzeng G-H (2010) A dominance-based rough set approach to customer behavior in the airline market. Inf Sci 180(11):2230–2238
4. Pritscher L, Feyen H (2001) Data mining and strategic marketing in the airline industry. Data Mining for Marketing Applications. Citeseer: http://citeseerx.ist.psu.edu/viewdoc/summary?doi=10.1.1.124.7062.
5. Malthouse EC, Blattberg RC (2005) Journal of Interactive Marketing. Can we predict customer lifetime value? Wiley Online Library: http://www.researchgate.net/publication/227633642_Can_we_predict_customer_lifetime_value/file/60b7d517fd5bb2905e.pdf.
6. Aeroplan loyalty program, http://en.wikipedia.org/wiki/Aeroplan
7. Smith BC, Leimkuhler JF, Darrow RM (1992) Yield management at American airlines. Interfaces 22(1):8–31
8. Burges CJ (1998) A tutorial on support vector machines for pattern recognition. Data Min Knowl Disc 2(2):121–167
9. (2013) Greg Ridgeway with contributions from others. gbm: Generalized Boosted Regression Models. R package version 2.0-8. http://CRAN.R-project.org/package=gbm
10. Ian M (2012) glm2: Fitting Generalized Linear Models. R package version 1.1.1. http://CRAN.R-project.org/package=glm2
11. Valentini G, Masulli F (2002) Ensembles of learning machines. Neural Nets. Springer, Berlin Heidelberg, pp 3–20

4

Intrusion detection and Big Heterogeneous Data: a Survey

Richard Zuech*, Taghi M Khoshgoftaar and Randall Wald

*Correspondence: rzuech@fau.edu
Florida Atlantic University, 777
Glades Road, Boca Raton, FL, USA

Abstract

Intrusion Detection has been heavily studied in both industry and academia, but cybersecurity analysts still desire much more alert accuracy and overall threat analysis in order to secure their systems within cyberspace. Improvements to Intrusion Detection could be achieved by embracing a more comprehensive approach in monitoring security events from many different heterogeneous sources. Correlating security events from heterogeneous sources can grant a more holistic view and greater situational awareness of cyber threats. One problem with this approach is that currently, even a single event source (e.g., network traffic) can experience Big Data challenges when considered alone. Attempts to use more heterogeneous data sources pose an even greater Big Data challenge. Big Data technologies for Intrusion Detection can help solve these Big Heterogeneous Data challenges. In this paper, we review the scope of works considering the problem of heterogeneous data and in particular Big Heterogeneous Data. We discuss the specific issues of Data Fusion, Heterogeneous Intrusion Detection Architectures, and Security Information and Event Management (SIEM) systems, as well as presenting areas where more research opportunities exist. Overall, both cyber threat analysis and cyber intelligence could be enhanced by correlating security events across many diverse heterogeneous sources.

Keywords: Intrusion detection; Big data; Security; IDS; SIEM; Data fusion; Heterogeneous; Hadoop; Cloud; Feature selection; Situational awareness; Big Heterogeneous Data

Introduction

Cybersecurity is critical as society becomes increasingly dependent on computerized systems for its finances, industry, medicine, and other important aspects. One of the most important considerations in cybersecurity is Intrusion Detection. In order to mitigate or prevent attacks, awareness of an attack is essential to being able to react and defend against attackers. Cyber Defenses can be further improved by utilizing Security Analytics and Intrusion Detection data to look for hidden attack patterns and trends. Intrusion Detection is also important for forensic purposes in order to identify successful breaches even after they have occurred. For example, it is important to know afterwards if information such as credit card data has already been stolen, in order to take additional precautions or possibly take law enforcement or legal actions. Intrusion Detection can also be very helpful beyond detecting cyber-attacks in noticing abnormal system behavior to detect accidents or undesired conditions. For example, an Intrusion Detection System

(IDS) could report anomalies where a malfunction or human error is causing customer credit card numbers to be erroneously charged multiple times. Or perhaps an IDS could alert on something out of the ordinary and detect a gas leak, and help prevent an explosion which could harm or even kill humans. Intrusion Detection can be helpful in providing early warnings and minimizing damage.

This study evaluates some of the advancements in Intrusion Detection technology along with important considerations like monitoring a wide array of heterogeneous security event sources. As cyber-attacks have evolved and grown in sophistication, Intrusion Detection products have also become much more sophisticated, monitoring an ever increasing amount of diverse heterogeneous security event sources. IDSs were the first specialized products developed to detect and alert for potential cyber-attacks, and they can either employ misuse detection or anomaly detection. An IDS utilizing misuse detection evaluates data it is monitoring against a database of known attack signatures to determine attack matches. An IDS utilizing anomaly detection, on the other hand, evaluates data it is monitoring against a normal baseline, and can issue alerts based on abnormal behavior.

One traditional IDS product is a Network Intrusion Detection System (NIDS) which monitors for cyber threats at the network layer by evaluating network traffic. Another traditional IDS product is a Host-based Intrusion Detection System (HIDS) which monitors for cyber threats directly on the computer hosts by monitoring a computer host's system logs, system processes, files, or network interface. An IDS can monitor specific protocols like a web server's Hyper Text Transfer Protocol (HTTP); this type of IDS is called a Protocol-based Intrusion Detection System (PIDS). IDSs can also be specialized to monitor application-specific protocols like an Application Protocol-based Intrusion Detection System (APIDS). An example for this could be an APIDS that monitors a database's Structured Query Language (SQL) protocol. Similar to the heterogeneity of the security event sources such as network and diverse host types, the IDSs themselves can be heterogeneous in their type, how they operate, and in their diverse alert output formats.

Today's Information Technology (IT) security systems and personnel can be inundated with an overload of ambiguous information or false alarms, and the cybersecurity domain frequently encounters problems dealing with Big Data from currently implemented systems. Compounding the problem further, existing IT security systems seldom integrate across a wide spectrum of an organization's information systems. For example, an organization can typically have the following systems: Firewalls, IDSs, computer workstations, Anti-virus software, Databases, end-user Applications, and a variety of other systems. However with traditional IDSs there is rarely any integration among them in the context of monitoring for security breach attempts, and very seldom is there any sort of integrated security monitoring approach across a large proportion of an organization's information systems. A basic illustration of what this paper evaluates is given in Figure 1, where security events from most (if not all) of an organization's computing assets are being monitored. This diagram exhibits the heterogeneity of a typical enterprise's network where security events from different workstations, servers, NIDSs, HIDs, firewall events, etc. can all be very different. For example, an organization might use different NIDS solutions to increase detection accuracy, and increase the heterogeneity of a single function in the security system. To improve Intrusion Detection these security events should be correlated with each other in order to improve alerting

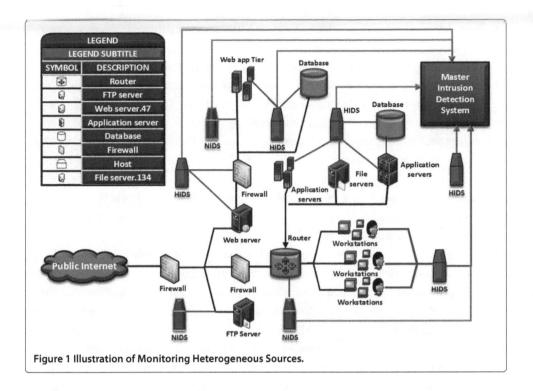

Figure 1 Illustration of Monitoring Heterogeneous Sources.

accuracy as well as give a more comprehensive overview of cyber threats from an overall perspective.

Intrusion Detection frequently involves analysis of Big Data, which is defined as research problems where mainstream computing technologies cannot handle the quantity of data. Even a single security event source such as network traffic data can cause Big Data challenges. According to Nassar et al. [1], merely 1Gbps of sustained network traffic can cause Big Data challenges for Intrusion Detection while using deep packet inspection. Another Big Data challenge that larger organizations can face is having an incredible amount of host log event data. The Cloud Security Alliance reported [2] that in 2013, it is estimated that an enterprise like HP can "generate 1 trillion events per day or roughly 12 million events per second". They report that such large volumes of data are "overwhelming" and they even struggle to simply store the data. Enterprises dealing with such Big Data issues at this scale cannot use existing analytical techniques effectively, and so false alarms are especially problematic. Additionally, it can be very difficult to correlate events over such large amounts of data, especially when that data can be stored in many different formats. Relational database technology can commonly become a bottleneck in Big Data challenges. For example, commercial SIEMs that use relational database technologies for their storage repositories will find the databases becoming bottlenecks in deployments at larger enterprises: storage and retrieval of data begins to take longer than is acceptable. Zions Bancorporation conducted a case study [3] where it would take their traditional SIEM systems between 20 minutes to an hour to query a month's worth of security data, however when using tools with Hadoop technology it would only take about one minute to achieve the same results. It is a clear sign that Intrusion Detection is facing Big Data challenges when a mainstream technology like relational databases becomes a bottleneck. Next generational Big Data storage technologies like Hadoop can help address these problems.

While traditional Intrusion Detection Systems (IDSs) are a critical component of Intrusion Detection, more focus should be placed on gathering security data from a wider variety of heterogeneous sources and correlating events across them to gain better situational awareness and holistic comprehension of cybersecurity. Analyzing security data across heterogeneous sources can be difficult for Intrusion Detection where homogeneous sources already face Big Data challenges. By analyzing additional heterogeneous sources, the problem can be compounded into a more significant Big Heterogeneous Data challenge as each source can potentially have Big Data. Improving situational awareness by correlating security events or alert data across heterogeneous sources where each can have Big Data challenges is a much more significant problem than performing Intrusion Detection independently on each homogeneous Big Data source, and this is the Big Heterogeneous Data challenge for Intrusion Detection.

A larger IT infrastructure can cause Big Heterogeneous Data challenges with its diversity of input event sources such as various hosts. Correlating among diverse sources like workstations, various application servers, and the network can be a significant problem when facing Big Data challenges. Compounding the problem further is that both the security alerting devices (e.g., IDSs, SIEMS, etc) as well as alert messages can be heterogeneous in nature. The typical enterprise can have a myriad of different security products which do not integrate well, and this heterogeneity causes difficulty for Intrusion Detection. Gartner Research Director Lawrence Pingree addresses this difficulty with a concept called "intelligence awareness" which is the capability of automated intelligence sharing and alerting across a myriad of security systems, and further explains that security systems must become "adaptable based on contextual awareness, situational awareness and controls themselves can inform each other and perform policy enforcement based on degrees or gradients of threat and trust levels" [4]. Ed Billis, CEO of Risk I/O further elaborates on this problem where security products are silo'ed from each other: "SIEMs weren't originally designed to consume much more than syslog or netflow information with a few exceptions around configuration or vulnerability assessment. Security analytics is more than just big data – it's also diverse data. This causes serious technical architectural limitations that aren't easy to overcome with just SIEM" [5].

In addition, industrial processes should also be monitored for Intrusion Detection as industrial systems are increasingly computerized. One example is the nation's electrical grid where most equipment has been computerized that is used to monitor the real-world physical sensors that measure electrical properties like power, voltage, and current. Being computerized, they should be monitored for Intrusion Detection as well. However, the overall Intrusion Detection system can also enhance its capabilities by considering abnormal operational electrical readings and even correlating those real-world events to security events in cyberspace, thus further enhancing situational awareness. Kezunovic et al. [6] discuss the role of Big Data in the electric power industry, and IBM [7] further describes the Big Data challenges faced in this industry along with the need for security monitoring. Clearly, all this Big Data must be monitored in the context of Intrusion Detection. Since real-world physical sensors from the electrical grid can generate Big Data separately, these sensors from the physical world constitute another heterogeneous data source beyond cyberspace and contribute another dimension of heterogeneity as an input to Big Heterogeneous Data. Other industrial applications and processes have increasingly been computerized, with their real-world physical sensors also having Big Data.

They can enhance their overall situational awareness by utilizing those physical sensors as inputs into their Intrusion Detection architecture. When doing so, organizations should be aware of the Big Heterogeneous Data challenges they will face.

Even though there have been other survey papers on the Intrusion Detection topic, our paper is unique compared to these prior surveys. We focus on improving intrusion detection from the perspective of aggregating security sensor data from systems and devices which exhibit a great deal of heterogeneity. At the same time, we consider the fundamental Big Data problems that are inherent with such forms of heterogeneous security data. One survey by Modi et al. [8] is especially relevant when considering our work as they focus on Intrusion Detection in the Cloud. Their work does a fantastic job of describing the great deal of heterogeneity of security data and systems encountered in the cloud, and this is increasingly relevant as cloud computing becomes more pervasive and presents more Big Data challenges. Another survey by Zhou et al. [9] is also relevant to ours as they consider heterogeneous architectures for IDSs which collaborate in teams to improve detection accuracy, but they do not consider the Big Data ramifications.

While this paper covers a large variety of issues, there are two main themes of this survey:

1. Cybersecurity Data across Heterogeneous Sources.
2. Big Heterogeneous Data for Intrusion Detection.

The remainder of this paper is presented as follows: The INTRUSION DETECTION AND BIG DATA BACKGROUND section presents a background on Intrusion Detection and some Big Data implications and challenges. The SECURITY DATA ACROSS HETEROGENEOUS SOURCES section covers Security Data across Heterogeneous Sources. The BIG HETEROGENEOUS DATA FOR INTRUSION DETECTION section discusses Big Heterogeneous Data for Intrusion Detection. The DISCUSSION section provides further discussion and insights about the issues covered. Finally, the CONCLUSION section concludes the work presented in this paper.

Intrusion detection and big data background

The purpose of this section is to briefly give a general background on Big Data, as well as insight into Big Data challenges facing Intrusion Detection. Some background information is also provided with regards to challenges in security learning such as utilizing publicly available data sets and feature selection. Finally, some examples are provided illustrating how Big Data technologies can be utilized to address Big Data challenges in Intrusion Detection.

Big Data is typically defined in terms of 3Vs, a designation originally developed by Gartner analyst Doug Laney [10] in 2001: Volume, Velocity, and Variety. Volume refers to the amount of data, and there certainly can be a Big Data challenge when large amounts of data pose challenges to processing with traditional computing or techniques (which is also referred to as "Big Volume"). Velocity refers to the speed at which data is processed, and there can be a Big Data challenge when the rate of data is moving too quickly to process with traditional computing or techniques (which is also referred to as "Big Velocity"). Variety refers to the complexity of the data, and there can be a Big Data challenge when the data includes complex problems such as high dimensionality, data from many sources, or data having many different data structures: all of these problems can cause difficulty in processing with traditional computing or techniques (which is also referred to as "Big Variety"). There are many other definitions of Big Data, such as the 5Vs defined by Zikopoulous [11] that adds Veracity and Value to the already existing 3Vs of Volume, Velocity, and Variety. Veracity accounts for the correctness of the data, and can include data quality problems such as noise or missing values (which is also referred to as "Big Veracity"). Value accounts for Big Data in the sense that if particular data does not provide significance (value), it is not relevant for Big Data analysis (which is also referred to as "Big Value"). However for simplicity, Big Data can just be summarized as any time current mainstream computing or techniques cannot process data effectively.

For Intrusion Detection, Big Data is currently a major challenge and has been a prevailing theme for quite some time. In 1994, a study by Frank [12] for Intrusion Detection focusing on data reduction and classification found: "a user typically generates between 3 - 35 Megabytes of data in an eight hour period and it can take several hours to analyze a single hour's worth of data". They further suggested that filtering, clustering, and feature selection on the data is "important if real-time detection is desired," which can improve detection accuracy. This example indicates that Intrusion Detection has been facing Big Data challenges long before the "Big Data" term was introduced.

While a more comprehensive security monitoring system across heterogeneous systems could improve security, it would further exacerbate the Big Data challenge for Intrusion Detection which is already present in isolated systems. Integrating across more security sensors would increase Big Data issues in terms of: Volume in having to store more information collectively, Velocity in that more information would be flowing collectively at a higher rate in and out of the monitoring system, and especially Variety in terms of many different types of information coming from very different sources and also collectively yielding higher dimensionality.

A more comprehensive approach for monitoring a myriad of diverse heterogeneous event sources for Intrusion Detection can yield a better situational awareness of the threats in cyberspace, and thus improve detection accuracy and minimize false alarms by correlating security events among these diverse sources. Experiments have indicated that embracing a more diverse heterogeneous approach to Intrusion Detection does yield better situational awareness and improve accuracy. However, Big Data challenges already exist in some of the individual sources, and when they are aggregated the existing Big Data problem is compounded into a more significant Big Heterogeneous Data problem. When Big Data challenges are already present in any of the underlying inputs or outputs for Intrusion Detection, the overall system will likely experience Big Data challenges as well unless the Big Data bottleneck is eliminated. One way to remove this Big Data challenge is by filtering out (removing) the Big Data from a subsystem. However this is not ideal if valuable information is lost. New techniques or Big Data technologies can alleviate the challenges and costs that Big Data impose for Intrusion Detection.

Big Heterogeneous Data definitions

When Big Data is present in heterogeneous forms, it can be considered Big Heterogeneous Data regardless of whether that data is input(s) or output(s) of the system. For example, this can arise due to the additive properties of Big Data. If one input is deemed

Big Data and is added to another input which is not Big Data, the result will still be Big Data. This can be shown in Equation 1 below:

$$BD(\text{``}BigData\text{''}) + NBD(\text{``}NotBigData\text{''}) = BD(\text{``}BigData\text{''}) \tag{1}$$

Similarly if some advanced data correlation (or data fusion which is presented in the SECURITY DATA ACROSS HETEROGENEOUS SOURCES section) for analysis is occurring and the Big Data is being combined with "Not Big Data" in a multiplicative manner, the result will still be Big Data. This can be shown in Equation 2 below (assuming "Not Big Data" is greater than one):

$$BD(\text{``}BigData\text{''}) \times NBD(\text{``}NotBigData\text{''}) = BD(\text{``}BigData\text{''}) \tag{2}$$

Therefore, when Big Data is being combined with other data that is not classified as Big Data, the result will still be Big Data.

Another important consideration is that Big Data Challenges can quickly escalate into a significantly larger Big Data problem when combining multiple heterogeneous sources for analysis where each of the sources can have Big Data challenges individually. An example of this would be if two or more heterogeneous sources which separately contain Big Data challenges individually were then analyzed with advanced data correlation techniques (or data fusion which is presented in the SECURITY DATA ACROSS HETERO-GENEOUS SOURCES section) in order to give better accuracy through superior situational awareness. For complex systems such as Intrusion Detection where a large amount of heterogeneous sources are common and can contain Big Data challenges, the problem can quickly escalate into a more difficult Big Heterogeneous Data challenge. This can be shown in Equation 3 below (where n refers to the number of heterogeneous data sources that contain Big Data, and $n > 1$):

$$BHD(\text{``}BigHeterogeneousData\text{''}) = \prod_{i=1}^{n} BHDSi(\text{``}BigHeterogenousDataSourcei\text{''}) \tag{3}$$

The above generalizations do not always apply and even if parts of the system (e.g., a subsystem) contains Big Data challenges, these do not always propagate throughout the rest of the system. Big Data can be effectively removed in one or more of the subsystems by filtering (removal), and then the Big Data would not necessarily propagate throughout the rest of the system. This is not always an ideal approach if the Big Data being filtered out contains value, but it is still necessary at times if retaining the Big Data is too costly. An example for this would be if netflow traffic was analyzed for a NIDS instead of deep packet inspection. The deep packet inspection will yield superior detection accuracy. However the cost may be prohibitive in doing so. Another example might be the time retention policy for very detailed forensic data, where costs can prevent this Big Data from being stored indefinitely. This is illustrated in Equation 4 below (where the subtraction operator is essentially filtering or removal of the Big Data):

$$BD(\text{``}BigData\text{''}) - BD(\text{``}BigData\text{''}) = NBD(\text{``}NotBigData\text{''}) \tag{4}$$

As the above scenario is a cost and benefit tradeoff, Big Data challenges can also be removed by some of the following "Big Data Handlers": Big Data technologies, natural technology evolution (e.g., Storage or Processing evolutions such as Moore's Law), or novel techniques (or new approaches). For example, if it is desired to retain forensic data longer and a "Big Data Handler" technology like Hadoop permits this to be performed in a cost permissible fashion, then the "Big Data Challenge" can be removed and the "Handled Big Data" can be retained in a manner that is within cost constraints. This is illustrated in Equation 5 below (where the addition operator is enabling the Big Data to be handled in a cost effective manner):

$$BDC(\text{``BigDataChallenge''}) + BDH(\text{``BigDataHandler''}) = HBD(\text{``HandledBigData''})$$

$$(5)$$

Essentially, when dealing with Big Data challenges and heterogeneous inputs or outputs, the resulting data will still be Big Data if the Big Data Challenge is not eliminated in some way. For example, if there was a "Big Data Challenge" like a particular data source that had very high dimensionality and if a "Big Data Handler" like feature selection could be effectively used to create "Handled Big Data", then the "Big Data Challenge" will either remain or be eliminated depending on whether an effective "Big Data Handler" was used. In this case, if feature selection was effectively employed as a "Big Data Handler", then the "Big Data Challenge" would be removed and we would have "Handled Big Data". Likewise, if feature selection was not effective (or used), then the "Big Data Challenge" would remain and we were not able to effectively handle the particular challenges from Big Data.

Accordingly, when considering Big Data with heterogeneous sources or outputs, it can be better described as Big Heterogeneous Data so long as the Big Data Challenges are not eliminated in some way. The reason Big Heterogeneous Data is a more descriptive term is because typically the Big Data Challenges will be even more pronounced (i.e., magnified) when dealing with extreme heterogeneity in the input(s) or output(s) of Intrusion Detection Big Data within cyberspace. The BIG HETEROGENEOUS DATA FOR INTRUSION DETECTION section will further elaborate on Big Heterogeneous Data in terms of inputs and output categories now that the rationale behind the Big Heterogeneous Data terminology has been presented. This Big Heterogeneous Data challenge can become more pronounced while attempting to enhance Intrusion Detection through superior situational awareness by adopting more heterogeneity in the inputs, outputs, and architectural components as mentioned throughout this survey.

Important considerations for intrusion detection

With a more comprehensive security monitoring system, improvements to computer security do not need to be restricted to merely detecting security intrusions. Such a system could be extended to actually prevent security intrusions by integrating with technologies such as Intrusion Prevention Systems (IPSs), and embracing more of a "Defense in Depth" strategy [13]. Naturally, an IPS would require close to real-time detection. Note that this study is not limited to Intrusion Detection with the "real-time" distinction, and also includes offline forensic and security analytic capabilities.

This survey is not similar to previous Intrusion Detection surveys in that it evaluates the Intrusion Detection problem with an emphasis on aggregating security sensor data across many different systems and devices with the motivation of further improving security alerting accuracy. In addition, we consider the Big Data issues that arise when handling such forms of heterogeneous security data.

In the earlier days of computing, security monitoring was primarily performed by system administrators checking the log files of their servers. Then in the 1980s, the concept of the Intrusion Detection System was introduced, where a separate monitoring device would look for suspicious behavior at the network or computer host level. Denning [14] produced what many consider to be the first landmark research paper for Intrusion Detection System (IDS) research back in 1987. A good example of an IDS is the common and widely known open source IDS called Snort [15,16].

Intrusion Detection is a very active research area with important implications. The Center for Strategic and International Studies and McAfee conducted a study [17] and analyzed monetary losses from cybercrime and cyber espionage: "for the US, for example, our best guess is that losses may reach $100 billion annually." They approximate these global losses to be about $300 billion annually. In 2012 through more than 250 client engagements, the Verizon RISK Team [18] found over 47,000 confirmed security incidents, with 92% of data breaches perpetuated by outsiders in their engagements with clients. In a study [19] by the Ponemon Institute, for the FY 2012 it was determined that the most expensive cybercrime category was "Detection" costing 26% (followed by: Recovery, Ex-post Response, Containment, Investigation, Incident management). These studies clearly demonstrate that cybersecurity (and specifically Intrusion Detection) have significant economic impact.

Julisch and Dacier [20] discuss how Intrusion Detection can have many false alarms: "IDSs can easily trigger thousands of alarms per day, up to 99% of which are false positives." It is not uncommon for security analysts to grow numb to a flood of meaningless false alarms. Xu and Ning [21] state that in terms of detection rate, IDSs are typically not completely accurate, and can have an unacceptable number of False Negatives ("may miss some attacks").

Intrusion Detection is inherently a Big Data problem according to Suthaharan and Panchagnula [22]: "However the biggest challenge is the 'Big-Data' problem associated with the large amount of network traffic data collected dynamically in the intrusion detection dataset". Bhatti et al. [23] discuss how even current technologies cannot cope well with the Big Data challenges of Intrusion Detection: "Security analytics in a big data environment presents a unique set of challenges, not properly addressed by the existing security incident and event monitoring (or SIEM) systems that typically work with a limited set of traditional data sources (firewall, IDS, etc.) in an enterprise network". From a study by Enterprise Strategy Group at the end of 2012, Olsten [24] discusses that: "44% of enterprise organizations consider their security analytics 'big data' today, while another 44% believe that their security analytics requirements will be regarded as 'big data' within the next two years". Clearly, Intrusion Detection can be a Big Data challenge.

Challenges of machine learning in cybersecurity

This section addresses some issues found with Intrusion Detection data set challenges and feature selection. This background is very relevant for Intrusion Detection in general especially considering the widespread criticism of the publicly available data sets, and yet the majority of the research uses these criticized data sets. Accordingly, it is important that the reader understands that many of the experiments considered in this paper suffer the same criticisms when using an experiment with data sets (unless otherwise noted). Some researchers openly admit that the underlying data sets themselves have inherent flaws. Nonetheless, researchers continue to use them because essentially it is the best they have to work with.

A brief background is also given on feature selection and its application to Intrusion Detection data sets. This too can be important for considering experiments with data sets for Intrusion Detection, and especially more so when utilizing data sets from a multitude of diverse heterogeneous sources. The reason for this is the landscape for cybersecurity can change extremely rapidly, and accordingly can undermine the stability of the feature selection sets in general and especially so for real-time Intrusion Detection. These issues will also be evaluated from the perspective of Big Data.

Intrusion detection data set challenges

Many authors discuss the problems with existing public Intrusion Detection data sets: for example, Sommer and Paxson [25] give an excellent summary regarding some of the underlying reasons why this is a significant problem. The cybersecurity landscape has changed significantly over the last decade, and many don't even consider experiments that use older data sets to even be relevant today according to Sommer and Paxson. Unfortunately, organizations can be reluctant or even legally constrained from divulging sensitive data that these types of data sets can contain, and Coull et al. [26] note that attempts to anonymize sensitive data are not always effective. In addition, lab simulation of real-world network traffic to generate data sets is often not very realistic. As shown in a survey by Azad and Jha [27], the two most popular data sets used for research in Intrusion Detection are DARPA and KDD Cup where out of the 75 studies discussed, 46 used one of these data sets while only 29 chose a different one. This is disappointing because the DARPA and KDD Cup data sets are over a decade old, and even recent studies still frequently use them. The cybersecurity landscape has changed significantly over the last decade, and many don't consider experiments that use those data sets to be relevant today [25]. To make matters even worse, it became widely known shortly after the initial release of those data sets that they contained inherent flaws, as discussed by McHugh [28] and Mahoney and Chan [29]. Nonetheless, the DARPA and KDD data sets are still widely used even today. Some of the more commonly used data sets can be seen in Table 1.

These flawed public data sets lack Veracity from the perspective of Big Data, and so they would not be relevant as a consequence of having poor quality. Due to this low Veracity, these data sets would also lack Value as well, further reducing their relevancy.

Table 1 Summary of popular datasets in the intrusion detection domain [30]

Data source	Dataset name	Abbreviation
Network Traffic	DARPA 1998 TCPDump Files	DARPA98
	DARPA 1999 TCPDump Files	DARPA99
	KDD99 Dataset	KDD99
	10% KDD99 Dataset	KDD99-10
	Internet Exploration Shootout Dataset	IES
User behavior	Unix User Dataset	UNIXDS
System call sequences	DARPA 1998 BSM Files	BSM 98
	DARPA 1998 BSM Files	BSM 99
	University of New Mexico Dataset	UNM

A few other data sets of note are: ISCX [31], MAWI [32], NSA Data Capture [33], and the Internet Storm Center [34] (which also hosts the dshield.org data set). However, these more recent data sets are not used as frequently as the DARPA and KDD data sets, even in recent studies.

Song et al. took an interesting approach [35] in building their own data set by using honeypot data. A honeypot is a system that is not completely patched in order to draw attention from attackers. They also placed a machine in the network to generate normal traffic, and so any activity related to that machine was labeled as normal (it did not receive much attack traffic) while all traffic related to the honeypots were labeled as an attack. Overall there were approximately 93,000,000 total sessions generated, with about 50,000,000 being normal sessions and the remainder being attack sessions. Also of interest, was that their IDSs and anti-virus did not successfully classify about 426,000 of the sessions as attacks, even though they were able to more correctly classify them as attacks upon deeper inspection of the shellcodes. Because this data did not come from an actual client or pertain to ongoing business efforts, Song et al. did not need to worry about the sensitivity of the data. Also, their data set is roughly balanced between the classes of normal and attack.

While there are some drawbacks to this approach (for example, the normal class could be considered too "simulated"), it shows good promise for future work. More researchers could take this or a similar approach instead of continuing to use datasets that are not very relevant from over a decade ago. Another option for researchers to generate more adequate data sets might be for them to actually launch attacks in honeypot networks with simulated normal traffic, or possibly even do so in a real-world environment if they can properly sanitize sensitive data or ensure the absence of sensitive data in the first place. Generating data sets at even larger scales with honeypots could also lead to Big Data challenges in terms of Volume, Variety, and even Velocity in having to accommodate such large amounts, speed, and variety of Intrusion Detection data.

Intrusion detection and feature selection opportunities

Feature selection is an important technique in addressing Big Data challenges posed by Intrusion Detection, and when applied properly it can significantly improve classification processing times. In some cases, it can even improve classification accuracy by removing misleading noise. However, one should take caution in how feature selection is applied and especially with regards to research studies versus real-world application in terms of both relevancy and efficiency.

Many studies (even recent studies) are essentially using static data sets (i.e., DARPA, KDD, etc.) in the sense that the labeled instances might not anticipate newer real-world attacks such as "zero-day exploits", and this is especially important in the domain of cybersecurity because it is inherently a dynamically changing landscape. Newer attacks can be significantly more diverse than old attacks in terms of both technical implementation as well as the underlying methods themselves in the ongoing arms race between attackers and defenders. So in terms of feature selection in Intrusion Detection, yesterday's selected features from a static data set might not be relevant for tomorrow's dynamically different data set. A new attack class can make different features important, and different feature sets may or may not be relevant even at the millisecond scale. Thus, it is important to rethink the relevancy of feature sets from data sets that are older, lack diversity, or are very static.

A smaller number of relevant features will improve classification processing times from an efficiency standpoint. However, the process of performing feature selection in some cases can take a considerable amount of computation time. Applying feature selection to a data set where its attributes can change both rapidly and diversely might not be able to generate feature sets in close to real-time. In certain scenarios where generating feature sets takes too long for the effectiveness of the system, perhaps generating feature selection sets could be delegated to an offline process similar to what Bass proposed for offline Data Mining [36]. Those feature selection sets could be applied by the Intrusion Detection templates which are then used at the various sensors. In this manner, some static and stable feature sets could be used for Intrusion Detection. However, it cannot be assumed that all feature selection sets will be stable, especially when they are built from a myriad of heterogeneous sources in a constantly evolving and hostile environment where the diversity in attributes of data sets can vary considerably.

Wang et al. [37] conducted an experiment employing feature selection, specifically to address the so-called "dimensional disaster" problem which often prevents multi-sensor fusion from being applied to Network Security. In their experiment the original number of features was 84, which took 2.66 seconds of CPU time to process the test set. When they reduced the number of features to 37, it only took 1.54 seconds to process the test set. While they only assessed network data (some classification errors were higher or lower depending on the attack type), they asserted that fusing from other heterogeneous sources such as a host log could be beneficial. Perhaps different feature selection techniques could have further reduced the number of features without significantly sacrificing classification accuracy.

Tsang et al. use a MOGFIDS (fuzzy-logic based) feature selection technique on KDD-Cup99 [38] and achieved the best overall feature selection results as compared to eleven other techniques in terms of classification accuracy. Chebrulu et al. [39] present an ensemble approach of feature selection and are able to achieve higher classification accuracies with the combination of feature selection techniques versus using each technique independently, and in their case they did improve overall Intrusion Detection accuracy for all attack categories and the normal class of the DARPA dataset by using an ensemble of Bayesian Networks and Classification and Regression Tress. Chen et al. [40] show that classification times can be sometimes be reduced in half when using SVM and C4.5 feature selection techniques on the KDD datasets, and they also evaluate Random Forest (RF) as a feature selection technique but they do not provide classification times for all the features of RF to compare its performance of classification times. Elngar et al. [41] use a Particle Swarm Optimization (PSO-Discretize-HNB) technique which uses feature selection to reduce the feature set size from 41 to 11 features, and with the smaller feature set Detection Accuracy improved from 97.7

Clearly feature selection can be beneficial with Intrusion Detection. However care must be taken in its application, as the nature of attack threats changes, so can the data. Correspondingly, the feature sets also change. Also similar to other domains, feature selection can be used to address Big Data challenges. Feature Selection can help reduce the dimensionality of the data being processed with Intrusion Detection, and it has the potential to mitigate Big Variety challenges simply through reduction of certain features.

However, feature selection can also introduce additional Big Variety challenges when feature sets are highly unstable and a large Variety of different feature sets need to be utilized. Any time feature selection is used it can help address Big Volume challenges simply by collecting less data from the removal of certain features. Similarly, feature selection can be especially helpful in reducing Big Velocity challenges by increasing processing speeds. For example, Elngar et al. [41] found they could reduce processing times by a factor of ten simply by reducing 41 features to 11 features. Feature selection shows good promise for addressing Big Data challenges found within Intrusion Detection.

Using Hadoop to ddress big data challenges for intrusion detection

Traditional computing storage platforms like relational databases do not scale effectively against the onslaught of Big Data challenges posed by Intrusion Detection. Hadoop, an open-source distributed storage platform that can run on commodity hardware, has been utilized to better accommodate the Big Data storage requirements of massive Volume and fast Velocity along with potentially very diverse heterogeneous data structures. Collectively, Hadoop can refer to several technologies such as HDFS, Hive, MapReduce, Pig, etc. HDFS is the Hadoop Distributed File System, Hive is a data warehouse implementation for Hadoop, MapReduce is a programming model in Hadoop, and Pig is a querying language for Hadoop which has similarities to the SQL language for relational databases. Refer to [42] for further details on Hadoop.

Suthaharan [43] proposes the use of Big Data technologies like Hadoop, Hive, and the Cloud. He argues that before Big Data technologies should be employed to address Intrusion Detection, it should first be apparent that there are Big Data challenges present so as to not unnecessarily deploy Big Data technologies. Suthaharan argues that the current 3Vs of Volume, Variety, and Velocity cannot adequately provide for the early detection of Big Data, and so he proposes 3Cs of Cardinality, Continuity, and Complexity to more easily develop metrics with mathematical and statistical tools. A brief summary of the definitions for the proposed 3Cs follows:

Cardinality - number of records at an instant
Continuity - (1) continuous functions represent data; (2) continuous growth with respect to time
Complexity - (1) data type variety is large; (2) high dimensionality; (3) high speed data processing

Suthaharan proposes a Big Data model to deal with Intrusion Detection as shown in Figure 2. The User Interaction and Learning System (UILS) performs the learning on the data, permits users to interact with the system, and can control the storage requirements. The Network Traffic Recording System (NTRS) simply captures the network traffic and either stores it locally in the Hadoop Distributed File System (HDFS) or the Cloud Computing Storage System (CCSS). If data is needed immediately it is stored locally in the HDFS, otherwise it can be stored in the CCSS and can be processed later. Also, for Machine Learning in Intrusion Detection and Big Data, Suthaharan recommends the following should receive more attention: multi-domain representation-learning, cross-domain representation-learning, and machine lifelong learning.

Whitworth and Suthaharan [44] address the security challenges introduced with a model that can utilize the public Internet and the Cloud. Even though storage in

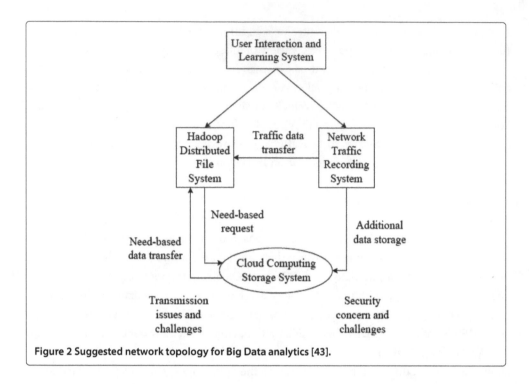

Figure 2 Suggested network topology for Big Data analytics [43].

the Cloud can incur a significant communication cost, higher latency, and additional security challenges, the authors contend that the Cloud can extend storage beyond a local network's capacity in an elastic and "cost effective and efficient manner" using Infrastructure as a Service (IaaS). Trust levels are proposed to assess varying levels of encryption requirements based on weighted values of cloud provider "risk level" and the sensitivity of the data. A Data Key Store (DKS) is also proposed to manage security and efficiently provide for data retrievability (ensuring the data is unchanged and available).

Jeong et al. [45] give an overview of issues encountered with Intrusion Detection and Big Data and how various Hadoop technologies can address these challenges, specifically focusing on anomaly-based (misuse) IDSs. They describe various techniques and issues found with Intrusion Detection, as well as what some of the main issues are in applying Hadoop technologies for Intrusion Detection. Their study provides a good introduction for readers not already familiar with Hadoop technologies and how they can be applied to Big Data challenges found with Intrusion Detection.

Lee and Lee [46] conducted an experiment with Hadoop technologies (e.g., HDFS, MapReduce, and Hive) to measure and analyze Internet traffic for a DDOS Detector. In their experiment they were able to achieve throughput speeds of up to 14 Gbps in some scenarios, and some of their slower results were close to 6 Gbps for some analysis types while using 30 or more nodes in a cluster. Several options were tested in the experiment, such as varying the number of cluster nodes (specifically, there were either 30 more powerful nodes or 300 less powerful nodes), and they also varied the file size of the playback file from 1 TB to 5 TB while performing 5 different types of analysis. Their study only considered previously recorded traffic data from files and not real-time traffic monitoring. However, they indicated that they plan to support real-time traffic monitoring with future work. Hadoop and its related technologies show good feasibility as an Intrusion Detection tool as they were able to achieve up to 14 Gbps for a DDOS detector, and this is only a preliminary experiment with future improvements planned.

Cheon and Choe [47] propose a distributed IDS architecture based on Snort and Hadoop technologies. They performed an experiment to see if additional Hadoop-based nodes for analysis could increase processing efficiency. Their methodology was to use replay files rather than real-time data, and then to evaluate the efficiency in terms of total processing time of the replay files while varying the number of Hadoop-based analysis nodes from zero to eight. A total of nine computers were used in the experiment with one acting as the "master node". They discovered that the performance efficiency increased (it took less time to process the dataset) as they increased the number of Hadoop-based nodes. However, processing efficiency actually decreased with only one Hadoop-based analysis node. When all eight nodes were used, they saw an increase of 424% in performance as compared to using the stand-alone machine without any distributed nodes of Hadoop analysis slaves. It would be interesting to repeat the experiment with significantly more Hadoop-based nodes in order to see how far this methodology can scale out and if a certain threshold would offer diminishing returns.

Veetil and Gao [48] conducted an experiment and created Hadoop clusters to implement the Naïve Bayes algorithm in a distributed fashion. With a 6 node "homogeneous" Hadoop-based cluster where the nodes had similar hardware, they were able perform classification 37% quicker than a stand-alone machine could. While the experiment was successful as a proof of concept to use a distributed Hadoop-based cluster to implement Naïve Bayes classifier, it could only classify an average of 434 packets per minute. Much more research and experimentation can be done to implement Hadoop technologies to improve Intrusion Detection efficiency and classification accuracy.

Security data across heterogeneous sources

The purpose of this section is to describe various techniques and architectures to accommodate diverse heterogeneous sources for Intrusion Detection. In order to not deviate from that focus since it is a central theme for this study, the Big Data implications of these systems will only be partially addressed within this section. Overall, Intrusion Detection systems need to consider more diverse heterogeneous sources to provide better situational awareness within cyberspace. This can yield significant improvements to cybersecurity as Intrusion Detection is one of the core pillars of any cyber defense system. The first section gives a background on how data fusion can be used to improve situational awareness as has been done in other domains like Military applications. In the second section for illustrative purposes, a small sampling from academic studies of Intrusion Detection architectures with heterogeneous sources will be presented to give a brief overview and background of these systems. In the third section, several studies regarding SIEM systems will be presented, as well as some of the issues surrounding their deployment in the commercial sector. SIEM technology is not simply just another type of heterogeneous IDS architecture, but rather is a completely different architecture in its own right with an approach to heterogeneous data for Intrusion Detection which also provides for security analytics and forensic capabilities.

Enhancing situational awareness in cyberspace with data fusion

In 2000, Bass [36] made a major contribution to Intrusion Detection research by suggesting data fusion as a technique to aggregate Intrusion Detection data from many different heterogeneous sources such as "numerous distributed packet sniffers, system log files, SNMP traps and queries, user profile databases, system messages, and operator commands". Essentially, data fusion is a technique to make overall sense of data from different sources which commonly have different data structures. Bass also elaborated extensively on using data fusion online (near real-time) in conjunction with data mining offline in order to process the enormous amount of cybersecurity data more effectively so that it could be useful for Intrusion Detection purposes. The purpose of the data mining is to discover previously undetected intrusions based on past data, and use these to build Intrusion Detection templates. This is not performed in real-time because the data mining operations cannot always be performed quickly enough to perform near real-time reactions for Intrusion Detection (which also suggests that Big Velocity was causing problems for real-time Intrusion Detection back in 2000). These Intrusion Detection templates are applied to the online (near real-time) data fusion operations in order to better assess possible threats.

Bass [36] described that he borrowed some concepts directly from military applications such as multisensor data fusion, where on the battlefield or in military theaters a widely diverse array of heterogeneous sources can be employed. He also described using a methodology discovered by the military's concept of Observe, Orient, Decide, and Act (OODA) to gain an overall higher cyberspace situational awareness by using data fusion for Intrusion Detection, and that data fusion can provide varying levels of inference from being merely aware of an intrusion attempt up to being able to analyze the threat and vulnerability. In "Multisensor data fusion for next generation distributed intrusion detection systems" [49], Bass elaborated further on his proposed model and provides further details on data fusion. Bass's approach of analyzing Intrusion Detection data across many different types of devices and systems concurrently is an excellent example of utilizing many diverse heterogeneous sources, helping researchers gain enhanced insight into cybersecurity (particularly in the context of Big Data challenges).

Similar to Bass's approach, Lan et al. [50] utilized data fusion across diverse heterogeneous sources with the explicit goal of improving Intrusion Detection through superior situational awareness. They warned that traditional deployments of security products such as Firewalls, IDSs, and security scanners rarely work together and only possess very minimal knowledge of the network assets they are protecting. In order to bolster cyber defense through a superior situational awareness, the authors proposed using a form of data fusion known as Dempster-Shafer (D-S) evidence theory in order to make good sense out of the heterogeneous sources. D-S evidence theory is a fairly common data fusion technique utilized by researchers using data fusion within the Intrusion Detection domain, which applies probabilistic techniques to the current observations of the system. Providing details for D-S evidence theory is beyond the scope of this study, so refer to [50] for more details.

A prevailing theme encountered by Lan et al. [50] was the Big Data challenges encountered when combining events from heterogeneous sources (e.g., IDS, firewall, host log files, netflow, etc.) to achieve better situational awareness. They discuss how Big Velocity problems can make it hard "to obtain the security state of the whole network precisely when facing too much warning information". Big Volume issues exist in collecting, fusing, and analyzing "a great deal of information". With diverse heterogeneous sources, the Big Variety challenges were very clear: "the complexities and diversities of security alert data on modern networks make such analysis extremely difficult". They conducted an experiment with the DARPA2000 data set, and by using data fusion were able to simplify alert messages from a total count of 64,481 to 6,164, which is an order of magnitude improvement. While this experiment shows data fusion can be an effective technique, further experiments using more modern and robust data sets would likely be of greater interest.

It is important to caution that just arbitrarily adding a multitude of sensors and fusing them all together does not necessarily improve accuracy. This is a phenomenon described by Mitchell [51] as "catastrophic fusion" where often the performance of an entire data fusion system is worse than that of the individual sensors. Careful design and consideration must be given to properly construct a data fusion system. Further background information regarding data fusion especially with regards to Intrusion Detection can be found in [52] by Hall.

This section described the importance of enhancing cyber defense through improving situational awareness. Just like data fusion is used in other domains for improving situational awareness, it can also be applied to Intrusion Detection. Research applying data fusion to Intrusion Detection shows good potential for improving the state of the art; however, researchers should carefully consider Big Data challenges that can exist within Intrusion Detection when applying data fusion.

A sampling of various heterogeneous intrusion detection architectures

The studies presented in this section give a brief conceptual overview of the various Intrusion Detection architectures found in academic studies when dealing with heterogeneous sources. Given that the previous section illustrated the importance of considering heterogeneous sources to improve cybersecurity, the purpose of this section is to explore the architectural issues of these systems identified by researchers. Following are five different examples of architectures proposed by researchers to accommodate diverse heterogeneous event sources.

In one study, Fessi et al. [53] consider Intrusion Detection across heterogeneous sources. A good illustration for this is given in Figure 3 where multiple distributed "Observers" harvest data from various heterogeneous sources (e.g., both network and various host-based monitoring) and a "Global Analyzer" makes the ultimate decision for whether security events originating from the "Observers" are security incidents. In making its final decision, this "Global Analyzer" will perform data fusion across the various "Analyzers" to gain a better situational awareness across the multiple analyzers especially in the case of distributed attacks. One of the interesting aspects of this model is that the "Analyzers" themselves can be heterogeneous, and different types of "Analyzers" such as misuse detection or anomaly detection could simultaneously be used for the same events from observers. So essentially, each observer could be associated to one or more "Analyzers" for the motivation of detecting different classes of attacks. This model could scale well in the face of Big Data challenges given some of its distributed characteristics, which enables "Observers" and "Analyzers" to be added for scalability. However if there is only one centralized "Global Analyzer", it could become a bottleneck in the face of very

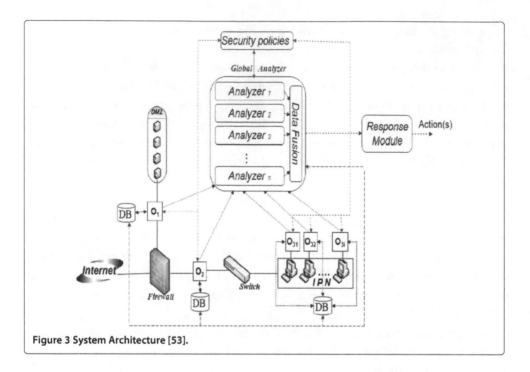

Figure 3 System Architecture [53].

Big Data or it could also be problematic if it was successfully attacked or had reliability faults.

To take more of a global view of Intrusion Detection, Ganame et al. [54] extend upon their earlier work with a centralized Security Operation Center (SOC) called a SOCBox, and develop an enhanced version called Distributed Security Operation Center (DSOC). Their architecture allows an organization to scale the system across the Internet to provide even better correlation across geographical boundaries and provide enhanced defense resiliency if one site comes under attack. Obviously, this architecture could even scale beyond multiple organizations.

One of the reasons Ganame et al. [54] extended the original centralized SOC architecture to DSOC was that the SOC architecture could be compromised by an attacker flooding the network on one site, and the Centralized SOC wouldn't be able to receive all the security events, allowing attackers to evade detection. They presented several examples of being able to compromise the SOC with "flood" attacks, demonstrating that the original SOC architecture was suspect to "flood" attacks and faced a Big Volume problem. The DSOC was able to overcome this problem by using a Local Analyzer (LA) at each site to assess intrusion detection by collecting, analyzing, and correlating alert security events locally. Each LA would then transmit a smaller and more intelligible payload of alerts to a Global Analyzer (GA) which would then perform further aggregation and analysis of alerts sent from all LAs in order to build better global awareness for Intrusion Detection (and the GA can be mirrored for redundancy and fault tolerance).

Ganame et al. [54] also describe the benefit of using diverse heterogeneous sources to correlate events across multiple sources in order to successfully detect attacks, and give an example where most homogeneous NIDS systems would be unable to detect certain multi-step attacks. Importantly, they were able to experimentally show that utilizing heterogeneous sources yielded superior Intrusion Detection capabilities over what most homogeneous approaches such as NIDS are capable of with more advanced attacks. The

DSOC system utilizes diverse heterogeneous sources and accordingly monitors all network components such as "IDS, IPS, firewall, router, work-station, etc." to yield a more comprehensive situational awareness. Refer to Figure 4 for an illustration of examples that a Local Analyzer could use as diverse heterogeneous sources. The system also employs Protocol Agents and Application Agents to better facilitate harvesting the information from the source events in an understandable format as well as in a redundant fashion and with encrypted transmission. One other interesting aspect they discussed was the need for common message formats among different devices and protocols like the Intrusion Detection Message Exchange Format (IDMEF). However, they found that the XML bus used for IDMEF was "too heavy and resource consuming," especially for event correlation. The authors implemented a separate translation process to overcome this Big Velocity challenge.

This study demonstrates a couple of Big Volume challenges in that their original SOC architecture was prone to "flood" attacks, and that they could not directly use standard IDMEF formatting due to poor event correlation performance. Also, the use of heterogeneous data sources gave superior detection accuracy over homogeneous sources in some cases.

A Collaborative Intrusion Detection System (CIDS) is presented by Bye et al. in [55], where multiple "participants" (e.g., IDSs) form teams to work together to better assess Intrusion Detection collectively. As IDS technology has proliferated, the deployment of multiple IDSs within one environment has become more prevalent. A CIDS is a way for the multiple (and even different) IDSs to work together in teams. This allows a "Bigger Picture" to be realized through collaboration. The authors present a framework which

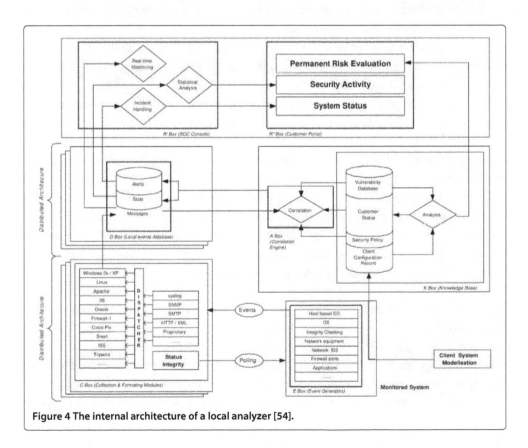

Figure 4 The internal architecture of a local analyzer [54].

can work across many different heterogeneous sources called Collaborative Intrusion Detection Framework (CIDF), and a set of mechanisms is used for a given detection or correlation algorithm to enable the Collaboration among IDSs. An "agent" is a participant in the CIDF which is also a member of a "detection group," possibly including other agents. These groups/subsets of agents have the same objective (such as anomaly detection), while another group/subset of agents may have a different objective (such as misuse detection). This study is relevant in that the authors are formally defining a framework for how CIDSs operate in general as well as how to cope with more complex issues such as security (and other issues) while collaborating. The authors also give examples of heterogeneous sources being used such as DSHIELD. Another interesting aspect is the overall heterogeneity of the framework, beyond just heterogeneous event sources. Agents within a group can themselves be comprised of heterogeneous "agents" (for example, by having different IDSs), and even the "detection groups" can be tasked with heterogeneous Intrusion Detection roles.

A Distributed Intrusion Detection System (DIDS) model is proposed by Bartos and Rehak [56] to overcome one major shortcoming of traditional IDSs: operating in isolation. Their main motivation is to increase overall accuracy and detect more threats. Importantly, their proposed DIDS can also accommodate heterogeneous sources, and their study gives examples of different event sources. The distributed IDS nodes are referred to as "sensors", and they have the capability to conduct data fusion to correlate different event types (i.e., if they are in different formats). Overall, every "sensor" IDS can communicate with every other sensor in the network with the motivation of redundancy as well as extra resiliency against attack. Each IDS "sensor" can tune itself to specialize its detection capabilities in order to improve accuracy for that specific attack class, and rely on other IDS "sensors" to evaluate other attack classes. Also, the IDS "sensors" can send requests for assistance when suspect behavior is encountered. Bartos and Rehak conducted an experiment for the proposed architecture and found that they could improve detection accuracy while keeping the false alarms constant. Their study is interesting in that data fusion across heterogeneous sources can help detection accuracy, but it is also interesting that it could not reduce false alarms especially considering that their architecture has a more global view. It would be interesting to evaluate the performance of this approach on a larger scale; however, it is a fairly novel exploration into utilizing distributed IDSs along with heterogeneous sources.

In evaluating DIDSs, Cai and Wu [57] discuss the software agent based approach for host-based systems where the agent monitors all relevant information of the host "including file system, logs and the kernel". While they also discuss the NIDS components, this is yet another example where more diverse heterogeneous sources are being monitored, enabling analysts "to get a broader view of what is occurring on their network as a whole". Cai and Wu also discuss the benefits of correlating IDS alerts across the Internet, similar to what Ganame et al. refer to in [54], and Bartos and Rehak also share this global view for Intrusion Detection in [56]. Other studies such as [58,59] show alert correlation across geographical boundaries to be an important cyber defense strategy for the enterprise as a whole. In these studies, a prevailing theme is that more diverse heterogeneous sources will enhance Intrusion Detection capabilities through event correlation and a better comprehension of situational awareness of cyber threats.

Security information and event management systems

SIEM systems are architecturally different than typical IDS solutions, and are the result of computer security vendors in the commercial sector seeking to profit by solving problems that enterprises were experiencing. The SIEM term was first coined in 2005 by Gartner Analysts Mark Nicolett and Amrit Williams [60] to describe how the industry was converging Security Information Management (SIM) and Security Event Management (SEM) technologies. SEM primarily dealt with real-time analysis for the purposes of incident response, and SIM mostly dealt with the long-term storage for the purposes of historical and trend analysis as well as providing forensic capabilities. Anuar et al. [61] discuss additional background information on SIEM technology, specifically in terms of comparing SIEM products to more traditional IDS and IPS products. SIEM systems take a more comprehensive approach beyond traditional IDSs with the motivation of giving a better holistic view of an organization's IT security, and a good definition is given by Rouse [62] in that a SIEM gives the ability to see trends and patterns of security data from a single point of view even though the security data can originate from diverse heterogeneous sources such as the network, end-user devices, servers, firewalls, antivirus systems, and intrusion prevention systems.

According to Gartner [63] SIEM software sales was $976.4 million in 2012 with 27.5 percent growth, and for comparison the overall security software market grew from $17.7 billion in 2011 to $19.1 billion in 2012 as tracked by Gartner (with SIEM software comprising about 5% of the total market share in security software). Per Mosaic Security Research [64], there are currently 65 SIEM products as of this writing with 6 of them being classified as freeware. As SIEM technology is relatively new as compared to IDS technology, there are still many academic research opportunities especially considering the widespread commercial growth of SIEM technology. Following is a brief overview of SIEM technology. SIEM products can differ from each other in how they operate and in terms of features they provide, and one particular SIEM definition might not universally apply to all SIEM products. Aguirre and Alonso [65] generalize the major SIEM functionalities as the following: "aggregates data from many sources, continuously monitors incidents, correlates events, and issues alert notifications". In their study, they also contend it is important for organizations to aggregate SIEM information across their multiple domains and they propose a federation of SIEMs to accomplish that goal.

Similarly, after analyzing SIEM systems, Kotenko et al. [66] contend the four main SIEM components are the following: "event filtering, aggregation, abstraction, and correlation; reasoning and visualization; decision support reaction and counter measures; attack modeling and security evaluation".

Either definition is sufficient for SIEMs, especially since Kotenko et al. drew their definition from the most advanced SIEMs as defined by Gartner Analysts Nicolett and Kavanagh in [67], while Aguirre and Alonso apply their generalization to a broader range of SIEM products.

Kotenko et al. [66] also discuss the various standards used by SIEMs to represent security events and incidents in standardized formats: SCAP [68], Common Base Event (CBE) [69], and Common Information Model (CIM) [70]. One of the main design motivations of SIEM technology is that vendors will typically try to ensure all the security data sensor sources have as common a format as possible in order to minimize the amount of "data fusion" analysis that needs to be performed. They also discuss the inadequacy found in all the major and widespread SIEM systems in that they use a traditional relational database for the storage and querying of the security data, and that the relational database model that the SIEMs are using is often overloaded. To overcome this limitation, they recommend using a hybrid database approach for the SIEM repository where a traditional RDBMS is used in conjunction with both XML-based databases and a triplet store ("A triple store is a purpose-built database for the storage and retrieval of RDF metadata" [71] and the triple is based on the "subject-predicate-object" methodology). It would be interesting to determine whether Hadoop technologies could provide any storage repository benefits as that was not mentioned by Kotenko et al.

The fact that traditional RDBMSs are a performance bottleneck for SIEM systems demonstrates that they face major Big Data challenges. This makes sense as they are analyzing security data across a myriad of diverse heterogeneous sources, whereas this survey points out numerous times that Big Data challenges can be encountered at only single sources for Intrusion Detection. Kotenko and Chechulin [72] propose an interesting attack modeling framework for SIEM systems in [72] called Attack Modeling and Security Evaluation Component (AMSEC) to address both known and unknown (zero day) vulnerabilities.

Metzger et al. [59] conducted a study in Higher Education Institutes (HEIs) regarding Intrusion Detection and how it can be applied with SIEM technology in conjunction with formalized Incident Management techniques. The overall system can react to security events either automatically or manually through a Computer Security Incident Response Team (CSIRT). HEIs can be highly targeted among botnets, email spammers, and others for their high bandwidth capabilities among other reasons. The authors propose a framework where in addition to the traditional SIEM approach, a couple of other non-traditional sources for the SIEM system are considered: Manual Reporting and the "DFN-CERT service". Manual Reporting allows outside organizations or individuals, internal Administrators or Support staff, and Help Desk tickets to report security incidents and information directly to the system for automated processing. This extra source can benefit Intrusion Detection for the SIEM system with increased detection accuracy as it broadens the scope of events being monitored. The SIEM can also correlate its other events with this new source for increased benefit. The "DFN-CERT service" is a worldwide service to automatically report malicious behavior and metadata to the local SIEM system, with the similar benefit of enhanced detection and correlation capabilities for the SIEM. These two other methods are used in conjunction with the traditional SIEM monitoring, correlation, and analysis functionalities. Additionally, their model includes having the SIEM either take automatic responses to events or to notify appropriate Administrators for action based on configurable policies and/or threshold measurements of events. With their model, they were able to automatically react (at least partially) to more than 85% of all abuse cases in their HEI study. This is important in that it shows more heterogeneous sources can enhance detection, correlation, and reaction capabilities of SIEM systems, especially with regards to reporting more diverse security events and metadata to the local SIEM system. Benefit can also be gained with the local SIEM receiving cybersecurity intelligence from a worldwide network. Also, it is important to note that heterogeneous sources need not be limited to cyberspace as shown in this study, and that reports from humans can enhance the situational awareness as well. A major motivation for the system implementation was to automate everything as much as possible in a formalized manner.

In a study evaluating systems to monitor security for cloud computing, Diego et al. [73] conclude that no single solution can currently cover all existing security threats for Infrastructure as a Service (IaaS) platforms. To enhance the overall infrastructure security it is recommended to use more diverse and heterogeneous solutions. Diego et al. give an example that two different types of SIEMs could detect more threats than just one. In addition, this study proposes a Quality of Protection (QoP) in terms of both better fault tolerance and enhanced security for the security system itself by using systematic redundancy (i.e., if one part of the system fails or comes under attack then a redundant piece can still function). An experiment was carried out with the commercial ArcSight SIEM product to test the throughput when using redundant SIEMs in a Byzantine fault tolerant architecture. A total of 4 ArcSight SIEM "replicas" were used with one being allowed to be faulty, and over 250,000 events per second could be processed. They determined the system was bound by resource exhaustion, and additional resources could further increase event throughput. This study did not elaborate on the methodology of storage and querying of the events into the archival repository with regards to forensic purposes and how the archival repository would scale out as additional SIEMs were added to the system. This study is interesting from a Big Data standpoint in that it shows good experimental results in the scalability of SIEM technology, but there is no clear indication in whether SIEM technology would face a scalability threshold with relational databases still being the prevalent storage engine. However, recently some vendors such as Splunk [74] have adopted relational database technologies in order to better address Big Data challenges.

In an effort to make SIEM technology more effective in defending against rapidly evolving cyber threats, Li et al. [75] recommend an Enterprise Security Monitoring (ESM) solution. Large enterprises are facing increasingly challenging attacks such as Advanced Persistent Threats (APTs), and one major problem these large enterprises can have is their various security teams might be fragmented into different organizational silos which can cause difficulties in sharing security intelligence information across these boundaries to better correlate events, especially against more advanced attacks. Their proposal to advance cyber defense to face these challenges is to use SIEM technology as a core component, and use this in conjunction with Enterprise Security Intelligence (ESI) to enhance overall next generation cyber defense architectures. Essentially, ESI will extend the overall security intelligence of the SIEM capabilities similar to how Business Intelligence (BI) is traditionally applied, and would allow more advanced security intelligence analytics to be developed and utilized in order to adapt to more advanced threats. For example, to provide improved situational awareness with ESI, business context information specific to the organization could be combined with alerts generated from the SIEM as well as various intelligence sources (i.e., those reported by humans or systems).

As originally put forth by Gartner in [76], Li et al. explain the six design principals of the next generation ESM shown in Table 2 (Refer to Figure 5 for a visual illustration).

The creation of a "fusion center" for the enterprise is recommended by the authors where the ESM is collaboratively utilized across organizational boundaries in a variety of ways especially regarding any aspects that could be fragmented (e.g., planning, risk assessment, data sources, intelligence analysis, etc.). They also contend that different

Table 2 Six design principals of the next generation ESM

1. "Comprehensive Enterprise Coverage"	The entire production IT stack (e.g., "networks, hosts, applications, databases, identities") for the enterprise must be monitored by the ESM regardless of environment (i.e., onsite or in the cloud).
2. "Information Interaction and Correlation"	All meaningful events, logs, and similar from input sources in #1 must be capable of being collected for correlation.
3. "Technology Interaction and Correlation"	The SIEM will serve as the foundation of the correlation engine, however it should also integrate with other important security technologies such as: Firewalls, IDSs/IPSs, DLPs, Vulnerability Management, and Anti-Malware.
4. "Business Interaction and Correlation"	The ESM must be aware and tuned to the specifics of the organization's business context to better assess an attacker's motivation and yield better correlation and intelligence.
5. "Cross-Boundary Intelligence for Better Decision Making"	The ESM solution must span organizational boundaries across the entire enterprise in a cohesive and collaborative manner, and not permit fragmentation with regards to its overall cyber defense.
6. "Visualized Output for Dynamic and Real-time Defense"	The output of the system must be easily visualized and understandable by end user analysts in an effective manner.

organizations could even benefit by collaborating and sharing security information with each other. However they emphasize the great difficulty posed by this because of competitive, technical, legal, and possibly embarrassing reasons (i.e., disclosing certain breaches could harm their image). In order to better cope with the Big Data challenges of processing and storing "massive amounts of data", Li et al. suggest that technologies like Hadoop could be leveraged. They also recommend cloud-based Enterprise Security Monitoring vendors as a "natural solution" for Big Data and scalability issues of enterprises.

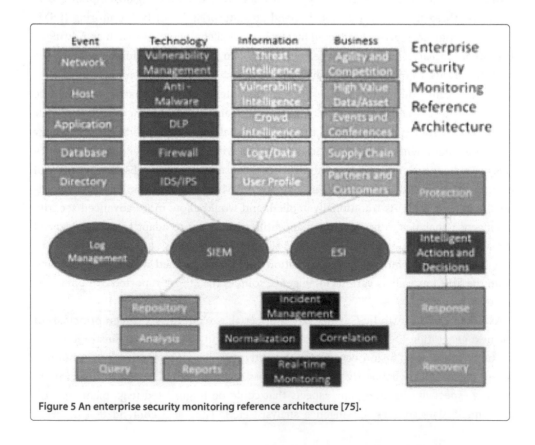

Figure 5 An enterprise security monitoring reference architecture [75].

Big heterogeneous data for intrusion detection

The purpose of this section is to describe Big Heterogeneous Data in terms of different categories to illustrate the various underlying levels of heterogeneity for Big Data within Intrusion Detection. At a high level, Big Heterogeneous Data can be described in terms of being input or output data. Big Heterogeneous Input Data can be further categorized into traditional Big Cyberspace Data and Big Industrial Data (i.e., data from industrial processes in the real physical world). Big Heterogeneous Output Data will be presented in the categories of Big Archival Security Data (which considers the long term storage aspects) and Big Alert Data (which will present Big Data issues surrounding alert data).

Big Heterogeneous input data

Big Heterogeneous Input Data is essentially just the types of input data in the spirit of Big Heterogeneous Data from the previous section (security data across heterogeneous sources). It can be considered simply as just heterogeneous input Big Data. The following sections each discuss one particular type of heterogeneous input Big Data grouped by higher-level categories. It is important to consider that a great deal of heterogeneity among the sources can be present within these categories. First, the traditional cyberspace input Big Data is presented. Then, Big Heterogeneous Industrial Data beyond cyberspace is discussed, and this section gives examples of Big Data from the physical world outside of cyberspace (e.g., industrial process data) which can further improve situational awareness even in cyberspace.

Big Heterogeneous cyberspace data

Big Heterogeneous Cyberspace Data are the traditional input types of data which are commonly considered in Intrusion Detection literature, but here they are presented in the context of Big Data. Both network layer and host layer event sources are considered. The network layer coverage is essentially just the network traffic that traditional approaches like NIDSs (e.g., Snort) monitor with a focus on Big Data. The host layer coverage focuses on Big Data challenges with different host sources, and is equivalent to the traditional HIDS approaches where computer servers, workstations, devices, etc. are being monitored. Again, it is important to consider that a great deal of diverse heterogeneity can occur among event sources in this category.

Nassar et al. [1] contend that outsourcing flow-based network monitoring and Intrusion Detection to cloud providers can be cost effective if done so in a secure manner. They give an example of Big Data with a university network that produces an average load of 650 Mbps and peaks up to 1.0 Gbps, and assert that because of such Big Network Data that "many monitoring systems have already shifted from the deep packet inspection to the aggregated flow data level". In other words, because of such Big Velocity at the network level, more accurate techniques of intrusion detection such as deep packet inspection are being abandoned in favor of less computationally intensive techniques such as monitoring at the network flow data level. Nassar et al. discuss privacy and anonymization issues in being able to securely outsource network monitoring, and that a university network with an average load of 650 Mbps posing Big Velocity challenges is of particular interest.

In order to evaluate Big Network Data, Sitaram et al. [77] consider network-based IDS challenges faced by large cloud providers or those with fat network pipes such as OC-192 and OC-768 links. They consider such data as a "clear representation of big data streams in its most raw form (which is hundreds of thousands of TCP/IP packets per second)". Sitaram et al. envision building a NIDS capable of handling Big Data network streams such as these by utilizing Big Data tools such as Hadoop and a network monitoring tool called PacketPig [78]. According to the authors, PacketPig is capable of Deep Packet Inspection, deep network analysis, and even full packet capture when using it with Hadoop. In this study, they mainly consider the effectiveness of clustering algorithms for analyzing packet classification. Their experiment with the KDD data set found the K-means clustering algorithm to generally outperform the Expectation-Maximization and DBSCAN Clustering algorithms. However, their future work sounds especially interesting if it can successfully operate in terms of such Big Velocity.

Beyond the network, host-based event log data has traditionally been one of the main sources for Intrusion Detection monitoring. An organization can have a multitude of computing hosts both in quantity as well as diversity in terms of the different types of log files being generated. All of this log data can quickly add up to Big Host Event Log Data in that it can be very high in Volume, Velocity, and Variety.

The hosts that produce these logs can have Variety such as end-user computer workstations, computer infrastructure servers, devices, appliances, virtualization hosts, or even cloud-based hosts. The types of logs being generated are heterogeneous and can vary from Operating System events to a wide variety of application events such as antivirus software, firewall logs, honeypot activity, web server logs, ftp server logs, email server logs, domain controller logs, web proxy logs, VPN logs, DHCP server logs, etc. While this is not a comprehensive listing of the various types of logs one can encounter in the typical organization, it illustrates that the various types of logs can pose Big Variety challenges in having to correlate security events across a wide range of heterogeneous log types.

To better cope with Big Data challenges organizations can face with their log data, Yen et al. [79] developed a system called Beehive which performs "large-scale log analysis for detecting suspicious activity in enterprise networks". They report that organizations are facing Big Volume challenges in terms of the logs being "very large in volume", and implemented their system at a large enterprise, EMC, for two weeks. At EMC, they describe their major challenges as the "Big Data problem" where 1.4 billion log messages are generated on average per day (about 1 terabyte). This also suggests Big Velocity challenges in dealing with such a high data rate as well. They also discuss the problem of organizations implementing a variety of different security products which generate logs whose formats vary widely, and this suggests a Big Variety challenge. Also, they note that these logs from various security products may have problems such as incompleteness or even inconsistency, and so they describe logs with these challenges as being "dirty".

Beehive monitors the communication of dedicated hosts (e.g., workstations) with other host targets. This is accomplished by monitoring logs from a wide range of network devices such as web proxies, DHCP servers, VPN servers, windows domain controllers, and antivirus software. The logs are ultimately stored in a commercial SIEM system. They reported all the log information being stored in the SIEM as "a big data problem", and that "efficient data-reduction algorithms and techniques" are required to cope with such Big Data logging challenges. Another major challenge they encountered with the logs stored in the SIEM was that the information which was actually being stored proved difficult to correlate against other events because of the underlying quality of the data. As an example, logs could have the incorrect time stamp because of being in a different time zone. Another log format difficulty encountered was that typically only IP addresses were stored, and it was difficult to associate events to specific hosts given that IP addresses could change via DHCP. So, correlation against additional logs was necessary to properly identify hosts.

In terms of detecting security incidents, the Beehive project proved fairly successful versus the enterprise's state of the art security tools. Over a period of two weeks, 784 security incidents were discovered by Beehive whereas the enterprise's existing security tools only detected 8 of these incidents. So, a large number of security incidents were in fact unknown with the existing security tools. One source which was especially beneficial was the web proxy logs, where suspicious traffic activity or questionable destinations could be discovered. Yen et al. [79] were able to effectively reduce the amount of messages inspected by 74% simply by filtering out whitelisted target hosts. This is an interesting study in the effectiveness of the approach, especially considering the Big Data challenges encountered. It would be interesting to see if future similar work could perhaps extend beyond workstations to server log behavior.

According to Myers et al. [80], event correlation is frequently not performed with log analysis due to "difficulties and inadequacies with current technologies". One reason they indicate that organizations have difficulties analyzing security logs is because of "the sheer volume of data to collect, process and store". This suggests that log analysis with event correlation for Intrusion Detection is a Big Data challenge in the contexts of both volume and velocity. Myers et al. conducted an experiment on web server logs to evaluate the effectiveness of applying event correlation in a distributed fashion, and their results showed this technique could effectively detect many common web application attacks while maintaining a low false positive rate. Their distributed approach also showed a reduction in network traffic of syslog messages by 99.88%. This distributed approach illustrates good potential for addressing Big Velocity found in security network traffic by reducing that amount of traffic.

Big Heterogeneous industrial data

Cyber threats can damage and even destroy real-world physical targets beyond cyberspace. Industrial and Utility operations are especially prone to this exposure given their evolution of integrating and automating their physical operations with Information Technology from cyberspace. Even when these systems are "air gapped" and physically disconnected from the public Internet and other networks, these cyber threats can still be catastrophic in nature to real-world objects. An example of a successful attack occurred against Iran's nuclear program with the Stuxnet virus, and some of Iran's nuclear centrifuges were destroyed in the attack. Further details of this incident are given by Langner [81].

Therefore, it can also be important to include heterogeneous sources from the physical world to better improve overall situational awareness for security. A good conceptual illustration for how to extend monitoring beyond cyberspace is given in Figure 6, and this shows different Host, Network, and Device IDSs harvesting information into a centralized SIEM system with the goal of improving Intrusion Detection by also analyzing data from Process Control System sensors. This illustration is from a study performed by Valdes and Cheung [82] with the explicit goal of gaining better situational awareness in process control systems. The motivation was to extend the existing functionality of

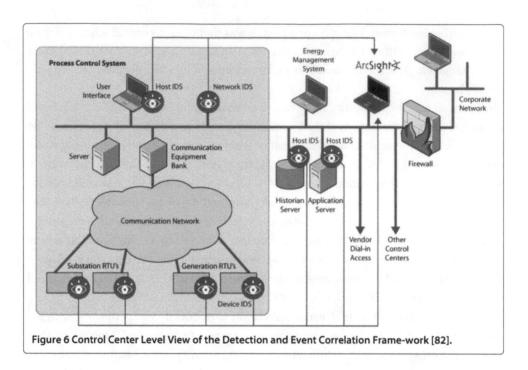

Figure 6 Control Center Level View of the Detection and Event Correlation Frame-work [82].

a SIEM product (ArcSight) to correlate control/process system alarms with IDS events from the SIEM, and thus extend situational awareness beyond cyberspace to also include industrial physical process control systems by correlating IDS data with measurements from underlying physical process data such as electrical current, pressure, flow rate, and similar industrial measurements. This is an interesting concept in that cyberspace situational awareness can be improved by correlating data from heterogeneous sources in the physical world beyond cyberspace, and that Intrusion Detection need not be merely limited to cyberspace sources. The authors indicate that important industries such as refining, pipelines, and electric power can benefit from this approach of utilizing more diverse heterogeneous sources, while cautioning that the stakes are especially high for detecting cyber-attacks against those platforms, as damage can also be physically harmful or even deadly, such as releasing hazardous materials into the environment. Refer to [83] for further background information and also the final report [84].

According to Xiao-bo et al. in [85], Data from Industrial and Utility operations certainly can have Big Data. They design "a big data acquisition engine based on rule engine" to better handle Big Data acquisition flow problems when industrial processes face such challenges. Their study describes how supervisory control and data acquisition (SCADA) systems are evolving and increasingly using Ethernet-based networks rather than traditional serial port connections. SCADA systems are essentially Industrial Control Systems which are based on computers, and they control and monitor industrial processes in the physical world. Xiao-bo et al. propose a rule engine implemented in Java Expert System Shell (JESS), and seek to improve performance and quality from industrial Big Data acquisition flows. Their design accommodates the real-time demands of SCADA systems, and can be used for data analysis, alarming, and forecasting. It is interesting that they chose to address Big Data challenges as a cornerstone of their design in dealing with data flows from SCADA systems.

A study conducted by Datta Ray et al. [86] evaluates Security and Big Data challenges that the electric power grid is facing. They assert that a paradigm shift is required to properly address the cybersecurity demands of the smart grid (i.e., electric power grid). Even more diverse heterogeneous event sources will need to be monitored, and this will further exacerbate the "Big Data onslaught" the utilities are currently facing. Additionally, a Formal Risk Management system should make "the analysis of such Big Data manageable, scalable, and effective." A more formal Return On Investment (ROI) analysis should rigorously address an enterprise's multitude of security and risk contexts.

When it comes to cybersecurity, Datta Ray et al. contend that "the crux of the problem is that organizations have taken a piecemeal approach to security". Various security products such as firewalls and antivirus software do not communicate systematically with each other to yield "holistic intelligence", and typically by the time meaningful patterns are found it is too late and the damage has already occurred. They further assert "these point or perimeter solutions applied to host computers, networks, or applications often work with little knowledge of each other's functions and capabilities". In order to be successful in achieving a holistic risk management system, a major design consideration is interoperability between a diverse myriad of devices such as "meters, synchrophasors, IEDs, firewalls, field devices, etc." This interoperability is important, and should even consider both structured and unstructured data from the sources. By interoperating among "existing point, perimeter, and defense-in-depth security solutions with actionable insights", a more systematic and superior cyber defense can be realized.

In this spirit of considering more diverse heterogeneous security event sources, Datta Ray et al. provide great detail on enhancing overall security by integrating security event sources beyond cyberspace and the Big Data challenges of doing so. The model that they use to illustrate this is by categorizing traditional cyberspace event sources as Utility Business Information Technology (IT), and by categorizing event sources beyond cyberspace as Power System Operation Technologies (OT). For example, IT event sources could be typical cyberspace components such as firewalls, and OT event sources could be a meter that measures electrical quantities such as power, voltage, and current.

By combining and correlating security events across both IT and OT sources, an improved situational awareness can be realized. However, both the IT or OT sources can face Big Data challenges, and Datta Ray et al. propose a model shown in Figure 7 on how to cope with the Big Data onslaught in a systemic manner to improve risk management. In addition to diverse heterogeneous sources, the model also considers "exogenous and endogenous sources of intelligence and asynchronous and real time interactions among its various components". The model indicates how the system can provide feedback in near real time to react to specific events, and that the intelligence of the system is based on an aggregate of Big Data IT and OT inputs.

By unifying the IT and OT domains and correlating events across the entire spectrum, the overall quality of the entire smart grid can be enhanced even while processing a Big Velocity of information from a Big Variety of diverse sources which can lead to valuable insights from previously unknown correlations and hidden patterns. The smart grid faces all of the "3Vs" of Big Data criteria: "huge volume, diverse sources and types and the varied speed of the incoming data". The amount of data the smart grid faces is so large that it has "surpassed the ability of traditional relational and scan/sort systems to process the data".

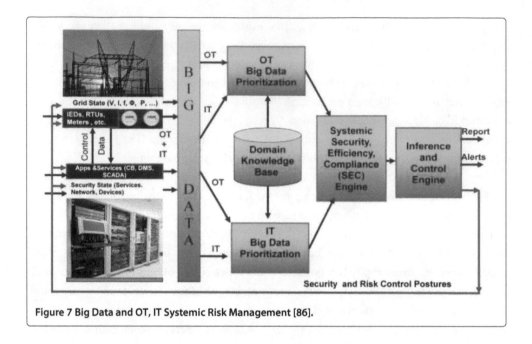

Figure 7 Big Data and OT, IT Systemic Risk Management [86].

Formal Risk Management and ROI analyses are very important considerations in how utility companies process Big Data, as the risks are high. While financial risks such as electrical theft or outages are obvious, the loss of human life is possible in extreme cases like a gas explosion from a leak, or if a hospital (or home) that uses life-support systems were to be maliciously denied electricity. Instead of merely "drowning in data", Big Data can be used as an advantage to improve risk analysis and combined with ROI analysis can more effectively prioritize information assets in terms of effectiveness, scalability, and protection.

Big heterogeneous output data

Big Heterogeneous Data can be output data as well, and this is classified as Big Heterogeneous Output Data. This section addresses the heterogeneity of output Big Data for Intrusion Detection in two main categories: Big Archival Data and Big Alert Data. Big Archival Security Data is output data which is being archived either for the purpose of forensics or Security Analytics, while Big Alert Data is output data either for further alerting analysis or for notifying an administrator or system component to take action. Both of these Big Heterogeneous Outputs can have very pronounced Big Data attributes in terms of Volume, Velocity, and Variety.

Big archival security data

A very important aspect for Intrusion Detection is long-term storage of certain security data. Essentially, there are two main goals for the archival of security data. The first goal is to improve Intrusion Detection capabilities even in real-time with offline data mining operations and Security Analytics. This offline data mining operation on security data can further try to identify previously unknown cyber threats, and then update the real-time detection capabilities with additional new signatures or behavior traits. The second goal is to provide forensic capabilities with this data so that in the event of a security breach, forensic evidence is available to assist the investigation. This data can also be used as evidence in legal proceedings if properly maintained. Typically not every single piece of computing data will be kept in the offline repository store, and care must be taken to properly filter out what is not necessary.

In an experiment using log data generated from anti-malware software, Hoppe et al. [87] use data mining to search for patterns among malware infections in the archived storage repository of a SIEM. They described difficulties in performing the data mining in dealing with such a large amount of data, and that a critical success factor was utilizing the formal CRISP-DM data mining process. In addition, they also described that in IS infrastructures: "the amount of data is enormous". Big Data challenges were a factor in their study especially in the context of Big Volume, given that their data mining operations were performed offline and not for real-time Intrusion Detection. In their study they found that the age and gender of workstation users could infer high or low risk of malware infection. However it was also found that users with or without administrator rights on their workstations did not influence malware infection. Hoppe et al. contend that in specific scenarios, performing data mining on data collected by SIEM systems can enhance the quality of Information Security Infrastructure for companies. This is an illustration that feedback from the offline archive store of a SIEM can be useful for better real-time inference of events which might even possibly yield better situational awareness.

A model proposed by Hunt et al. [88] seeks to both enhance real-time adaptive security while improving long-term forensic capabilities. They point out that security data "arriving too fast to store" and process can now be better addressed with new terabyte storage devices, parallel processing, clustered computers, and even super computers. To give a point of reference, a network with a 10Gbps flow over one hour of incoming traffic requires 5 terabytes of storage. They assert that such infrastructure is currently out of reach for medium sized organizations. Given the processing and storage problems and the application of super computers, there are clear Big Data challenges, especially in the context of Volume and Velocity.

According to the Hunt et al., most IDS/IPS and firewall systems even when reporting information to SIEM systems frequently do not capture sufficient information for robust forensic capabilities as they do not create "digital evidence bags". These systems usually do not sufficiently automatically react in real-time or provide sufficient "traceback" functionality. "Traceback" functionality is the ability to correlate already identified malicious sources (e.g., source IP, port, ISP, etc.) with other real-time components of the network as well as for future forensic purposes. In their model, they also suggest that honeypots, honeynets, and sinkholes are important components for the overall system. Sinkholes can be summarized as a way to draw these packets into a "sinkhole" and allow the malicious packets in so that they can be recorded for forensics as well as later correlation of suspicious behavior, versus having a firewall merely dropping packets with malicious characteristics. These malicious packets are ultimately drowned and not permitted to propagate past the sinkhole, as another firewall explicitly blocks these packets.

Hunt et al. also assert that Data Loss Prevention (DLP) systems are mature in some regards. However their capability to link back to the original events pertaining to breaches with forensics is "largely lacking". They emphasize that DLPs should integrate better with SIEM systems to improve the "very serious" situation of needing better forensic capabilities. Importantly they realize it is "inevitable" that for both real-time security and forensics the focus needs to shift from network protection to data centric protection (i.e., data leakage from the database). Intuitively, this is a compelling argument given that gaining access to such data is a major motivation for attackers.

While their model gives many interesting details, a few examples will be briefly mentioned. One of the recommendations is to use encryption for the log devices from all sources, and to use a "digital evidence bag" for the purposes of forensically sound data (including the possibility of using a kernel security module to mitigate interception attacks). Also emphasized is that a proper chain of custody must be employed in order to be able to properly prosecute perpetrators, and a couple of helpful items for this would be cryptographic hashes and key management for all evidence.

Their proposed model seeks to improve upon existing forensic capabilities while also enhancing real-time Intrusion Detection with additional correlation sources. The authors emphasize that not all systems have these weaknesses, although many do. They also indicate that the extent to which correlated data can adapt firewall rules in the real-time is an open research question.

Big alert data

Intrusion Detection Systems and other security systems produce alerts to notify administrators of suspicious activity. Even an individual IDS can trigger many alerts, and the problem becomes even more prominent when dealing with heterogeneous sources such as a wide array of sensors or multiple IDSs. The basic problem is that a single security inspection event can trigger many alarms even if it is a single incident, or many false alarms can even be raised with normal traffic.

A common technique which is used to stop a flood of alerts is called alert correlation. The basic concept of alert correlation is that when the same characteristic is causing the same alarm, the system should filter and aggregate multiple alarms into one alarm so that a flood of alarms of the same type does not occur (instead just a count of those same alarm types could be reported). An illustrative example of alert correlation is given in Figure 8

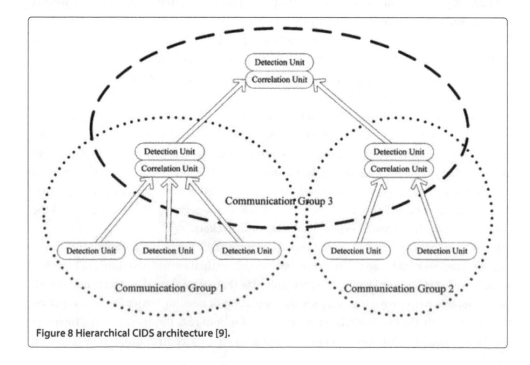

Figure 8 Hierarchical CIDS architecture [9].

where alerts are initially correlated locally in a hierarchical fashion. They are subsequently correlated again at a more global level.

The process of generating alerts certainly can involve Big Data challenges in terms of Volume, Velocity, and Variety. Big Volume and Big Velocity challenges for alert generation can involve correlation with other alerts, events, rules, or knowledge bases. These correlation activities can involve massive processing power, storage requirements, and network traffic. Big Variety challenges for alert generation can involve correlation among alert generators such as IDSs that can have many different formats for their alert messages or event data. It is common for organizations to have security products with many different proprietary alert formats, even though efforts are still being made to standardize. Semantically, alerts can either be considered inputs or outputs as they can also serve as inputs for alert correlation purposes. Alerts always operate at least once in an output capacity, but alerts do not always operate in an input capacity. Since alerts are typically considered outputs conceptually for notification purposes as well as for archiving and forensic purposes, they will be categorized as outputs for this study's organizational purposes.

The actual alerts themselves can indeed pose Big Data challenges, and a study by Sundaramurthy et al. [89] gives an example where they analyzed a data set with over 35 billion alerts from the HP TippingPoint IPS product. This data was collected over a 5 year period in over 1,000 customer networks worldwide. The data mining analytics posed the most significant Big Data challenges given the sheer volume and processing requirements which included correlating the alert data with the filter metadata (which contains further details about the actual alert). One interesting insight learned from the data was that with the Denial of Service (DOS) or Distributed Denial of Service (DDOS) attacks, the majority of these attacks were actually attacking the application layer instead of the network layer. Traditionally, DOS attacks are at the network layer where a bunch of packets "chokes" a device. However, newer attacks can more effectively attack the application layer by sending a specially crafted malicious packet which will cause the application to consume significant resources. They found 78.65% of the DOS alerts were from application-layer attacks, and only 21.35% of the DOS alerts were from network-layer attacks. DOS attacks can present Big Data challenges in themselves. If alerts from these DOS attacks are not properly handled via alert correlation or similar techniques, then the alerts themselves can actually compound the Big Data problems from the DOS attacks with alert floods. These DOS attacks pose a Big Velocity problem, and their corresponding alerts could as well if not properly handled.

For Collaborative Intrusion Detection Systems (CIDSs), Zhou et al. [58] found that a decentralized approach for alert correlation versus a centralized approach could significantly reduce the processing time and number of alarms while not significantly sacrificing detection accuracy. This is especially important given that one of their major challenges was a Big Data challenge with the alert messages themselves being bottlenecked at a centralized alert correlation server: "the scalability problem addresses the challenge of how to cope with the huge volume of raw alerts that can be generated by each participating IDS in the system". They were able to solve this bottleneck problem by utilizing a hierarchical alert correlation architecture as shown in Figure 8. For a given stealthy scan scenario, they were able to significantly increase detection accuracy with their probabilistic threshold approach versus a naïve scheme that used the same threshold. This architecture was able to accommodate multi-dimensional data sources by restricting their analysis to only four specific features (Source IP Address, Source Port, Destination Port, and Protocol), and Zhou et al. applied these four features to evaluate eight different combinations containing them. Admittedly their approach had drawbacks such as not being able to always properly detect if the attacker spread their attack over a longer period of time than the threshold could handle. Future work for their architecture should also address security counter-measures if distributed node(s) are compromised, which is quite possible considering that this architecture is a distributed system that could span across the public Internet. Their study is interesting from a Big Data perspective in that they could significantly improve overall detection time by actually benefiting from the increased message routing and processing time in a distributed architecture. However, their study obviously only con-sidered network traffic features and was not a comprehensive evaluation across hetero-geneous sources beyond network traffic features. More work in this area should evaluate just that.

The processing for alert correlation is clearly a Big Data challenge. Roschke et al. conducted an experiment [90] to evaluate the efficiency of alert correlation with three different database architectures: traditional row-based DBMS (e.g., MySQL), memory-based column database (e.g., MonetDB), and a custom built in-memory database. In all cases, the in-memory database yielded far superior processing for alert correlation with the authors concluding that the row-based database showed "poor performance" for clus-tering and correlation. While the column database performed better than the row-based database in terms of alert clustering and correlation analysis, the column database per-formed extremely poor in terms of record insertion, being able to only insert 63 records per second, and so the authors concluded that particular database was "unfeasible" for general IDS utility and only useful for analytic purposes. The authors do point out that the utility of the in-memory database is obviously limited by the amount of memory available which will give an upper limit to the amount of alerts that can be correlated (or clustered), whereas traditional databases do not have this limitation. They propose limiting the time window in which alerts can be correlated or clustered to avoid this problem. This exper-iment shows that alert correlation is a Big Velocity challenge, although this experiment was limited to only evaluating network-based alerts via Snort. Big Data challenges for alert correlation would be further exacerbated if additional diverse heterogeneous sources were utilized as the number of alerts could increase, in addition to the broader need to perform data fusion across the different sources.

Discussion

When it comes to Intrusion Detection for Big Heterogeneous Data, a great deal of future work can be done with research. If it can be presumed that the annual cost in the USA for cybercrime is $100 Billion annually [17] and that organizations spend about 26% on Detection [19], obviously it cannot be inferred that Intrusion Detection is costing $26 Billion annually (as the total national cost for Intrusion Detection cannot be directly extrapolated from amounts spent by organizations for Intrusion Detection and national Cybercrime costs). However, even if these numbers are only estimates it can be gauged in terms of the order of magnitude that the national costs for Intrusion Detection are very large. Analyzing much more heterogeneous security data can yield significant improvements to the Intrusion Detection domain, and employing Big Data technologies and techniques will allow more of this Big Heterogeneous Data to be utilized.

Promising future research in this spirit will be presented in the following main areas: Data Sets, Feature Selection, Data Fusion, SIEMs, Database Issues, and Other Architectural Considerations.

Data sets

Clearly, the relative lack of high-quality Intrusion Detection data sets is a problem for the academic research community. Some researchers have been building their own data sets due to the lack of existing relevant ones. However one difficulty with this approach is how to accurately label Intrusion Detection data as either attack or normal. Honeypots, honeynets, and sinkholes as well as intentionally cyber-attacking for the purposes of generating data sets might be able to help with labeling data as an attack, but there are still challenges with these approaches. Also, other traffic cannot always be assumed to be normal as it could also be contaminated with attack data. Synthesizing both attack and normal data might not build robust enough datasets in that they are not similar enough to the real world. Another issue is that data sets should constantly be updated as time progresses with new instances containing new normal traffic (i.e., new technologies, applications, and users) and attacks (i.e., new techniques or exploits) to keep research relevant as well as to better train learning systems for Intrusion Detection in an iterative fashion as technology and cyber-attacks evolve.

High quality, robust, and heterogeneously diverse public data sets are so fundamental to Intrusion Detection experimentation and research that the availability of such data sets is fundamentally a significant research problem in its own right. Actual research into the production of these data sets could allow researchers to make better overall progress in the Intrusion Detection arms race. Various techniques and issues such as those mentioned in the preceding paragraph and in the Intrusion Detection Data Set Challenges section should be considered when developing such data sets. Another important consideration is that Intrusion Detection data sets should also accommodate many diverse heterogeneous security sources to adequately address the issue of improving situational awareness. In addition, perhaps Intrusion Detection may need to use more than binary classification in some scenarios and use multiple classifications (i.e., "attack", "normal", "suspicious", "unknown", etc.).

Feature selection

The application of feature selection can be helpful for real-time intrusion detection in terms of reducing detection classification times and even sometimes improving classification accuracy, but care must be taken in the application of feature selection. It is important to understand where and how feature selection can be applied effectively, especially with regards to unstable Intrusion Detection data sets. More specifically, how can feature selection play a role in security event data that is constantly evolving with new characteristics due to issues such as new technologies as well as new cyber-attacks? Thus, the stability of feature sets is very significant in the cybersecurity domain where the landscape is extremely dynamic and not as static as some other domains (e.g., bioinformatics) where feature selection is applied. Feature selection could play a very prominent role where many diverse heterogeneous sources are being analyzed and correlated as feature reduction could significantly reduce storage Volume, processing Velocity, and complex Variety.

Data fusion

Data Fusion has not been widely adopted within the Intrusion Detection domain as compared to other domains like military applications that have a multitude of diverse heterogeneous sensors. A considerable amount of research has been conducted for alert correlation with Intrusion Detection, but very few works consider event fusion or other types of data fusion. Many more experiments with different data fusion techniques should be performed, especially in the context of many more diverse heterogeneous sources which contain Big Data. The question is therefore raised: can significant improvements be realized for Intrusion Detection by doing this, or would the costs be too high?

SIEMs

SIEM technology is proprietary and it is difficult to speculate on some of the internals of different product offerings, but it is apparent that SIEMs do attempt to normalize the data sources into as common formats as possible (e.g., SCAP, CBE, and CEE). While standardizing the formats of security events is good in the sense of reducing some of the more challenging data fusion aspects and to increase performance, in some cases it could possibly be detrimental if valuable information for a particular source is being lost or minimized. However, standardized message formats are not a reality in the real-world in many situations due to a wide variety of security products simply still using different formats. More experimentation into how SIEMs compare to traditional data fusion approaches might be beneficial. Obviously there are benefits to formatting all security event sources into as common formats as possible. However what are the drawbacks with the common format approach from actual experiments?

NIDSs and HIDSs still play a prominent role in the commercial sector. However SIEMs seem to have recently taken the security industry by storm for larger organizations with their ability to both detect cyber-attacks in the real-time, and provide offline security analytics and forensics. But the research community still seems too narrowly focused on the Intrusion Detection problem by conducting much more research on traditional IDSs than a more heterogeneous approach such as SIEMs. SIEMs should be evaluated much more by the research community, especially with regards to experimentation. Furthermore, the research community could further evaluate how to extend SIEM functionality in novel ways as SIEMs have not been Intrusion Detection's "silver bullet".

Database issues

When Big Data poses challenges for Intrusion Detection, whether it is in standalone subsystem event sources or major architectural components for a heterogeneous system, how can technologies like Hadoop and similar technologies improve upon the state of the art and solve pressing problems? More experimentation is needed in this regard. Specifically for SIEMs (or their research-based data fusion equivalents), how can we improve the efficiency of the offline repository stores (which are used for both forensics as well as offline security analytics which provide feedback to the online system?) Many SIEMs use traditional RDBMS technology for this purpose, and more experiments could be conducted to see how other approaches such as columnar databases, xml databases, Hadoop technologies, or hybrids thereof could make these repository stores more efficient and effective. Research into using better storage platforms effectively is needed for the enormous Volume, fast Velocity, and complex Variety processing requirements for Intrusion Detection.

Other architectural considerations

From a general conceptual framework, more experimentation is needed into what Bass [36] proposed, which explored how data mining from offline repositories can give useful feedback to effectively and efficiently benefit real-time Intrusion Detection. Bass's concept was fairly sophisticated and very highly cited by the research community. However there has not been significant experimental research with this model. A good deal of experimentation is still needed to explore the effectiveness of Bass's model with concepts such as real-time feedback and utilizing different Intrusion Detection "feature templates" based on the current situation. Similarly, SIEMs do afford archive repository storage for security analytics and forensics, and researchers could evaluate how to further improve the real-time Intrusion Detection component with this repository store.

In general, more experimentation is needed to illustrate the effectiveness of the cloud in solving Big Heterogeneous Data challenges for Intrusion Detection. More studies and experiments to illustrate the costs involved with utilizing the cloud platform would be beneficial in terms of network bandwidth, processing, and storage requirements. An important consideration is to determine what data gets filtered out, which is an important consequence in terms of establishing good ground truth for Intrusion Detection as well as regarding forensic capabilities.

Some good preliminary research has been conducted regarding architectural topology in terms of Centralized, Distributed, or Hybrid approaches for Sensors, IDSs, and Analyzers. Typically SIEMs will use a Centralized approach for the decision unit which possesses advantages and disadvantages. More experiments could be conducted to further refine these. Also, more research into how SIEM systems can scale out with multiple SIEMs would be beneficial as well. Some benefits have been realized with distributed or hierarchical architectures for IDSs and analyzers, but much more potential experimentation is yet to be realized especially in terms of utilizing more data fusion.

Heterogeneity among the actual Sensors, IDSs, Analyzers, or even SIEMs can be beneficial for Intrusion Detection where detection accuracy can be improved. For example, different IDSs working in teams to evaluate the same security events can improve detection accuracy, and the same can be accomplished with using more than one type of SIEM to analyze the same security events. So far, this type of Detector heterogeneity has showed good benefits. Even more research should be conducted into this area especially in terms of being sensitive to the additional costs versus the benefits.

Greater geographical and organizational heterogeneity should be employed for Intrusion Detection. Alert and event correlation beyond geographical and organizational boundaries could further improve situational awareness. Projects such as the Internet Storm Center [34] for honeypots and collecting malicious Intrusion Detection metadata. However organizations could participate much more actively. Will a natural evolution be to outsource the Intrusion Detection function to Managed Service Providers (MSPs)? Will these MSPs be able to more cost effectively manage Intrusion Detection through scaling out with a more comprehensive Intrusion Detection knowledge base and better core competency? More research should evaluate how significantly sharing of Intrusion Detection events, alerts, analysis, and knowledge across many organizations could enhance the state of the art. Are there ways for even competing organizations to share cyber-threat security event data for their collective good while still protecting their competitive interests? A prevalent consensus among the research community is that greater sharing for Intrusion Detection is necessary, and more research should be conducted to evaluate this on a significantly larger scale of sharing.

Conclusion

Historically most of the academic research for Intrusion Detection has focused too narrowly on the network layer with NIDs and to some extent at the host level with HIDSs. The academic research community should actively embrace a more diverse heterogeneous-based event source approach and follow the lead of the commercial sector where the rapid proliferation of SIEM technology has blossomed into a billion dollar industry (despite the term "SIEMS" having only been coined in 2005). This proliferation of SIEM technology throughout industry is an important consideration, given that one of the inherent features in this technology is to correlate security events from a wide array of diverse heterogeneous sources, and its successes in the commercial sector should give credence to this approach.

Both cybersecurity and physical security for organizations such as those in the utility and the industrial sector can even be enhanced by correlating traditional IT security events with those beyond cyberspace such as sensor devices measuring anomalous real-world quantities like gas leaks, electrical power/voltage/current, temperature, fire alarms, or many other sensors. Correlating security events from physical world sensors with cyberspace is becoming significantly more important as the utility and industrial sectors are becoming increasingly computerized for automation, and thus exposing their physical infrastructures to new cyber threats such as malicious attackers or "cyber accidents".

More diverse heterogeneous sources can provide for improved situational awareness within the Intrusion Detection domain similar to the military's use of diverse heterogeneous sources in its doctrines, strategies, tactics, and engagements. The onslaught of all this Big Input Data drives the engine for an onslaught of Big Output Data. For Intrusion Detection, great heterogeneous diversity in both its input and output data poses significant Big Heterogeneous Data challenges.

While Intrusion Detection does not always face Big Data challenges, it does face Big Data challenges more often as time progresses and especially more so for larger private and government organizations. This trend of Big Data challenges will continue as a multitude of more heterogeneous sources are analyzed. Even medium and smaller organizations will need to assess whether their Intrusion Detection architecture or Security Analytics merit the deployment costs of Big Data technologies. Big Data challenges for Intrusion Detection already exist for the nation's electric grid given its tight integration with computers, and will become even more pronounced as many more diverse cyber and non-cyber heterogeneous sources are brought online to enhance overall cyber defense and improve situational awareness for critical infrastructure.

Competing interests
The authors declare that they have no competing interests.

Authors' contributions
RZ performed the primary literature review and analysis for this work, and also drafted the manuscript. RW worked with RZ to develop the article's framework and focus. TMK introduced this topic to RZ and RW, and coordinated the other authors to complete and finalize this work. All authors read and approved the final manuscript.

Acknowledgements

We thank the reviewers for their constructive comments.

References

1. Nassar M, al Bouna B, Malluhi Q (2013) Secure outsourcing of network flow data analysis. In: Big Data (BigData Congress), 2013 IEEE International Congress On. IEEE, Santa Clara, CA, USA. pp 431–432
2. Group BDW (2013) Big Data Analytics for Security Intelligence. https://downloads.cloudsecurityalliance.org/initiatives/bdwg/Big_Data_Analytics_for_Security_Intelligence.pdf. Accessed 2015-1-10
3. Chickowski E (2012) A Case Study In Security Big Data Analysis. http://www.darkreading.com/analytics/security-monitoring/a-case-study-in-security-big-data-analysis/d/d-id/1137299?. Accessed 2015-1-10
4. Chickowski E (2013) Moving Beyond SIEM For Strong Security Analytics. http://www.darkreading.com/moving-beyond-siem-for-strong-security-analytics/d/d-id/1141069?. Accessed 2015-1-10
5. Marko K (2014) Big Data: Cyber Security's Silver Bullet? Intel Makes the Case. http://www.forbes.com/sites/kurtmarko/2014/11/09/big-data-cyber-security/. Accessed 2015-1-10
6. Kezunovic M, Xie L, Grijalva S (2013) The role of big data in improving power system operation and protection. In: Bulk Power System Dynamics and Control - IX Optimization, Security and Control of the Emerging Power Grid (IREP), 2013 IREP Symposium. IEEE, Rethymno, Greece. pp 1–9
7. Software I (2013) Managing big data for smart grids and smart meters. http://www-935.ibm.com/services/multimedia/Managing_big_data_for_smart_grids_and_smart_meters.pdf. Accessed 2015-1-10
8. Modi C, Patel D, Borisaniya B, Patel H, Patel A, Rajarajan M (2013) A survey of intrusion detection techniques in cloud. J Netw Comput Appl 36(1):42–57
9. Zhou CV, Leckie C, Karunasekera S (2010) A survey of coordinated attacks and collaborative intrusion detection. Comput Secur 29(1):124–140
10. Laney D (2001) 3d data management: Controlling data volume, velocity and variety. Technical Report 949, META Group (now Gartner). http://blogs.gartner.com/doug-laney/files/2012/01/ad949-3D-Data-Management-Controlling-Data-Volume-Velocity-and-Variety.pdf
11. Zikopoulos P, Parasuraman K, Deutsch T, Giles J, Corrigan D (2012) Harness the power of big data The IBM big data platform. McGraw Hill Professional, New York, NY. http://books.google.com/books?id=HhSON0xOCQ0C
12. Frank J (1994) Artificial intelligence and intrusion detection: current and future directions. In: Proceedings of the 17th national computer security conference. Vol. 10. Citeseer, Baltimore, MD, USA. pp 1–12
13. Information Assurance Solutions Group (2015) Defense in depth. Technical report, National Security Agency. http://www.nsa.gov/ia/_files/support/defenseindepth.pdf. Accessed 2015-1-10
14. Denning DE (1987) An intrusion-detection model. Softw Eng IEEE Trans SE-13(2):222–232. doi:10.1109/TSE.1987.232894
15. Sourcefire (2015) Snort, Home Page. http://www.snort.org/. Accessed 2015-1-10
16. Roesch M (1999) Snort: Lightweight intrusion detection for networks. In: LISA. Vol. 99. USENIX, Seattle, WA, USA. pp 229–238
17. Center for Strategic and International Studies (2013) The economic impact of cybercrime and cyber espionage. Technical report. McAfee http://www.mcafee.com/us/resources/reports/rp-economic-impact-cybercrime.pdf
18. Verizon RISK Team (2013) 2013 data breach investigations report. Technical report. Verizon http://www.verizonenterprise.com/resources/reports/rp_data-breach-investigations-report-2013_en_xg.pdf
19. Ponemon Institute LLC (2012) 2012 cost of cyber crime study: United states. Technical report. Ponemon Institute http://www.ponemon.org/local/upload/file/2012_US_Cost_of_Cyber_Crime_Study_FINAL6%20.pdf
20. Julisch K, Dacier M (2002) Mining intrusion detection alarms for actionable knowledge. In: Proceedings of the Eighth ACM SIGKDD International Conference on Knowledge Discovery and Data Mining. ACM, Edmonton, Alberta, Canada. pp 366–375
21. Xu D, Ning P (2008) Correlation analysis of intrusion alerts. Intrusion Detect Syst 38:65–92
22. Suthaharan S, Panchagnula T (2012) Relevance feature selection with data cleaning for intrusion detection system. In: Southeastcon, 2012 Proceedings of IEEE. IEEE, Orlando, FL, USA. pp 1–6
23. Bhatti R, LaSalle R, Bird R, Grance T, Bertino E (2012) Emerging trends around big data analytics and security: Panel. In: Proceedings of the 17th ACM Symposium on Access Control Models and Technologies SACMAT '12. ACM, New York, NY, USA. pp 67–68. doi:10.1145/2295136.2295148. http://doi.acm.org/10.1145/2295136.2295148
24. Oltsik J (2013) Defining Big Data Security Analytics. Networking Nuggets and Security Snippets (Blog). http://www.networkworld.com/community/blog/defining-big-data-security-analytics. Accessed 2014-5-23
25. Sommer R, Paxson V (2010) Outside the closed world: On using machine learning for network intrusion detection. In: Security and Privacy (SP), 2010 IEEE Symposium On. IEEE, Oakland, CA, USA. pp 305–316
26. Coull SE, Wright CV, Monrose F, Collins MP, Reiter MK (2007) Playing devil's advocate: Inferring sensitive information from anonymized network traces. In: NDSS. Vol. 7. Internet Society, San Diego, CA, USA. pp 35–47
27. Azad C, Jha VK (2013) Data mining in intrusion detection: a comparative study of methods, types and data sets. Int J Inf Technol Comput Sci 5(8):75–90
28. McHugh J (2000) Testing intrusion detection systems: a critique of the 1998 and 1999 darpa intrusion detection system evaluations as performed by lincoln laboratory. ACM Trans Inf Syst Secur 3(4):262–294
29. Mahoney MV, Chan PK (2003) An analysis of the 1999 darpa/lincoln laboratory evaluation data for network anomaly detection. In: Recent advances in intrusion detection. Springer, Berlin Heidelberg. pp 220–237
30. Wu SX, Banzhaf W (2010) The use of computational intelligence in intrusion detection systems: A review. Appl Soft Comput 10(1):1–35
31. Shiravi A, Shiravi H, Tavallaee M, Ghorbani AA (2012) Toward developing a systematic approach to generate benchmark datasets for intrusion detection. Comput Secur 31(3):357–374. doi:10.1016/j.cose.2011.12.012

32. Fontugne R, Borgnat P, Abry P, Fukuda K (2010) Mawilab: Combining diverse anomaly detectors for automated anomaly labeling and performance benchmarking. In: Proceedings of the 6th International COnference. Co-NEXT '10. ACM, New York, NY, USA. pp 8–1812. doi:10.1145/1921168.1921179. http://doi.acm.org/10.1145/1921168.1921179

33. United States Marine Academy – West Point (2015) Cyber Research Center – DataSets. http://www.usma.edu/crc/SitePages/DataSets.aspx. Accessed 2015-1-10

34. Internet Storm Center (2015) Reports – Internet Security | SANS ISC. https://isc.sans.edu/reports.html. Accessed 2015-1-10

35. Song J, Takakura H, Okabe Y, Eto M, Inoue D, Nakao K (2011) Statistical analysis of honeypot data and building of kyoto 2006+ dataset for nids evaluation. In: Proceedings of the First Workshop on Building Analysis Datasets and Gathering Experience Returns for Security. ACM, Salzburg, Austria. pp 29–36

36. Bass T (2000) Intrusion detection systems and multisensor data fusion. Commun ACM 43(4):99–105

37. Wang H, Liu X, Lai J, Liang Y (2007) Network security situation awareness based on heterogeneous multi-sensor data fusion and neural network. In: Computer and Computational Sciences, 2007. IMSCCS 2007. Second International Multi-Symposiums On. IEEE, Iowa City, IA, USA. pp 352–359

38. Tsang C-H, Kwong S, Wang H (2007) Genetic-fuzzy rule mining approach and evaluation of feature selection techniques for anomaly intrusion detection. Pattern Recognit 40(9):2373–2391

39. Chebrolu S, Abraham A, Thomas JP (2005) Feature deduction and ensemble design of intrusion detection systems. Comput Secur 24(4):295–307

40. Chen Y, Li Y, Cheng X-Q, Guo L (2006) Survey and taxonomy of feature selection algorithms in intrusion detection system. In: Lipmaa H, Yung M, Lin D (eds). Information Security and Cryptology. Lecture Notes in Computer Science. Vol. 4318. Springer, Berlin Heidelberg. pp 153–167

41. Elngar A, Mohamed D, Ghaleb F (2013) A real-time anomaly network intrusion detection system with high accuracy. Inf Sci Lett Int J 2(2):49–56

42. The Apache Software Foundation (2015) Welcome to Apache Hadoop!. http://hadoop.apache.org/. Accessed 2015-1-10

43. Suthaharan S (2013) Big data classification: problems and challenges in network intrusion prediction with machine learning. In: Big Data Analytics Workshop, in Conjunction with ACM Sigmetrics. ACM, Pittsburgh, PA, USA

44. Whitworth J, Suthaharan S (2013) Security problems and challenges in a machine learning-based hybrid big data processing network systems. In: ACM Sigmetrics 2013 (Big Data Analytics Workshop). ACM, Pittsburgh, PA, USA

45. Jeong H, Hyun W, Lim J, You I (2012) Anomaly teletraffic intrusion detection systems on hadoop-based platforms: A survey of some problems and solutions. In: Network-Based Information Systems (NBiS), 2012 15th international conference on. IEEE, Melbourne, Australia. pp 766–770

46. Lee Y, Lee Y (2013) Toward scalable internet traffic measurement and analysis with hadoop. ACM SIGCOMM Comput Commun Rev 43(1):5–13

47. Cheon J, Choe T-Y (2013) Distributed processing of snort alert log using hadoop. Int J Eng Technol(0975-4024) 5(3):2685–2690

48. VeetiL S, Gao Q (2013) A real-time intrusion detection system by integrating hadoop and naive bayes classification. In: Dalhousie Computer Science In-house Conference (DCSI). Dalhousie University, Halifax, Canada

49. Bass T (1999) Multisensor data fusion for next generation distributed intrusion detection systems. In: IRIS National Symposium. IRIS National Symposium, Laurel, MD, USA

50. Lan F, Chunlei W, Guoqing M (2010) A framework for network security situation awareness based on knowledge discovery. In: Computer Engineering and Technology (ICCET), 2010 2nd international conference on. Vol. 1. IEEE, Chengdu, China. pp 1–226

51. Mitchell HB (2012) Data fusion: concepts and ideas. Springer, New York, NY. http://books.google.com/books?id=ZyPYGh-WAgYC

52. Hall DL, Llinas J (1997) An introduction to multisensor data fusion. Proc IEEE 85(1):6–23

53. Fessi B, Benabdallah S, Hamdi M, Rekhis S, Boudriga N (2010) Data collection for information security system. In: Engineering Systems Management and Its Applications (ICESMA), 2010 second international conference on. IEEE, Sharjah, United Arab Emirates. pp 1–8

54. Karim Ganame A, Bourgeois J, Bidou R, Spies F (2008) A global security architecture for intrusion detection on computer networks. Comput Secur 27(1):30–47

55. Bye R, Camtepe SA, Albayrak S (2010) Collaborative intrusion detection framework: characteristics, adversarial opportunities and countermeasures. In: Proceedings of CollSec: Usenix Workshop on Collaborative Methods for security and privacy. USENIX, Washington, DC, USA

56. Bartos K, Rehak M (2012) Self-organized mechanism for distributed setup of multiple heterogeneous intrusion detection systems. In: Self-Adaptive and Self-Organizing Systems Workshops (SASOW), 2012 IEEE sixth international conference on. IEEE, Lyon, France. pp 31–38

57. Cai H, Wu N (2010) Design and implementation of a dids. In: 2010 IEEE International Conference on Wireless Communications, Networking and Information Security. IEEE, Beijing, China. pp 340–342

58. Vincent Zhou C, Leckie C, Karunasekera S (2009) Decentralized multi-dimensional alert correlation for collaborative intrusion detection. J Netw Comput Appl 32(5):1106–1123

59. Metzger S, Hommel W, Reiser H (2011) Integrated security incident management–concepts and real-world experiences. In: IT Security Incident Management and IT Forensics (IMF), 2011 Sixth International Conference On. IEEE, Stuttgart, Germany. pp 107–121

60. Williams A (2007) The Future of SIEM – The market will begin to diverge. http://techbuddha.wordpress.com/2007/01/01/the-future-of-siem-%E2%80%93-the-market-will-begin-to-diverge/

61. Anuar NB, Papadaki M, Furnell S, Clarke N (2010) An investigation and survey of response options for intrusion response systems (irss). In: Information Security for South Africa (ISSA), 2010. IEEE, Johannesburg, South Africa. pp 1–8

62. Rouse M (2012) security information and event management (SIEM). http://searchsecurity.techtarget.com/definition/security-information-and-event-management-SIEM

63. Messmer E (2013) Gartner security report: McAfee up, Trend Micro down. http://www.networkworld.com/news/2013/053013-gartner-security-survey-270297.html
64. Mosaic Security Research Log Management & Security Information and Event Management (SIEM) Software Guide | Mosaic Security Research. http://mosaicsecurity.com/categories/85-log-management-security-information-and-event-management. Accessed 2014-5-23
65. Aguirre I, Alonso S (2012) Improving the automation of security information management: A collaborative approach. Secur Privacy IEEE 10(1):55–59
66. Kotenko I, Polubelova O, Saenko I (2012) The ontological approach for siem data repository implementation. In: Green Computing and Communications (GreenCom), 2012 IEEE international conference on. IEEE, Besancon, France. pp 761–766
67. Nicolett M, Kavanagh KM (2011) Critical capabilities for security information and event management technology. Gartner Report
68. Radack S, Kuhn R (2011) Managing security: the security content automation protocol. In: IT Professional. IEEE 9(13):9–11
69. Ogle D, Kreger H, Salahshour A, Cornpropst J, Labadie E, Chessell M, Horn B, Gerken J, Schoech J, Wamboldt M (2002) Canonical situation data format: the common base event v1.1.1. IBM Corporation. http://xml.coverpages.org/IBMCommonBaseEventV111.pdf. Accessed 2015-1-10
70. Distributed Management Task Force Inc (2014) Common Information Model (CIM). http://dmtf.org/standards/cim. Accessed 2014-5-23
71. Revelytix Inc. (2010) Triple store evaluation analysis report. Technical report, Revelytix. http://www.algebraixdata.com/wp-content/uploads/2014/02/Revelytix-Triplestore-Evaluation-Analysis-Results.pdf
72. Kotenko I, Chechulin A (2012) Common framework for attack modeling and security evaluation in siem systems. In: Green Computing and Communications (GreenCom), 2012 IEEE international conference on. IEEE, Besancon, France. pp 94–101
73. Kreutz D, Casimiro A, Pasin M (2012) A trustworthy and resilient event broker for monitoring cloud infrastructures. In: Distributed applications and interoperable systems. Springer, Berlin Heidelberg. pp 87–95
74. Splunk Inc. Operational Intelligence, Log Management, Application Management, Enterprise Security and Compliance | Splunk. http://www.splunk.com/. Accessed 2014-5-23.
75. Li Y, Liu Y, Zhang H (2012) Cross-boundary enterprise security monitoring. In: Computational Problem-Solving (ICCP), 2012 international conference on. IEEE, Leshan, China. pp 127–136
76. Blum D, Schacter P, Maiwald E, Krikken R, Henry T, de Boer M, Chuvakin A (2011) 2012 planning guide: Security and risk management. Technical Report G00224667 Gartner, Inc.
77. Sitaram D, Sharma M, Zain M, Sastry A, Todi R (2013) Intrusion detection system for high volume and high velocity packet streams: A clustering approach. Int J Innovation Manag Technol 4(5):480–485
78. Kaszuba G (2013) packetloop/packetpig. GitHub.0 https://github.com/packetloop/packetpig
79. Yen T-F, Oprea A, Onarlioglu K, Leetham T, Robertson W, Juels A, Kirda E (2013) Beehive: large-scale log analysis for detecting suspicious activity in enterprise networks. In: Proceedings of the 29th Annual Computer Security Applications Conference. ACM, New Orleans, LA, USA. pp 199–208
80. Myers J, Grimaila MR, Mills RF (2011) Log-based distributed security event detection using simple event correlator. In: System Sciences (HICSS), 2011 44th Hawaii International Conference on. IEEE, Kauai, HI, USA. pp 1–7
81. Langner R (2011) Stuxnet: Dissecting a cyberwarfare weapon. Secur Privacy IEEE 9(3):49–51
82. Valdes A, Cheung S (2009) Intrusion monitoring in process control systems. In: System Sciences, 2009. HICSS'09. 42nd Hawaii international conference on. IEEE, Waikoloa, Big Island, HI, USA. pp 1–7
83. SRI International (2014) Detection and Analysis of Threats to the Energy Sector (DATES). http://www.csl.sri.com/projects/dates/. Accessed 2014-5-23
84. Valdes A (2010) Detection and analysis of threats to the energy sector: Dates. Technical report, SRI International
85. XU X-b, YANG Z-q, XIU J-p, LIU C (2013) A big data acquisition engine based on rule engine. J China Universities Posts Telecommunications 20:45–49
86. Ray PD, Reed C, Gray J, Agarwal A, Seth S (2012) Improving roi on big data through formal security and efficiency risk management for interoperating ot and it systems. In: Grid-Interop Forum 2012, Irving, Texas, USA
87. Gabriel R, Hoppe T, Pastwa A, Sowa S (2009) Analyzing malware log data to support security information and event management: Some research results. In: Advances in databases, knowledge, and data applications, 2009. DBKDA'09. First international conference on. IEEE, Cancun, Mexico. pp 108–113
88. Hunt R, Slay J (2010) The design of real-time adaptive forensically sound secure critical infrastructure. In: Network and System Security (NSS), 2010 4th International conference on. IEEE, Melbourne, Australia. pp 328–333
89. Sundaramurthy SC, Bhatt S, Eisenbarth MR (2012) Examining intrusion prevention system events from worldwide networks. In: Proceedings of the 2012 ACM workshop on building analysis datasets and gathering experience returns for security. ACM, Raleigh, NC, USA. pp 5–12
90. Roschke S, Cheng F, Meinel C (2010) A flexible and efficient alert correlation platform for distributed ids. In: Network and System Security (NSS), 2010 4th international conference on. IEEE, Melbourne, Australia. pp 24–31

5

A survey on platforms for big data analytics

Dilpreet Singh and Chandan K Reddy*

* Correspondence:
reddy@cs.wayne.edu
Department of Computer Science,
Wayne State University, Detroit, MI
48202, USA

Abstract

The primary purpose of this paper is to provide an in-depth analysis of different platforms available for performing big data analytics. This paper surveys different hardware platforms available for big data analytics and assesses the advantages and drawbacks of each of these platforms based on various metrics such as scalability, data I/O rate, fault tolerance, real-time processing, data size supported and iterative task support. In addition to the hardware, a detailed description of the software frameworks used within each of these platforms is also discussed along with their strengths and drawbacks. Some of the critical characteristics described here can potentially aid the readers in making an informed decision about the right choice of platforms depending on their computational needs. Using a star ratings table, a rigorous qualitative comparison between different platforms is also discussed for each of the six characteristics that are critical for the algorithms of big data analytics. In order to provide more insights into the effectiveness of each of the platform in the context of big data analytics, specific implementation level details of the widely used k-means clustering algorithm on various platforms are also described in the form pseudocode.

Keywords: Big data; MapReduce; graphics processing units; scalability; big data analytics; big data platforms; k-means clustering; real-time processing

Introduction

This is an era of Big Data. Big Data is driving radical changes in traditional data analysis platforms. To perform any kind of analysis on such voluminous and complex data, scaling up the hardware platforms becomes imminent and choosing the right hardware/ software platforms becomes a crucial decision if the user's requirements are to be satisfied in a reasonable amount of time. Researchers have been working on building novel data analysis techniques for big data more than ever before which has led to the continuous development of many different algorithms and platforms.

There are several big data platforms available with different characteristics and choosing the right platform requires an in-depth knowledge about the capabilities of all these platforms [1]. Especially, the ability of the platform to adapt to increased data processing demands plays a critical role in deciding if it is appropriate to build the analytics based solutions on a particular platform. To this end, we will first provide a thorough understanding of all the popular big data platforms that are currently being used in practice and highlight the advantages and drawbacks of each of them.

Typically, when the user has to decide the right platforms to choose from, he/she will have to investigate what their application/algorithm needs are. One will come across a few fundamental issues in their mind before making the right decisions.

- How quickly do we need to get the results?
- How big is the data to be processed?
- Does the model building require several iterations or a single iteration?

Clearly, these concerns are application/algorithm dependent that one needs to address before analyzing the systems/platform-level requirements. At the systems level, one has to meticulously look into the following concerns:

- Will there be a need for more data processing capability in the future?
- Is the rate of data transfer critical for this application?
- Is there a need for handling hardware failures within the application?

In this paper, we will provide a more rigorous analysis of these concerns and provide a score for each of the big data platforms with respect to these issues.

While there are several works that partly describe some of the above mentioned concerns, to the best of our knowledge, there is no existing work that compares different platforms based on these essential components of big data analytics. Our work primarily aims at characterizing these concerns and focuses on comparing all the platforms based on these various optimal characteristics, thus providing some guidelines about the suitability of different platforms for various kinds of scenarios that arise while performing big data analytics in practice.

In order to provide a more comprehensive understanding of the different aspects of the big data problem and how they are being handled by these platforms, we will provide a case study on the implementation of k-means clustering algorithm on various big data platforms. The k-means clustering was chosen here not only because of its popularity, but also due to the various dimensions of complexity involved with the algorithm such as being iterative, compute-intensive, and having the ability to parallelize some of the computations. We will provide a detailed pseudocode of the implementation of the k-means clustering algorithm on different hardware and software platforms and provide an in-depth analysis and insights into the algorithmic details.

The major contributions of this paper are as follows:

- Illustrate the scaling of various big data analytics platforms and demonstrate the advantages and drawbacks of each of these platforms including the software frameworks.
- Provide a systematic evaluation of various big data platforms based on important characteristics that are pertinent to big data analytics in order to aid the users with a better understanding about the suitability of these platforms for different problem scenarios.
- Demonstrate a case study on the k-means clustering algorithm (a representative analytics procedure) and describe the implementation level details of its functioning on various big data platforms.

The remainder of the paper is organized as follows: the fundamental scaling concepts along with the advantages and drawbacks of horizontal and vertical scaling are explained in Section "Scaling". Section "Horizontal scaling platforms" describes various horizontal scaling platforms including peer-to-peer networks, Hadoop and Spark. In section "Vertical scaling platforms", various vertical platforms graphics processing units and high performance clusters are described. Section "Comparison of different platforms" provides thorough comparisons between different platforms based on several characteristics that are important in the context of big data analytics. Section "How to choose a platform for big data analytics?" discusses various details about choosing the right platform for a particular big data application. A case study on k-means clustering algorithm along with its implementation level details on each of the big data platform is described in Section "K-means clustering on different platforms". Finally, the "Conclusion" section concludes our discussion along with future directions.

Scaling

Scaling is the ability of the system to adapt to increased demands in terms of data processing. To support big data processing, different platforms incorporate scaling in different forms. From a broader perspective, the big data platforms can be categorized into the following two types of scaling:

- **Horizontal Scaling:** Horizontal scaling involves distributing the workload across many servers which may be even commodity machines. It is also known as "scale out", where multiple independent machines are added together in order to improve the processing capability. Typically, multiple instances of the operating system are running on separate machines.
- **Vertical Scaling:** Vertical Scaling involves installing more processors, more memory and faster hardware, typically, within a single server. It is also known as "scale up" and it usually involves a single instance of an operating system.

Table 1 compares the advantages and drawbacks of horizontal and vertical scaling. While scaling up vertically can make the management and installation straight-forward,

Table 1 A comparison of advantages and drawbacks of horizontal and vertical scaling

Scaling	Advantages	Drawbacks
Horizontal scaling	→ Increases performance in small steps as needed	→ Software has to handle all the data distribution and parallel processing complexities
	→ Financial investment to upgrade is relatively less	→ Limited number of software are available that can take advantage of horizontal scaling
	→ Can scale out the system as much as needed	
Vertical scaling	→ Most of the software can easily take advantage of vertical scaling	→ Requires substantial financial investment
	→ Easy to manage and install hardware within a single machine	→ System has to be more powerful to handle future workloads and initially the additional performance in not fully utilized
		→ It is not possible to scale up vertically after a certain limit

it limits the scaling ability of a platform since it will require substantial financial investment. To handle future workloads, one always will have to add hardware which is more powerful than the current requirements due to limited space and the number of expansion slots available in a single machine. This forces the user to invest more than what is required for his current processing needs.

On the other hand, horizontal scale out gives users the ability to increase the performance in small increments which lowers the financial investment. Also, there is no limit on the amount of scaling that can done and one can horizontally scale out the system as much as needed. In spite of these advantages, the main drawback is the limited availability of software frameworks that can effectively utilize horizontal scaling.

Horizontal scaling platforms

Some of the prominent horizontal scale out platforms include peer-to-peer networks and Apache Hadoop. Recently, researchers have also been working on developing the next generation of horizontal scale out tools such as Spark [2] to overcome the limitations of other platforms. We will now discuss each of these platforms in more detail in this section.

Peer-to-peer networks

Peer-to-Peer networks [3,4] involve millions of machines connected in a network. It is a decentralized and distributed network architecture where the nodes in the networks (known as peers) serve as well as consume resources. It is one of the oldest distributed computing platforms in existence. Typically, Message Passing Interface (MPI) is the communication scheme used in such a setup to communicate and exchange the data between peers. Each node can store the data instances and the scale out is practically unlimited (can be millions of nodes).

The major bottleneck in such a setup arises in the communication between different nodes. Broadcasting messages in a peer-to-peer network is cheaper but the aggregation of data/results is much more expensive. In addition, the messages are sent over the network in the form of a spanning tree with an arbitrary node as the root where the broadcasting is initiated.

MPI, which is the standard software communication paradigm used in this network, has been in use for several years and is well-established and thoroughly debugged. One of the main features of MPI includes the state preserving process i.e., processes can live as long as the system runs and there is no need to read the same data again and again as in the case of other frameworks such as MapReduce (explained in section "Apache hadoop"). All the parameters can be preserved locally. Hence, unlike MapReduce, MPI is well suited for iterative processing [5]. Another feature of MPI is the hierarchical master/slave paradigm. When MPI is deployed in the master–slave model, the slave machine can become the master for other processes. This can be extremely useful for dynamic resource allocation where the slaves have large amounts of data to process.

MPI is available for many programming languages. It includes methods to send and receive messages and data. Some other methods available with MPI are 'Broadcast', which is used to broadcast the data or messages over all the nodes and 'Barrier', which is another method that can put a barrier and allows all the processes to synchronize and reach up to a certain point before proceeding further.

Although MPI appears to be perfect for developing algorithms for big data analytics, it has some major drawbacks. One of the primary drawbacks is the fault intolerance since MPI has no mechanism to handle faults. When used on top of peer-to-peer networks, which is a completely unreliable hardware, a single node failure can cause the entire system to shut down. Users have to implement some kind of fault tolerance mechanism within the program to avoid such unfortunate situations. With other frameworks such as Hadoop (that are robust to fault tolerance) becoming widely popular, MPI is not being widely used anymore.

Apache hadoop

Apache Hadoop [6] is an open source framework for storing and processing large data-sets using clusters of commodity hardware. Hadoop is designed to scale up to hundreds and even thousands of nodes and is also highly fault tolerant. The various components of a Hadoop Stack are shown in Figure 1. The Hadoop platform contains the following two important components:

- Distributed File System (HDFS) [7] is a distributed file system that is used to store data across cluster of commodity machines while providing high availability and fault tolerance.
- Hadoop YARN [8] is a resource management layer and schedules the jobs across the cluster.

MapReduce

The programming model used in Hadoop is MapReduce [9] which was proposed by Dean and Ghemawat at Google. MapReduce is the basic data processing scheme used in Hadoop which includes breaking the entire task into two parts, known as mappers and reducers. At a high-level, mappers read the data from HDFS, process it and generate some intermediate results to the reducers. Reducers are used to aggregate the intermediate results to generate the final output which is again written to HDFS. A typical Hadoop job involves running several mappers and reducers across different nodes in the cluster. A good survey about MapReduce for parallel data processing is available in [10].

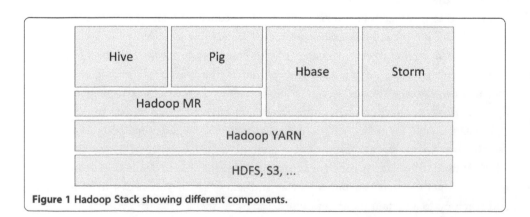

Figure 1 Hadoop Stack showing different components.

MapReduce wrappers

A certain set of wrappers are currently being developed for MapReduce. These wrappers can provide a better control over the MapReduce code and aid in the source code development. The following wrappers are being widely used in combination with MapReduce.

- **Apache Pig** is a SQL-like environment developed at Yahoo [11] is being used by many organizations like Yahoo, Twitter, AOL, LinkedIn etc. **Hive** is another MapReduce wrapper developed by Facebook [12]. These two wrappers provide a better environment and make the code development simpler since the programmers do not have to deal with the complexities of MapReduce coding.

- Programming environments such as **DryadLINQ**, on the other hand, provide the end users with more flexibility over the MapReduce by allowing the users to have more control over the coding. It is a C# like environment developed at Microsoft Research [13]. It uses LINQ (a parallel language) and a cluster execution environment called Dryad. The advantages include better debugging and development using Visual Studio as the tool and interoperation with other languages such as standard .NET.

In addition to these wrappers, some researchers have also developed scalable machine learning libraries such as Mahout [14] using MapReduce paradigm.

Limitations of MapReduce

One of the major drawbacks of MapReduce is its inefficiency in running iterative algorithms. MapReduce is not designed for iterative processes. Mappers read the same data again and again from the disk. Hence, after each iteration, the results have to be written to the disk to pass them onto the next iteration. This makes disk access a major bottleneck which significantly degrades the performance. For each iteration, a new mapper and reducer have to be initialized. Sometimes the MapReduce jobs are short-lived in which case the overhead of initialization of that task becomes a significant overhead to the task itself. Some workarounds such as forward scheduling (setting up the next MapReduce job before the previous one finishes) have been proposed. However, these approaches introduce additional levels of complexity in the source code. One such work called HaLoop [15] extends MapReduce with programming support for iterative algorithms and improves efficiency by adding caching mechanisms. CGL MapReduce [16,17] is another work that focuses on improving the performance of MapReduce iterative tasks. Other examples of iterative MapReduce include Twister [18] and imapreduce [19].

Spark: next generation data analysis paradigm

Spark is a next generation paradigm for big data processing developed by researchers at the University of California at Berkeley. It is an alternative to Hadoop which is designed to overcome the disk I/O limitations and improve the performance of earlier systems. The major feature of Spark that makes it unique is its ability to perform in-memory computations. It allows the data to be cached in memory, thus eliminating the Hadoop's disk overhead limitation for iterative tasks. Spark is a general engine for large-scale data processing that supports Java, Scala and Python and for certain tasks it is tested to be up to 100× faster than Hadoop MapReduce when the data can fit in the memory, and up to 10× faster when data resides on the disk. It can run on Hadoop Yarn manager and can read data from HDFS. This makes it extremely versatile to run on different systems.

Berkeley data analytics stack (BDAS)

The Spark developers have also proposed an entire data processing stack called Berkeley Data Analytics Stack (BDAS) [20] which is shown in Figure 2. At the lowest level of this stack, there is a component called Tachyon [21] which is based on HDFS. It is a fault tolerant distributed file system which enables file sharing at memory-speed (data I/O speed comparable to system memory) across a cluster. It works with cluster frameworks such as Spark and MapReduce. The major advantage of Tachyon over Hadoop HDFS is its high performance which is achieved by using memory more aggressively. Tachyon can detect the frequently read files and cache them in memory thus minimizing the disk access by different jobs/queries. This enables the cached files to be read at memory speed. Another feature of Tachyon is its compatibility with Hadoop MapReduce. MapReduce programs can run over Tachyon without any modifications. The other advantage of using Tachyon is its support for raw tables. Tables with hundreds of columns can be loaded easily and the user can specify the frequently used columns to be loaded in memory for faster access.

The second component in BDAS, which is the layer above Tachyon, is called Apache Mesos. Mesos is a cluster manager that provides efficient resource isolation and sharing across distributed applications/frameworks. It supports Hadoop, Spark, Aurora [22], and other applications on a dynamically shared pool of resources. With Mesos, scalability can be increased to tens of thousands of nodes. APIs are available in java, python and C++ for developing new parallel applications. It also includes multi-resource scheduling capabilities.

The third component running on top of Mesos is Spark which takes the place of Hadoop MapReduce in the BDAS architecture. On the top of the stack are many Spark wrappers such as Spark Streaming (Large Scale real-time stream processing), Blink DB (queries with bounded errors and bounded response times on very large data) [23], GraphX (Resilient distributed Graph System on Spark) [24] and MLBase (distributed machine learning library based on Spark) [25].

Recently, BDAS and Spark have been receiving a lot of attention due to their performance gain over Hadoop. Now, it is even possible to run Spark on Amazon Elastic Map-Reduce [26]. Although BDAS consists of many useful components in the top layer

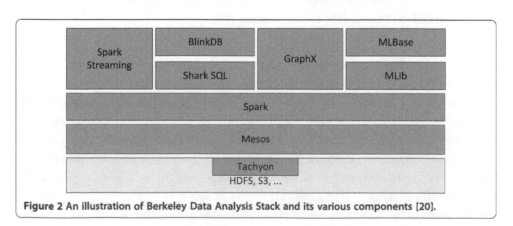

Figure 2 An illustration of Berkeley Data Analysis Stack and its various components [20].

(for various applications), many of them are still in the early stages of development and hence the support is rather limited. Due to the vast number of tools that are already available for Hadoop MapReduce, it is still the most widely used distributed data processing framework.

Vertical scaling platforms

The most popular vertical scale up paradigms are High Performance Computing Clusters (HPC), Multicore processors, Graphics Processing Unit (GPU) and Field Programmable Gate Arrays (FPGA). We describe each of these platforms and their capabilities in the following sections.

High performance computing (HPC) clusters

HPC clusters [27], also called as blades or supercomputers, are machines with thousands of cores. They can have a different variety of disk organization, cache, communication mechanism etc. depending upon the user requirement. These systems use well-built powerful hardware which is optimized for speed and throughput. Because of the top quality high-end hardware, fault tolerance in such systems is not problematic since hardware failures are extremely rare. The initial cost of deploying such a system can be very high because of the use of the high-end hardware. They are not as scalable as Hadoop or Spark clusters but they are still capable of processing terabytes of data. The cost of scaling up such a system is much higher compared to Hadoop or Spark clusters. The communication scheme used for such platforms is typically MPI. We already discussed about MPI in the peer-to-peer systems (see section "Peer-to-peer networks"). Since fault tolerance is not an important issue in this case, MPIs' lack of fault tolerance mechanism does not come as a significant drawback here.

Multicore CPU

Multicore refers to one machine having dozens of processing cores [28]. They usually have shared memory but only one disk. Over the past few years, CPUs have gained internal parallelism. More recently, the number of cores per chip and the number of operations that a core can perform has increased significantly. Newer breeds of motherboards allow multiple CPUs within a single machine thereby increasing the parallelism. Until the last few years, CPUs were mainly responsible for accelerating the algorithms for big data analytics.

Figure 3(a) shows a high-level CPU architecture with four cores. The parallelism in CPUs is mainly achieved through multithreading [29]. All the cores share the same memory. The task has to be broken down into threads. Each thread is executed in parallel on different CPU cores. Most of the programming languages provide libraries to create threads and use CPU parallelism. The most popular choice of such programming languages is Java. Since multicore CPUs have been around for several years, a large number of software applications and programming environments are well developed for this platform. The developments in CPUs are not at the same pace compared to GPUs. The number of cores per CPU is still in double digits with the processing power close to 10Gflops while a single GPU has more than 2500 processing cores with

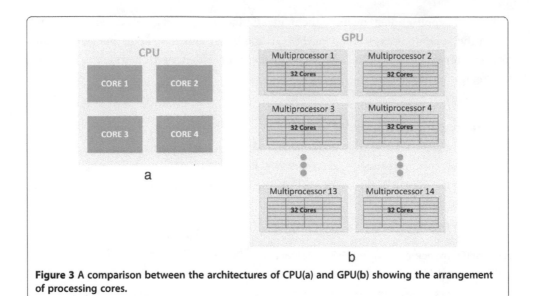

Figure 3 A comparison between the architectures of CPU(a) and GPU(b) showing the arrangement of processing cores.

1000Tflops of processing power. This massive parallelism in GPU makes it a more appealing option for parallel computing applications.

The drawback of CPUs is their limited number of processing cores and their primary dependence on the system memory for data access. System memory is limited to a few hundred gigabytes and this limits the size of the data that a CPU can process efficiently. Once the data size exceeds the system memory, disk access becomes a huge bottleneck. Even if the data fits into the system memory, CPU can process data at a much faster rate than the memory access speed which makes memory access a bottleneck. GPU avoids this by making use of DDR5 memory compared to a slower DDR3 memory used in a system. Also, GPU has high speed cache for each multiprocessor which speeds up the data access.

Graphics processing unit (GPU)

Graphics Processing Unit (GPUs) is a specialized hardware designed to accelerate the creation of images in a frame buffer intended for display output [30]. Until the past few years, GPUs were primarily used for graphical operations such as video and image editing, accelerating graphics-related processing etc. However, due to their massively parallel architecture, recent developments in GPU hardware and related programming frameworks have given rise to GPGPU (general-purpose computing on graphics processing units) [31]. GPU has large number of processing cores (typically around 2500+ to date) as compared to a multicore CPU. In addition to the processing cores, GPU has its own high throughput DDR5 memory which is many times faster than a typical DDR3 memory. GPU performance has increased significantly in the past few years compared to that of CPU. Recently, Nvidia has launched Tesla series of GPUs which are specifically designed for high performance computing. Nvidia has released the CUDA framework which made GPU programming accessible to all programmers without delving into the hardware details. These developments suggest that GPGPU is indeed gaining more popularity. Figure 3(b) shows a high-level GPU architecture with 14 multiprocessors and 32 streaming processors per block. It usually has two levels of parallelism. At the first level, there are several multiprocessors (MPs) and within each multiprocessor there are several streaming processors (SPs). To use this setup, GPU program is broken down into threads which execute on SPs and these threads are grouped together to form thread blocks which run on a multiprocessor. Each thread within a block can communicate with each other and synchronize with other threads in the same block. Each of these threads has access to small but extremely fast shared cache memory and larger global main memory. Threads in one block cannot communicate with the threads in the other block as they may be scheduled at different times. This architecture implies that for any job to be run on GPU, it has to be broken into blocks of computation that can run independently without communicating with each other [32]. These blocks will have to be further broken down into smaller tasks that execute on an individual thread that may communicate with other threads in the same block.

GPUs have been used in the development of faster machine learning algorithms. Some libraries such as GPUMiner [33] implement few machine learning algorithms on GPU using the CUDA framework. Experiments have shown many folds speedup using the GPU compared to a multicore CPU.

GPU has its own drawbacks. The primary drawback is the limited memory that it contains. With a maximum of 12GB memory per GPU (as of current generation), it is not suitable to handle terabyte scale data. Once the data size is more than the size of the GPU memory, the performance decreases significantly as the disk access becomes the primary bottleneck. Another drawback is the limited amount of software and algorithms that are available for GPUs. Because of the way in which the task breakdown is required for GPUs, not many existing analytical algorithms are easily portable to GPUs.

Field programmable gate arrays (FPGA)

FPGAs are highly specialized hardware units which are custom-built for specific applications [34]. FPGAs can be highly optimized for speed and can be orders of magnitude faster compared to other platforms for certain applications. They are programmed using Hardware descriptive language (HDL) [35]. Due to customized hardware, the development cost is typically much higher compared to other platforms. On the software side, coding has to be done in HDL with a low-level knowledge of the hardware which increases the algorithm development cost. User has to carefully investigate the suitability of a particular application for FPGA as they are effective only for a certain set of applications.

FPGAs are used in a variety of real-world applications [36, 37]. One example where FPGA was successfully deployed is in the network security applications [38]. In one such application, FPGA is used as a hardware firewall and is much faster than the software firewalls in scanning large amounts of network data [39]. In the recent years, the speed of multicore processors is reaching closer to that of FPGAs.

Comparison of different platforms

We will now provide a more detailed comparison of different platforms using the (star) ratings, where 5 stars correspond to the best possible rating and 1 star corresponds to the lowest possible rating for any given platform for a particular characteristic. Table 2

Table 2 Comparison of different platforms (along with their communication mechanisms) based on various characteristics

Scaling type	Platforms (Communication Scheme)	System/Platform			Application/Algorithm		
		Scalability	Data I/O performance	Fault tolerance	Real-time processing	Data size supported	Iterative task support
Horizontal scaling	Peer-to-Peer (TCP/IP)	★★★★★	★	★	★	★★★★★	★★
	Virtual clusters (MapRedce/MPI)	★★★★★	★★	★★★★★	★★	★★★★	★★
	Virtual clusters (Spark)	★★★★★	★★★	★★★★★	★★	★★★★	★★★
Vertical scaling	HPC clusters (MPI/Mapreduce)	★★★	★★★★	★★★★	★★★	★★★★	★★★★
	Multicore (Multithreading)	★★	★★★★	★★★★	★★★	★★	★★★★
	GPU (CUDA)	★★	★★★★★	★★★★	★★★★★	★★	★★★★
	FPGA (HDL)	★	★★★★★	★★★★	★★★★★	★★	★★★★

compares the different platforms based on the following characteristics: scalability, data I/O performance, fault tolerance, real-time processing, data size support and the support for iterative tasks. Clearly, the first three characteristics are system/platform dependent and last three are application/algorithm dependent. We will provide more details about each of these characteristics and evaluate the "goodness" of each platform for that particular characteristic by providing the star ratings for each of the platform with respect to these characteristics. It should be noted that this table provides a mere qualitative comparisons between the platforms and is not intended to bring any quantitative judgments about these platforms. In other words, a rating of two stars for a platform should be interpreted as better than having a one star and does not necessarily mean that it is two times better than the platform with a one star. Similarly, if a platform X is rated with four stars, platform Y is rated with two stars, and platform Z is rated with one star, then it should be interpreted as platform X is significantly better than platform Z compared to platform Y. It should also be noted that it is almost impossible to quantify this significance in a general scenario and one can only do so in the context of a specific application or a problem at hand. However, we anticipate that this rating table provides a snapshot of the general strengths and weaknesses of various platforms available in the context of the critical characteristics related to big data analytics.

Scalability

Scalability is defined as the ability of the system to handle growing amount of work load in a capable manner or its ability to be enlarged to accommodate that growth. In our case, scalability is considered to be the ability to add more hardware (scale up or scale out) to improve the capacity and performance of a system.

In this category, the virtual clusters and peer-to-peer networks will get 5 stars since these systems are highly scalable. In these two platforms, it is relatively easy to add more machines and scale out these systems to any extent needed. The HPC clusters will receive a 3 star rating because it becomes difficult to scale up these systems after a certain extent. HPC clusters can have thousands of cores but once deployed, they are expensive to scale up. 2 Stars for GPU shows that the scalability is not the strength of

GPUs. There is a limit on the number of GPUs a single machine can have and adding more machines will create data transfer bottleneck over the network. 1 star rating for FPGA is due to the fact that once FPGA is developed and deployed, scaling up and modifying becomes extremely costly.

Data I/O performance

Data I/O performance refers to the rate at which the data is transferred to/from a peripheral device. In the context of big data analytics, this can be viewed as the rate at which the data is read and written to the memory (or disk) or the data transfer rate between the nodes in a cluster. GPU and FPGA receive 5 stars since they have high throughput memory and the data I/O operations are extremely fast. The current generation GPUs are available with DDR5 memory which is many times faster than the DDR3 system memory. HPC clusters and Multicore will fall next in this category with 4 stars. These systems usually make use of system memory which is reasonably faster compared to disk access. Since HPC clusters and Multicore are usually single machines, network access is not a bottleneck.

Virtual clusters using the Spark framework receive 3 stars since Spark makes use of system memory which gives it an edge over Hadoop. Although system memory is fast, the data transfer between different nodes still takes place over the network. This makes the network access a bottleneck for data I/O. Virtual clusters using MapReduce over Hadoop receive 2 stars as they primarily read data from the disk which is a rather slow and time consuming process. In addition, the communication over the network degrades the performance.

Peer-to-peer systems are the worst in this category and will receive only 1 star. These systems use disks for the data access. In addition, the unmanaged and complex network scheme makes it very inefficient to aggregate the results over a single node and makes network communication even slower compared to the virtual clusters. These flaws degrade the data I/O performance.

Fault tolerance

Fault tolerance [40] is the characteristic of a system to continue operating properly in the event of a failure of one or more components. Since we created this table with an intent to compare the platforms of similar capacity, we additionally consider the chances of failure in a system and give a high rating if system failures are extremely rare even though it may not have any fault tolerance mechanism. This enables us to make an unbiased comparison between unreliable systems with fault tolerance and reliable hardware with not so good fault tolerance mechanism.

Virtual clusters get 5 stars since they primarily use MapReduce or Spark, running on frameworks such as Hadoop which have efficient in-built fault tolerant mechanisms.

On the other hand, HPC clusters, Multicore, GPU and FPGA get 4 stars. Although none of these contain the state-of-the-art fault tolerant mechanisms, they have the most reliable and well-built hardware which makes the hardware failure an extremely rare event. They get a slightly lower rating compared to the virtual clusters because of the occasional hardware failures that can still happen in spite of their rarity. 1 star rating is given to peer-to-peer networks, which shows their inability to handle system failures. They do not have any in-built fault tolerance mechanisms and additionally these networks mainly consist of commodity machines which are highly susceptible to hardware failures.

Real-time processing

Real-time processing of a system is its ability to process the data and produce the results strictly within certain time constrains. Real-time responses are often delivered in the order of milliseconds and sometimes microseconds depending on the application and the user requirements.

In this category, FPGA and GPU score 5 stars and outperform other platforms. GPU with its thousands of processing cores and high memory bandwidth is well suited for real-time data processing. Although their memory is limited, GPUs are optimized for speed and are often used for online processing. Similarly, FPGAs are specially built hardware optimized for speed and are suitable for real-time data processing.

Multicores and HPC clusters get 3 stars. They have reasonable real-time processing capabilities (though not as good as GPU and FPGA) with many processing cores and high bandwidth memory. Virtual clusters with 2 stars are not typically used for handling real-time processing tasks. They are slow in data I/O between the nodes and do not contain powerful and optimized hardware. Peer-to-Peer networks are the worst performers in this category and hence they receive only 1 star. They are slow with respect to real-time data processing because of the network communication overhead and commodity hardware.

Data size supported

Data size support is the size of the dataset that a system can process and handle efficiently. In this category, peer-to-peer networks will receive 5 stars since they can handle even petabytes of data and can theoretically scale out to unlimited number of nodes. Virtual clusters and HPC clusters can handle terabytes of data and thus will receive 4 stars. Virtual clusters can scale up to tens of thousands of nodes and frameworks like Hadoop and Spark are capable of processing and handling such large datasets.

Multicore, GPU and FPGA are not well suited for processing large data sets. All these systems get 2 stars for the limited size of the data that they can support. GPUs have a limited on-board memory in the order of several gigabytes. Similarly, Multicore systems rely on system memory which can only be up to hundreds of gigabytes.

Iterative tasks support

This is the ability of a system to efficiently support iterative tasks. Since many of the data analysis tasks and algorithms are iterative in nature, it is an important metric to compare different platforms, especially in the context of big data analytics.

HPC clusters, Multicore, GPU and FPGA score 4 stars in this category and all of them are highly suitable for iterative algorithms. However, all the iterative algorithms cannot be easily modified to run on each of these platforms which is the primary reason for giving 4 stars instead of 5 stars. These platforms are perfectly suitable for iterative algorithms since the result of one iteration can be easily used in the next iteration and all the parameters can be stored locally. Processes can reside and can keep running as long as the machine is running [41].

Virtual clusters using spark receive only 3 stars. The ability of the spark framework to use system memory for storing the data significantly reduces the data I/O overhead. The iterative tasks can still run in such cases but not as efficiently as the other platforms mentioned earlier. Data still has to be written to the memory after every iteration.

Virtual clusters using MapReduce and peer-to-peer frameworks are not designed to handle iterative tasks and hence received only 2 stars. MapReduce is not designed for iterative processing and the data has to be written onto the disk after every iteration, thus making the disk I/O a huge bottleneck. Some recent developments such as HaLoop improves MapReduce performance for iterative tasks to a certain extent which is why it was not given a 1 star. Peer-to-peer networks using TCP/IP are overwhelmed by the network communication overhead. To combine the results from different nodes after every iteration presents a significant challenge due to the complex network structure.

How to choose a platform for big data analytics?

The star ratings provided in Table 2 gives a bird's eye view of the capabilities and features of different platforms. The decision to choose a particular platform for a certain application usually depends on the following important factors: data size, speed or throughput optimization and model development. We will now provide more details about each of these factors.

Data size

The size of data that is being considered for processing is probably the most important factor. If the data can fit into the system memory, then clusters are usually not required and the entire data can be processed on a single machine. The platforms such as GPU, Multicore CPUs etc. can be used to speed up the data processing in this case. If the data does not fit into the system memory, then one has to look at other cluster options such as Hadoop, Spark etc. Again, Hadoop and Spark clusters can handle large amount of data but Hadoop has well developed tools and frameworks although it is slower for iterative tasks. The user has to decide if he needs to use off-the-shelf tools which are available for Hadoop or if he wants to optimize the cluster performance in which case Spark is more appropriate.

Speed or throughput optimization

Here, speed refers to the ability of the platform to process data in real-time whereas throughput refers to the amount of data that system is capable of handling and processing simultaneously. The users will need to be clear about whether the goal is to optimize the system for speed or throughput. If one needs to process large amount of data and do not have strict constraints on the processing time, then one can look into systems which can scale out to process huge amounts of data such as Hadoop, Peer-to-Peer networks, etc. These platforms can handle large-scale data but usually take more time to deliver the results. On the other hand, if one needs to optimize the system for speed rather than the size of the data, then they need to consider systems which are more capable of real-time processing such as GPU, FPGA etc. These platforms are capable of processing the data in real-time but the size of the data supported is rather limited.

Training/Applying a model

In data analytics, training of the model is typically done offline and it usually takes a significant amount of time. A model is typically applied in an online environment where the user expects the results within a short period of time (almost instantaneously). This creates a strong need for investigating different platforms for training and applying a model depending on the end-user application. Usually, during the training process, the user needs to deal with large amount of training data and since training is done offline, the processing time is not critical. This makes horizontal scale out platforms suitable for training a model. When a model is applied, results are expected in real-time and vertical scale up platforms are usually preferred. GPUs are preferable over other platforms when the user has strict real-time constraints and the data can be fit into the system memory. On the other hand, the HPC clusters can handle more data compared to GPUs but are not suitable for real-time processing compared to GPUs.

Practical implications

This work can provide useful insights for a wide variety of practical applications. Many users and researchers working in different areas of big data ranging from real-time systems to large-scale data processing applications can assess the advantages and disadvantages of the platforms they are currently using. This survey will be immensely helpful for them to understand if they can improve the existing systems by choosing the right platform. The strengths and weaknesses of each of the platforms are clearly highlighted in this paper. More specifically, for big data applications, there is often a trade-off between the real-time analysis requirements and the scalability of the data being processed. For the former, GPUs will be optimal choice and for the latter horizontal scaling platforms such as Hadoop and Spark are optimal choices. For example, in some of the recommendation problems dealing with millions of users, it is extremely important to have a scalable platform that can handle huge amounts of data processing and it is not absolutely required to have the results in a real-time manner. In web search applications, due to the billions of webpages available, the webpage indexing process will require a highly scalable platform which can accurately index the webpages offline. However, for the actual online component where the user enters the query and the results are expected to be obtained in real-time, vertical scaling platforms might be more suitable. Hence, depending on the application, one can probably define the most critical needs and then choose the right kind of platform accordingly. In the previous section, we characterized several such needs for practical applications.

K-means clustering on different platforms

In order to provide more insights into the analytics algorithms on different platforms, we will demonstrate the implementation of the K-Means clustering algorithm on these platforms presented so far. The choice of the K-Means algorithm was made not only because of its popularity and wide usage [42, 43], but also due to some of its critical elements that can demonstrate the ability of various platforms in handling other analytics procedures. Some of these characteristics include:

- Iterative nature of the algorithm wherein the current iteration results are needed before proceeding to the next iteration.
- Compute-intensive task of calculating the centroids from a set of datapoints.
- Aggregation of the local results to obtain a global solution when the algorithm is parallelized.

It should be noted that many of the analytics algorithms share atleast some of these characteristics. Hence, it is important to understand how these characteristics of K-means clustering algorithm are being handled using different platforms. Figure 4 explains the different steps involved in a basic K-means clustering algorithm. The algorithm starts by initializing the cluster centroids. In the next step, each data point is associated with closest centroid and in the third step, the centroids are recalculated for all the associated data instances for a given cluster. The second and third steps are repeated until the centroids converge (or after a pre-defined number of iterations).

We will now discuss the implementation details of this algorithm on different platforms to get a deeper understanding of how such iterative algorithms are modified to fit different communication schemes.

K-means on MapReduce

MapReduce is not an ideal choice for iterative algorithms such as K-Means clustering. This will be clearly shown in this section as we explain the K-Means clustering using MapReduce. The pseudocode for mapper and reducer functions for k-means clustering algorithm is given in Figure 5. Basically, mappers read the data and the centroids from the disk. These mappers then assign data instances to clusters. Once every mapper has completed their operation, reducers compute the new centroids by calculating the average of data points present in each cluster. Now, these new centroids are written to the disk. These centroids are then read by the mappers for the next iteration and the entire process is repeated until the algorithm converges. This shows the disk access bottleneck of MapReduce for iterative tasks as the data has to be written to the disk after every iteration.

> **The k-means Clustering Algorithm**
> Input : Data points D, Number of clusters k
> Step 1: Initialize k centroids randomly
> Step 2: Associate each data point in D with the nearest centroid. This will divide the data points into k clusters.
> Step 3: Recalculate the position of centroids.
> Repeat steps 2 and 3 until there are no more changes in the membership of the data points
> Output : Data points with cluster memberships

Figure 4 The pseudocode of the K-means clustering algorithm.

> **k-means::Map**
> Input: Data points D, number of clusters k and centroids
> 1: for each data point d Є D do
> 2:   Assign d to the closest centroid
> Output: centroids with associated data points
>
> ---
>
> **k-means::Reduce**
> Input: Centroids with associated data points
> 1: Compute the new centroids by calculating the average of data points in cluster
> 2: Write the global centroids to the disk
> Output: New centroids

Figure 5 Pseudocode of MapReduce based K-means clustering algorithm. The first part shows the map function and the second part shows the reduce function.

K-means on MPI

MPI [44] typically have a master–slave setting and the data is usually distributed among the slaves. Figure 6 explains the pseudocode for K-means using MPI. In the first step, the slaves read their portion of the data. In the second step, the master broadcasts the centroids to the slaves. Next, the slaves assign data instances to the clusters and compute new local centroids which are then sent back to the master. Master will then compute new global centroids by aggregating local centroids weighted by local cluster sizes. These new global centroids are then again broadcasted back to the slaves for the next iteration of K-means. In this manner, the process continues until the centroids converge. In this implementation, the data is not written to the disk but the primary bottleneck lies in the communication when MPI is used with peer-to-peer networks since aggregation is costly and the network performance will be low.

K-means on GPU

GPU has a large number of processing cores. Hence, in order to effectively utilize all the cores, the algorithm will need to be modified cautiously. Figure 7 shows the pseudocode of K-means using GPU. In the case of K-means, each processor is given a small task (assigning a data vector to a centroid). Also, a single core in a GPU is not very powerful which is why the centroid recalculation is done on the CPU. The centroids are uploaded to the shared memory of the GPU and the datapoints are partitioned and uploaded into each multiprocessor. These multiprocessors work on one data vector at a

> **k-means::MPI**
> Input: Data points D, number of clusters k
> 1: Slaves read their part of data
> 2: do until global centroids converge
> 3:   Master broadcasts the centroids to the slaves
> 4:   Slaves assign data instances to the closest centroids
> 5:   Slaves compute the new local centroids and local cluster sizes
> 6:   Slaves send local centroids and cluster sizes to the master
> 7:   Master aggregates local centroids weighted by local cluster sizes into global centroids.
> Output: Data points with cluster memberships

Figure 6 Pseudocode of k-means clustering algorithm using MPI in a master–slave configuration.

> ***k*-means::GPU**
> Input: Data points D, number of clusters k
> 1: do until global centroids converge
> 2:   Upload data points to each multiprocessor and centroids to the shared memory
> 3:   Multiprocessor works with one data vector at a time and associate it with the closest centroid
> 4:   Centroid recalculation is done on CPU

Figure 7 The pseudocode of the K-means clustering algorithm on GPU.

time and associate it with the closest centroid. Once all the points are assigned to the centroids, CPU recalculates the centroids and again will upload the new centroids to the multiprocessors. This process is repeated until the centroids converge or until a pre-defined number of iterations are completed. Another aspect to consider here is the density of the data. If the data is sparse, many multiprocessors will stall due to scarcity of data vectors to compute, which will eventually degrade the performance. In a nutshell, the performance of GPUs will be the best when the data is relatively denser and when the algorithm is carefully modified to take advantage of processing cores.

K-means on other platforms

K-means implementation on Spark is similar to the MapReduce-based implementation described in Section K-means on MapReduce. Instead of writing the global centroids to the disk, they are written into the memory which speeds up the processing and reduces the disk I/O overhead. In addition, the data will be loaded into the system memory in order to provide faster access. The K-means clustering on CPU involves multithreading where each thread associates a data vector to a centroid and finally the centroids are recomputed for the next iteration. On the other hand, K-means implementation on FPGA depends upon the FPGA architecture used and may differ significantly depending on the type of FPGA being used.

Conclusion and future directions

This paper surveys various data processing platforms that are currently available and discusses the advantages and drawbacks for each of them. Several details on each of these hardware platforms along with some of the popular software frameworks such as Hadoop and Spark are also provided. A thorough comparison between different platforms based on some of the important characteristics (such as scalability and real-time processing) has also been made through star based ratings. The widely used k-means clustering algorithm was chosen as a case study to demonstrate the strengths and weaknesses of different platforms. Some of the important characteristics of k-means algorithm such as its iterative nature, compute-intensive calculations and aggregating local results in a parallel setting makes it an ideal choice to better understand the various big data platforms. It should be noted that many of the analytical algorithms share these characteristics as well. This article provides the readers with a comprehensive review of different platforms which can potentially aid them in making the right decisions in choosing the platforms based on their data/computational requirements.

The future work involves investigating more algorithms such as decision trees, nearest neighbor, pagerank etc. over different platforms. For empirical evaluation, different experiments involving varying data size and response times can be performed over various platforms for different algorithms. Through such an analysis we will get valuable insights which can be useful in many practical and research applications. One other important direction of research will be to choose the right platform for a particular application. Based on the specific application needs, one can tailor their platform specific factors such as the amount of hard disk, memory and the speed required for optimally running the application. This study will provide a first step to analyze the effectiveness of each of the platforms and especially the strengths of them for handling real-world applications. Another direction will be to investigate the possibility of combining multiple platforms to solve a particular application problem. For example, attempting to merge the horizontal scaling platforms such as Hadoop with vertical scaling platforms such as GPUs is also gaining some recent attention. This involves several non-trivial tasks not only at the platform level but also becomes challenging to decompose the algorithm into parts and running various algorithmic components in various platforms. A combination of platforms might be more suitable for a particular algorithm and can potentially resolve the issue of making it highly scalable (through horizontal scaling) as well as performing real-time analysis (through vertical scaling).

Competing interests

The authors declare that they have no competing interests.

Authors' contributions

DS worked on the preparation of the manuscript. He also worked on the pseudocodes presented in the paper. CKR is responsible for the overall organization and the content of this survey article. All authors read and approved the final manuscript.

Acknowledgements

This work was supported in part by the National Institutes of Health award R21CA175974 and the US National Science Foundation grants IIS-1231742 and IIS-1242304.

References

1. Agneeswaran VS, Tonpay P, Tiwary J (2013) Paradigms for realizing machine learning algorithms. Big Data 1(4):207–214
2. Zaharia M, Chowdhury M, Franklin MJ, Shenker S, Spark SI (2010) Cluster Computing with Working Sets. In: Proceedings of the 2nd USENIX Conference on Hot Topics in Cloud Computing., pp 10–10
3. Milojicic DS, Kalogeraki V, Lukose R, Nagaraja K, Pruyne J, Richard B, Rollins S, Xu Z (2002) Peer-to-peer computing. Technical Report HPL-2002-57, HP Labs
4. Steinmetz R, Wehrle K (2005) Peer-to-Peer Systems and Applications. Springer Berlin, Heidelberg
5. Sievert O, Casanova H (2004) A simple MPI process swapping architecture for iterative applications. Int J High Perform Comput Appl 18(3):341–352
6. Hadoop. http://hadoop.apache.org/
7. Borthakur D (2008) HDFS architecture guide. HADOOP APACHE PROJECT. http://hadoop.apache.org/docs/r1.2.1/hdfs_design.pdf
8. Vavilapalli VK, Murthy AC, Douglas C, Agarwal S, Konar M, Evans R, Graves T, Lowe J, Shah H, Seth S (2013) Apache hadoop yarn: Yet another resource negotiator. In: Proceedings of the 4th annual Symposium on Cloud Computing., p 5
9. Dean J, Ghemawat S (2008) MapReduce: simplified data processing on large clusters. Commun ACM 51(1):107–113
10. Lee K-H, Lee Y-J, Choi H, Chung YD, Moon B (2012) Parallel data processing with MapReduce: a survey. ACM SIGMOD Record 40(4):11–20
11. Olston C, Reed B, Srivastava U, Kumar R, Tomkins A (2008) Pig latin: a not-so-foreign language for data processing. In: Proceedings of the ACM SIGMOD international conference on Management of Data. ACM, pp 1099–1110
12. Thusoo A, Sarma JS, Jain N, Shao Z, Chakka P, Anthony S, Liu H, Wyckoff P, Murthy R (2009) Hive: a warehousing solution over a map-reduce framework. Proceedings of the VLDB Endowment 2(2):1626–1629
13. Yu Y, Isard M, Fetterly D, Budiu M, Erlingsson Ú, Gunda PK, Currey J (2008) DryadLINQ: A System for General-Purpose Distributed Data-Parallel Computing Using a High-Level Language. In: OSDI., pp 1–14
14. Owen S, Anil R, Dunning T, Friedman E (2011) Mahout in Action. Manning
15. Bu Y, Howe B, Balazinska M, Ernst MD (2010) HaLoop: efficient iterative data processing on large clusters. Proceedings of the VLDB Endowment 3(1–2):285–296
16. Ekanayake J, Pallickara S, Fox G (2008) Mapreduce for data intensive scientific analyses. In: Proceesings of IEEE Fourth International Conference on eScience., pp 277–284

17. Palit I, Reddy CK (2012) Scalable and parallel boosting with MapReduce. IEEE Trans Knowl Data Eng 24(10):1904–1916
18. Ekanayake J, Li H, Zhang B, Gunarathne T, Bae S-H, Qiu J, Fox G (2010) Twister: a runtime for iterative mapreduce. In: Proceedings of the 19th ACM International Symposium on High Performance Distributed Computing. ACM, pp 810–818
19. Zhang Y, Gao Q, Gao L, Wang C (2012) Imapreduce: a distributed computing framework for iterative computation. J Grid Comput 10(1):47–68
20. Berkeley Data Analysis Stack. https://amplab.cs.berkeley.edu/software/
21. Tachyon. http://tachyon-project.org/
22. Aurora. https://incubator.apache.org/projects/aurora.html
23. Agarwal S, Mozafari B, Panda A, Milner H, Madden S, Stoica I (2013) BlinkDB: Queries with Bounded Errors and Bounded Response times on very Large Data. In: Proceedings of the 8th ACM European Conference on Computer Systems., pp 29–42
24. Xin RS, Gonzalez JE, Franklin MJ, Stoica I (2013) Graphx: A resilient distributed graph system on spark. In: First International Workshop on Graph Data Management Experiences and Systems., p 2
25. Kraska T, Talwalkar A, Duchi JC, Griffith R, Franklin MJ, Jordan MI (2013) MLbase: A Distributed Machine-learning System. In: Proceedings of Sixth Biennial Conference on Innovative Data Systems Research
26. Amazon Elastic MapReduce http://aws.amazon.com/
27. Buyya R (1999) High Performance Cluster Computing: Architectures and Systems (Volume 1). Prentice Hall, Upper SaddleRiver, NJ, USA
28. Bekkerman R, Bilenko M, Langford J (2012) Scaling up Machine Learning: Parallel and Distributed Approaches. Cambridge University Press
29. Tullsen DM, Eggers SJ, Levy HM (1995) Simultaneous Multithreading: Maximizing on-Chip Parallelism. In: ACM SIGARCH Computer Architecture News., pp 392–403
30. Owens JD, Houston M, Luebke D, Green S, Stone JE, Phillips JC (2008) GPU computing. Proc IEEE 96(5):879–899
31. Nickolls J, Dally WJ (2010) The GPU computing era. IEEE Micro 30(2):56–69
32. Hong S, Kim H (2009) An analytical Model for a GPU Architecture with Memory-Level and Thread-Level Parallelism Awareness. In: ACM SIGARCH Computer Architecture News., pp 152–163
33. Fang W, Lau KK, Lu M, Xiao X, Lam CK, Yang PY, He B, Luo Q, Sander PV, Yang K (2008) Parallel data mining on graphics processors. Hong Kong University of Science and Technology, Tech Rep HKUST-CS08-07 2
34. Francis RJ, Rose J, Vranesic ZG (1992) Field Programmable Gate Arrays, vol 180. Springer
35. Thomas DE, Moorby PR (2002) The Verilog Hardware Description Language, vol 2. Springer
36. Monmasson E, Idkhajine L, Cirstea MN, Bahri I, Tisan A, Naouar MW (2011) FPGAs in industrial control applications. IEEE Trans Ind Informat 7(2):224–243
37. Bouldin D (2004) Impacting education using FPGAs. In: Proceedings of 18th International conference on Parallel and Distributed Processing Symposium., p 142
38. Chen H, Chen Y, Summerville DH (2011) A survey on the application of FPGAs for network infrastructure security. IEEE Commun Surv Tutor 13(4):541–561
39. Jedhe GS, Ramamoorthy A, Varghese K (2008) A scalable high throughput firewall in FPGA. In: Proceedings of 16th International Symposium on Field-Programmable Custom Computing Machines., pp 43–52
40. Fault Tolerance. http://en.wikipedia.org/wiki/Fault_tolerance
41. Snir M (1998) MPI–the Complete Reference: The MPI core, vol 1. MIT press
42. Jain AK (2010) Data clustering: 50 years beyond K-means. Pattern Recogn Lett 31(8):651–666
43. Reddy CK, Vinzamuri B (2013) A Survey of Partitional and Hierarchical Clustering Algorithms. Data Clustering: Algorithms and Applications., p 87
44. Gropp W, Lusk E, Skjellum A (1999) Using MPI: Portable Parallel Programming with the Message-Passing Interface, Vol 1. MIT press

6

Contextual anomaly detection framework for big sensor data

Michael A Hayes and Miriam AM Capretz[*]

*Correspondence:
mcapretz@uwo.ca
Department of Electrical and
Computer Engineering, Western
University, London, Canada

Abstract

The ability to detect and process anomalies for Big Data in real-time is a difficult task. The volume and velocity of the data within many systems makes it difficult for typical algorithms to scale and retain their real-time characteristics. The pervasiveness of data combined with the problem that many existing algorithms only consider the content of the data source; e.g. a sensor reading itself without concern for its context, leaves room for potential improvement. The proposed work defines a contextual anomaly detection framework. It is composed of two distinct steps: content detection and context detection. The content detector is used to determine anomalies in real-time, while possibly, and likely, identifying false positives. The context detector is used to prune the output of the content detector, identifying those anomalies which are considered both content and contextually anomalous. The context detector utilizes the concept of profiles, which are groups of similarly grouped data points generated by a multivariate clustering algorithm. The research has been evaluated against two real-world sensor datasets provided by a local company in Brampton, Canada. Additionally, the framework has been evaluated against the open-source Dodgers dataset, available at the UCI machine learning repository, and against the R statistical toolbox.

Keywords: Big data analytics; Contextual anomaly detection; Predictive modelling; Multivariate clustering; Streaming sensors

Introduction

Anomalies are abnormal events or patterns that do not conform to expected events or patterns [1]. Identifying anomalies is important in a broad set of disciplines; including, medical diagnosis, insurance and identity fraud, network intrusion, and programming defects. Anomalies are generally categorized into three types: point, or content anomalies; context anomalies, and collective anomalies. Point anomalies occur for data points that are considered abnormal when viewed against the whole dataset. Context anomalies are data points that are considered abnormal when viewed against meta-information associated with the data points. Finally, collective anomalies are data points which are considered anomalies when viewed with other data points, against the rest of the dataset.

Algorithms to detect anomalies generally fall into three types: unsupervised, supervised, and semi-supervised [1]. These techniques range from training the detection algorithm using completely unlabelled data, to having a pre-formed dataset with entries labelled *normal* or *abnormal*, and to those that rely only partially on external input. A common output of these techniques is a trained categorical classifier which receives a new data entry as the input, and outputs a hypothesis for the data points abnormality. One problem with standard anomaly detection approaches is that there is little concern for the context of the data content. For example, a sensor reading may determine that a particular electrical box is consuming an abnormally high amount of energy. However, when viewed in context with the location of the sensor, current weather conditions, and time of year, it is well within normal bounds. These types of anomalies are commonly found in fields with spatial, sequential, or temporal attributes that can be associated with the sensor [1].

One interesting, and growing, field where anomaly detection is prevalent is in *Big Data*, and in particular, sensor data. Sensor data that is streamed from sources such as electrical outlets, water pipes, telecommunications, Web logs, and many other areas, generally follows the template of large amounts of data that is input very frequently. For example, in Web logs, anomaly detection can be used to identify abnormal behavior, such as identify fraud. In many of these areas one difficulty is coping with the velocity and volume of the data while still providing real-time support for detection of anomalies. Further, future prediction, energy usage reduction strategies, and anomaly detection are popular sources of new technological developments, many aimed at creating intelligent buildings. Intelligent builds are those that can manage, optimize, and reduce their own energy consumption, based on Big sensor Data [2].

There is also much discussion on the types of algorithms applied to anomaly detection; some consider that there is a paradigm shift in the types of algorithms used: from computationally expensive algorithms to computationally inexpensive algorithms [3]. The inexpensive algorithms may have much higher training accuracy error; that is, the error accumulated per record when training. However, when normalized over the entire, large, dataset, the higher training accuracy error converges to a lesser prediction error. Prediction error is defined as the error accumulated when predicting new values from a trained predictor [4]. The prediction error for the inexpensive algorithm is within similar ranges as those found with the computationally more expensive algorithm, yet occurring over a much smaller time frame. A motivation of this work is to then take this notion and shift it to incorporate these computationally expensive algorithms which still generally perform better.

Contextual anomaly detection seeks to find relationships within datasets where variations in external behavioural attributes well describe anomalous results in the data. For example, viewing data in the context of time, or in the context of time-related concepts such as seasons, weekdays and weekends, workdays and time-off, can reveal anomalous behaviour directly correlated with such context. This is distinct from content anomalies which can be defined as abnormal instances in data with respect to the implicit data alone. An example of a content anomaly is an abnormal spike in user logins on a website, independent from external reasons. An example for contextual anomalies can be found in a use-case such as power consumption likely has context-based, time-related relationships: it makes sense to posit that the power consumption of an office building is much higher during midday, during a work day, compared to at night, during a weekend. One aspect of this work is to explore, and show the work is successfully applied, for these more obvious relationships while also remaining expandable to learning and revealing complex contextually anomalous behaviours.

Some related works have focused on anomaly detection in data with spatial relationships [5], while others propose methods to define outliers based on relational class attributes [6]. A prevalent issue in these works is their scalability to large amounts of data. In most cases the algorithms have increased their complexity to overcome more naive methods, but in doing so have limited their application scope to offline detection. This problem is compounded as *Big Data* requirements are found not only in giant corporations such as Amazon or Google, but in more and more small companies that require storage, retrieval, and querying over very large scale systems. Additionally, where an algorithm may have excelled in its serial elision, it is now necessary to view the algorithm in parallel; using concepts such as divide and conquer, or MapReduce [7]. Many common anomaly detection algorithms such as k-nearest neighbour, single class support vector machines, and outlier-based cluster analysis are designed for single machines [8].

The research in this paper will describe a technique to detect contextually anomalous values in streaming sensor systems. This research is based on the notion that anomalies have dimensional and contextual locality. That is, the dimensional locality will identify those abnormalities which are found to be structurally different based on the sensor reading. Contextually, however, the sensors may introduce new information which diminishes or enhances the abnormality of the anomaly. Further, the technique will use a two-part detection scheme to ensure that point anomalies are detected in real-time and then evaluated using contextual clustering. The latter evaluation will be performed based on *sensor profiles* which are defined by identifying sensors that are used in similar contexts. The primary goal of this technique is to provide a scalable way to detect, classify, and interpret anomalies in sensor-based systems. This ensures that real-time anomaly detection can occur. The proposed approach is novel in its application to very large scale systems, and in particular, its use of contextual information to reduce the rate of false positives. Further, we posit that our work can be extended by defining a third step based on the semantic locality of the data, providing a further reduction in the number of anomalies which are false positive.

The following sections of the paper are organized as follows: the "Background and literature review" section will describe related works in the field of anomaly detection in streaming sensor systems. The "Research design and methodology" section will outline the approach taken by the proposed research. The framework will be applied on three datasets in the "Results and discussion" section. Finally, the "Conclusions" section will describe concluding thoughts and ideas for future work in this area.

Background and literature review

Anomaly detection is involved in a variety of applications, across many disciplines. As such, terminology and background will be introduced to facilitate understanding for the rest of the paper. Anomaly detection algorithms can be categorized as point detection, collective detection, or context-aware detection algorithms [1]. Contextual detection is the root of the work presented in this paper and so will be the focus on much of the related works. Contextual anomalies exist where the dataset includes a combination of *behavioural* and *contextual* attributes. These terms are also defined as *environmental* and *indicator* attributes, as introduced by Song et al. [9]. Behavioural attributes are attributes such as the sensor reading itself. Contextual attributes take on one of four forms, defined in Table 1.

Table 1 Definitions for types of contextual attributes

Term	Definition
Spatial	The records in the dataset include features which identify locational information for the record. For example, a sensor reading may have spatial attributes for the city, province, and country the sensor is located in; it could also include finer-grained information about the sensors location within a building, such as floor, room, and building number.
Graphs	The records are related to other records as per some graph structure. The graph structure then defines a spatial neighbourhood whereby these relationships can be considered as contextual indicators.
Sequential	The records can be considered as a sequence within one another. That is, there is meaning in defining a set of records that are positioned one after another. For example, this is extremely prevalent in time-series data whereby the records are timestamped and can thus be positioned relative to each other based on time readings.
Profile	The records can be clustered within profiles that may not have explicit temporal or spatial contextualities. This is common in anomaly detection systems where, for example, a company defines profiles for their users; should a new record violate the existing user profile, that record is declared anomalous.

Contextual anomaly applications are normally handled in one of two ways. First, the context anomaly problem is transformed into a point anomaly problem. That is, the application attempts to apply separate point anomaly detection techniques to the same dataset, within different contexts. In this approach, it is necessary to define the contexts of normal and anomalous records apriori, which is not always possible within many applications. This is true for the Big sensor Data use case, where it is difficult to define the entire set of known anomalous records. The second approach to handling contextual anomaly applications is to utilize the existing structure within the records to detect anomalies using all the data concurrently. This is especially useful when the context of the data cannot be broken into discrete categories, or when new records cannot easily be placed within one of the given contexts. The second approach generally requires a higher computational complexity than the first approach as the underlying algebra in calculating a contextual anomaly is computationally expensive.

Many previous anomaly detection algorithms in the sensoring domain focus on using the sequential information of the reading to predict a possible value and then comparing this value to the actual reading. Hill and Minsker [10] propose a data-driven modelling approach to identify point anomalies in such a way. In their work they propose several *one-step ahead* predictors; i.e. based on a sliding window of previous data, predict the new output and compare it to the actual output. Hill and Minsker [10] note that their work does not easily integrate several sensor streams to help detect anomalies. This is in contrast to the work outlined in this paper where the proposed technique includes a contextual detection step that includes historical information for several streams of data, and their context. In an earlier work, Hill et al. [11] proposed an approach to use several streams of data by employing a real-time Bayesian anomaly detector. The Bayesian detector algorithm can be used for single sensor streams, or multiple sensor streams. However, their approach relies strictly on the sequential sensor data without including context. Focusing an algorithm purely on detection point anomalies in the sensoring domain has some drawbacks. First, it is likely to miss important relationships between similar sensors within the network as point anomaly detectors work on the global view of the data. Second, it is likely to generate a false positive anomaly when context such as the time of day, time of year, or type of location is missing. For example, hydro sensor readings in the winter may fluctuate outside the acceptable anomaly identification range, but this could be due to varying external temperatures influencing how a building manages their heating and ventilation.

Little work has been performed in providing context-aware anomaly detection algorithms. Srivastava and Srivastava [12], proposed an approach to bias anomaly detectors using functional and contextual constraints. Their work provides *meaningful* anomalies in the same way as a post-processing algorithm would, however, their approach requires an expensive dimensionality reduction step to flatten the semantically relevant data with the content data. Mahapatra et al. [13] propose a contextual anomaly detection framework for use in text data. Their work focuses on exploiting the semantic nature and relationships of words, with case studies specifically addressing *tags* and *topic* keywords. They had some promising results, including a reduction in the number of false positives identified without using contextual information. Their approach was able to use well-defined semantic similarity algorithms specifically for identifying relationships between words. This is in contrast to the work proposed in this paper as we are concerned with contextual information such as spatio-temporal relationships between sensors. Similar to the work proposed in this paper is their use of contextual detection as a post-processing step. This allows the algorithm to be compared and optimized at two distinct steps: point anomaly detection, and contextual anomaly detection.

A different approach for contextual detection is that work of AlEroud et al. [14], who apply contextual anomaly detection to uncover zero-day cyber attacks. Their work involves two distinct steps, similar to the modules described in this paper: contextual misuse module, and an anomaly detection technique. There are other minor modules, such as data pre-processing, and profile sampling. The first major component, contextual misuse, utilizes a conditional entropy-based technique to identify those records that are relevant to specific, useful, contexts. The second component, anomaly detection, uses a 1-nearest neighbour approach to identify anomalies based on some distance measure. This component is evaluated over the records individually to determine whether connections between records indicate anomalous values. The work presented by AlEroud et al. [14] is similar to the work presented in this paper in that the detection is composed of two distinct modules. However, the content component of their work involves calculating difficult distance measures that are not always easily definable. For example, when faced with many features that each have different data types or domains, it is difficult to calculate suitable distance metrics as finding a common method to aggregate the features is also difficult. Another drawback is that each module is normally evaluated for all new incoming values. While the authors do say that the first component aims to reduce the dimensionality required for the second component, they go on to mention that both the contextual component and anomaly detection component are calculated individually to evaluate the anomaly detection prowess of the approach.

Miller et al. [15] discuss anomaly detection in the domain of attributed graphs. Their work allows for contextual data to be included within a graph structure. One interesting result is that considering additional metadata forced the algorithm to explore parts of the graph that were previously less emphasized. A drawback of Miller et al.'s [15] work is that their full algorithm is difficult for use in real-time analytics. To compensate, they provide an estimation of their algorithm for use in real-time analytics, however the estimation is not explored in detail and so it is difficult to determine its usefulness in the real-time detection domain.

Other work has been done in computationally more expensive algorithms, such as support vector machines (SVMs) and neural networks. In general, these algorithms require a large amount of training time, and little testing time. In most cases this is acceptable as models can be trained in an offline manner, and then evaluated in real-time. One disadvantage to using these classification-based algorithms is that many require accurate labels for normal classes within the training data [8]. This is difficult in scenarios such as environmental sensor networks where there is little to no labelling for each sensor value. Shilton et al. [16] propose a SVM approach to multiclass classification and anomaly detection in wireless sensor networks. Their work requires data to have known classes to be classified into, and then those data points which cannot be classified are considered anomalous. One issue that the authors present is the difficulty in setting one of the algorithm's parameters. To reduce the effect of the computational complexity of these algorithms, Lee et al. [17] have proposed work to detect anomalies by leveraging Hadoop. Hadoop is an open-source software framework that supports applications to run on distributed machines. Their work is preliminary in nature and mostly addresses concerns and discussion related to anomaly detection in Big Data. Another online anomaly detection algorithm has been proposed by Xie et al. [18]. Their work uses a histogram-based approach to detect anomalies within hierarchical wireless sensor networks. A drawback to their approach is their lack of consideration for multivariate data. That is, their work focuses strictly on developing histograms for the data content but not the context of the data.

Another component of the work presented in this paper is deploying a modular, hierarchical, framework to ensure the algorithm can cope with the velocity and volume of Big Data. Other work by Kittler et al. [19] present a system architecture to detect anomalies in the machine perception domain. In particular, they propose a set of definitions and taxonomies to clearly define the roles and boundaries within their anomaly detection architecture. Their work is underlined with a Bayesian probabilistic predictor which is enhanced by concepts such as outlier, noise, distribution drift, novelty detection and rare events. These concepts are used to extend their application to other domains that consider similar concepts. This approach is in distinct contrast to the work proposed by this paper. Concretely, Kittler et al. [19] present context as more analagous to *semantics* in that the additional information they add is similar to domain ontologies rather than contextual information inherently associated within the data.

Research design and methodology

The work proposed in this paper describes a framework consisting of two distinct components: the content anomaly detector and the contextual anomaly detector. The work is described as a framework as it provides an extendible and modular approach to anomaly detection, not requiring specific implementations for each module: the content and context detectors in particular. The rest of this paper will propose one possible solution for the modules, which works particularly well for the streaming sensor use-case.

The primary reason for creating a separation of concerns between content and context is in the interest of scalability for large amounts of data. The content-based detector will be capable of processing every new piece of data being sent to a central repository as it will use an algorithm with a fast testing time. In contrast to this, the context-based detector will be used in two situations: to help determine if the anomaly detected by the content detector is a false positive, and to randomly ensure that the sensor is not producing wholly anomalous results. The latter reason being that a sensor may be acting non-anomalous within its own history of values, but not when viewed with sensors with similar context. Sub-section "Contextual anomaly detection" will also outline the technique to train the *sensor profiles*, thus determining which sensors are contextually similar. We define here a *sensor profile* as a contextually aware representation of the sensor as a subset of its attributes. Comparing an incoming sensor value with the corresponding sensor profile consists of comparing the incoming value with an average of all the sensor values composing the corresponding sensor profile. This creates two levels of abstraction for the contextual detector. First, since similar sensors are combined into sensor profiles, a level of context is created at a sensor attribute level. Second, the contextual detection uses a correlation matrix of the attributes for the sensors to further apply context to incoming values for comparison. The use of clustering is also used for two purposes. First, clustering helps reduce the population size by creating sub-tasks that run against the computationally expensive contextually anomaly detection function. Second, clustering provides early insight into the context of the new sensor value. Again, this early context picture is further enhanced when the contextual detector is applied. A pictorial representation of the sensor profile concept is illustrated in Figure 1.

Algorithm 1 illustrates the process of the technique from a component-level. The `UnivariateGaussianPredictor` function evaluates the sensor against historical values taken from the same sensor. The function will calculate a prediction based on the previous values and compare that prediction against the actual result. This algorithm corresponds with the diagram shown in Figure 2. The `GetSensorProfile` function will request the other sensors that are contextually similar to the sensor being

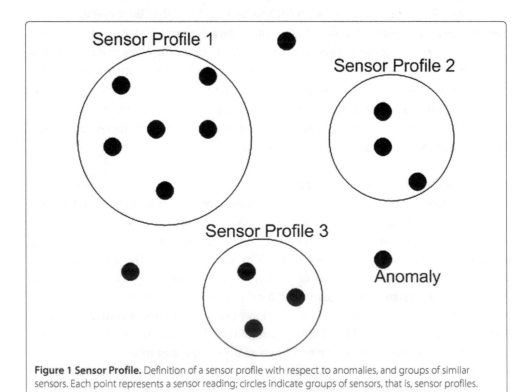

Figure 1 Sensor Profile. Definition of a sensor profile with respect to anomalies, and groups of similar sensors. Each point represents a sensor reading; circles indicate groups of sensors, that is, sensor profiles.

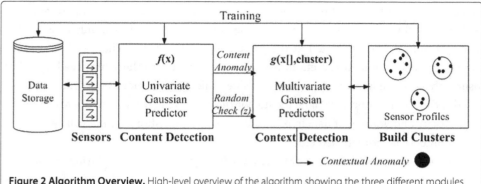

Figure 2 Algorithm Overview. High-level overview of the algorithm showing the three different modules and how they interact with one another. Additionally shows the input and output for each module.

evaluated. `MultivariateGaussianPredictor` then compares the sensor value with a mean value from the sensors found in the sensor profile. Again, based on the result of this evaluation, the anomaly can be rejected as being anomalous or confirmed as being both a content and context-based anomaly. Another important note is the `IsRandomContextCheck` function which is part of the if-statement. This will determine whether a random, perhaps non-anomalous, sensor value be sent to the context-based detector. The reason for this is primarily to check whether the sensor is behaving anomalous with respect to the sensor profile.

Algorithm 1: Contextual Anomaly Detection

---

input : *SensorValue*
output: *Anomaly*

content ← `UnivariateGaussianPredictor` (*SensorValue*)

if `IsAnomalous` *(content)* ‖ `IsRandomContextCheck` *(content)* **then**
    profile ← `GetSensorProfile` (*SensorValue*); context ←
    `MultivariateGaussianPredictor` (*SensorValue, profile*);
    if `IsAnomalous` *(context)* **then**
      | return *Anomaly*=true;
    end if
    else
      | return *Anomaly*=false;
    end if
end if
else
| return *Anomaly*=false;
end if

Content anomaly detection

Content anomaly detection, or point anomaly detection, has been well explored in literature. In particular, the proposed content anomaly detection technique will use a *univariate Gaussian predictor* to determine point anomalies. Univariate Gaussian predictors build a historical model of the data, and then predict and compare new values based on the model. The predictor will be univariate in that it will only consider the historical sensor readings to adjust the parameters of the model. There will be no consideration for the contextual meta-information associated with the sensor readings. This ensures that the predictor can classify new values quickly while sacrificing some accuracy. Speed is the most important characteristic for the point detector as it needs to evaluate a high velocity and volume of data in real-time. The accuracy shortcoming will be handled by the contextual anomaly detector.

The univariate Gaussian predictor relies on defining two parameters during the training of the algorithm, μ and σ^2. Equation (1) and Equation (2) show how these two parameters are set, where m is the number of training values, and $x^{(i)}$ is the sensor reading for training value i. An anomaly is detected when $p(x) < \epsilon$, where ϵ is a threshold value set during implementation.

$$\mu = \frac{1}{m} \sum_{i=1}^{m} x^{(i)} \tag{1}$$

$$\sigma^2 = \frac{1}{m} \sum_{i=1}^{m} \left(x^{(i)} - \mu\right)^2 \tag{2}$$

$$p(\bar{x}) = \prod_{j=1}^{n} \frac{1}{\sqrt{2\pi}\sigma} \exp - \frac{\left(\bar{x}_j - \mu_j\right)^2}{2\sigma^2}$$

$$= \frac{1}{\sqrt{2\pi}\sigma} \exp - \frac{(\bar{x} - \mu)^2}{2\sigma^2} (\because n = 1) \tag{3}$$

Contextual anomaly detection

The contextual anomaly detector is based on two concepts: defining the *sensor profiles* and assigning each sensor to one of the sensor profiles, and evaluating the current sensor value (declared anomalous by the content anomaly detector) against the sensor profile's average expected value. The sensor profiles are defined using a multivariate clustering algorithm; the algorithm is multivariate to include the sensors multidimensional contextual metadata which may include location, building, ownership company, time of year, time of day, and weather phenomena. The clustering algorithm will place each sensor within a sensor profile and then assign that profile group to the sensor. When a sensor has been declared anomalous by the content anomaly detector, the context anomaly detector will determine the average expected value of the sensor group. Then, in a similar way as in Equation 3, the context anomaly detector will determine whether the sensor value falls within the acceptable prediction interval.

The k-means clustering algorithm will iterate through the following steps:

1. Randomly initiate K random clusters
2. Partition the dataset into the K random clusters, based on Equation 4; placing items into each cluster based on the smallest distance to the cluster
3. Re-calculate the centroids for each cluster
4. Repeat Step 2 until Step 3 does not modify cluster centroids

$$\min_s \sum_{i=1}^{k} \sum_{x_j} ||x_j - \mu_i||^2 \tag{4}$$

Once the clusters have been formed using k-means clustering, we define a Gaussian predictor for the *subset* of sensors which belong to each sensor profile. Then, each sensor profile has a specific Gaussian predictor which can be used to determine if a new sensor value is anomalous for that particular sensor profile family. Equations 5, 6, and 7 define the mean, sigma, and prediction function for the Gaussian predictor, where $\mu \in \mathbb{R}^n$, $\Sigma \in \mathbb{R}^{n \times n}$. Σ refers to the covariance matrix of the features used to define the Gaussian predictor. Also, $|\Sigma|$ refers to calculating the determinant of the covariance matrix. The new sensor values that are passed from the content anomaly detector are evaluated with respect to Equation 7. The value, $p(x)$ is compared against some threshold, ϵ, and is flagged as anomalous if it is less than ϵ.

$$\mu = \frac{1}{m} \sum_{i=1}^{m} x^{(i)} \tag{5}$$

$$\Sigma = \frac{1}{m} \sum_{i=1}^{m} \left(x^{(i)} - \mu\right)\left(x^{(i)} - \mu\right)^T \tag{6}$$

$$p(\bar{x}) = \frac{1}{(2\pi)^{(\frac{n}{2})}|\Sigma|^{(\frac{1}{2})}} \exp\left(-\frac{1}{2}(\bar{x} - \mu)^T \Sigma^{-1}(\bar{x} - \mu)\right) \tag{7}$$

To summarize, the context anomaly detection algorithm proceeds as follows:

1. Offline: generate k clusters for each sensor profile
2. Offline: generate k Gaussian classifiers for each sensor profile
3. Online: evaluate corresponding Gaussian classifier when receiving a value by the content detector

Complexity and parameter discussion

The contextual detection algorithm works on multiple dimensions of the dataset, and thus has a higher computational complexity in comparison to the content detector. To cope with higher computational complexity, the proposed framework utilizes parallelization and data reduction in an important way. The anomaly detection evaluation uses the notion of data reduction by only evaluating the computationally more expensive contextual anomaly detector on a very small subset of the data. The modularity of the content detector and the context detector allows the proposed research to be implemented in a large distributed environment. The content detectors can independently process information in parallel on distributed machines and only need to share findings to the context detector when an anomaly is detected. Then, the framework can horizontally scale by adding additional machines to indepdently process new data.

Another important aspect of the proposed algorithms is the selection of some of the parameters. For example, selection of the k in the k-means clustering algorithm will have a large impact on the accuracy of the Gaussian predictors. The problem of parameter selection is well-known in data mining but a work entitled *k-means++* by Arthur and Vassilvitskii [20] attempts to overcome this issue, specifically for k-means clustering. Therefore, the implementation of this work will utilize the k-means++ algorithm in place of the classic k-means algorithm. This does not change the sets of equations listed earlier in this section.

Results and discussion

The preliminary evaluation of this work was primarily done in conjunction with Powersmiths, a company specializing in providing sensor equipment to businesses to help build a sustainable future [21]. Figure 3 illustrates a general sensor streaming application. To do this, Powersmiths uses sensor data that is pulled from the electrical, water, and gas systems within the business. This data is pushed to a cloud-based data storage solution where some analysis is completed and pushed back to the consumer. Currently, customers may have tens to hundreds of sensors, each with the ability to produce sensor data on the order of a few seconds, to several minutes.

The evaluation of the proposed technique was done using their existing system. Preliminary studies were not done in real-time but rather trained in batch over their historical data and validated using a test dataset. To test the implementation offline, while emulating a real-time environment, several pseudo data streams were created and pushed to the detector at regular intervals mirroring the real world case. The following sub-sections will detail the implementation of the technique, and the results. The evaluation of the proposed work will also be shown on the open-source Dodgers dataset, available from the UCI Machine Learning repository [22,23].

Powersmiths and the Datasets

Powersmiths collects a wide-range of data; including: sensor streams (as byte arrays) with temporal information, sensor spatial information, consumer profile information (i.e. name, location, etc), and multi-media including videos, images, and audio. For the purposes of anomaly detection, Powersmiths has provided a subset of their data which includes electricity sensor streams and temperature sensor streams, and their related temporal and spatial context. A table of the electrical data is shown in Table 2, for each time input, there are corresponding values for each of the four sensors (labelled Sensor

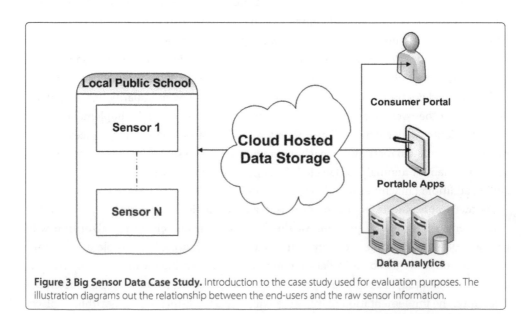

Figure 3 Big Sensor Data Case Study. Introduction to the case study used for evaluation purposes. The illustration diagrams out the relationship between the end-users and the raw sensor information.

Table 2 Dataset and feature domains

Feature	Domain
Time	DD/MM/YYYY HH:MM
Sensor 1	0.00 - 100.00
Sensor 1 Location	[a-zA-Z0-9]
Sensor 2	0.00 - 100.00
Sensor 2 Location	[a-zA-Z0-9]
Sensor 3	0.00 - 100.00
Sensor 3 Location	[a-zA-Z0-9]
Sensor 4	0.00 - 100.00
Sensor 4 Location	[a-zA-Z0-9]
Day of the Week	0 - 7
Time of Day	0,1,2

1...Sensor 4) and the physical location of the sensor (labelled Sensor 1 Location...Sensor 4 Location). For the purposes of expanding the contextual information for the sensors, the *Time* feature has been discretized into two new features: *Day of the Week* and *Time of Day*. Time of Day is discretized into three values: 0 representing readings occurring outside normal, 9-5, office hours; 1 representing values occurring during morning, 9-1, office hours; and 2 representing values occurring during afternoon, 2-5, office hours. These features are shown below the break in Table 2. One can consider the values for *Day of the Week*, *Time of Day*, and the set of locations as contextual information for the sensors; while the content itself is simply the sensor reading at the given time.

The given Powersmiths dataset for the electrical dataset includes 101,384 tuples; where 85% were used for training, and 15% were used for testing. As mentioned earlier, the testing dataset has been modified to simulate a real-world streaming environment from multiple sensors. This was done by using the time stamp and individual sensors to produce four test datasets (one for each sensor). The simulation environment processes concurrent sensors streaming data in every 10ms. The authors acknowledge that a static write frequency is the optimal case and does not wholly represent a real-world simulation; however, the results can still show how the proposed research responds in such an environment. The second dataset, for temperature streaming sensor readings, consists of 26,943 readings. Again, for testing and evaluation purposes this dataset was split into 85% for training, and 15% for evaluation. The dataset consists of five sensors; their meta-information is shown in Table 3. The dataset consists of five sensors that are recording temperature readings, in degrees Celsius. The sensors are again distributed across the building's main office; both recording values of rooms themselves, as well as latent temperatures of the walls. Like dataset 1, there is additional contextual information that can be extracted from the *Time* attribute, as shown in Table 4.

The implementation for the framework was completed using a virtualized sensor stream. That is, the application was built around an old view of the *Big Sensor Data* dataset, and not done over the real, live, data. To ensure the data was still tested as though it was real-time, a virtualized sensor stream was created. This was accomplished by extracting the different sensors from the entire dataset into their own individual datasets. The queue would then be incrementally evaluated and removed. A code listing for this process can be found in Listing 1. Another important implementation detail is the determination in the number of sensor profiles to create during the contextual detection

Table 3 Sensor dataset 2: temperature

Location	Sensor location	Associated	Unit
Main	Head Office	Forge Hallway	Celsius
Main	Head Office	Forge Room	Celsius
Main	Head Office	IT Closet	Celsius
Main	Head Office	South Wall	Celsius
Main	Head Office	North Wall	Celsius

process. Determining the number of profiles was done as a pre-processing step, iteratively increasing the number of sensor profiles until the accuracy was no longer improved. Empirically this was determined to be three clusters for the Powersmiths datasets. Logically this also made sense as Powersmiths provides three types of sensoring to their clients.

Listing 1 Code Snippet for Virtualized Sensor Stream

```java
//Instantiate Queue
Queue virtualQueue = new LinkedList();
...
//Concurrently write new sensor values
synchronized(virtualQueue) {
    virtualQueue.add(sensorValue);
}
...
//Evaluate the top-most queue against
//the real-time model
while(true) {
    if(virtualQueue.poll() != null) {
        String val[] = virtualQueue.remove();
        boolean isAnomalous =
            checkValueWithRealTime(
        Double.parseDouble(val[1]));
        if (isAnomalous) anomalyArray.add(
                    value);
    }
}
```

Dataset 1 implementation and results: HVAC

The preliminary implementation for this work was completed in Java using the Weka [24] open-source data mining library for building the clusters. There were four sensors included in the HVAC dataset, all measuring the electricity from power meters located in different areas within the building. For example, there were sensors for the two research

Table 4 Dataset example

Date Time	Sensor 1	Sensor 2	Sensor 3	Sensor 4	Sensor 5	Day	Time of Day
03/01/2011 09:00	20.86	22.32	26.69	2.27	1.78	2	0
03/01/2011 10:00	20.32	21.63	26.05	0.88	-2.14	2	0
03/01/2011 11:00	20.11	21.62	25.87	-2.44	-3.24	2	0

and development areas, existing on two floors. Also, there were sensors for the two administrative sectors of the building. Information on the location, as well as the sensor reading time as described in Table 2 were included.

The initial Gaussian anomaly predictor using only content information (i.e. the data stream itself) was built using all the sensor values in the training dataset. This predictor is labelled as `Univariate Gaussian Predictor` in Algorithm 1 and Figure 2. For the purposes of this proof of concept, the parameters μ and σ^2, from Equation (1) and Equation (2), were determined iteratively. In further studies the authors would like to show relative speed-ups and trade-offs in parallelizing this step of the algorithm. Evaluating the sensor data was done in real-time as the simulator streamed in values. Given the low computational expense of this step, parallelization may not provide a large performance increase.

We empirically determined that three clusters were appropriate for building a clustering model; beyond three the clustering algorithm saw little improvement. The cluster process is shown as `Build Clusters` in Figure 2. After determining the sensor profiles by clustering, a contextual Gaussian predictor was built for each contextual cluster, or *sensor profile* as defined in the "Research design and methodology" section. Algorithm 1 labels this as `Multivariate Gaussian Predictor`. Again, for the purposes of this proof of concept, the arrays of μ and Σ for each sensor profile were determined iteratively. This would need to be compared to a parallel elision as future work.

The results of our work can be described in two steps. The first step is in the algorithms ability to determine the point anomalies in real-time. The second step is to determine which of these anomalies are contextually anomalous, as well as point anomalous. In

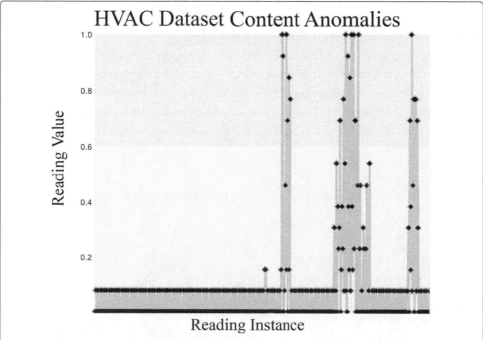

Figure 4 Content Anomaly Detection. The results of the proposed work on the HVAC sensor dataset. Each black circle represents a sensor reading, the readings are interconnected with dark grey lines. Additionally, the points highlighted in grey at the top of the image are those which have been identified as anomalous with respect to their content alone.

Figure 4 the results of the point anomaly detector are shown. The upper portion of the figure, shaded in grey, shows those values which were determined to be anomalous. Over the course of the simulation, 23 of the sensor values were considered to be point anomalies. Concretely, this means that 23 of the values were seen to be anomalous with respect to the expected value of that particular sensor, using only the sensor value. This means that less than 0.01% of the values were found to be anomalous, which is reasonable for the context of sensor streaming in a commercial building.

The second part of the results is determining which of those 23 sensor values are contextually anomalous. That is, based on the contextual information of: sensor physical locations, sensor reading time of day, sensor reading day of the week, and correlations between other sensors; which values remain anomalous? In Figure 5, a pie graph indicating the number of point anomalies, 23, and the number of contextually insignificant sensor values, 2. This figure outlines the reduction in the total number of anomalies detected by removing those that were considered contextually normal. The figure also illustrates that 9% of the potential point anomalies were cleared by the context detection process. Concretely, the approach determined that two of the point anomalies should not be considered as anomalous when including contextual information such as *Time of Day*, *Day of the Week*, and sensor spatial information.

Thus, we can say that the algorithm reduced the number of false-positive anomalies by 2. The other benefit we see here is that the more computationally expensive contextual detector only needed to evaluate 23 sensor readings, instead of the tens of thousands that are streamed to the point detector. Therefore, as the detection algorithm scales to more volumes of data, with higher velocities of data streams, the algorithm will still be able to evaluate the computationally more expensive contextual detector while still providing real-time detection.

Dataset 2 implementation and results: temperature

Synonymous to dataset 1, the first component to evaluate is the content detection for the temperature dataset. In testing the proposed work's content detection using the test data, the content detector was able to find 254 anomalies. These anomalies are considered to be point anomalous. This is strictly larger than the previous dataset results; however, when taking a closer look at those values labelled as anomalous, the readings are consistent with

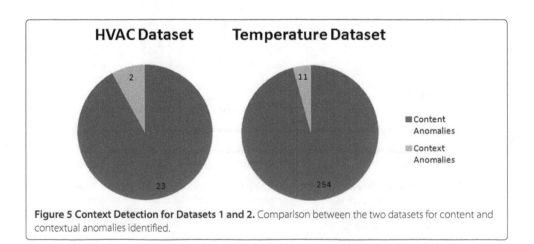

Figure 5 Context Detection for Datasets 1 and 2. Comparison between the two datasets for content and contextual anomalies identified.

a failed sensor. These results are shown in Figure 6. More discussion on this will occur after addressing the context detection component.

The second major component to be evaluated is the context detection. To perform context detection, the proposed framework first needs to determine the sensor profiles for the temperature sensors. For dataset 2, it was determined that two sensor profiles existed within the dataset; adding more clusters did not increase the effectiveness of the context detector. Further, the two sensor profiles that were revealed included one group for the two temperature sensors that record latent temperatures, and three sensors that record room temperature. Once determining the two sensor profile groups, two multivariate Gaussian predictors were trained, one for each cluster. The results of the contextual detector determined that 11 of the 254 point anomalies could be cleared as being non-anomalous with respect to their context. It was also found that when training the context detector with one sensor profile, i.e. not including the initial context of the data, there were no contextual anomalies cleared. Additionally, when removing the *Day* and *Time-OfDay*(TOD) attributes, no contextual anomalies were found. This further shows that the addition of the context detector has a positive impact of determining anomalous readings. The results of running the simulation using the contextual detection with the content detection for both datasets are shown in Figure 5. The figure shows the distribution of context anomalies found within the content anomalies.

The results for dataset 2 were also promising with anomalous examples shown in Table 5. The framework efficiently determined content based anomalies in real-time using the virtualized sensor streaming implementation. Details on the running times for the components is shown in Table 6.

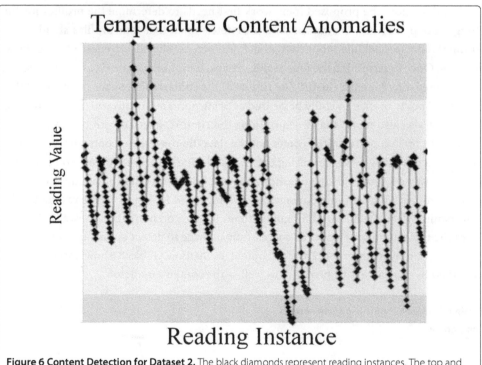

Figure 6 Content Detection for Dataset 2. The black diamonds represent reading instances. The top and bottom highlighted portions in grey identify reading instances that were considered anomalous with respect to their content for the temperature dataset.

Table 5 Anomalous examples for dataset 2

Sen. 1	Sen. 2	Sen. 3	Sen. 4	Sen. 5	Day	TOD
15.12	15.25	18.71	5.35	3.71	7	1
17.42	19.09	24.53	1.05	3.56	3	0
17.22	18.18	23.18	4.08	6.88	1	0
0	0	0	0	-1.26	4	2
0	0	0	0	-1.43	7	0
0	0	0	0	-1.47	7	0

Dataset 3 implementation and results: dodger loop

The final dataset used for evaluation is based on data collected by the Freeway Performance Measurement System (PeMS) in California. The data was collected for the *Dodgers Loop* in Los Angeles, for times when the Los Angeles Dodgers were playing baseball games. The initial goal of the data was to predict days when there were Dodgers games, based on the traffic seen at the Dodgers Loop. The data includes observations over 25 weeks, at 288 time slices per day. In total, there are three attributes, two contextual, one behavioural, and 50,400 tuples.

Synonymous to the Powersmiths datasets, the first component to evaluate is the content detection for the Dodgers Loop dataset. In testing the proposed work's content detection using the test data, the content detector was able to find 17 anomalies. These anomalies are considered to be point anomalous. These anomalies were *all* injected into the dataset as there were no anomalies found when initially running the algorithm. The authors attempted to inject values that should be considered anomalies (i.e. abnormally high amounts of traffic for early mornings where there was certainly no Dodger baseball game).

The second major component to be evaluated is the context detection. To perform context detection, the proposed framework first needs to determine the profiles for the Dodger Loop readings. For dataset 3, it was determined that four profiles should exist within the dataset; adding more clusters did not increase the effectiveness of the context detector. Once determining the four profile groups, four multivariate Gaussian predictors were trained, one for each cluster. The results of the contextual detector determined that 1 of the 17 point anomalies could be cleared as being non-anomalous with respect to their context. It was also found that when training the context detector with one sensor profile, i.e. not including the initial context of the data, there were no contextual anomalies cleared. Additionally, when removing the *Day* and *TimeOfDay* attributes, no contextual anomalies were found. This further shows that the addition of the context detector has a positive impact of determining anomalous readings, and is akin to earlier results for the Powersmiths data. Details on the running times for the components is shown in Table 7. From the table: the framework can successfully manage to detect anomalies in real-time, only using an average of 1432ns per content evaluation. Table 8 show the anomalies identified by the contextual predictor as well as the content predictor.

Table 6 Dataset 2 running time results

Component	Time
ReadCSV	1.145 sec
BuildContextModel	2.343 sec
BuildRealtimeModel	0.021 sec
CheckRealTime (average)	933 ns

Table 7 Dataset 3 running time results

Component	Time
ReadCSV	1.145 sec
BuildContextModel	0.063 sec
BuildRealtimeModel	0.011 sec
CheckRealTime (average)	1432 ns

Validation and cross-validation

We present the validation of our work in two ways. First, we discuss our work in comparison with other views on the same datasets we used, as well as other works in the area of anomaly detection. Second, we discuss our work with respect to Powersmiths use-case, and specifically related to the apriori knowledge they have provided. First, it is difficult to compare anomaly detection algorithms as the definition for an anomaly is highly dependent on the use-case. For example, Powersmiths may consider abnormal values within 10% deviation an anomaly, whereas another energy management company considers values within 8% deviation an anomaly. With this in consideration, we present a major benefit of our work: a sliding detection threshold. That is, the threshold for an anomaly to be considered abnormal can be configured dynamically based on the use case. A second way in which we validated our work is to compare it with the standard R statistical toolbox, and specifically the *outlier* function in the *outliers* package.

The previous evaluation sections attempted to provide insight into the validity of the proposed work with respect to real-world data. This section will further compare the results of the earlier sections to results from the popular **R** application for statistical computing. Figure 7 shows the results of running the outliers package on dataset 2. The largest section indicates the highest density statistical probability for dataset 2, while the other two dense sections indicate lesser populated areas. The anomalies are noted by black numbers; as seen in Figure 7, there are anomalous values in both sections. A summary of the comparison between the work presented in this paper and the **R** outliers package is shown in Table 9. Concretely, we can conclude that our proposed framework performed as well as the R outliers package in detecting the anomalies, and is much more scalable, and applicable to real-time detection.

When given thess datasets, Powersmiths mentioned that there were lengths of time when various sensors failed at their headquarters. Specifically in the temperature dataset, where the framework was able to successfully identify these anomalous readings, as shown below the double-line break in Table 5. This is promising as it validates the approach for the real-world data, knowing a set of values that were previously considered anomalous by Powersmiths. The detector additionally determined a set of anomalies that were not purely based on a totally failed sensor; these are shown above the double-line in Table 5. One of the difficulties with validating any anomaly detection approach is that the definition of an anomaly changes depending on the owner of the dataset, and their view over what should be considered anomalous. Therefore, a first step in validation is determining that the framework could initially identify all values which were considered anomalous by the dataset owner: Powersmiths themselves. Another consideration is performing cross-validation, that is, using different subsets of the dataset for training and

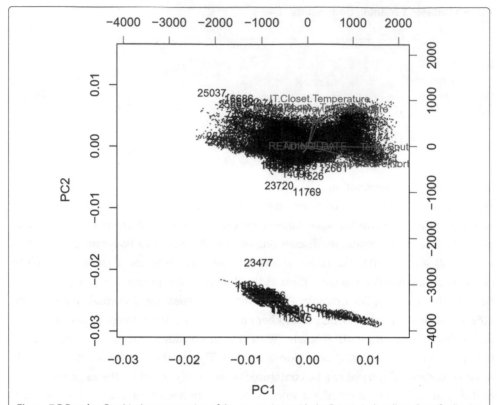

Figure 7 R Results. Graphical representation of the comparison with the R statistical toolbox. Specifically, the numbered points are those that were identified as anomalous with respect to the context of the sensor readings.

testing to ensure that the framework still identifies those values as anomalous in different subsets of the dataset.

Cross-validation was performed for the temperature dataset and found that the anomalous values presented by Powersmiths were again detected. In fact, one of the subsets for cross-validation included a subset of 15% of the dataset where there were *no* anomalies identified by Powersmiths. Indeed, the framework did not detect any anomalies for this subset of the data. To summarize the validation of the framework for the presented datasets, the approach was four-fold:

- Confirm that the framework is able to identify anomalies with respect to those identified by Powersmiths, the dataset owner, themselves.
- Validate that the framework is able to identify injected anomalies by the author; these are values that fall well out of the parameters of one or more of the attributes in the dataset.

Table 8 Anomalous Examples for dataset 3

Time	Day Of Week	Cars Per 5 min	Time Of Day
2760	3	76	0
3060	3	44	0
2820	4	0	0
0	0	0	0
540	0	-8	0

Table 9 Results comparison with the R outliers package

Concept	Discussion
Running time	A major difference between the work presented in this paper and the R outliers package is in the running time of both algorithms. One of the major design considerations for the proposed work was the ability to run in real-time. The R outliers package runs in batch over the entire set of data and runs on the order of minutes to completion, whereas our work runs on the order of seconds.
Anomalies found	The work presented in this paper and R outliers package detected a number of equivalent anomalies. The huge list of anomalies pertaining to the failed sensors identified apriori by Powersmiths were found by both detectors. Further, the work presented in this paper detected all of the anomalies detected by the R outliers package, including those that were contextually cleared.

- Compare the results with the R statistical toolbox to ensure that the results found by the framework are consistent with the offline approach of the R statistical toolbox.
- Cross-validate the results of the dataset with other subsets of the dataset. That is, use different subsets of 15% to compare and confirm that the framework still identifies all the anomalous values.

Random positive detection: implementation and results

In addition to implementing the framework's content and context detection, and evaluating three large datasets using each module, we have also explored the random positive detection module. The first approach we used was implementing a naive random detection module, which simply randomly passed *any* value that was flagged to be passed to the context detector. This approach was used with an implementation-defined random value, 0.01%. However, initial results for this approach proved the *base rate fallacy*: essentially outlining that our initial assumption for the random detection still being able to detect the anomalies is false. In other words, following the Bayes theorem, attempting to detect anomalies using this form of random detection has the following property:

$$P(anomaly|rand) = \frac{P(rand|anomaly) * P(anomaly)}{P(rand)} \tag{8}$$

From Equation 8, we can see that the probability that we randomly detect an event that already has a small percentage of occurring is very low. Due to this property, it is necessary to rethink the approach in determining the random values. Before continuing our approach for these three datasets, we attempted to determine, offline, whether there were any values to randomly detect. Concretely, we tested whether there were any contextual anomalies that were not passed to the context detector from the content detector. In running *only* the context detector over the entire test dataset, the results showed that there were no context anomalies that were not passed to the content detector. Therefore, for the three datasets used for the evaluation of this work, none contained anomalies that were normal with respect to their content, but abnormal with respect to their context.

Conclusions

The work presented in the paper describes a novel framework for anomaly detection in Big Data. Specifically, the framework utilizes a hierarchical approach to identify anomalies in real-time, while also detecting a number of false positives. Then, a contextual anomaly detection algorithm is used to prune the anomalies detected by the content detector, but using the meta-information associated with the data points. To cope with the velocity and volume of Big Data, the anomaly detection algorithm relies on a fast, albeit less accurate, point anomaly detection algorithm to find anomalies in real-time from sensor streams. These anomalies can then be processed by a contextually aware, more computationally expensive, anomaly detection algorithm to determine whether the anomaly was contextually anomalous. This approach allows the algorithm to scale to Big Data requirements as the computationally more expensive algorithm is only needed on a very small set of the data, i.e. the already determined anomalies.

The evaluation of the framework was also discussed based on the implementation details provided in this paper. The evaluation of the framework was performed using three sets of data; one for a set of HVAC electricity sensors, one for a set of temperature sensors, and a third set for a traffic system in California. The evaluation provided some conclusions of the work:

- The framework was able to positively detect, in real-time, content based anomalies for the datasets. Further, the context detector was able to determine some anomalies that should not be considered anomalous when evaluated with respect to context.

- The framework was able to positively detect anomalies that were determined apriori by the owner of the datasets. In particular, the framework determined a large set of anomalous readings which occurred when Powersmiths indicated a massive sensor failure.

- The framework performed competitively with the R outlier statistical package. The framework performed in real-time, in comparison with the batch approach provided by the R application.

One of the major goals of the framework was to remain modular and scalable for future works. As a result, there are several areas of future work that would be interesting to explore:

- The datasets considered in the evaluation section are only one type of Big Data: *tall* datasets. It is important to consider the other common type of application: *wide* datasets. These are attributed by a large number of features, with a smaller number of records. One of the major benefits of this work is that the hierarchy of content to contextual detection ensures that a computationally inexpensive algorithm reduces the number of records evaluated by the contextual detector.

- The framework has been tested in the simulated, virtualized, sensor streaming environment. Therefore, a logical future work would be to implement the framework within a working business environment that is streaming live data to the central repository.

- The framework could also be integrated with decision making systems within a live environment. The output of the framework is an indication that a sensor is acting anomalous. This information can be exploited by a decision making algorithm, such as a complex event processing framework, to coordinate changes within the business environment.

- The modularity of the framework allows further components to be added, or updated, in the framework. This introduces two such avenues of future work: first, the proposed modules can be modifed and updated with other types of algorithms. Second, additional modules could be added to the framework itself. For example, a semantic detection module can be included.

Competing interests

The authors declare that they have no competing interests.

Authors' contributions

MAH is the principal researcher for the work proposed in this article. His contributions include the underlying idea, background investigation, initial drafting of the article, and results implementation. MAMC guided the initial research idea, and played a pivotal role in editing the article. Both authors read and approved the final manuscript.

Acknowledgements

This research was supported by an NSERC CGS-M research grant to Michael Hayes at Western University (CGSM-444130-2013). The authors would also like to acknowledge the support provided by Powersmiths.

References
1. Chandola V, Banerjee A, Kumar V (2009) Anomaly detection: a survey. ACM Comput Surv 41(3):1–58
2. Chan H, Chou P, Duri S, Lei H, Reason J (2009) The design and implementation of a smart building control system. In: e-Business Engineering, 2009. ICEBE '09. IEEE International Conference On. IEEE. pp 255–262
3. Fan J, Han F, Liu H (2014) Challenges of big data analysis. Natl Sci Rev. Oxford University Press
4. Dalessandro B (2013) Bring the noise: Embracing randomness is the key to scaling up machine learning algorithms. Big Data 1(2):110–112
5. He Z, Xu X, Huang JZ, Deng S (2004) Mining class outliers: concepts, algorithms and applications in crm. Expert Syst Appl 27(4):681–697
6. Kou Y, Lu C-T (2006) Spatial weighted outlier detection. In: Proceedings of SIAM Conference on Data Mining. SIAM
7. Dean J, Ghemawat S (2008) MapReduce: Simplified data processing on large clusters. Commun ACM 51(1):107–113
8. Rajasegarar S, Leckie C, Palaniswami M (2008) Anomaly detection in wireless sensor networks. Wireless Commun IEEE 15(4):34–40
9. Song X, Wu M, Jermaine C, Ranka S (2007) Conditional anomaly detection. Knowl Data Eng IEEE Trans 19(5):631–645
10. Hill DJ, Minsker BS (2010) Anomaly detection in streaming environmental sensor data: A data-driven modeling approach. Environ Model Softw 25(9):1014–1022
11. Hill DJ, Minsker BS, Amir E (2009) Real-time bayesian anomaly detection in streaming environmental data. Water Resources Res 45(4)
12. Srivastava N, Srivastava J (2010) A hybrid-logic approach towards fault detection in complex cyber-physical systems. In: Prognostics and Health Management Society, 2010 Annual Conference of The. IEEE. pp 13–24
13. Mahapatra A, Srivastava N, Srivastava J (2012) Contextual anomaly detection in text data. Algorithms 5(4):469–489
14. AlEroud A, Karabatis G (2012) A contextual anomaly detection approach to discover zero-day attacks. In: Cyber Security, 2012 International Conference On. IEEE. pp 40–45
15. Miller BA, Arcolano N, Bliss NT (2013) Efficient anomaly detection in dynamic, attributed graphs: Emerging phenomena and big data. In: Intelligence and Security Informatics (ISI), 2013 IEEE International Conference On. IEEE. pp 179–184
16. Shilton A, Rajasegarar S, Palaniswami M (2013) Combined multiclass classification and anomaly detection for large-scale wireless sensor networks. In: Intelligent Sensors, Sensor Networks and Information Processing, 2013 IEEE Eighth International Conference On. IEEE. pp 491–496
17. Lee JR, Ye S-K, Jeong H-DJ (2013) Detecting anomaly teletraffic using stochastic self-similarity based on Hadoop. In: Network-Based Information Systems (NBiS), 2013 16th International Conference On. IEEE. pp 282–287
18. Xie M, Hu J, Tian B (2012) Histogram based online anomaly detection in hierarchical wireless sensor networks. In: Trust, Security and Privacy in Computing and Communications, 2012 IEEE 11th International Conference On. IEEE. pp 751–759
19. Kittler J, Christmas W, Campos TD, Windridge D, Yan F, Illingworth J, Osman M (2013) Domain anomaly detection in machine perception: a system architecture and taxonomy. IEEE Trans Pattern Anal Mach Intell 99(PrePrints):1
20. Arthur D, Vassilvitskii S (2007) K-means++: The advantages of careful seeding. In: Proceedings of the Eighteenth Annual ACM-SIAM Symposium on Discrete Algorithms. SODA '07, Society for Industrial and Applied Mathematics, Philadelphia, PA, USA. pp 1027–1035. http://dl.acm.org/citation.cfm?id=1283383.1283494
21. Powersmiths (2010) Powersmiths: Power for the Future. http://ww2.powersmiths.com/index.php?q=content/powersmiths/about-us
22. Bache K, Lichman M (2013) UCI Machine Learning Repository. http://archive.ics.uci.edu/ml
23. Hutchins J (2013) Freeway Performance Measurement System (PeMS). http://pems.dot.ca.gov/
24. Machine Learning Group (2012) Weka 3 - Data Mining with Open Source Machine Learning Software in Java. http://www.cs.waikato.ac.nz/ml/weka/

v-TerraFly: large scale distributed spatial data visualization with autonomic resource management

Yun Lu[*], Ming Zhao, Lixi Wang and Naphtali Rishe

* Correspondence: yun@cs.fiu.edu
School of Computing and
Information Sciences, Florida
International University, Miami, FL
33199, USA

Abstract

GIS application hosts are becoming more and more complicated. Theses hosts' management is becoming more time consuming and less reliabale decreases with the increase in complexity of GIS applications. The resource management of GIS applications is becoming increasingly important in order to deliver to the user the desired Quality of Service. Map systems often serve dynamic web workloads and involve multiple CPU- and I/O-intensive tiers, which makes it challenging to meet the response time targets of map requests while using the resources efficiently. This paper proposes a virtualized web map service system, v-TerraFly, and its autonomic resource management in order to address this challenge. Virtualization facilitates the deployment of web map services and improves their resource utilization through encapsulation and consolidation. Autonomic resource management allows resources to be automatically provisioned to a map service and its internal tiers on demand. Specifically, this paper proposes new techniques to predict the demand of map workloads online and optimize resource allocations considering both response time and data freshness as the QoS target. The proposed v-TerraFly system is prototyped on TerraFly, a production web map service, and evaluated using real TerraFly workloads. The results show that v-TerraFly can accurately predict the workload demands: 18.91% more accurate; and efficiently allocate resources to meet the QoS target: improves the QoS by 26.19% and saves resource usages by 20.83% compared to traditional peak-load-based resource allocation.

Introduction

With the exponential growth of the World Wide Web, there are more domains open to Geographic Information System (GIS) applications. Internet can provide information to a multitude of users, making GIS available to a wider range of public users than ever before. Web-based map services are the most important application of modern GIS systems. For example, Google Maps has more than 350 million users. There is also a rapidly growing number of geo-enabled applications which consume web map services on traditional computing platforms as well as the emerging mobile devices.

Virtual machines (VM) are powerful platforms for hosting web map service systems. VMs support flexible resource allocation to both meet web map services system demands and share resources with other applications. Virtualization is also enabling technology for the emerging cloud computing paradigm, which further allows highly scalable and cost-effective web map services hosting leveraging its elastic resource availability and pay-as-you-go economic model [1].

However, due to the highly complex and dynamic nature of web map service systems, it is challenging to efficiently host them using virtualized resources. First, typical web map services have to serve dynamically changing workloads, which makes it difficult to host map services on shared resources without compromising performance or wasting resources. Second, a web map service often consists of several tiers which have different intensive resource needs and result in dynamic internal resource contention. Third, for a typical web map service, both response time for requests and the freshness of the returned data are critical factors of the Quality of Service (QoS) required by users.

To address the above challenges, this paper presents v-TerraFly, an autonomic resource management approach for virtualized map service systems, which can automatically optimize the QoS (considering both response time and data freshness) while minimizing the resource cost [2-4]. *First*, v-TerraFly can accurately predict the workload demands of a web map service online based on a novel two-way forecasting algorithm that considers both historical hourly patterns and daily patterns. *Second*, based on the predicted workload, v-TerraFly can automatically estimate the resource demands of its various tiers based on performance profiles created using machine learning techniques. *Third*, v-TerraFly employs a new QoS model that captures the balance between response time and data freshness and uses this model to automatically optimize the resource allocation of a web map service system [5].

This proposed v-TerraFly system is realized on Hyper-V virtual machine environments and evaluated by experiments using real workloads collected from the production TerraFly system. The results show that the proposed two-level workload prediction method is outperforms traditional exponential smoothing prediction by 18.91%, and the system improves the QoS by 26.19% compared to traditional statically node allocation. In the meantime, it saves resource usages by 20.83% compared to traditional peak-load-based resource allocation.

In summary, this paper's main contributions are: (1) created a VM-based map service system, v-TerraFly, which virtualizes all tiers of a typical web map service and supports dynamic resource allocations to the different tiers; (2) proposed a novel autonomic resource management approach for virtualized map services, which automatically allocates resources to different tiers of the service and optimizes the allocations based on the performance and data freshness tradeoff; (3) evaluated v-TerraFly using real workloads collected from production web map service system, which shows substantial improvement on QoS and resource efficiency.

The rest of this paper is organized as follows: Section Background presents the background and motivations; Sections v-TerraFly describes the architecture of v-TerraFly; Section Autonomic Resource Management in v-TerraFly explains the autonomic resource management of v-TerraFly; Section Evaluation presents an experimental evaluation; Section Related work examines related work; and Section Conclusions and future work concludes the paper.

Background
Web map services
As a promising new application of GIS, web map service exhibits its excellence in serving online map requests responsively and delivering geographical information precisely

over the Internet [6]. A typical web map service, such as Google maps, Bing maps, and Yahoo maps [7], are usually built upon several major tiers (Figure 1). A *Preprocessor* preloads images and geographic features from raw data repository and splits them into grid format, known as image tiles, to facilitate the *Processor* quickly locating and fetching data. Then a tile *Processor* retrieves and integrates all tiles needed in a customer's query. As its upper tier, a generic map interface accesses this imagery by geo-location, and a client app (or browser) to show the map to end-users.

In this paper, we use TerraFly as a case study of a web map system [1]. TerraFly serves worldwide web map requests, providing users with customized aerial photography, satellite imagery and various overlays, such as street names, roads, restaurants, services and demographic data. Following the typical architecture described above, TerraFly contains two major tiers (Figure 1): the Image *Loader Tier* preprocesses the raw imagery data from repository; the Image *Reader Tier* processes image tiles and retrieves queried images [8]. These tiers are further described in Section v-TerraFly.

Traditionally, web map services are hosted on dedicated physical servers with sufficient hardware resources to satisfy their expected peak workloads in order to provide responsive web services to the users. However, this becomes inefficient for real-world situations where the workloads are intrinsically dynamic in terms of their busty arrival patterns and ever changing unit processing costs [9]. Consequently, peak-load-based resource provision often leads to underutilization of resources for normal state workloads and causes substantial overhead.

Using VMs to host multi-tier web map services can effectively address this limitation because virtualized resources, including CPU, memory, and I/O, are decoupled from their physical infrastructures and can be flexibly allocated to different tiers of the web map system [10]. This approach allows the resource capacity of each tier to elastically grow and shrink to serve its dynamic. In this way, different tiers transparently share the consolidated resources with each other and/or other applications with strong isolation. Such benefits are important to the efficiency of web map service hosting in both typical data centers and emerging cloud systems. On one hand, users need to pay for only the resources their services actually consume. On the other hand, resource providers only

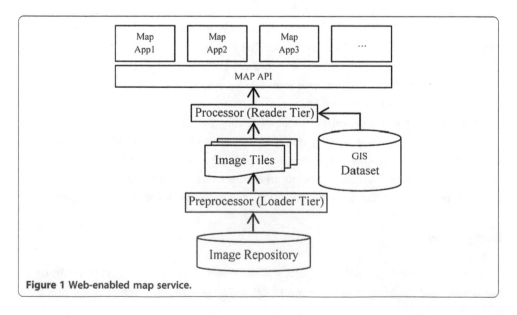

Figure 1 Web-enabled map service.

need to allocate resources as required by the services while saving valuable resources for hosting other applications [11].

Virtualization also offers a new paradigm for web map service deployments. Modern web map services are sophisticated systems, where their installation and configuration require substantial domain knowledge and experience as well as considerable efforts from the administrators. VM-based web map service hosting allows carefully installed software to be distributed as simply as copying the data that represents the VMs. In addition, this approach allows web map services to be quickly replicated and distributed for performance and reliability improvements.

Research design and methodology

v-TerraFly Architecture

To enable the autonomic resource management in TerraFly, we leverage VM techniques to virtualize this multi-tier system, denoted as v-TerraFly. The two critical resource intensive tiers of TerraFly, the image *Loader* and *Reader Tier*s, are deployed on the VMs instead of physical servers.

Figure 2 shows the architecture of this v-TerraFly. The users interact with the application tier which handles most of the business logic and provides advanced application services, such as universal mapping and application specific mapping (e.g. real estate, water management), by sending the mapping queries including position and resolution requirements to the tiers below. Then the image *Reader Tier* is invoked to compute and locate associated map tiles from indexed imagery database according to the requests from the application. To maintain data freshness, the organized imagery database is updated by the *Loader Tier* periodically at the same time. *Loader* contiguously extracts the incoming raw map data from the raw imagery repository, preprocesses and organizes the raw data to destination projection, and then converts the data into the destination file type, and finally updates the data into the organized imagery database.

Due to the structure of the mapping service system, these two tiers of v-TerraFly exhibit distinct resource usage behaviors in the production environment. On one hand, the *Reader Tier* may experience different number of concurrent users during different periods of a day, which results in highly dynamic workloads with varying intensity against the *Loader*. On the other hand, the *Loader* does not have as

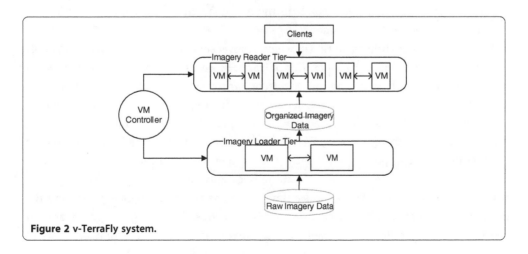

Figure 2 v-TerraFly system.

stringent performance requirement as the *Roader* does but still needs reserved resource to guarantee data freshness. Therefore, it is beneficial to host these two tiers together on virtualized cluster nodes to multiplex the common computing resources so that the total resource capacity can be better utilized among different tiers. For example, more VMs are allocated to the *Reader Tier* during daytime when peak-load of user requests is expected to happen but the loading process is less active; but shifting more VMs to the *Loader* over night to allow data updates accumulated in daytime.

Virtualization in TerraFly also improves the flexibility in terms of the system reliability and scalability. VM is the computing resource in both *Loader* and *Reader Tier*s. With the load balance in both tiers, the work load of each VM is the same; therefore, the VMs in the same tier are considered identical. Since the computing resources can be partitioned through VM nodes, the network bandwidth, which is always a bottleneck in the original system, can now be well balanced among VMs. Furthermore, by pairing every two VMs as complementary *Reader* nodes, it is able to provide more reliable service under unexpected system failure by simply replacing the failed VM with its corresponding back-upped VM [12,13].

Motivating examples

In this section, we demonstrate both the necessity and benefits of resource consolidation in a map service system.

For web map services, the performance of *Reader Tier* and *Loader Tier* are both important. Better *Reader Tier* performance provides shorter page response time; better *Loader Tier* performance provides faster loading of new map data. But both tiers are resource-intensive and they will compete with each other on resource allocation. The goal is to balance the two tiers to achieve best quality of service when we have limited resources.

The workloads of web map service can be highly dynamic over time. Based on the analysis on the web service logs of TerraFly, it is observed that there were millions of web requests received on the *Reader* server over the year of 2012, i.e., more than 450 visits per second on average. However, this workload varies significantly on hourly basis. Figure 3 shows a typical one-day TerraFly workload trace. It shows that the request rate drops to 150 (visits per second) in the morning (around 9:00 am) while rising quickly up to 900 (visits per second) in the afternoon. It would be more efficient to turn off some *Reader* VMs at times.

Assuming the variation in workload which follows such a time-related pattern is predictable, by virtualizing the *Reader Tier* of TerraFly we can easily save resources when the workload intensity is low by simply turning off some *Reader* VMs, and as the workload intensity increases, we can bring back them online to process the additional requests.

To further quantify the resource savings, we replay this one-day trace using two deployment schemes for the *Reader Tier*: the static scheme deploys the Reader tier on the fixed number of computing nodes throughout the entire experiment (2, 4, 6, 8 and 10 nodes respectively); the dynamic schema only assigns sufficient nodes needed by the workload in every hour. The response time is used as the performance metric and the desired QoS target is set to (0.7 s). Figure 4 compares the average response time in every hour using different schemes. We use *node-hour* as the cost unit in terms of

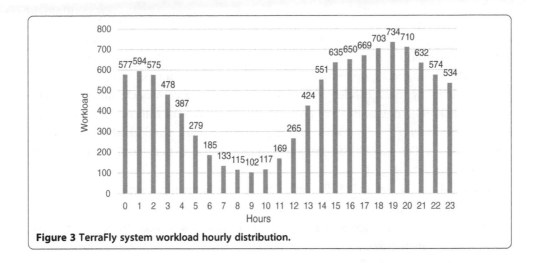

Figure 3 TerraFly system workload hourly distribution.

computing resource. By measuring the number N_i of active nodes used in the ith hour, the total amount of the resource during certain time period T (hours) can be computed as $\sum_{i}^{T} N_i$.

Figure 4 compared the measured response times in every hour using different deployments as well as the total resource costs needed in one day. As we can see among the static deployment configurations, only the 10-node configuration can always meet the desired target, however at the cost of the highest total resource amount (240 *node-hour*); others suffer different levels of QoS violation as the workload changes dynamically.

In contrast, the dynamic deployment scheme is able to track the QoS target all the time with only 148 *node-hour*, saving about 23% of the resources compared to the static 8-node configuration which cannot satisfy the QoS target, and saving 38% of the resources compared to the static 10-node configuration which can satisfy the QoS target. Its resource utilization is as efficient as the 6-node configuration but delivers much better performance.

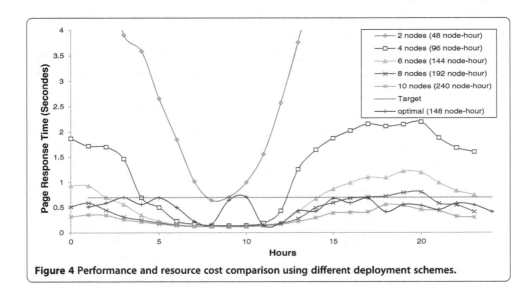

Figure 4 Performance and resource cost comparison using different deployment schemes.

The above example shows strong evidence of the importance of map service virtualization and its online resource management. Currently, our traditional TerraFly system is deployed on the 8 physical *Reader Tier* nodes and 2 *Loader Tier* nodes. It works well for supporting up to 800 concurrent users, and about 6GB fresh data can be load each hour by the 2 *Loader* nodes (Refer to 4.3 Resource Model); but the system scalability is limited due to its fixed physical capacity. It cannot shift resources between *Reader* and *Loader Tier*s even when one tier has idle resource and another has insufficient resources. The inability of shifting resources between tiers results the waste of resources.

However, there are several challenges to dynamic resource management of a virtualized web map service. First, the dynamics in the realistic workload causes the demand of CPU consumption change over time; second, resources also need to be dynamically allocated between the *Reader Tier* to optimize response time and the *Loader Tier* to keep the data fresh.

These challenges can be well addressed by an autonomic VM-based resource management solution which can flexibly partition shared resources and allocate resource on-demand for dynamic workload in order to guarantee performance and improve resource utilization.

Autonomic resource management in v-TerraFly
General approach

Figure 5 illustrates the framework of our proposed autonomic resource management system for v-TerraFly, which consists of three key modules. Please see the notes in Table 1 Parameter description. In this paper, we focus on the resource management for both *Reader* and *Loader Tier*s, since they are the most resource intensive tiers in v-TerraFly.

As a workload executes on the VMs, the *Workload Sensor* monitors the actual workload at current time step, noted as $w(t)$. The *Workload Predictor* then forecasts the future workload $w(t + 1)$ for the next time step based on a prediction model. Based on the predicted workload, the *Reader* profile and *Loader* profile which are trained offline are used to estimate their resource demands for time $t + 1$, denoted by $rR(t + 1)$ and $rL(t + 1)$ respectively. The estimated resource demands are then used by the *Resource Allocator* to make the actual allocations by assigning appropriate number of VMs to the *Reader Tier* and *Loader Tier*. Together, these modules form a closed-loop which runs continuously (e.g., every hour), for v-TerraFly's resource control and optimization.

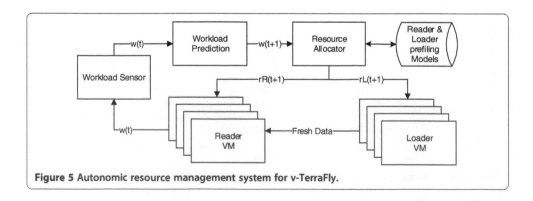

Figure 5 Autonomic resource management system for v-TerraFly.

Table 1 Parameter description

Parameter	Description
$w(t)$	Workload at time t
$rR(t)$	Reader VM CPU resource need at time t
$rL(t)$	Loader VM CPU resource need at time t
w_h^{Des}	Horizontal double exponential smoothing prediction
w_d^{Des}	Vertical double exponential smoothing prediction
w'	Two-level double exponential smoothing

In the rest of this section, we describe the key components of this autonomic system in details.

Workload prediction

In order to accurately and timely predict the workload on v-TerraFly, we propose new forecasting techniques to discover and exploit patterns in user visiting behaviors such as those observed in Figure 3. Specifically, we propose a new two-level time series prediction approach to build a prediction model based on the historical workload measurements, i.e., the request rate observed from the *Reader Tier* of v-TerraFly. Based on such a model, the workload predictor in v-TerraFly is able to estimate the workload intensity for the next time period.

Time series analysis techniques are widely applied in economic data analysis to provide statistical prediction and therefore guide business decisions. A variety of time series prediction methods are available such as the *Moving Averages*, *Linear Regression* and *Exponential Smoothing* [14-16]. In this paper, the TerraFly workload prediction based on the double exponential smoothing (DES) method [17] which is suitable for discrete data sequence with repeated changing patterns.

DES is a smoothing-based forecasting method that can be applied to time series data, a sequence of observations with equally spaced intervals, expressed as $\{Y(0),\ Y(1),..,\ Y(t)\}$. Then in DES, the estimate for the $t+1$ time intervals can be computed as:

$$Y^{Des}(t+1) = 2S'(t) - S''(t) + \left(\frac{\alpha}{1-\alpha}\right)\left(S'(t) - S''(t)\right)$$

$$S'(t) = \alpha Y(t) + (1-\alpha)S'(t-1)$$

$$S''(t) = \alpha S'(t) + (1-\alpha)S''(t-1)$$

The equation shows a linear combination of smoothing based statistics associated with a smoothing weight α. The first two components reflect the variation of mean of the overall data while the third tracks the trend of the data. S' is denoted as the singly-smoothed series which smoothed the next measure by assigning a exponentially decreased smoothing weight to the data of the series and computing the weighted average of the observed series. More intuitively, the most recent data is of more importance to the current estimates, i.e., the weight assigned to the data k periods old is $(1-\alpha)^k$, therefore the closer to 1 of the value of α, less smoothing effect but greater weight to the recent changes. S'' is denoted as the doubly-smoothed series computed by recursively applying the same exponential smoothing operation to the singly-smoothed series S' using the same smoothing weight.

In order to perform the time-series-based forecast in v-TerraFly, the workload can be represented as a sequence of intensity measurements that come from a continuing time series at time intervals T, denoted as $\{... \ w(t\text{-}2\ T),\ w(t\text{-}T),\ w(t)\}$. More specifically, the workload measurement can be either the average request rate or the number of concurrent client sessions observed in every hour; the time interval T can be either one hour or one day (24 hour).

We propose a new two-level double exponential smoothing forecasting model to capture both the daily pattern and hourly pattern of v-TerraFly workload as follows.

$$w'(t+1) = \mu_h w_h^{Des}(t+1) + \mu_d w_d^{Des}(t+1) \tag{1}$$

where w_h^{Des} is the *horizontal* double exponential smoothing prediction based on the hourly pattern in the workload, and w_d^{Des} is the *vertical* double exponential smoothing prediction based on the daily pattern of the workload.

$$w_h^{Des}(t) = 2S'(t\text{-}1)\text{-}S''(t\text{-}1) + \left(\frac{\alpha_h}{1-\alpha_h}\right)\left(S'(t\text{-}1)\text{-}S''(t\text{-}1)\right) \tag{2}$$

$$w_d^{Des}(t) = 2S'(t\text{-}24)\text{-}S''(t\text{-}24) + \left(\frac{\alpha_d}{1-\alpha_d}\right)\left(S'(t\text{-}24)\text{-}S''(t\text{-}24)\right) \tag{3}$$

More specifically, $w_h^{Des}(t)$, called horizontal prediction, is predicted based on $\{\ w(t-3),\ w(t-2), w(t-1)\}$ from a hourly series; while $w_d^{Des}(t)$, vertical prediction, is based on the observation series $\{\ w(t-48), w(t-24), w(t)\}$ that are extracted vertically at the same hours but from continuing days, i.e., a 24-hour vertical time span. The associated μ factors which are set between 0 to 1 are used to balance the importance between three components.

Since each level of DES operation is associated with a smoothing weights, we denote the weights in horizontal and vertical predictions as α_h and α_d respectively. Then the proposed two-level DES model can be considered as a function of α_h and α_d, given observed workload series. Therefore the workload model is trained continuously online as soon as the new measurement is observed by optimizing both α_h and α_d to minimize the weighted sum of squared errors between the prediction and the actual observation. Once the model is updated, it applies to the system immediately for the next prediction.

Performance profiling

Performance profiles relate the workload of the *Reader* and *Loader Tier*s to their resource demands according to the desired performance. Taking the predicted workload $w(t+1)$ as the input, these profiles are used by the *Resource Allocator* to allocate resources to the *Reader* and *Loader Tier*s dynamically in order to achieve the desired QoS.

For the *Reader Tier*, since the workload consists of online web requests, the intensity of the workload is specified by request rate $w(t)$ as discussed in Section Workload prediction. The relevant performance metric is the average response time $RT(t)$ of the requests completed during each control period (e.g., one hour). It can be considered as a function of the workload and the number of VM nodes $rR(t)$ allocated to *Reader Tier*. Thus,

$$RT(t) = \varnothing(w(t), rR(t)) \tag{4}$$

The strategy to build this mapping is offline profiling. Given a specific workload w, we map the number of nodes n allocated to the *Reader Tier* to the performance RT by iterating over the allocation space and collecting corresponding performance measurements under each allocation candidate. Then we repeat the above step under different workloads by varying the number of the concurrent users in v-TerraFly. Figure 6 illustrates the mapping results by using two to ten *Reader* nodes to serve a workload with 40 to 240 concurrent users. Such a mapping provides the least number of VM nodes needed for a given workload to meet a specific QoS target. For example, if desired response time is set to 0.7 second, then the minimal number of VMs needed is two for a workload with about 40 users and 10 when there are more than 230 concurrent users.

In order to reduce the time required for performance profiling, we collected only a subset of the *Reader* configurations under a subset of the workload intensities, and use linear regression to build the *Reader Tier* entire performance profile. As shown in Figure 7, we got the profile mode and the R square is 0.9131.

We profiled both the CPU and I/O resource usages of the *Reader Tier*, as shown in Figure 7. The results show that both the CPU and I/O demands follow the exact same pattern as the workload varies, which validates the use of identical VM nodes as the resource allocation unit of the *Reader Tier*.

For the *Loader Tier*, since the workload mainly consists of batch jobs which loads raw data into organized repository, the workload intensity is given by the concurrency level, i.e., the average throughput achieved every control period. Allocating more VMs to the *Loader Tier* allows it to obtain higher throughout and finish the loading process sooner. We use offline profiling to create a model for *Loader* that represents the relationship between the throughput (I/O) and the number of VM nodes for the *Loader Tier*. We use different amount of map *Loader* nodes to load a given imagery dataset

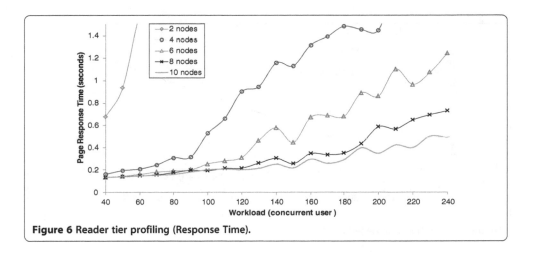

Figure 6 Reader tier profiling (Response Time).

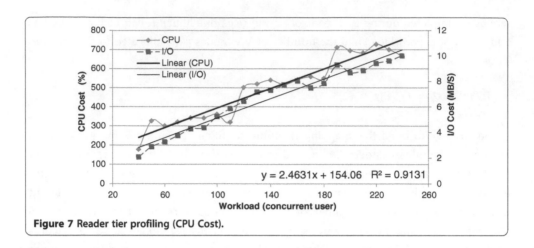

Figure 7 Reader tier profiling (CPU Cost).

and monitor the throughput. We then use linear regression to learn the entire model based on the training data. As shown in Figure 8, the throughput of *Loader Tier* is almost linear with respect to the number of *Loader* VMs. Using linear regression, the R square is only 0.9996.

QoS model

In this section, we propose a novel QoS model to consider both the responsiveness in serving user mapping requests and the quality of returning geographic information. In a virtualized web mapping system, both *Reader* and *Loader* VMs are usually co-hosted in a cluster/data center and compete for the common physical resources, while the former guarantees acceptable response time and the latter keeps the imagery data up to date. Since the performances from both tiers are critical, we need to well balance the importance between them especially when the total resource capacity is constrained. Therefore, a new QoS model is defined to represent the overall system performance at measuring time period t.

$$QoS(t) = r(t) \times f(t) \tag{5}$$

where $r(t)$ and $f(t)$ are the performance metrics for the *Reader* and *Loader Tier* respectively.

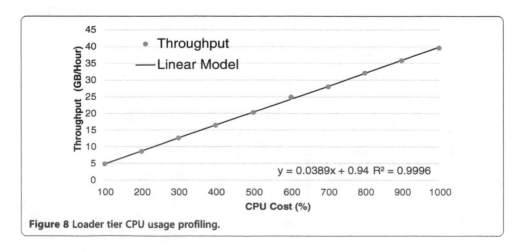

Figure 8 Loader tier CPU usage profiling.

The former QoS component r(t) is called the normalized response time, which measures the quality of web mapping services at time t and can be calculated as following:

$$r(t) = RT_{ref} / RT(t) \qquad (6)$$

where RT_{ref} is the desired average response time at *Reader Tier* and $RT(t)$ is the actual performance measurement at time t. The higher of the value, the quicker the user requests served at *Reader Tier*.

The latter QoS component $f(t)$ is called the cumulative data freshness which measures the quality of data-loading process at *Loader Tier* at time t. It is calculated recursively based on the previous data freshness value and the current data incremental rate, expressed as following:

$$f(t) = (1-\rho) \times f(t-1) + \Delta D(t)/D_{ref} \qquad (7)$$

where ρ is the decaying factor (predefined in the range of 0 to 1) indicating the data quality loss in terms of freshness during the past time period; D_{ref} is the desired amount of fresh data per time period, $\Delta D(t)$ is the actual amount of data loaded during time period t. Initially phase $t = 0, f(0) = \Delta D(0)/D_{ref}$.

For instance, assuming we need to maintain $D_{ref} = 300GB$ amount of fresh data in repository every control period and the data freshness value at previous time period was f $(t-1) = 0.9$ will be reduced to 0.864 at current time t given a decaying factor of 4.0%. If there is 15GB data loaded during current time period, then the incremental rate is 0.05 and therefore the freshness value $f(t) = 0.864 + 0.05 = 0.914$. Intuitively, we can say the current data quality is 91.4% fresh. Note that it is evident that the data freshness can be adjusted by controlling data incremental rate via resource management at *Loader Tier*.

By maximizing the QoS as computed above, the v-TerraFly resource management system automatically optimize the response time and data freshness simultaneously, which are both important to the map service received by users.

Results and discussion
Setup
This section evaluates the proposed virtual web map service system and its autonomic resource management using the v-TerraFly prototype and real traces collected from the TerraFly production system. As a typical web application, TerraFly usually provides a variety of web services via IIS (Internet Information Services) to serve online web requests. The test bed is set up on two Dell PowerEdge 2970 servers, each with two six-core 2.4GHz AMD Opteron CPUs, 32GB of RAM, and one 1 TB 7.2 RPM SAS disk. Windows Server 2008 and Hyper-V are installed to provide the virtualization environment for v-TerraFly. The resource management system for v-TerraFly is hosted on the hypervisor's management VM. All guest VMs including both *Reader* and *Loader Tier* of TerraFly are installed Windows Server 2008 Data Center as the OS. Each Reader and Loader VM is configured with one core CPU, 2G memory, and 64 GB disk. The resource allocation is done by starting or stopping VMs via Hyper-V PowerShell Script.

Workload prediction

We first evaluate the accuracy of our proposed two-level DES workload prediction algorithm by comparing it to two one-level DES approaches based on hourly pattern only (*Horizontal*) and daily pattern only (*Vertical*) respectively, as well as history average statistics (*History Average*). The evaluation is performed using a real one-month workload trace of the November 2012 extracted from the production TerraFly system's logs. To conduct the experiment more efficiently, the real trace is replayed with a 60-fold speedup, i.e., using one minute in the experiment to simulate one hour in real world. The prediction and updates of the workload models (*smoothing weights* α_h and α_d, refer to Eqs. 2 and 3) are performed every minute to adapt to the dynamics.

Figure 9 compares the online prediction errors of different approaches. Our proposed two-level prediction method delivers significantly better accuracy in predicting the request rate of one month workload. Overall, the 90 percentile average error rate of our two-level method is 10.01% with the lowest standard deviation of 145.3, both much lower than the other three prediction approaches which are 45.67% (*Horizontal*), 28.92% (*Vertical*), and 25.14% (*History Average*) respectively. These results demonstrate that our proposed method can effectively exploit both the hourly pattern and daily pattern in the workload and achieve accurate workload prediction.

Resource management of *Reader Tier*

As discussed in Section Performance profiling, based on the predicted workload, the v-TerraFly resource management system automatically allocates resources to the *Reader* and *Loader Tier*s in order to optimize the QoS. This section evaluates the resource management for the *Reader Tier* alone and demonstrates whether it can achieve the *Reader Tier*'s response time target with the least amount of resources.

In the experiment, a real daily workload trace of October 4th 2012 is replayed against v-TerraFly with a 60-fold speedup. The resource allocator adjusts resources allocation every 1 minute. The QoS target is set to 0.7 s in response time. Based on the profiling, the performance model of *Reader Tier* is $R(t) = 2.4631\,W(t) + 154.06$, (as shown in Figure 7).

Figures 10 and 11 compare the response time and allocations of our dynamic approach to static 6, 8, 9 and 10-node deployment plans respectively. From the results,

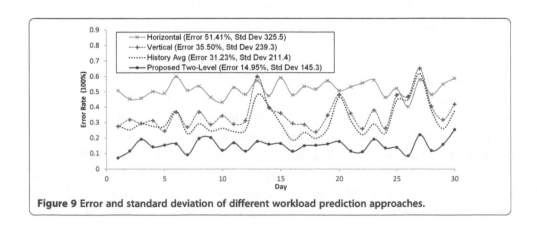

Figure 9 Error and standard deviation of different workload prediction approaches.

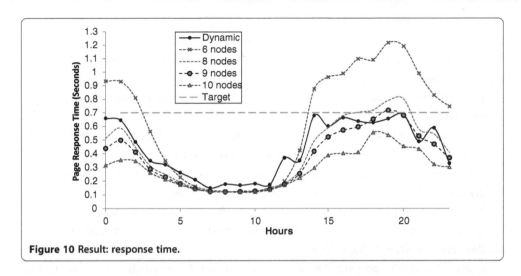

Figure 10 Result: response time.

we can see that the online dynamic approach is able to achieve the response time target all the time throughout the entire experiment. Compared to the 6-node static plan which achieves 0.634 second in average page response time, the online dynamic plan improves the performance by 32.18%, i.e., 0.430 second in average response time, but at the cost of only 5.6% more resource allocation, i.e., 8 additional *node-hour*. There are 13 data points where its response time exceeds 0.7 second in the 6-node static plan, which causes as much as 54.17% QoS violation; in contrast, no QoS violation occurs in the dynamic plan.

Compared to the 8-node static plan, the dynamic plan saves as much as 20.83% of total resources, i.e., 40 *node-hour*. Although the static 8-node plan allocates substantially more with surplus resources, it still causes three QoS violations during the experiment. The 9-node static plan meets the QoS target all the time except the 19th hour, and it costs 29.63% more total resources than the dynamic plan. The 10-node static plan is the only static plan that meets the QoS target all the time, but it costs 36.67% more total resources than the dynamic plan.

Overall, it is evident that the online dynamic deployment plan can efficiently allocate resources to the *Reader Tier* while at the same time meet the response time target by flexibly adjusting its VM assignments in an online manner.

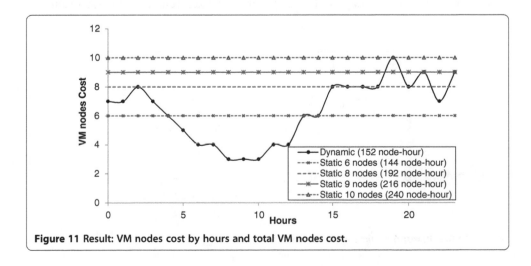

Figure 11 Result: VM nodes cost by hours and total VM nodes cost.

Resource management of both *Reader* and *Loader Tiers*

This section evaluates the proposed autonomic resource management approach for both *Reader* and *Loader Tier*s. Based on the QoS model defined in Section QoS model, the importance of both tiers needs to be balanced in order to optimize an overall QoS value which not only guarantees the responsiveness of map service but also maintains the data freshness of returned maps.

In the experiment, we use the same workload trace described in Section Resource management of *Reader Tier*, and compare our proposed approach to the traditional static deployment plan. The traditional method allocates a fixed number of nodes to *Reader Tier* to satisfy average response time by past experience and gives rest nodes to *Loader Tier*. Specifically, it assigns 7 nodes to the *Read Tier* and 3 nodes to the *Loader Tier* in order to achieve an average response time of 0.9 second and 303.3GB fresh data per day (average $f(t) = 0.809$, refer to Eq. 7).

Figures 12 and 13 compare the performance of the proposed dynamic plan to the traditional static plan in both response time of the *Reader Tier* and throughput of the *Loader Tier*. The static plan achieves an average response time of 0.897 seconds, while the dynamic plan shows slightly better 0.873 seconds. The latter also achieves higher average throughput (194.6 thousands requests per day) than the static one (185.1 thousands requests per day).

Although the performance improvement on the *Reader Tier* is not significant, Figure 14 shows that the proposed dynamic plan achieves much better overall QoS (26.19% improvement). The reason behind this substantial improvement is because the dynamic plan saves resources from the *Reader Tier* and allocates them to the *Loader Tier*, thereby making data loading faster without sacrificing *Reader* performance. Resources are dynamically balanced between these two tiers as the workload changes, where the autonomic resource management allocates only the necessary number of VM nodes to the *Reader Tier* to satisfy current workload, and reserve the rest to *Loader Tier* to load new data.

For example, as showed in Figure 15, from Hour 7 to 10, since the workload on *Reader Tier* is less intense, the dynamic plan allocates more resource to the *Loader Tier* to allow the new data to be loaded as fast as possible. As a result, the dynamic plan loads much more new data (473.3GB Per day) at a varying loading rate than the traditional plan (303.3GB Per day), which loads data at a fixed rate. And the QoS value of

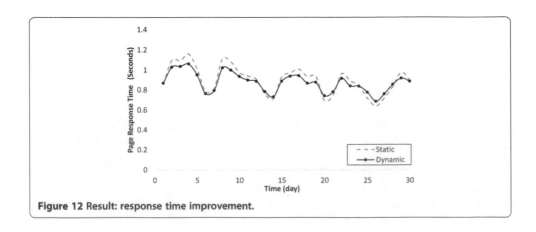

Figure 12 Result: response time improvement.

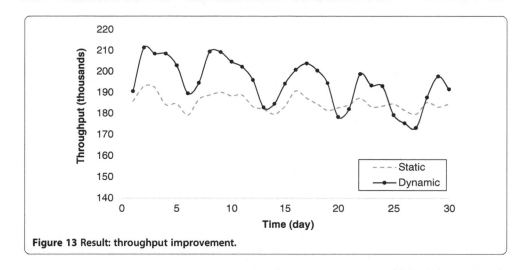

Figure 13 Result: throughput improvement.

the dynamic plan (*Avg QoS = 1.079,* refer to Eq. 5) is *26.20%* higher the traditional plan (*Avg QoS = 0.855,* refer to Eq. 5).

In summary, our proposed autonomic resource management approach is able to automatically optimize the tradeoff between service responsiveness and data freshness by balancing the resource allocations between the *Reader* and *Loader Tiers.*

Related work

In the geospatial discipline, web-based map services can significantly reduce the data volume and required computing resources at the end-user side [18]. To the best of our knowledge, v-TerraFly is the first to study the virtualization of typical web map services and propose QoS-driven resource management for a virtualized web map service through workload forecasting and dynamic resource allocation [19].

Various automatic forecasting algorithms have been studied in the related work [20], including different kinds of exponential smoothing. The work of Brown [16] and Gardner [17] led to the use of exponential smoothing in automatic forecasting for example, like Stellwagen & Goodrich's research at 1999 [15-17]. Hyndman (2002) developed a more general class of methods with a uniform approach to calculate the prediction interval [14,15]. The workload prediction algorithm proposed in this paper

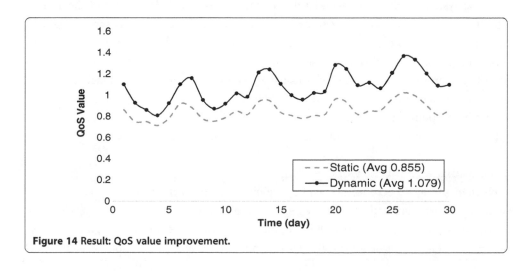

Figure 14 Result: QoS value improvement.

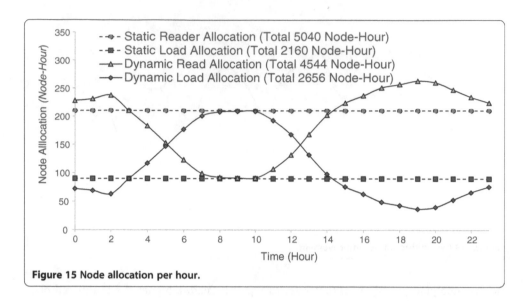

Figure 15 Node allocation per hour.

is based on exponential smoothing, but it is novel in the use of two levels of double exponential smoothing to capture both hourly pattern and daily pattern in the workload, which achieves much higher accuracy than traditional exponential smoothing methods.

In particular, Dinda *et al.* studied prediction-based best-effort real-time service to support distributed, interactive applications in shared computing environments. Two of the examples are an earthquake visualization tool and a GIS map display tool, which were shown to benefit from the service [21]. However, the workload prediction is based on linear prediction which is often not sufficient for real-world dynamic workloads. In this paper, we proposed a two-level exponential smoothing algorithm which shows good prediction accuracy for real TerraFly workloads.

Various types of solutions have been studied in the literature to address the problem of autonomic VM resource management. Different machine learning algorithms have been considered to model VM resource usages [22-25]. Although this article focused on virtualized geo-databases, we believe that our proposed VM resource allocation approach is generally applicable to the virtual resource management for other types of Big Data handling applications. The application-specific part of this approach is geo-database system applications with large numbers of users. Feedback control theory has also been used to adjust VM resource allocations, which are often based on models trained to identify the system and build the controller [26-29]. These various solutions are complementary to this paper's work which focuses on the management of virtualized web map services. Meanwhile, this paper proposes a unique QoS model to capture multiple important objectives and a new method to optimize resource allocation across multiple competing tiers, which has not been studied in the related work and can be applied to manage other multi-tier applications with similar characteristics.

Conclusions and future work

Web map services become increasingly widely used for various commercial and personal uses. Virtualization can greatly facilitate the deployment of web map service systems and substantially improve their resource utilization. To fulfill this potential, the resource management of a virtualized web map system needs to be able to handle the dynamic workloads that the system typically serves and satisfy the often competing demands of the various tiers of the system.

This paper presents a solution, v-TerraFly, to address these challenges. v-TerraFly is created by virtualizing the various tiers of a typical map service system and allowing resources to be dynamically allocated across the tiers. The resource management is done by predicting the workload intensity based on historical data and estimating the resource needs of the map service's *Reader* and *Loader Tiers* based on their performance models. A unique QoS metric is then defined to capture the tradeoff between the service responsiveness and data freshness, and it is used to optimize the resource allocation to the *Reader* and *Loader* VMs.

Experiments based on real TerraFly workload show that our system can accurately predict the workload's resource demands online and automatically allocate the resources accordingly to meet the performance target and save substantial resource cost compared to peak-load-based resource allocation. It can also automatically optimize the tradeoff between responsiveness and data freshness by dynamically balancing the shared resources between the *Reader* and *Loader* VMs.

In our future work, we will improve the scale of v-TerraFly, conducting larger experiments and employing live VM migration as an additional mechanism for optimizing resource management. We will also explore how to apply the principle of v-TerraFly to other applications that have similar dynamic and multi-tier characteristics as a web map service.

Competing interests
The authors declare that they have no competing interests.

Authors' contributions
YL carried out the TerraFly deployment pattern studies and v-TerraFly design, participated in the sequence experiment and drafted much of the manuscript. MZ participated the system design, advised and designed most of the experiment and analyzed the experiments results. LW participated in the VM node deployment and helped drafting the manuscript. NR developed the TerraFly technology and major algorithms, designed system layers design and partook in writing the manuscript. All authors read and approved the final manuscript.

Acknowledgement
This material is based in part upon work supported by the National Science Foundation under Grant Nos. MRI CNS-0821345, MRI CNS-1126619, CREST HRD-0833093, I/UCRC IIP-1338922, I/UCRC IIP-0829576, RAPID CNS-1057661, RAPID IIS-1052625, MRI CNS-0959985, AIR IIP-1237818, SBIR IIP-1330943, FRP IIP-1230661, III-Large IIS-1213026, SBIR IIP-1058428, SBIR IIP-1026265, SBIR IIP-1058606, SBIR IIP-1127251, SBIR IIP-1127412, SBIR IIP-1118610, SBIR IIP-1230265, SBIR IIP-1256641, HECURA CCF-0938045, CAREER CNS-1253944. Includes material licensed by TerraFly (http://terrafly.com) and the NSF CAKE Center (http://cake.fiu.edu).

References
1. Wang L, Xu J, Zhao M, Tu Y, Fortes JA (2011) Fuzzy modeling based resource management for virtualized database systems. In: Modeling, Analysis & Simulation of Computer and Telecommunication Systems (MASCOTS), 2011 IEEE 19th International Symposium on IEEE, pp. 32-42.
2. Rishe N, Chen SC, Prabakar N, Weiss MA, Sun W, Selivonenko A, Davis-Chu D (2001) TERRAFLY: A High-Performance Web-based Digital Library System for Spatial Data Access. In: CDE Demo Sessions, pp 17–19
3. Martin P, Elnaffar S, Wasserman T (2006) Workload Models for Autonomic Database Management Systems. ICAS
4. Padala P, Hou K, Shin K, Zhu X, Uysal M, Wang Z, Singhal S, Merchant A (2009) Automated Control of Multiple Virtualized Resources. SIGOPS/EuroSys
5. Kusic D, Kephart JO, Hanson JE, Kandasamy N, Jiang G (2009) Power and performance management of virtualized computing environments via lookahead control. Clust Comput 12(1):1–15. Special Issue on Autonomic Computing
6. Lu Y, Zhang M, Li T, Guang Y, Rishe N (2013) Online spatial data analysis and visualization system. In: Proceedings of the ACM SIGKDD Workshop on Interactive Data Exploration and Analytics, pp 73-79. ACM
7. Craig B (2007) Online Satellite and Aerial Images: Issues and Analysis. North Dakota Law Review 85, pp 547
8. Lu Y, Zhang M, Li T, Liu C, Edrosa E, Rishe N (2013) TerraFly GeoCloud: online spatial data analysis system. In: Proceedings of the 22nd ACM international conference on Conference on information & knowledge management, pp 2457–2460. ACM

9. Lu Y, Zhang M, Witherspoon S, Yesha Y, Rishe N (2013) sksOpen: Efficient Indexing, Querying, and Visualization of Geo-spatial Big Data. In: Proceedings of the 12th International Conference on Machine Learning and Applications (ICMLA'13). IEEE, DOI 10.1109/ICMLA.2013.161 pp 485-490

10. Anderson TE, Peterson LL, Shenker S, Turner JS (2005) Overcoming the internet impasse through visualization. IEEE Comp 38(4):34–41

11. Bennani MN, Menasce DA (2005) Resource allocation for autonomic data centers using analytic performance models. In: Autonomic Computing, 2005. ICAC 2005. Proceedings. Second International Conference on IEEE, pp 229–240

12. Baran ME, Wu FF (1989) Network reconfiguration in distribution systems for loss reduction and load balancing. Power Delivery, IEEE Transactions 4(2):1401-1407

13. Wood T, Cherkasova L, Ozonat K, Shenoy P (2008) Profiling and Modeling Resource Usage of Virtualized Applications. Middleware

14. Hyndman R, Koehler AB, Ord JK, Snyder RD (2008) Forecasting with Exponential Smoothing: The State Space Approach. XIII, 362 p

15. Hyndman RJ, Koehler AB, Snyder RD, Grose S (2002) A state space framework for automatic forecasting using exponential smoothing methods. Int J Forecast 18:439–454

16. Brown RG, Meyer RF (1961) The Fundamental Theorem of Exponential Smoothing. Oper Res 9:673–685

17. Gardner ES, Jr (2006) Exponential smoothing: The state of the art—Part II. International Journal of Forecasting 22(4):637-666

18. Lu Y, Zhao M, Zhao G, Wang L, Rishe N (2013) Massive GIS Database System with Autonomic Resource Management. In Proceedings of the 12th International Conference on Machine Learning and Applications (ICMLA'13). IEEE, DOI 10.1109/ICMLA.2013.161 pp 451-456

19. Yue P, Di L, Yang W, Yu G, Zhao P (2007) Semantics-based automatic composition of geospatial Web service chains. Comput Geosci 33(5):649-665

20. Morato D, Aracil J, Diez LA, Izal M, Magana E (2001) On linear prediction of Internet traffic for packet and burst switching networks. In: Computer Communications and Networks, 2001. Proceedings. Tenth International Conference on IEEE, pp 138-143

21. Dinda PA, Lowekamp B, Kallivokas LF, O'hallaron DR (1999) The case for prediction-based best-effort real-time systems. Springer Berlin Heidelberg, pp 309-318

22. Wildstrom J, Stone P, Witchel E (2008) CARVE: A Cognitive Agent for Resource Value Estimation. ICAC

23. Rao J, Bu X, Xu C, Wang L, Yin G (2009) VCONF: A Reinforcement Learning Approach to Virtual Machines Auto-configuration. ICAC

24. Wang L, Xu J, Zhao M, Tu Y, Fortes JAB (2011) Fuzzy Modeling Based Resource Management for Virtualized Database Systems. MASCOTS

25. Xu J, Zhao M, Fortes J (2008) Autonomic Resource Management in Virtualized Data Centers Using Fuzzy-logic-based Control. Cluster Computing

26. Padala P, Hou K, Shin K, Zhu X, Uysal M, Wang Z, Singhal S, Merchant A (2009) Automated Control of Multiple Virtualized Resources. SIGOPS/EuroSys

27. Liu X, Zhu X, Padala P, Wang Z, Singhal S (2007) Optimal Multivariate Control for Differentiated Services on a Shared Hosting Platform. CDC

28. Lama P, Zhou X (2011) PERFUME: Power and Performance Guarantee with Fuzzy MIMO Control in Virtualized Servers. IWQoS

29. Wang L, Xu J, Zhao M, Fortes J (2011) Adaptive virtual resource management with fuzzy model predictive control. In Proceedings of the 8th ACM international conference on Autonomic computing, pp 191-192. ACM

8

DCMS: A data analytics and management system for molecular simulation

Anand Kumar[1], Vladimir Grupcev[1], Meryem Berrada[1], Joseph C Fogarty[2], Yi-Cheng Tu[1]*, Xingquan Zhu[3], Sagar A Pandit[2] and Yuni Xia[4]

*Correspondence: ytu@cse.usf.edu
[1] Department of Computer Science and Engineering, University of South Florida, 4202 E. Fowler Ave., ENB118, 33620 Tampa, Florida, USA
Full list of author information is available at the end of the article

Abstract

Molecular Simulation (MS) is a powerful tool for studying physical/chemical features of large systems and has seen applications in many scientific and engineering domains. During the simulation process, the experiments generate a very large number of atoms and intend to observe their spatial and temporal relationships for scientific analysis. The sheer data volumes and their intensive interactions impose significant challenges for data accessing, managing, and analysis. To date, existing MS software systems fall short on storage and handling of MS data, mainly because of the missing of a platform to support applications that involve intensive data access and analytical process. In this paper, we present the database-centric molecular simulation (DCMS) system our team developed in the past few years. The main idea behind DCMS is to store MS data in a relational database management system (DBMS) to take advantage of the declarative query interface (*i.e.*, SQL), data access methods, query processing, and optimization mechanisms of modern DBMSs. A unique challenge is to handle the analytical queries that are often compute-intensive. For that, we developed novel indexing and query processing strategies (including algorithms running on modern co-processors) as integrated components of the DBMS. As a result, researchers can upload and analyze their data using efficient functions implemented inside the DBMS. Index structures are generated to store analysis results that may be interesting to other users, so that the results are readily available without duplicating the analysis. We have developed a prototype of DCMS based on the PostgreSQL system and experiments using real MS data and workload show that DCMS significantly outperforms existing MS software systems. We also used it as a platform to test other data management issues such as security and compression.

Keywords: Scientific database; Molecular simulation; Molecular dynamics; Data compression; Spatiotemporal database

Background

Recent advancement in computing and networking technologies has witnessed the rising and flourishing of data-intensive applications that severely challenge the existing data management and computing systems. In a narrow sense, data-intensive applications commonly require significant storage space and intensive computing power. The demand of such resources alone, however, is not the only fundamental challenge of dealing with big data [1-3]. Instead, the complications of big data are mainly driven by the complexity and the variety of the data generated from different domains [4]. For example, online social media has now been popularly used to collect real-time public feedback related to specific topics or products [5]. Data storage and management systems should support high throughput data access with millions of tweets generated each second [4]. Meanwhile, the tweets may be generated from different geographic regions, using different languages, and many of them may contain spam messages, typos, and malicious links etc. In addition to the low level data cleansing, access, and management issues, user privacy and public policies should also be considered (and integrated) in the analytical process for meaningful outcomes.

For many other application domains, such as scientific data analysis, the above big data complications also commonly exist. For example, particle simulation is a major computational method in many scientific and engineering fields for studying physical/chemical features of natural systems. In such simulations, a system of interest is treated as a collection of potentially large number of particles (*e.g.*, atoms, stars) that interact under classical physics rules. In the molecular and structural biology world, such simulations are generally called Molecular Simulations (MS). By providing a model description for biochemical and biophysical processes at a nanoscopic scale, MS is a powerful tool towards fundamental understanding of biological systems.

At present time, the field of MS has a handful of software systems employing their proprietary or open formats for data storage [6-8]. Although many of them are carefully designed to achieve maximum computational performance in simulation, they significantly fall short on storage and handling of the large scale data output. The MS by their nature generate a large amount of data in a streaming fashion - a system could consist of millions of atoms and one single simulation can easily run for tens of thousands of time steps. Figure 1 shows two (small) examples of such simulations. One salient problem of existing systems is the lack of efficient data retrieval and analytical query processing mechanisms.

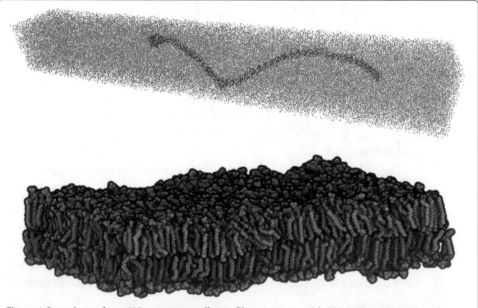

Figure 1 Snapshots of two MS systems: a collagen fiber structure with 890,000 atoms (top) and a dipalmitoylphosphatidylcholine (DPPC) bi-layer lipid system with 402,400 atoms (bottom).

In this paper, we present our recent research efforts in advancing big data analytic and management systems for scientific simulation domains, which usually generate large datasets with temporal and spatial correlations for analysis. Our research mainly emphasizes on the design of the data management system in supporting intensive data access, query processing, and optimization mechanisms for MS data. The main objective of our study is to produce high performance techniques for the MS community to accelerate the discovery process in biological/medical research. In particular, we introduce the design and development of a Database-Centric Molecular Simulation (DCMS) framework that allows scientists to efficiently retrieve, query, analyze, and share MS data.

A unique feature of DCMS is to build the system framework on top of a relational database management system (RDBMS). Such a decision is justified by careful analysis of the data processing requirements of the target application: since MS data is spatiotemporal in nature, existing DBMS provides significant advantages in modeling and application development. Plus, we can leverage the results of decades of research in spatiotemporal databases that are often (at least partially) implemented in RDBMSs. On the other hand, the unique features of MS data analysis/querying workload call for significant improvement and new functionalities in existing RDBMSs. A salient problem we face is the high computational complexity in processing analytical queries that are not seen in typical databases, demonstrating another dimension of difficulty shared by many of today's big data applications. For MS, there are also data compression and data security issues that require innovative solutions. Therefore, our work in DCMS focuses on meeting those challenges by augmenting the DBMS kernel with novel data structures and query processing/optimization algorithms. As a result, our system achieves significant improvement in data processing efficiency as compared to legacy solutions.

Related work

In current MS software [9-11], simulation data is typically stored in data files, which are further organized into various levels of directories. Data access is enabled by encoding the descriptions of the content in files into the names of files and directories, or storing more detailed descriptions about the file content in separate *metadata* files. Under the traditional file-based scheme, data/information sharing among MS community involves shipping the raw data packed in files along with the required format information and analysis tools. Due to the sheer volume of MS data, such sharing is extremely difficult, if possible at all. Two MS data analysis projects, BioSimGrid [12] and SimDB [13], store data and perform analysis at the same computer system and allow users remotely send in queries and get back results. This approach is based on the premises that: (1) analysis of MS data involves projection and/or reduction of data to smaller volume; (2) users need to exchange the reduced representation of data, rather than the whole raw data. In a similar project [14], databases are used to store digital movies generated from visualization of MS datasets.

In BioSimGrid and SimDB, relational databases are used to store and manage the metadata information. However, both systems *store raw MS data as flat files instead of database records*. Thus, the database only helps in locating the files of interest by querying the metadata. Further data retrieval and analysis are performed by opening and scanning the files located. Such an approach suffers from the following drawbacks: (1) *Difficulties in the development and maintenance of application programs.* Specific programs have to be coded for each specific type of queries using a general-purpose programming language such as C. This creates high demand for experienced programmers and thus limits the type of queries the system can support. (2) *Lack of a systematic scheme for efficient data retrieval and analysis.* An operating system views data as continuous bytes and only provides simple data access interfaces such as *seek* (i.e., jumping to a specific position of the file). Without data structures that semantically organize data records, data retrieval is often accomplished by sequentially scanning all relevant files. There is also a lack of efficient algorithms for processing queries that are often analytical in nature - most of existing algorithms are brute-force solutions. (3) *Other issues* such as data security and data compression are not sufficiently addressed.

The MDDB system [8] is close in spirit to DCMS. However, it focuses on data exploration and analysis within the simulation process rather than post-simulation data management. Another project named Dynameomics [15] coincided with the development of DCMS and delivered a database containing data from 11,000 protein simulations. Note that the main objective of the DCMS project is to provide a systematic solution to the problems mentioned above. To that end, most of our work is done within the kernel space of an open-source DBMS. In contrast to that, Dynameomics uses a commercial DBMS in its current form and attempts to optimize data management tasks at the application layer. We believe the DCMS approach has significant advantages in solving the last two issues mentioned above.

Case description

Issues

Here we summarize the data management challenges in typical MS applications.

MS Data A typical simulation outputs multiple *trajectory files* containing a number of snapshots (named *frames*) of the simulated system. Depending on the software and format, such data may be stored in binary form and undergo simple lossless compression. The main part of the data is very similar to those found in spatio-temporal databases. A typical trajectory file has some global data, which is used to identify the simulation, and a set of frames arranged in a sequential manner. Each frame may contain data entries that are independent of the atom index. The main part of trajectory frame is a sequential list of atoms with their positions, velocities, perhaps forces, masses, and types. These entries may contain additional quantities like identifiers to place an atom in particular residue or molecule. In file-based approach, the bond structure of residues is stored separately in *topology* files and the control parameters of a simulation are kept separately in *control* files. Hence, any sharing of data or analysis requires consistent exchange or availability of three types of files. Further complications in data exchange/use is due to different naming and storage convention used by individual researchers.

MS Queries Unlike traditional DBMSs where data retrieval is the main task, the mainstream queries in DCMS are analytical in nature. In general, an analytical query in MS is a mathematical function that maps the readings of a group of atoms to a scalar, vector, a matrix, or a data cube [13]. For the purpose of studying the statistical feature of the system, popular queries in this category include density, first-order statistics, second-order statistics, and histograms. Conceptually, to process such queries, we first need to retrieve the group of atoms of interest, and then compute the mathematical function. Current MS analysis toolboxes [6,7,9,11] accomplish these steps in an (algorithmically) straightforward way. Some of the analytical queries are computationally expensive. Popular queries can be found in Table 1 and we will elaborate more on those in Section "Analytical queries in DCMS". Many types of analytical queries are unique to the MS field, especially those that require the counting of all *n*-body interactions (thus named *n-body correlation functions*). For example, the spatial distance histogram (SDH) is a 2-body correlation function in which all pairwise distances are to be counted. The query processing engines in traditional DBMSs are designed with only simple aggregate queries in mind. Therefore, one major challenge of this project is to design mechanisms for efficient processing of analytical queries in MS that go far beyond simple aggregates.

While analytical queries are the workhorse tools for scientific discovery, many require retrieval of data as the first step. Furthermore, visualization tools also interact with the database retrieving subsets of the data points. By studying the data access patterns of the analytical queries and such tools, we identify the following data access queries that are relevant in DCMS:

- *Point queries* are equivalent to accessing a single point at the 3D space, e.g., find the location and/or other physical measurements of an atom at a specific time frame. Such queries are extremely useful for many visualization tools. A typical scenario is: the visualization tool asks for a sample of *n* data points within a specific region that reflects the underlying distribution. This is done by issuing queries with randomly generated atom IDs.

Table 1 Popular analytical queries in MS

Query name	Definition/Description
Moment of inertia	$I = \sum_{i=1}^{n} m_i \mathbf{r}_i$
Moment of inertia on z axis	$I_z = \sum_{i=1}^{n} m_i r_{zi}$
Sum of masses	$M = \sum_{i=1}^{n} m_i$
Center of mass	$C = \frac{I}{M}$
Radius of gyration	$RG = \sqrt{\frac{I_z}{M}}$
Dipole moment	$D = \sum_{i=1}^{n} q_i \mathbf{r}_i$
Dipole histogram	$D_z = \sum_{i=1}^{n} \frac{D}{z}$
Electron density	$ED = \frac{\sum_{i=1}^{n}(e_i - q_i)}{dz * x * y}$
Heat capacity	$\frac{3000\sqrt{T}*boltz}{2*\sqrt{T} - n*df*VarT}$
Isothermal compressibility	$\frac{VarV}{V_{avg}*boltz*T*PresFac}$
Mean square displacement	$msd = \langle (r_{t+\Delta_t} - r_t) \rangle$
Diffusion constant	$D_t = \frac{6*msd(t)}{t}$
Velocity autocorrelation	$V_{acor} = \langle (V_{t+\Delta_t} * V_t) \rangle$
Force autocorrelation	$F_{acor} = \langle (F_{t+\Delta_t} * F_t) \rangle$
Density function	Histogram of atom counts
Spatial distance histogram (SDH)	Histogram of all atom-to-atom distances
RDF	$rdf(r) = \frac{SDH(r)}{4*\pi*r^2*\sigma_r*\rho}$

- *Trajectory queries* retrieve all data points by fixing the value in one dimension. Two queries in this category are very popular in MS analysis: (1) single-atom trajectory (TRJ) query that retrieves the readings of a specific atom along time, and (2) frame (FRM) query that asks for the readings of all atoms in a specific time frame. These two queries, especially the second, are often issued to retrieve data points for various analytical queries such as the diffusion coefficient, in which we compute the root mean square displacement of all atoms in a frame.

- *Range (RNG) queries* are generalized trajectory queries with range predicates on one or more dimensions. For example, find all atoms in a specific region of the simulated space, or, find all atoms with velocity greater than 50 and smaller than 75. Range queries are the main building blocks of many analytical queries and visualization tasks.

- *Nearest neighbor (NN) queries* ask for the point(s) in a multidimensional space that are closest to a given point. For example, *retrieve the 20 closest atoms to a given iron atom*. This may help us locate unique structural features, e.g., certain part of the protein where a metal ion is bound to.

DCMS architecture

The architecture of the DCMS framework is illustrated in Figure 2, where the solid lines represent command flow and dotted lines represent data flow. At the core of DCMS is an integrated database system, including simulation parameters/states, simulation output data, and metadata for efficient data retrieval. An important design goal of DCMS is to allow scientists to easily transfer, interrogate, visualize, and hypothesize from integrated information obtained from a user-friendly interface as opposed to dealing with raw simulation data. To that end, DCMS provides various user interfaces for data input and query processing.

Data loader The data loader is responsible for transforming simulation data to the format required for storage in the database system. First, it can read and understand data

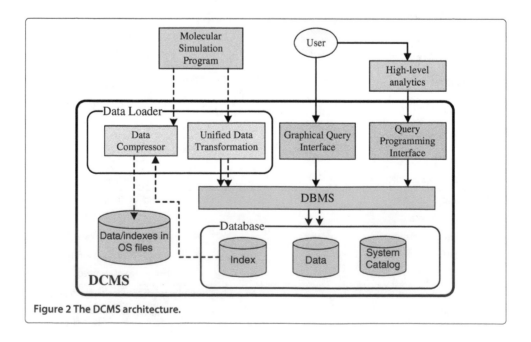

Figure 2 The DCMS architecture.

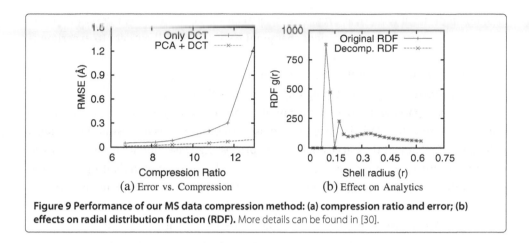

Figure 9 Performance of our MS data compression method: (a) compression ratio and error; (b) effects on radial distribution function (RDF). More details can be found in [30].

Other related work

Traditionally, database systems are mainly designed for commercial data and applications. In recent years, the scientific community has also adopted database technology in processing scientific data. However, scientific data are different from commercial data in that: (1) the volume of scientific data can be orders of magnitude larger; (2) data are often multidimensional and continuous; and (3) queries against scientific data are more complex. The above differences bring significant challenges to system design in scientific databases.

In summary, scientific database research fall into the following three types. The first is to build databases on top of out-of-box DBMS products, as seen in the following examples: GenBank (http://www.ncbi.nlm.nih.gov/Genbank) provides public access to about 80 million gene sequences; the Sloan Digital Sky Survey [33] enables astronomers to explore millions of objects in the sky; and the PeriScope [34] project explores declarative queries against biological sequence data. The second type focuses on extending the kernel functionalities of DBMSs to meet challenges in scientific data management. This includes work that deals with query language [35], data storage [36,37], data compression [38,39], index design [40], I/O scheduling [41], and data provenance [42]. The last type takes a more aggressive path by designing new DBMS architectures and building the DBMS from scratch. Most efforts along this direction happened in the past few years [43-46]. The SciDB project advocates a new data model (i.e., the multidimensional array model) for scientific domains and releases a prototype that enables parallel processing of data in a highly distributed environment. Clearly, our strategy of building DCMS falls into the second category.

Conclusions

Despite the importance of MS as a major research tool in many scientific and engineering fields, there is a lack of systems for effective data management. To that end, we developed a unified Information Integration and Informatics framework named Database-centric Molecular Simulations (DCMS). DCMS is designed to store simulation data collected from various sources, provide standard APIs for efficient data retrieval and analysis, and allow global data access to the research community. This framework is also a portal for registering well–accepted queries that in turn serve as building blocks for more complex high–level analytical programs. Users can develop these high–level programs into applications such as, applications that grant easy access of their data to experimentalists, visualize data, and provide feedback which can be used in the steering of MS. A fundamental component of the DCMS system is a relational database, which allows scientists to concentrate on developing high-level analytical tools using declarative query languages while passing the low-level details (e.g., primary query processing, data storage, basic access control) to DCMS. One of the most serious problems in existing MS systems is the low efficiency of data access and query processing. The unique query patterns of MS applications impose interesting challenges and also provide abundant optimization opportunities to DCMS design. To meet such challenges, we augmented an open-source DBMS with novel data structures and algorithms for efficient data retrieval and query processing. We focused on creative indexing and data organization techniques, query processing algorithms and optimization strategies. The DCMS system was also used as a platform to evaluate data compression algorithms specifically designed for MS data that can significantly reduce the size of the data.

Immediate work within DCMS will be focused on sharing computations (especially I/O operations) among different queries. Unlike traditional database applications, MS analysis normally centers around a small number of analytical queries (Table 1). Therefore, we can pro-actively run all relevant analytics at the time when the data is being loaded to DCMS. The advantage of this strategy is that only one I/O stream is needed - we have shown earlier that I/O can be the bottleneck in handling typical MS workloads. This requires us to modify the DBMS kernel to implement a master query processing algorithm to replace the ones dealing with individual queries. On the query processing side, utilization of other parallel hardware such as multi-core CPUs and FPGAs is definitely worth more efforts. Our current design of DCMS focuses on a single-node environment, deployment of DCMS on modern data processing platforms in a highly distributed environment (e.g., a computing cloud) will be an obvious direction for our future exploration.

Competing interests
The authors declare that they have no competing interests.

Authors' contributions
AK carried out the design, implementation, and experiments related to query processing, data compression, and data security. VG participated in experiments related to query processing and cache-based query optimization. MB designed and implemented index structures and the DCMS web interface. JF helped in the development of data loading and transformation module of DCMS. YT was in charge of the overall design of the DCMS system and algorithms related to analytical queries. XZ, SP, and YX participated in the system and web interface design. XZ also carried out the design and tuning of the data compression framework. YT drafted most parts of this manuscript while AK and VG also contributed to writing. All authors read and approved the final manuscript.

Acknowledgements
The project described here is supported by a research award (No. R01GM086707) from the US National Institutes of Health (NIH). Part of this work is also supported by two grants (IIS-1117699 and IIS-1253980) from US National Science Foundation (NSF), and gift from Nvidia via its CUDA Research Center program. The authors would like to thank the following collaborators for their contributions at various stages of this project: Anthony Casagrande, Shaoping Chen, Jin Huang, Jacob Israel, Dan Lin, Gang Shen, and Yongke Yuan.

Author details
[1]Department of Computer Science and Engineering, University of South Florida, 4202 E. Fowler Ave., ENB118, 33620 Tampa, Florida, USA. [2]Department of Physics, University of South Florida, 4202 E. Fowler Ave., PHY114, 33620 Tampa, Florida, USA. [3]Department of Electrical Engineering and Computer Science, Florida Atlantic University, 777 Glades Road, EE308, 33431 Boca Raton, Florida, USA. [4]Department of Computer Science, Indiana University - Purdue University Indianapolis, 723 W. Michigan St, SL280E, 46202 Indianapolis, Indiana, USA.

References

1. Howe D, Costanzo M, Fey P, Gojobori T, Hannick L, Hide W, Hill DP, Kania R, Schaeffer M, St. Pierre S, Twigger S, White O, Rhe SY (2008) Big data: The future of biocuration. Nature 455:47–50
2. Huberman B (2012) Sociology of science: Big data deserve a bigger audience. Nature 482:308
3. Centola D (2010) The spread of behavior in an online social network experiment. Science 329:1194–1197
4. Wu X, Zhu X, Wu G-Q, Ding W (2014) Data mining with big data. IEEE Trans Knowl Data Eng 26(1):97–107
5. J Bollen HM, Zeng X (2011) Twitter mood predicts the stock market. J Comput Sci 2:1–8
6. Michaud-Agrawal N, Denning E, Woolf T, Beckstein O (2011) MDAnalysis: A Toolkit for the Analysis of Molecular Dynamics Simulations. J Comput Chem 32(10):2319–2327
7. Humphrey W, Dalke A, Shulten K (1996) VMD: visual molecular dynamics. J Mol Graph 14(1):33–38
8. Nutanong S, Carey N, Ahmad Y, Szalay AS, Woolf TB (2013) Adaptive exploration for large-scale protein analysis in the molecular dynamics database. In: Proceedings of 25th Intl. Conf. Scientific and Statistical Database Management. SSDBM. ACM, New York, NY, USA. pp 45–1454
9. Hess B, Kutzner C, van der Spoel D, Lindahl E (2008) GROMACS 4: Algorithms for Highly Efficient, Load-Balanced, and Scalable Molecular Simulation. J Chem Theory Comput 4(3):435–447
10. Plimpton SJ (1995) Fast parallel algorithms for short range molecular dynamics. J Comput Phys 117:1–19
11. Brooks BR, Bruccoleri RE, Olafson BD, States DJ, Karplus M (1985) CHARMM: A program for macromolecular energy, minimization, and dynamics calculations. J Comput Chem 4:187–217
12. Ng MH, Johnston S, Wu B, Murdock SE, Tai K, Fangohr H, Cox SJ, Essex JW, Sansom MSP, Jeffreys P (2006) BioSimGrid: grid-enabled biomolecular simulation data storage and analysis. Future Generation Comput Systs 22(6):657–664
13. Feig M, Abdullah M, Johnsson L, Pettitt BM (1999) Large scale distributed data repository: design of a molecular dynamics trajectory database. Future Generation Comput Syst 16(1):101–110
14. Finocchiaro G, Wang T, Hoffmann R, Gonzalez A, Wade R (2003) DSMM: a database of simulated molecular motions. Nucleic Acids Res 31(1):456–457
15. van der Kamp M, Schaeffer R, Jonsson A, Scouras A, Simms A, Toofanny R, Benson N, Anderson P, Merkley E, Rysavy S, Bromley D, Beck D, Daggett V (2010) Dynameomics: a comprehensive database of protein dynamics. Structure 18(4):423–435
16. Frenkel D, Smit B (2002) Understanding molecular simulation: from algorithm to applications. Comput Sci Ser 1. Academic Press
17. Bamdad M, Alavi S, Najafi B, Keshavarzi E (2006) A new expression for radial distribution function and infinite shear modulus of lennard-jones fluids. Chem Phys 325:554–562
18. Stark JL, Murtagh F (2006) Astronomical image and data analysis. Springer, Berlin, Heidelberg
19. Wishart DS, Nip AM (1998) Protein chemical shift analysis: a practical guide. Biochem Cell Biol 76:153–163
20. Kim YJ, Patel JM (2007) Rethinking choices for multi-dimensional point indexing: making the case for the often ignored quadtree. In: Proceedings of the 3rd Biennial Conference on Innovative Data Systems Resarch (CIDR). pp 281–291. www.cidrdb.org
21. Nascimento M, Silva J (1998) Towards historical R-trees. In: Proceedings of ACM Symposium of Applied Computing (SAC). pp 235–240
22. Szalay A, Gray J, vandenBerg J (2002) Petabyte scale data mining: dream or reality. Technical Report MSR-TR-2002-84, Microsoft Research
23. Chen S, Tu Y-C, Xia Y (2011) Performance analysis of a dual-tree algorithm for computing spatial distance histograms. VLDB Journal 20(4):471–494
24. Grupcev V, Yuan Y, Tu Y-C, Huang J, Chen S, Pandit S, Weng M (2013) Approximate algorithms for computing spatial distance histograms with accuracy guarantees. IEEE Trans Knowl Data Eng 25(9):1982–1996
25. Kumar A, Grupcev V, Yuan Y, Tu Y-C, Huang J, Shen G (2014) Computing spatial distance histograms for large scientific datasets on-the-fly. IEEE Trans Knowl Data Eng 26(10):2410–2424
26. Halevy AY (2001) Answering queries using views: A survey. VLDB Journal 10(4):270–294
27. Afrati FN, Li C, Ullman JD (2007) Using views to generate efficient evaluation plans for queries. J Comput Syst Sci 73(5):703–724
28. Guttman A (1984) R-trees: a dynamic index structure for spatial searching. In: Proceedings of International Conference on Management of Data (SIGMOD). ACM Press, Boston, Massachusetts. pp 47–57
29. Omeltchenko A, Campbell TJ, Kalia RK, Liu X, Nakano A, Vashishta P (2000) Scalable I/O of large-scale molecular dynamics simulations: a data-compression algorithm. Comput Phys Commun 131:78–85
30. Kumar A, Zhu X, Tu Y-C, Pandit S (2013) Compression in molecular simulation datasets. In: 4th International Conference on Intelligence Science and Big Data Engineering (IScIDE). Springer, Beijing, China. pp 22–29
31. Aref WG, Ilyas IF (2001) SP-GIST: an extensible database index for supporting space partitioning trees. J Intell Inform Syst 17(2-3):215–240
32. Nvidia. http://www.nvidia.com/object/cuda_home_new.html
33. Szalay AS, Gray J, Thakar A, Kunszt PZ, Malik T, Raddick J, Stoughton C, vandenBerg J (2002) The SDSS Skyserver: Public Access to the Sloan Digital Sky Server Data. In: Proceedings of International Conference on Management of Data (SIGMOD). ACM, Madison, Wisconsin. pp 570–581
34. Patel JM (2003) The Role of Declarative Querying in Bioinformatics. OMICS: J Integr Biol 7(1):89–91
35. Chiu D, Agrawal G (2009) Enabling Ad Hoc Queries over Low-Level Scientific Data Sets. In: SSDBM. Springer, New Orleans, LA, USA. pp 218–236
36. Arya M, Cody WF, Faloutsos C, Richardson J, Toya A (1994) QBISM: Extending a DBMS to Support 3D Medical Images. In: ICDE. IEEE, Houston, Texas, USA. pp 314–325
37. Ivanova M, Kersten ML, Nes N (2008) Adaptive segmentation for scientific databases. In: ICDE. IEEE, Cancún, México. pp 1412–1414
38. Shahabi C, Jahangiri M, Banaei-Kashani F (2008) Proda: An end-to-end wavelet-based olap system for massive datasets. IEEE Comput 41(4):69–77

39. Chakrabarti K, Garofalakis M, Rastogi R, Shim K (2001) Approximate query processing using wavelets. VLDB J 10(2-3):199–223

40. Csabai I, Trencseni M, Dobos L, Jozsa P, Herczegh G, Purger N, Budavari T, Szalay AS (2007) Spatial indexing of large multidimensional databases. In: Proceedings of the 3rd Biennial Conference on Innovative Data Systems Resarch (CIDR). pp 207–218. www.cidrdb.org

41. Ma X, Winslett M, Norris J, Jiao X (2004) Godiva: Lightweight data management for scientific visualization applications. In: ICDE. IEEE Computer Society, Boston, MA, USA. pp 732–744

42. Chapman A, Jagadish HV, Ramanan P (2008) Efficient provenance storage. In: SIGMOD Conference. ACM, Vancouver, BC, Canada. pp 993–1006

43. Stonebraker M, Becla J, Dewitt D, Lim K-T, Maier D, Ratzesberger O (2009) Requirements for Science Data Bases and SciDB. In: CIDR 2009, Fourth Biennial Conference on Innovative Data Systems Research. www.cidrdb.org

44. Stonebraker M, Bear C, Cetintemel U, Cherniack M, Ge T, Hacham N, Harizopoulos S, Lifter J, Rogers J, Zdonik S (2007) One Size Fits All?- Part 2: Benchmarking Results. In: CIDR 2007, Third Biennial Conference on Innovative Data Systems Research. www.cidrdb.org

45. Stonebraker M, Madden S, Abadi DJ, Harizopoulos S, Hachem N, Helland P (2007) The End of an Architectural Era (It's Time for a Complete Rewrite). In: Proceedings of the 33rd International Conference on Very Large Data Bases. ACM, University of Vienna, Austria. pp 1150–1160

46. Sinha RR, Termehchy A, Mitra S, Winslett M (2007) Maitri Demonstration: Managing Large Scale Scientific Data (Demo). In: CIDR 2007, Third Biennial Conference on Innovative Data Systems Research, Asilomar, CA, USA. pp 219–224. www.cidrdb.org

9

Deep learning applications and challenges in big data analytics

Maryam M Najafabadi[1], Flavio Villanustre[2], Taghi M Khoshgoftaar[1], Naeem Seliya[1], Randall Wald[1*] and Edin Muharemagic[3]

*Correspondence: rwald1@fau.edu
[1] Florida Atlantic University, 777 Glades Road, Boca Raton, FL, USA
Full list of author information is available at the end of the article

Abstract

Big Data Analytics and Deep Learning are two high-focus of data science. Big Data has become important as many organizations both public and private have been collecting massive amounts of domain-specific information, which can contain useful information about problems such as national intelligence, cyber security, fraud detection, marketing, and medical informatics. Companies such as Google and Microsoft are analyzing large volumes of data for business analysis and decisions, impacting existing and future technology. Deep Learning algorithms extract high-level, complex abstractions as data representations through a hierarchical learning process. Complex abstractions are learnt at a given level based on relatively simpler abstractions formulated in the preceding level in the hierarchy. A key benefit of Deep Learning is the analysis and learning of massive amounts of unsupervised data, making it a valuable tool for Big Data Analytics where raw data is largely unlabeled and un-categorized. In the present study, we explore how Deep Learning can be utilized for addressing some important problems in Big Data Analytics, including extracting complex patterns from massive volumes of data, semantic indexing, data tagging, fast information retrieval, and simplifying discriminative tasks. We also investigate some aspects of Deep Learning research that need further exploration to incorporate specific challenges introduced by Big Data Analytics, including streaming data, high-dimensional data, scalability of models, and distributed computing. We conclude by presenting insights into relevant future works by posing some questions, including defining data sampling criteria, domain adaptation modeling, defining criteria for obtaining useful data abstractions, improving semantic indexing, semi-supervised learning, and active learning.

Keywords: Deep learning; Big data

Introduction

The general focus of machine learning is the representation of the input data and generalization of the learnt patterns for use on future unseen data. The goodness of the data representation has a large impact on the performance of machine learners on the data: a poor data representation is likely to reduce the performance of even an advanced, complex machine learner, while a good data representation can lead to high performance for a relatively simpler machine learner. Thus, feature engineering, which focuses on constructing features and data representations from raw data [1], is an important element of machine learning. Feature engineering consumes a large portion of the effort in a machine learning task, and is typically quite domain specific and involves considerable human input. For example, the Histogram of Oriented Gradients (HOG) [2] and Scale Invariant Feature Transform (SIFT) [3] are popular feature engineering algorithms developed specifically for the computer vision domain. Performing feature engineering in a more automated and general fashion would be a major breakthrough in machine learning as this would allow practitioners to automatically extract such features without direct human input.

Deep Learning algorithms are one promising avenue of research into the automated extraction of complex data representations (features) at high levels of abstraction. Such algorithms develop a layered, hierarchical architecture of learning and representing data, where higher-level (more abstract) features are defined in terms of lower-level (less abstract) features. The hierarchical learning architecture of Deep Learning algorithms is motivated by artificial intelligence emulating the deep, layered learning process of the primary sensorial areas of the neocortex in the human brain, which automatically extracts features and abstractions from the underlying data [4-6]. Deep Learning algorithms are quite beneficial when dealing with learning from large amounts of unsupervised data, and typically learn data representations in a greedy layer-wise fashion [7,8]. Empirical studies have demonstrated that data representations obtained from stacking up non-linear feature extractors (as in Deep Learning) often yield better machine learning results, e.g., improved classification modeling [9], better quality of generated samples by generative probabilistic models [10], and the invariant property of data representations [11]. Deep Learning solutions have yielded outstanding results in different machine learning applications, including speech recognition [12-16], computer vision [7,8,17], and natural language processing [18-20]. A more detailed overview of Deep Learning is presented in Section "Deep learning in data mining and machine learning".

Big Data represents the general realm of problems and techniques used for application domains that collect and maintain massive volumes of raw data for domain-specific data analysis. Modern data-intensive technologies as well as increased computational and data storage resources have contributed heavily to the development of Big Data science [21]. Technology based companies such as Google, Yahoo, Microsoft, and Amazon have collected and maintained data that is measured in exabyte proportions or larger. Moreover, social media organizations such as Facebook, YouTube, and Twitter have billions of users that constantly generate a very large quantity of data. Various organizations have invested in developing products using Big Data Analytics to addressing their monitoring, experimentation, data analysis, simulations, and other knowledge and business needs [22], making it a central topic in data science research.

Mining and extracting meaningful patterns from massive input data for decision-making, prediction, and other inferencing is at the core of Big Data Analytics. In addition to analyzing massive volumes of data, Big Data Analytics poses other unique challenges for machine learning and data analysis, including format variation of the raw data, fast-moving streaming data, trustworthiness of the data analysis, highly distributed input sources, noisy and poor quality data, high dimensionality, scalability of algorithms, imbalanced input data, unsupervised and un-categorized data, limited supervised/labeled data, etc. Adequate data storage, data indexing/tagging, and fast information retrieval are other key problems in Big Data Analytics. Consequently, innovative data analysis and data management solutions are warranted when working with Big Data. For example, in a recent work we examined the high-dimensionality of bioinformatics domain data and investigated feature selection techniques to address the problem [23]. A more detailed overview of Big Data Analytics is presented in Section "Big data analytics".

The knowledge learnt from (and made available by) Deep Learning algorithms has been largely untapped in the context of Big Data Analytics. Certain Big Data domains, such as computer vision [17] and speech recognition [13], have seen the application of Deep Learning largely to improve classification modeling results. The ability of Deep Learning to extract high-level, complex abstractions and data representations from large volumes of data, especially unsupervised data, makes it attractive as a valuable tool for Big Data Analtyics. More specifically, Big Data problems such as semantic indexing, data tagging, fast information retrieval, and discriminative modeling can be better addressed with the aid of Deep Learning. More traditional machine learning and feature engineering algorithms are not efficient enough to extract the complex and non-linear patterns generally observed in Big Data. By extracting such features, Deep Learning enables the use of relatively simpler linear models for Big Data analysis tasks, such as classification and prediction, which is important when developing models to deal with the scale of Big Data. The novelty of this study is that it explores the application of Deep Learning algorithms for key problems in Big Data Analytics, motivating further targeted research by experts in these two fields.

The paper focuses on two key topics: (1) how Deep Learning can assist with specific problems in Big Data Analytics, and (2) how specific areas of Deep Learning can be improved to reflect certain challenges associated with Big Data Analytics. With respect to the first topic, we explore the application of Deep Learning for specific Big Data Analytics, including learning from massive volumes of data, semantic indexing, discriminative tasks, and data tagging. Our investigation regarding the second topic focuses on specific challenges Deep Learning faces due to existing problems in Big Data Analytics, including learning from streaming data, dealing with high dimensionality of data, scalability of models, and distributed and parallel computing. We conclude by identifying important future areas needing innovation in Deep Learning for Big Data Analytics, including data sampling for generating useful high-level abstractions, domain (data distribution) adaption, defining criteria for extracting good data representations for discriminative and indexing tasks, semi-supervised learning, and active learning.

The remainder of the paper is structured as follows: Section "Deep learning in data mining and machine learning" presents an overview of Deep Learning for data analysis in data mining and machine learning; Section "Big data analytics" presents an overview of Big Data Analytics, including key characteristics of Big Data and identifying specific data analysis problems faced in Big Data Analytics; Section "Applications of deep learning in big data analytics" presents a targeted survey of works investigating Deep Learning based solutions for data analysis, and discusses how Deep Learning can be applied for Big Data Analytics problems; Section "Deep learning challenges in big data analytics" discusses some challenges faced by Deep Learning experts due to specific data analysis needs of Big Data; Section "Future work on deep learning in big data analytics" presents our insights into further works that are necessary for extending the application of Deep Learning in Big Data, and poses important questions to domain experts; and in Section "Conclusion" we reiterate the focus of the paper and summarize the work presented.

Deep learning in data mining and machine learning

The main concept in deep leaning algorithms is automating the extraction of representations (abstractions) from the data [5,24,25]. Deep learning algorithms use a huge amount of unsupervised data to automatically extract complex representation. These algorithms are largely motivated by the field of artificial intelligence, which has the general goal of emulating the human brain's ability to observe, analyze, learn, and make decisions, especially for extremely complex problems. Work pertaining to these complex challenges has been a key motivation behind Deep Learning algorithms which strive to emulate the hierarchical learning approach of the human brain. Models based on shallow learning architectures such as decision trees, support vector machines, and case-based reasoning may fall short when attempting to extract useful information from complex structures and relationships in the input corpus. In contrast, Deep Learning architectures have the capability to generalize in non-local and global ways, generating learning patterns and relationships beyond immediate neighbors in the data [4]. Deep learning is in fact an important step toward artificial intelligence. It not only provides complex representations of data which are suitable for AI tasks but also makes the machines independent of human knowledge which is the ultimate goal of AI. It extracts representations directly from unsupervised data without human interference.

A key concept underlying Deep Learning methods is distributed representations of the data, in which a large number of possible configurations of the abstract features of the input data are feasible, allowing for a compact representation of each sample and leading to a richer generalization. The number of possible configurations is exponentially related to the number of extracted abstract features. Noting that the observed data was generated through interactions of several known/unknown factors, and thus when a data pattern is obtained through some configurations of learnt factors, additional (unseen) data patterns can likely be described through new configurations of the learnt factors and patterns [5,24]. Compared to learning based on local generalizations, the number of patterns that can be obtained using a distributed representation scales quickly with the number of learnt factors.

Deep learning algorithms lead to abstract representations because more abstract representations are often constructed based on less abstract ones. An important advantage of more abstract representations is that they can be invariant to the local changes in the input data. Learning such invariant features is an ongoing major goal in pattern recognition (for example learning features that are invariant to the face orientation in a face recognition task). Beyond being invariant such representations can also disentangle the factors of variation in data. The real data used in AI-related tasks mostly arise from complicated interactions of many sources. For example an image is composed of different sources of variations such a light, object shapes, and object materials. The abstract representations provided by deep learning algorithms can separate the different sources of variations in data.

Deep learning algorithms are actually Deep architectures of consecutive layers. Each layer applies a nonlinear transformation on its input and provides a representation in its output. The objective is to learn a complicated and abstract representation of the data in a hierarchical manner by passing the data through multiple transformation layers. The sensory data (for example pixels in an image) is fed to the first layer. Consequently the output of each layer is provided as input to its next layer.

Stacking up the nonlinear transformation layers is the basic idea in deep learning algorithms. The more layers the data goes through in the deep architecture, the more complicated the nonlinear transformations which are constructed. These transformations represent the data, so Deep Learning can be considered as special case of representation learning algorithms which learn representations of the data in a Deep Architecture with multiple levels of representations. The achieved final representation is a highly non-linear function of the input data.

It is important to note that the transformations in the layers of deep architecture are non-linear transformations which try to extract underlying explanatory factors in the data. One cannot use a linear transformation like PCA as the transformation algorithms in the layers of the deep structure because the compositions of linear transformations yield another linear transformation. Therefore, there would be no point in having a deep architecture. For example by providing some face images to the Deep Learning algorithm, at the first layer it can learn the edges in different orientations; in the second layer it composes these edges to learn more complex features like different parts of a face such as lips, noses and eyes. In the third layer it composes these features to learn even more complex feature like face shapes of different persons. These final representations can be used as feature in applications of face recognition. This example is provided to simply explain in an understandable way how a deep learning algorithm finds more abstract and complicated representations of data by composing representations acquired in a hierarchical architecture. However, it must be considered that deep learning algorithms do not necessarily attempt to construct a pre-defined sequence of representations at each layer (such as edges, eyes, faces), but instead more generally perform non-linear transformations in different layers. These transformations tend to disentangle factors of variations in data. Translating this concept to appropriate training criteria is still one of the main open questions in deep learning algorithms [5].

The final representation of data constructed by the deep learning algorithm (output of the final layer) provides useful information from the data which can be used as features in building classifiers, or even can be used for data indexing and other applications which are more efficient when using abstract representations of data rather than high dimensional sensory data.

Learning the parameters in a deep architecture is a difficult optimization task, such as learning the parameters in neural networks with many hidden layers. In 2006 Hinton proposed learning deep architectures in an unsupervised greedy layer-wise learning manner [7]. At the beginning the sensory data is fed as learning data to the first layer. The first layer is then trained based on this data, and the output of the first layer (the first level of learnt representations) is provided as learning data to the second layer. Such iteration is done until the desired number of layers is obtained. At this point the deep network is trained. The representations learnt on the last layer can be used for different tasks. If the task is a classification task usually another supervised layer is put on top of the last layer and its parameters are learnt (either randomly or by using supervised data and keeping the rest of the network fixed). At the end the whole network is fine-tuned by providing supervised data to it.

Here we explain two fundamental building blocks, unsupervised single layer learning algorithms which are used to construct deeper models: Autoencoders and Restricted Boltzmann Machines (RBMs). These are often employed in tandem to construct stacked

Autoencoders [8,26] and Deep belief networks [7], which are constructed by stacking up Autoencoders and Restricted Boltzmann Machines respectively. Autoencoders, also called autoassociators [27], are networks constructed of 3 layers: input, hidden and output. Autoencoders try to learn some representations of the input in the hidden layer in a way that makes it possible to reconstruct the input in the output layer based on these intermediate representations. Thus, the target output is the input itself. A basic Autoencoder learns its parameters by minimizing the reconstruction error. This minimization is usually done by stochastic gradient descent (much like what is done in Multilayer Perceptron). If the hidden layer is linear and the mean squared error is used as the reconstruction criteria, then the Autoencoder will learn the first k principle components of the data. Alternative strategies are proposed to make Autoencoders nonlinear which are appropriate to build deep networks as well as to extract meaningful representations of data rather than performing just as a dimensionality reduction method. Bengio et al. have called these methods "regularized Autoencoders" in [5], and we refer an interested reader to that paper for more details on algorithms.

Another unsupervised single layer learning algorithm which is used as a building block in constructing Deep Belief Networks is the Restricted Boltzmann machine (RBM). RBMs are most likely the most popular version of Boltzmann machine [28]. They contains one visible layer and one hidden layer. The restriction is that there is no interaction between the units of the same layer and the connections are solely between units from different layers. The Contrastive Divergence algorithm [29] has mostly been used to train the Boltzmann machine.

Big data analytics

Big Data generally refers to data that exceeds the typical storage, processing, and computing capacity of conventional databases and data analysis techniques. As a resource, Big Data requires tools and methods that can be applied to analyze and extract patterns from large-scale data. The rise of Big Data has been caused by increased data storage capabilities, increased computational processing power, and availability of increased volumes of data, which give organization more data than they have computing resources and technologies to process. In addition to the obvious great volumes of data, Big Data is also associated with other specific complexities, often referred to as the four Vs: Volume, Variety, Velocity, and Veracity [22,30,31]. We note that the aim of this section is not to extensively cover Big Data, but present a brief overview of its key concepts and challenges while keeping in mind that the use of Deep Learning in Big Data Analytics is the focus of this paper.

The unmanageable large Volume of data poses an immediate challenge to conventional computing environments and requires scalable storage and a distributed strategy to data querying and analysis. However, this large Volume of data is also a major positive feature of Big Data. Many companies, such as Facebook, Yahoo, Google, already have large amounts of data and have recently begun tapping into its benefits [21]. A general theme in Big Data systems is that the raw data is increasingly diverse and complex, consisting of largely un-categorized/unsupervised data along with perhaps a small quantity of categorized/supervised data. Working with the Variety among different data representations in a given repository poses unique challenges with Big Data, which requires Big Data pre-processing of unstructured data in order to extract structured/ordered representations of the data for human and/or downstream consumption. In today's data-intensive technology era, data Velocity – the increasing rate at which data is collected and obtained – is just as important as the Volume and Variety characteristics of Big Data. While the possibility of data loss exists with streaming data if it is generally not immediately processed and analyzed, there is the option to save fast-moving data into bulk storage for batch processing at a later time. However, the practical importance of dealing with Velocity associated with Big Data is the quickness of the feedback loop, that is, process of translating data input into useable information. This is especially important in the case of time-sensitive information processing. Some companies such as Twitter, Yahoo, and IBM have developed products that address the analysis of streaming data [22]. Veracity in Big Data deals with the trustworthiness or usefulness of results obtained from data analysis, and brings to light the old adage "Garbage-In-Garbage-Out" for decision making based on Big Data Analytics. As the number of data sources and types increases, sustaining trust in Big Data Analytics presents a practical challenge.

Big Data Analytics faces a number of challenges beyond those implied by the four Vs. While not meant to be an exhaustive list, some key problem areas include: data quality and validation, data cleansing, feature engineering, high-dimensionality and data reduction, data representations and distributed data sources, data sampling, scalability of algorithms, data visualization, parallel and distributed data processing, real-time analysis and decision making, crowdsourcing and semantic input for improved data analysis, tracing and analyzing data provenance, data discovery and integration, parallel and distributed computing, exploratory data analysis and interpretation, integrating heterogenous data, and developing new models for massive data computation.

Applications of deep learning in big data analytics

As stated previously, Deep Learning algorithms extract meaningful abstract representations of the raw data through the use of an hierarchical multi-level learning approach, where in a higher-level more abstract and complex representations are learnt based on the less abstract concepts and representations in the lower level(s) of the learning hierarchy. While Deep Learning can be applied to learn from labeled data if it is available in sufficiently large amounts, it is primarily attractive for learning from large amounts of unlabeled/unsupervised data [4,5,25], making it attractive for extracting meaningful representations and patterns from Big Data.

Once the hierarchical data abstractions are learnt from unsupervised data with Deep Learning, more conventional discriminative models can be trained with the aid of relatively fewer supervised/labeled data points, where the labeled data is typically obtained through human/expert input. Deep Learning algorithms are shown to perform better at extracting non-local and global relationships and patterns in the data, compared to relatively shallow learning architectures [4]. Other useful characteristics of the learnt abstract representations by Deep Learning include: (1) relatively simple linear models can work effectively with the knowledge obtained from the more complex and more abstract data representations, (2) increased automation of data representation extraction from unsupervised data enables its broad application to different data types, such as image, textural, audio, etc., and (3) relational and semantic knowledge can be obtained at the higher levels of abstraction and representation of the raw data. While there are other useful aspects of Deep Learning based representations of data, the specific characteristics mentioned above are particularly important for Big Data Analytics.

Considering each of the four Vs of Big Data characteristics, i.e., Volume, Variety, Velocity, and Veracity, Deep Learning algorithms and architectures are more aptly suited to address issues related to Volume and Variety of Big Data Analytics. Deep Learning inherently exploits the availability of massive amounts of data, i.e. Volume in Big Data, where algorithms with shallow learning hierarchies fail to explore and understand the higher complexities of data patterns. Moreover, since Deep Learning deals with data abstraction and representations, it is quite likely suited for analyzing raw data presented in different formats and/or from different sources, i.e. Variety in Big Data, and may minimize need for input from human experts to extract features from every new data type observed in Big Data. While presenting different challenges for more conventional data analysis approaches, Big Data Analytics presents an important opportunity for developing novel algorithms and models to address specific issues related to Big Data. Deep Learning concepts provide one such solution venue for data analytics experts and practitioners. For example, the extracted representations by Deep Learning can be considered as a practical source of knowledge for decision-making, semantic indexing, information retrieval, and for other purposes in Big Data Analytics, and in addition, simple linear modeling techniques can be considered for Big Data Analytics when complex data is represented in higher forms of abstraction.

In the remainder of this section, we summarize some important works that have been performed in the field of Deep Learning algorithms and architectures, including semantic indexing, discriminative tasks, and data tagging. Our focus is that by presenting these works in Deep Learning, experts can observe the novel applicability of Deep Learning techniques in Big Data Analytics, particularly since some of the application domains in the works presented involve large scale data. Deep Learning algorithms are applicable to different kinds of input data; however, in this section we focus on its application on image, textual, and audio data.

Semantic indexing

A key task associated with Big Data Analytics is information retrieval [21]. Efficient storage and retrieval of information is a growing problem in Big Data, particularly since very large-scale quantities of data such as text, image, video, and audio are being collected and made available across various domains, e.g., social networks, security systems, shopping and marketing systems, defense systems, fraud detection, and cyber traffic monitoring. Previous strategies and solutions for information storage and retrieval are challenged by the massive volumes of data and different data representations, both associated with Big Data. In these systems, massive amounts of data are available that needs semantic indexing rather than being stored as data bit strings. Semantic indexing presents the data in a more efficient manner and makes it useful as a source for knowledge discovery and comprehension, for example by making search engines work more quickly and efficiently.

Instead of using raw input for data indexing, Deep Learning can be used to generate high-level abstract data representations which will be used for semantic indexing. These representations can reveal complex associations and factors (especially when the raw input was Big Data), leading to semantic knowledge and understanding. Data representations play an important role in the indexing of data, for example by allowing data points/instances with relatively similar representations to be stored closer to one another in memory, aiding in efficient information retrieval. It should be noted, however, that the high-level abstract data representations need to be meaningful and demonstrate relational and semantic association in order to actually confer a good semantic understanding and comprehension of the input.

While Deep Learning aids in providing a semantic and relational understanding of the data, a vector representation (corresponding to the extracted representations) of data instances would provide faster searching and information retrieval. More specifically, since the learnt complex data representations contain semantic and relational information instead of just raw bit data, they can directly be used for semantic indexing when each data point (for example a given text document) is presented by a vector representation, allowing for a vector-based comparison which is more efficient than comparing instances based directly on raw data. The data instances that have similar vector representations are likely to have similar semantic meaning. Thus, using vector representations of complex high-level data abstractions for indexing the data makes semantic indexing feasible. In the remainder of this section, we focus on document indexing based on knowledge gained from Deep Learning. However, the general idea of indexing based on data representations obtained from Deep Learning can be extended to other forms of data.

Document (or textual) representation is a key aspect in information retrieval for many domains. The goal of document representation is to create a representation that condenses specific and unique aspects of the document, e.g. document topic. Document retrieval and classification systems are largely based on word counts, representing the number of times each word occurs in the document. Various document retrieval schemas use such a strategy, e.g., TF-IDF [32] and BM25 [33]. Such document representation schemas consider individual words to be dimensions, with different dimensions being independent. In practice, it is often observed that the occurrence of words are highly correlated. Using Deep Learning techniques to extract meaningful data representations makes it possible to obtain semantic features from such high-dimensional textual data, which in turn also leads to the reduction of the dimensions of the document data representations.

Hinton et al. [34] describe a Deep Learning generative model to learn the binary codes for documents. The lowest layer of the Deep Learning network represents the word-count vector of the document which accounts as high-dimensional data, while the highest layer represents the learnt binary code of the document. Using 128-bit codes, the authors demonstrate that the binary codes of the documents that are semantically similar lay relatively closer in the Hamming space. The binary code of the documents can then be used for information retrieval. For each query document, its Hamming distance compared to all other documents in the data is computed and the top D similar documents are retrieved. Binary codes require relatively little storage space, and in addition they allow relatively quicker searches by using algorithms such as fast-bit counting to compute the Hamming distance between two binary codes. The authors conclude that using these binary codes for document retrieval is more accurate and faster than semantic-based analysis.

Deep Learning generative models can also be used to produce shorter binary codes by forcing the highest layer in the learning hierarchy to use a relatively small number of variables. These shorter binary codes can then simply be used as memory addresses. One word of memory is used to describe each document in such a way that a small Hamming-ball around that memory address contains semantically similar documents – such a technique is referred as "semantic hashing" [35]. Using such a strategy, one can perform information retrieval on a very large document set with the retrieval time being independent of the document set size. Techniques such as semantic hashing are quite attractive for information retrieval, because documents that are similar to the query document can be retrieved by finding all the memory addresses that differ from the memory address of the query document by a few bits. The authors demonstrate that "memory hashing" is much faster than locality-sensitive hashing, which is one of the fastest methods among existing algorithms. In addition, it is shown that by providing a document's binary codes to algorithms such as TF-IDF instead of providing the entire document, a higher level of accuracy can be achieved. While Deep Learning generative models can have a relatively slow learning/training time for producing binary codes for document retrieval, the resulting knowledge yields fast inferences which is one major goal of Big Data Analytics. More specifically, producing the binary code for a new document requires just a few vector matrix computations performing a feed-forward pass through the encoder component of the Deep Learning network architecture.

To learn better representations and abstractions, one can use some supervised data in training the Deep Learning model. Ranzato et al. [36] present a study in which parameters of the Deep Learning model are learnt based on both supervised and unsupervised data. The advantages of such a strategy are that there is no need to completely label a large collection of data (as some unlabeled data is expected) and that the model has some prior knowledge (via the supervised data) to capture relevant class/label information in the data. In other words, the model is required to learn data representations that produce good reconstructions of the input in addition to providing good predictions of document class labels. The authors show that for learning compact representations, Deep Learning models are better than shallow learning models. The compact representations are efficient because they require fewer computations when used in indexing, and in addition, also need less storage capacity.

Google's "word2vec" tool is another technique for automated extraction of semantic representations from Big Data. This tool takes a large-scale text corpus as input and produces the word vectors as output. It first constructs a vocabulary from the training text data and then learns vector representation of words, upon which the word vector file can be used as features in many Natural Language Processing (NLP) and machine learning applications. Miklov et al. [37] introduce techniques to learn high-quality word vectors from huge datasets with hundreds of millions of words (including some datasets containing 1.6 billion words), and with millions of distinct words in the vocabulary. They focus on artificial neural networks to learn the distributed representation of words. To train the network on such a massive dataset, the models are implemented on top of the large-scale distributed framework "DistBelief" [38]. The authors find that word vectors which are trained on massive amounts of data show subtle semantic relationships between words, such as a city and the country it belongs to – for example, Paris belongs to France and Berlin belongs to Germany. Word vectors with such semantic relationships could be used to improve many existing NLP applications, such as machine translation, information retrieval, and question response systems. For example, in a related work, Miklov et al. [39] demonstrate how word2vec can be applied for natural language translation.

Deep Learning algorithms make it possible to learn complex nonlinear representations between word occurrences, which allow the capture of high-level semantic aspects of the document (which could not normally be learned with linear models). Capturing these complex representations requires massive amounts of data for the input corpus, and producing labeled data from this massive input is a difficult task. With Deep Learning one can leverage unlabeled documents (unsupervised data) to have access to a much larger amount of input data, using a smaller amount of supervised data to improve the data representations and make them more related to the specific learning and inference tasks. The extracted data representations have been shown to be effective for retrieving documents, making them very useful for search engines.

Similar to textual data, Deep Learning can be used on other kinds of data to extract semantic representations from the input corpus, allowing for semantic indexing of that data. Given the relatively recent emergence of Deep Learning, additional work needs to be done on using its hierarchical learning strategy as a method for semantic indexing of Big Data. An remaining open question is what criteria is used to define "similar" when trying to extract data representations for indexing purposes (recall, data points that are semantically similar will have similar data representations in a specific distance space).

Discriminative tasks and semantic tagging

In performing discriminative tasks in Big Data Analytics one can use Deep Learning algorithms to extract complicated nonlinear features from the raw data, and then use simple linear models to perform discriminative tasks using the extracted features as input. This approach has two advantages: (1) extracting features with Deep Learning adds nonlinearity to the data analysis, associating the discriminative tasks closely to Artificial Intelligence, and (2) applying relatively simple linear analytical models on the extracted features is more computationally efficient, which is important for Big Data Analytics. The problem of developing efficient linear models for Big Data Analytics has been extensively investigated in the literature [21]. Hence, developing nonlinear features from massive amounts of input data allows the data analysts to benefit from the knowledge available through the massive amounts of data, by applying the learnt knowledge to simpler linear models for further analysis. This is an important benefit of using Deep Learning in Big Data Analytics, allowing practitioners to accomplish complicated tasks related to Artificial Intelligence, such as image comprehension, object recognition in images, etc., by using simpler models. Thus discriminative tasks are made relatively easier in Big Data Analytics with the aid of Deep Learning algorithms.

Discriminative analysis in Big Data Analytics can be the primary purpose of the data analysis, or it can be performed to conduct tagging (such as semantic tagging) on the data for the purpose of searching. For example, Li et al. [40] explore the Microsoft Research Audio Video Indexing System (MAVIS) that uses Deep Learning (with Artificial Neural Networks) based speech recognition technology to enable searching of audio and video files with speech. To converting digital audio and video signals into words, MAVIS automatically generates closed captions and keywords that can increase accessibility and discovery of audio and video files with speech content.

Considering the development of the Internet and the explosion of online users in recent years, there has been a very rapid increase in the size of digital image collections. These come from sources such as social networks, global positioning satellites, image sharing systems, medical imaging systems, military surveillance, and security systems. Google has explored and developed systems that provide image searches (e.g., the Google Images search service), including search systems that are only based on the image file name and document contents and do not consider/relate to the image content itself [41,42]. Towards achieving artificial intelligence in providing improved image searches, practitioners should move beyond just the textual relationships of images, especially since textual representations of images are not always available in massive image collection repositories. Experts should strive towards collecting and organizing these massive image data collections, such that they can be browsed, searched, and retrieved more efficiently. To deal with large scale image data collections, one approach to consider is to automate the process of tagging images and extracting semantic information from the images. Deep Learning presents new frontiers towards constructing complicated representations for image and video data as relatively high levels of abstractions, which can then be used for image annotation and tagging that is useful for image indexing and retrieval. In the context of Big Data Analytics, here Deep Learning would aid in the discriminative task of semantic tagging of data.

Data tagging is another way to semantically index the input data corpus. However, it should not be confused with semantic indexing as discussed in the prior section. In semantic indexing, the focus is on using the Deep Learning abstract representations directly for data indexing purposes. Here the abstract data representations are considered as features for performing the discriminative task of data tagging. This tagging on data can also be used for data indexing as well, but the primary idea here is that Deep Leaning makes it possible to tag massive amounts of data by applying simple linear modeling methods on complicated features that were extracted by Deep Learning algorithms. The remainder of this section focuses largely on some results from using Deep Leaning for discriminative tasks that involve data tagging.

At the ImageNet Computer Vision Competition, Hinton et al. [17] demonstrated an approach using Deep Learning and Convolutional Neural Networks which outperformed other existing approaches for image object recognition. Using the ImageNet dataset, one of the largest for image object recognition, Hinton's team showed the importance of Deep Learning for improving image searching. Dean et al. [38] demonstrated further success on ImageNet by using a similar Deep Learning modeling approach with a large-scale software infrastructure for training an artificial neural network.

Some other approaches have been tried for learning and extracting features from unlabeled image data, include Restricted Boltzmann Machines (RBMs) [7], autoencoders [26], and sparse coding [43]. However, these were only able to extract low-level features, such as edge and blob detection. Deep Learning can also be used to build very high-level features for image detection. For example, Google and Stanford formulated a very large deep neural network that was able to learn very high-level features, such as face detection or cat detection from scratch (without any priors) by just using unlabeled data [44]. Their work was a large scale investigation on the feasibility of building high-level features with Deep Learning using only unlabeled (unsupervised) data, and clearly demonstrated the benefits of using Deep Learning with unsupervised data. In Google's experimentation, they trained a 9-layered locally connected sparse autoencoder on 10 million 200×200 images downloaded randomly from the Internet. The model had 1 billion connections and the training time lasted for 3 days. A computational cluster of 1000 machines and 16000 cores was used to train the network with model parallelism and asynchronous SGD (Stochastic Gradient Descent). In their experiments they obtained neurons that function like face detectors, cat detectors, and human body detectors, and based on these features their approach also outperformed the state-of-the-art and recognized 22,000 object categories from the ImageNet dataset. This demonstrates the generalization ability of abstract representations extracted by Deep Learning algorithms on new/unseen data, i.e., using features extracted from a given dataset to successfully perform a discriminative task on another dataset. While Google's work involved the question of whether it is possible to build a face feature detector by just using unlabeled data, typically in computer vision labeled images are used to learn useful features [45]. For example, a large collection of face images with a bounding box around the faces can be used to learn a face detector feature. However, traditionally it would require a very large amount of labeled data to find the best features. The scarcity of labeled data in image data collections poses a challenging problem.

There are other Deep Learning works that have explored image tagging. Socher et al. [46] introduce recursive neural networks for predicting a tree structure for images in multiple modalities, and is the first Deep Learning method that achieves very good results on segmentation and annotation of complex image scenes. The recursive neural network architecture is able to predict hierarchical tree structures for scene images, and outperforms other methods based on conditional random fields or a combination of other methods, as well as outperforming other existing methods in segmentation, annotation and scene classification. Socher et al. [46] also show that their algorithm is a natural tool for predicting tree structures by using it to parse natural language sentences. This demonstrates the advantage of Deep Learning as an effective approach for extracting data representations from different varieties of data types. Kumar et al. [47] suggest that recurrent neural networks can be used to construct a meaningful search space via Deep Learning, where the search space can then be used for a designed-based search.

Le et al. [48] demonstrate that Deep Learning can be used for action scene recognition as well as video data tagging, by using an independent variant analysis to learn invariant spatio-temporal features from video data. Their approach outperforms other existing methods when combined with Deep Learning techniques such as stacking and convolution to learn hierarchical representations. Previous works used to adapt hand designed feature for images like SIFT and HOG to the video domain. The Le et al. [48] study shows that extracting features directly from video data is a very important research direction, which can be also generalized to many domains.

Deep Learning has achieved remarkable results in extracting useful features (i.e., representations) for performing discriminative tasks on image and video data, as well as extracting representations from other kinds of data. These discriminative results with Deep Learning are useful for data tagging and information retrieval and can be used in search engines. Thus, the high-level complex data representations obtained by Deep Learning are useful for the application of computationally feasible and relatively simpler linear models for Big Data Analytics. However, there is considerable work that remains for further exploration, including determining appropriate objectives in learning good representations for performing discriminative tasks in Big DataAnalytics [5,25].

Deep learning challenges in big data analytics

The prior section focused on emphasizing the applicability and benefits of Deep Learning algorithms for Big Data Analytics. However, certain characteristics associated with Big Data pose challenges for modifying and adapting Deep Learning to address those issues. This section presents some areas of Big Data where Deep Learning needs further exploration, specifically, learning with streaming data, dealing with high-dimensional data, scalability of models, and distributed computing.

Incremental learning for non-stationary data

One of the challenging aspects in Big Data Analytics is dealing with streaming and fast-moving input data. Such data analysis is useful in monitoring tasks, such as fraud detection. It is important to adapt Deep Learning to handle streaming data, as there is a need for algorithms that can deal with large amounts of continuous input data. In this section, we discuss some works associated with Deep Learning and streaming data, including incremental feature learning and extraction [49], denoising autoencoders [50], and deep belief networks [51].

Zhou et al. [49] describe how a Deep Learning algorithm can be used for incremental feature learning on very large datasets, employing denoising autoencoders [50]. Denoising autoencoders are a variant of autoencoders which extract features from corrupted input, where the extracted features are robust to noisy data and good for classification purposes. Deep Learning algorithms in general use hidden layers to contribute towards the extraction of features or data representations. In a denoising autoencoder, there is one hidden layer which extracts features, with the number of nodes in this hidden layer initially being the same as the number of features that would be extracted. Incrementally, the samples that do not conform to the given objective function (for example, their classification error is more than a threshold, or their reconstruction error is high) are collected and are used for adding new nodes to the hidden layer, with these new nodes being initialized based on those samples. Subsequently, incoming new data samples are used to jointly retrain all the features. This incremental feature learning and mapping can improve the discriminative or generative objective function; however, monotonically adding features can lead to having a lot of redundant features and overfitting of data. Consequently, similar features are merged to produce a more compact set of features. Zhou et al. [49] demonstrate that the incremental feature learning method quickly converges to the optimal number of features in a large-scale online setting. This kind of incremental feature extraction is useful in applications where the distribution of data changes with respect to time in massive online data streams. Incremental feature learning and extraction can be generalized for other Deep Learning algorithms, such as RBM [7], and makes it possible to adapt to new incoming stream of an online large-scale data. Moreover, it avoids expensive cross-validation analysis in selecting the number of features in large-scale datasets.

Calandra et al. [51] introduce adaptive deep belief networks which demonstrates how Deep Learning can be generalized to learn from online non-stationary and streaming data. Their study exploits the generative property of deep belief networks to mimic the samples from the original data, where these samples and the new observed samples are used to learn the new deep belief network which has adapted to the newly observed data. However, a downside of an adaptive deep belief network is the requirement for constant memory consumption.

The targeted works presented in this section provide empirical support to further explore and develop novel Deep Learning algorithms and architectures for analyzing large-scale, fast moving streaming data, as is encountered in some Big Data application domains such as social media feeds, marketing and financial data feeds, web click stream data, operational logs, and metering data. For example, Amazon Kinesis is a managed service designed to handle real-time streaming of Big Data – though it is not based on the Deep Learning approach.

High-dimensional data

Some Deep Learning algorithms can become prohibitively computationally-expensive when dealing with high-dimensional data, such as images, likely due to the often slow learning process associated with a deep layered hierarchy of learning data abstractions and representations from a lower-level layer to a higher-level layer. That is to say, these Deep Learning algorithms can be stymied when working with Big Data that exhibits large Volume, one of the four Vs associated with Big Data Analytics. A high-dimensional data source contributes heavily to the volume of the raw data, in addition to complicating learning from the data.

Chen et al. [52] introduce marginalized stacked denoising autoencoders (mSDAs) which scale effectively for high-dimensional data and is computationally faster than regular stacked denoising autoencoders (SDAs). Their approach marginalizes noise in SDA training and thus does not require stochastic gradient descent or other optimization algorithms to learn parameters. The marginalized denoising autoencoder layers to have hidden nodes, thus allowing a closed-form solution with substantial speed-ups. Moreover, marginalized SDA only has two free meta-parameters, controlling the amount of noise as well as the number of layers to be stacked, which greatly simplifies the model selection process. The fast training time, the capability to scale to large-scale and high-dimensional data, and implementation simplicity make mSDA a promising method with appeal to a large audience in data mining and machine learning.

Convolutional neural networks are another method which scales up effectively on high-dimensional data. Researchers have taken advantages of convolutional neural networks on ImageNet dataset with 256×256 RGB images to achieve state of the art results [17,26]. In convolutional neural networks, the neurons in the hidden layers units do not need to be connected to all of the nodes in the previous layer, but just to the neurons that are in the same spatial area. Moreover, the resolution of the image data is also reduced when moving toward higher layers in the network.

The application of Deep Learning algorithms for Big Data Analytics involving high-dimensional data remains largely unexplored, and warrants development of Deep Learning based solutions that either adapt approaches similar to the ones presented above or develop novel solutions for addressing the high-dimensionality found in some Big Data domains.

Large-scale models

From a computation and analytics point of view, how do we scale the recent successes of Deep Learning to much larger-scale models and massive datasets? Empirical results have demonstrated the effectiveness of large-scale models [53-55], with particular focus on models with a very large number of model parameters which are able to extract more complicated features and representations [38,56].

Dean et al. [38] consider the problem of training a Deep Learning neural network with billions of parameters using tens of thousands of CPU cores, in the context of speech recognition and computer vision. A software framework, DistBelief, is developed that can utilize computing clusters with thousands of machines to train large-scale models. The framework supports model parallelism both within a machine (via multithreading) and across machines (via message passing), with the details of parallelism, synchronization, and communication managed by DistBelief. In addition, the framework also supports data parallelism, where multiple replicas of a model are used to optimize a single objective. In order to make large-scale distributed training possible an asynchronous SGD as well as a distributed batch optimization procedure is developed that includes a distributed implementation of L-BFGS (Limited-memory Broyden-Fletcher-Goldfarb-Shanno, a quasi-Newton method for unconstrained optimization). The primary idea is to train multiple versions of the model in parallel, each running on a different node in the network and analyzing different subsets of data. The authors report that in addition to accelerating the training of conventional sized models, their framework can also train models that are larger than could be contemplated otherwise. Moreover, while the framework focuses on training large-scale neural networks, the underlying algorithms are applicable to other gradient-based learning techniques. It should be noted, however, that the extensive computational resources utilized by DistBelief are generally unavailable to a larger audience.

Coates et al. [56] leverage the relatively inexpensive computing power of a cluster of GPU servers. More specifically, they develop their own system (using neural networks) based on Commodity Off-The-Shelf High Performance Computing (COTS HPC) technology and introduce a high-speed communication infrastructure to coordinate distributed computations. The system is able to train 1 billion parameter networks on just 3 machines in a couple of days, and it can scale to networks with over 11 billion parameters using just 16 machines and where the scalability is comparable to that of DistBelief. In comparison to the computational resources used by DistBelief, the distributed system network based on COTS HPC is more generally available to a larger audience, making it a reasonable alternative for other Deep Learning experts exploring large-scale models.

Large-scale Deep Learning models are quite suited to handle massive volumes of input associated with Big Data, and as demonstrated in the above works they are also better at learning complex data patterns from large volumes of data. Determining the optimal number of model parameters in such large-scale models and improving their computational practicality pose challenges in Deep Learning for Big Data Analytics. In addition to the problem of handling massive volumes of data, large-scale Deep Learning models for Big Data Analytics also have to contend with other Big Data problems, such as domain adaptation (see next section) and streaming data. This lends to the need for further innovations in large-scale models for Deep Learning algorithms and architectures.

Future work on deep learning in big data analytics

In the prior sections, we discussed some recent applications of Deep Learning algorithms for Big Data Analytics, as well as identified some areas where Deep Learning research needs further exploration to address specific data analysis problems observed in Big Data.

Considering the low-maturity of Deep Learning, we note that considerable work remains to done. In this section, we discuss our insights on some remaining questions in Deep Learning research, especially on work needed for improving machine learning and the formulation of the high-level abstractions and data representations for Big Data.

An important problem is whether to utilize the entire Big Data input corpus available when analyzing data with Deep Learning algorithms. The general focus is to apply Deep Learning algorithms to train the high-level data representation patterns based on a portion of the available input corpus, and then utilize the remaining input corpus with the learnt patterns for extracting the data abstractions and representations. In the context of this problem, a question to explore is what volume of input data is generally necessary to train useful (good) data representations by Deep Learning algorithms which can then be generalized for new data in the specific Big Data application domain.

Upon further exploring the above problem, we recall the Variety characteristic of Big Data Analytics, which focuses on the variation of the input data types and domains in Big Data. here, by considering the shift between the input data source (for training the representations) and the target data source (for generalizing the representations), the problem becomes one of domain adaptation for Deep Learning in Big Data Analytics. Domain adaptation during learning is an important focus of study in Deep Learning [57,58], where the distribution of the training data (from which the representations are learnt) is different from the distribution of the test data (on which the learnt representations are deployed).

Glorot et al. [57] demonstrate that Deep Learning is able to discover intermediate data representations in a hierarchical learning manner, and that these representations are meaningful to, and can be shared among, different domains. In their work, a stacked denoising autoencoder is initially used to learn features and patterns from unlabeled data obtained from different source domains. Subsequently, a support vector machine (SVM) algorithm utilizes the learnt features and patterns for application on labeled data from a given source domain, resulting in a linear classification model that outperforms other methods. This domain adaptation study is successfully applied on a large industrial strength dataset consisting of 22 source domains. However, it should be noted that their study does not explicitly encode the distribution shift of the data between the source domain and the target domains. Chopra et al. [58] propose a Deep Learning model (based on neural networks) for domain adaptation which strives to learn a useful (for prediction purposes) representation of the unsupervised data by taking into consideration information available from the distribution shift between the training and test data. The focus is to hierarchically learn multiple intermediate representations along an interpolating path between the training and testing domains. In the context of object recognition, their study demonstrates an improvement over other methods. The two studies presented above raise the question about how to increase the generalization capacity of Deep Learning data representations and patterns, noting that the ability to generalize learnt patterns is an important requirement in Big Data Analytics where often there is a distribution shift between the input domain and the target domain.

Another key area of interest would be to explore the question of what criteria is necessary and should be defined for allowing the extracted data representations to provide useful semantic meaning to the Big Data. Earlier, we discussed some studies that utilize the data representations extracted through Deep Learning for semantic indexing. Bengio et al. [5] present some characteristics of what constitutes good data representations for performing discriminative tasks, and point to the open question regarding the definition of the criteria for learning good data representations in Deep Learning. Compared to more conventional learning algorithms where misclassification error is generally used as an important criterion for model training and learning patterns, defining a corresponding criteria for training Deep Learning algorithms with Big Data is unsuitable since most Big Data Analytics involve learning from largely unsupervised data. While availability of supervised data in some Big Data domains can be helpful, the question of defining the criteria for obtaining good data abstractions and representations still remains largely unexplored in Big Data Analytics. Moreover, the question of defining the criteria required for extracting good data representations leads to the question of what would constitute a good data representation that is effective for semantic indexing and/or data tagging.

In some Big Data domains, the input corpus consists of a mix of both labeled and unlabeled data, e.g., cyber security [59], fraud detection [60], and computer vision [45]. In such cases, Deep Learning algorithms can incorporate semi-supervised training methods towards the goal of defining criteria for good data representation learning. For example, following learning representations and patterns from the unlabeled/unsupervised data, the available labeled/supervised data can be exploited to further tune and improve the learnt representations and patterns for a specific analytics task, including semantic indexing or discriminative modeling. A variation of semi-supervised learning in data mining, active learning methods could also be applicable towards obtaining improved data representations where input from crowdsourcing or human experts can be used to obtain labels for some data samples which can then be used to better tune and improve the learnt data representations.

Conclusion

In contrast to more conventional machine learning and feature engineering algorithms, Deep Learning has an advantage of potentially providing a solution to address the data analysis and learning problems found in massive volumes of input data. More specifically, it aids in automatically extracting complex data representations from large volumes of unsupervised data. This makes it a valuable tool for Big Data Analytics, which involves data analysis from very large collections of raw data that is generally unsupervised and un-categorized. The hierarchical learning and extraction of different levels of complex, data abstractions in Deep Learning provides a certain degree of simplification for Big Data Analytics tasks, especially for analyzing massive volumes of data, semantic indexing, data tagging, information retrieval, and discriminative tasks such a classification and prediction.

In the context of discussing key works in the literature and providing our insights on those specific topics, this study focused on two important areas related to Deep Learning and Big Data: (1) the application of Deep Learning algorithms and architectures for Big Data Analytics, and (2) how certain characteristics and issues of Big Data Analytics pose unique challenges towards adapting Deep Learning algorithms for those problems. A targeted survey of important literature in Deep Learning research and application to different domains is presented in the paper as a means to identify how Deep Learning can be used for different purposes in Big Data Analytics.

The low-maturity of the Deep Learning field warrants extensive further research. In particular, more work is necessary on how we can adapt Deep Learning algorithms for problems associated with Big Data, including high dimensionality, streaming data analysis, scalability of Deep Learning models, improved formulation of data abstractions, distributed computing, semantic indexing, data tagging, information retrieval, criteria for extracting good data representations, and domain adaptation. Future works should focus on addressing one or more of these problems often seen in Big Data, thus contributing to the Deep Learning and Big Data Analytics research corpus.

Competing interests
The authors declare that they have no competing interests.

Authors' contributions
MMN performed the primary literature review and analysis for this work, and also drafted the manuscript. RW and NS worked with MMN to develop the article's framework and focus. TMK, FV and EM introduced this topic to MMN and TMK coordinated with the other authors to complete and finalize this work. All authors read and approved the final manuscript.

Author details
[1]Florida Atlantic University, 777 Glades Road, Boca Raton, FL, USA. [2]LexisNexis Business Information Solutions, 245 Peachtree Center Avenue, Atlanta, GA,USA. [3]LexisNexis Business Information Solutions, 6601 Park of Commerce Blvd, Boca Raton,FL, USA.

References
1. Domingos P (2012) A few useful things to know about machine learning. Commun ACM 55(10)
2. Dalal N, Triggs B (2005) Histograms of oriented gradients for human detection. In: Computer Vision and Pattern Recognition, 2005. CVPR 2005. IEEE Computer Society Conference On. IEEE Vol. 1. pp 886–893
3. Lowe DG (1999) Object recognition from local scale-invariant features. In: Computer Vision, 1999. The Proceedings of the Seventh IEEE International Conference On. IEEE Computer Society Vol. 2. pp 1150–1157
4. Bengio Y, LeCun Y (2007) Scaling learning algorithms towards, AI. In: Bottou L, Chapelle O, DeCoste D, Weston J (eds). Large Scale Kernel Machines. MIT Press, Cambridge, MA Vol. 34. pp 321–360. http://www.iro.umontreal.ca/~lisa/pointeurs/bengio+lecun_chapter2007.pdf
5. Bengio Y, Courville A, Vincent P (2013) Representation learning: A review and new perspectives. Pattern Analysis and Machine Intelligence, IEEE Transactions on 35(8):1798–1828. doi:10.1109/TPAMI.2013.50
6. Arel I, Rose DC, Karnowski TP (2010) Deep machine learning-a new frontier in artificial intelligence research [research frontier]. IEEE Comput Intell 5:13–18
7. Hinton GE, Osindero S, Teh Y-W (2006) A fast learning algorithm for deep belief nets. Neural Comput 18(7):1527–1554
8. Bengio Y, Lamblin P, Popovici D, Larochelle H (2007) Greedy layer-wise training of deep networks, Vol. 19
9. Larochelle H, Bengio Y, Louradour J, Lamblin P (2009) Exploring strategies for training deep neural networks. J Mach Learn Res 10:1–40
10. Salakhutdinov R, Hinton GE (2009) Deep boltzmann machines. In: International Conference on, Artificial Intelligence and Statistics. JMLR.org. pp 448–455
11. Goodfellow I, Lee H, Le QV, Saxe A, Ng AY (2009) Measuring invariances in deep networks. In: Advances in Neural Information Processing Systems. Curran Associates, Inc. pp 646–654
12. Dahl G, Ranzato M, Mohamed A-R, Hinton GE (2010) Phone recognition with the mean-covariance restricted boltzmann machine. In: Advances in Neural Information Processing Systems. Curran Associates, Inc. pp 469–477
13. Hinton G, Deng L, Yu D, Mohamed A-R, Jaitly N, Senior A, Vanhoucke V, Nguyen P, Sainath T, Dahl G, Kingsbury B (2012) Deep neural networks for acoustic modeling in speech recognition: The shared views of four research groups. Signal Process Mag IEEE 29(6):82–97
14. Seide F, Li G, Yu D (2011) Conversational speech transcription using context-dependent deep neural networks. In: INTERSPEECH. ISCA. pp 437–440
15. Mohamed A-R, Dahl GE, Hinton G (2012) Acoustic modeling using deep belief networks. Audio Speech Lang Process IEEE Trans 20(1):14–22
16. Dahl GE, Yu D, Deng L, Acero A (2012) Context-dependent pre-trained deep neural networks for large-vocabulary speech recognition. Audio Speech Lang Process IEEE Trans 20(1):30–42
17. Krizhevsky A, Sutskever I, Hinton G (2012) Imagenet classification with deep convolutional neural networks. In: Advances in Neural Information Processing Systems. Curran Associates, Inc. Vol. 25. pp 1106–1114
18. Mikolov T, Deoras A, Kombrink S, Burget L, Cernocký J (2011) Empirical evaluation and combination of advanced language modeling techniques. In: INTERSPEECH. ISCA. pp 605–608
19. Socher R, Huang EH, Pennin J, Manning CD, Ng A (2011) Dynamic pooling and unfolding recursive autoencoders for paraphrase detection. In: Advances in Neural Information Processing Systems. Curran Associates, Inc. pp 801–809
20. Bordes A, Glorot X, Weston J, Bengio Y (2012) Joint learning of words and meaning representations for open-text semantic parsing. In: International Conference on Artificial Intelligence and Statistics. JMLR.org. pp 127–135
21. National Research Council (2013) Frontiers in Massive Data Analysis. The National Academies Press, Washington, DC. http://www.nap.edu/openbook.php?record_id=18374
22. Dumbill E (2012) What Is Big Data? An Introduction to the Big Data Landscape. In: Strata 2012: Making Data Work. O'Reilly, Santa Clara, CA O'Reilly

23. Khoshgoftaar TM (2013) Overcoming big data challenges. In: Proceedings of the 25th International Conference on Software Engineering and Knowledge Engineering, Boston, MA. ICSE. Invited Keynote Speaker

24. Bengio Y (2009) Learning Deep Architectures for AI. Now Publishers Inc., Hanover, MA, USA

25. Bengio Y (2013) Deep learning of representations: Looking forward. In: Proceedings of the 1st International Conference on Statistical Language and Speech Processing. SLSP'13. Springer, Tarragona, Spain. pp 1–37. http://dx.doi.org/10.1007/978-3-642-39593-2_1

26. Hinton GE, Salakhutdinov RR (Science) Reducing the dimensionality of data with neural networks 313(5786):504–507

27. Hinton GE, Zemel RS (1994) Autoencoders, minimum description length, and helmholtz free energy. Adv Neural Inform Process Syst 6:3–10

28. Smolensky P (1986) Information processing in dynamical systems: foundations of harmony theory. In: Parallel Distributed Processing: Explorations in the Microstructure of Cognition. MIT Press. Vol. 1. pp 194–281

29. Hinton GE (2002) Training products of experts by minimizing contrastive divergence. Neural Comput 14(8):1771–1800

30. Garshol LM (2013) Introduction to Big Data/Machine Learning. Online Slide Show, http://www.slideshare.net/larsga/introduction-to-big-datamachine-learning. http://www.slideshare.net/larsga/introduction-to-big-datamachine-learning

31. Grobelnik M (2013) Big Data Tutorial. European Data Forum. http://www.slideshare.net/EUDataForum/edf2013-big-datatutorialmarkogrobelnik?related=1

32. Salton G, Buckley C (1988) Term-weighting approaches in automatic text retrieval. Inform Process Manag 24(5):513–523

33. Robertson SE, Walker S (1994) Some simple effective approximations to the 2-poisson model for probabilistic weighted retrieval. In: Proceedings of the 17th Annual International ACM SIGIR Conference on Research and Development in Information Retrieval. pp 232–241. Springer-Verlag New York, Inc

34. Hinton G, Salakhutdinov R (2011) Discovering binary codes for documents by learning deep generative models. Topics Cogn Sci 3(1):74–91

35. Salakhutdinov R, Hinton G (2009) Semantic hashing. Int J Approximate, Reasoning 50(7):969–978

36. Ranzato M, Szummer M (2008) Semi-supervised learning of compact document representations with deep networks. In: Proceedings of the 25th International Conference on Machine Learning. ACM. pp 792–799

37. Mikolov T, Chen K, Dean J (2013) Efficient estimation of word representations in vector space. CoRR: Computing Research Repository: 1–12. abs/1301.3781

38. Dean J, Corrado G, Monga R, Chen K, Devin M, Le Q, Mao M, Ranzato M, Senior A, Tucker P, Yang K, Ng A (2012) Large scale distributed deep networks. In: Bartlett P, Pereira FCN, Burges CJC, Bottou L, Weinberger KQ (eds). Advances in Neural Information Processing Systems Vol. 25. pp 1232–1240. http://books.nips.cc/papers/files/nips25/NIPS2012_0598.pdf

39. Mikolov T, Le QV, Sutskever I (2013) Exploiting similarities among languages for machine translation. CoRR: Comput Res Repository: 1–10. abs/1309.4168

40. Li G, Zhu H, Cheng G, Thambiratnam K, Chitsaz B, Yu D, Seide F (2012) Context-dependent deep neural networks for audio indexing of real-life data. In: Spoken Language Technology Workshop (SLT), 2012 IEEE. IEEE. pp 143–148

41. Zipern A (2001) A Quick Way to Search For Images on the Web. The New York Times. News Watch Article. http://www.nytimes.com/2001/07/12/technology/news-watch-a-quick-way-to-search-for-images-on-the-web.html

42. Cusumano MA (2005) Google: What it is and what it is not. Commun ACM - Med Image Moeling 48(2):15–17. doi:10.1145/1042091.1042107

43. Lee H, Battle A, Raina R, Ng A (2006) Efficient sparse coding algorithms. In: Advances in Neural Information Processing Systems. MIT Press. pp 801–808

44. Le Q, Ranzato M, Monga R, Devin M, Chen K, Corrado G, Dean J, Ng A (2012) Building high-level features using large scale unsupervised learning. In: Proceeding of the 29th International Conference in Machine Learning, Edingburgh, Scotland

45. Freytag A, Rodner E, Bodesheim P, Denzler J (2013) Labeling Examples that Matter: Relevance-Based Active Learning with Gaussian Processes. In: 35th German Conference on Pattern Recognition (GCPR). Saarland University and Max-Planck-Institute for Informatics, Germany. pp 282–291

46. Socher R, Lin CC, Ng A, Manning C (2011) Parsing natural scenes and natural language with recursive neural networks. In: Proceedings of the 28th International Conference on Machine Learning. Omnipress. pp 129–136

47. Kumar R, Talton JO, Ahmad S, Klemmer SR (2012) Data-driven web design. In: Proceedings of the 29th International Conference on Machine Learning. icml.cc/Omnipress

48. Le QV, Zou WY, Yeung SY, Ng AY (2011) Learning hierarchical invariant spatio-temporal features for action recognition with independent subspace analysis. In: Computer Vision and Pattern Recognition (CVPR) 2011 IEEE Conference On. IEEE. pp 3361–3368

49. Zhou G, Sohn K, Lee H (2012) Online incremental feature learning with denoising autoencoders. In: International Conference on Artificial Intelligence and Statistics. JMLR.org. pp 1453–1461

50. Vincent P, Larochelle H, Bengio Y, Manzagol P-A (2008) Extracting and composing robust features with denoising autoencoders. In: Proceedings of the 25th International Conference on Machine Learning. ACM. pp 1096–1103

51. Calandra R, Raiko T, Deisenroth MP, Pouzols FM (2012) Learning deep belief networks from non-stationary streams. In: Artificial Neural Networks and Machine Learning–ICANN 2012. Springer, Berlin Heidelberg. pp 379–386

52. Chen M, Xu ZE, Weinberger KQ, Sha F (2012) Marginalized denoising autoencoders for domain adaptation. In: Proceeding of the 29th International Conference in Machine Learning, Edingburgh, Scotland

53. Coates A, Ng A (2011) The importance of encoding versus training with sparse coding and vector quantization. In: Proceedings of the 28th International Conference on Machine Learning. Omnipress. pp 921–928

54. Hinton GE, Srivastava N, Krizhevsky A, Sutskever I, Salakhutdinov R (2012) Improving neural networks by preventing co-adaptation of feature detectors. CoRR: Comput Res Repository: 1–18. abs/1207.0580

55. Goodfellow IJ, Warde-Farley D, Mirza M, Courville A, Bengio Y (2013) Maxout networks. In: Proceeding of the 30th International Conference in Machine Learning, Atlanta, GA

56. Coates A, Huval B, Wang T, Wu D, Catanzaro B, Andrew N (2013) Deep learning with cots hpc systems. In: Proceedings of the 30th International Conference on Machine Learning. pp 1337–1345

57. Glorot X, Bordes A, Bengio Y (2011) Domain adaptation for large-scale sentiment classification: A deep learning approach. In: Proceedings of the 28th International Conference on Machine Learning (ICML-11). pp 513–520

58. Chopra S, Balakrishnan S, Gopalan R (2013) Dlid: Deep learning for domain adaptation by interpolating between domains. In: Workshop on Challenges in Representation Learning, Proceedings of the 30th International Conference on Machine Learning, Atlanta, GA

59. Suthaharan S (2013) Big data classification: Problems and challenges in network intrusion prediction with machine learning. In: ACM Sigmetrics: Big Data Analytics Workshop. ACM, Pittsburgh, PA

60. Wang W, Lu D, Zhou X, Zhang B, Mu J (2013) Statistical wavelet-based anomaly detection in big data with compressive sensing. EURASIP J Wireless Commun Netw 2013:269. http://www.bibsonomy.org/bibtex/25e432dc7230087ab1cdc65925be6d4cb/dblp

10

Comparative study between incremental and ensemble learning on data streams: Case study

Wenyu Zang[1,2]*, Peng Zhang[2], Chuan Zhou[2] and Li Guo[2]

*Correspondence:
zangwenyu@software.ict.ac.cn
[1] Institute of Computing
Technology, Chinese Academy of
Science, South Road of Chinese
Academy of Science, Beijing, China
[2] Institute of Information
Engineering, Chinese Academy of
Science, MinZhuang Road, Beijing,
China

Abstract

With unlimited growth of real-world data size and increasing requirement of real-time processing, immediate processing of big stream data has become an urgent problem. In stream data, hidden patterns commonly evolve over time (i.e.,concept drift), where many dynamic learning strategies have been proposed, such as the incremental learning and ensemble learning. To the best of our knowledge, there is no work systematically compare these two methods. In this paper we conduct comparative study between theses two learning methods. We first introduce the concept of "concept drift", and propose how to quantitatively measure it. Then, we recall the history of incremental learning and ensemble learning, introducing milestones of their developments. In experiments, we comprehensively compare and analyze their performances *w.r.t.* accuracy and time efficiency, under various concept drift scenarios. We conclude with several future possible research problems.

Keywords: Incremental learning; Ensemble learning; Concept drift; Big data streams

Background

We are now entering the era of big data. In government, business and industry domains, big data are generated rapidly and steadily, with a constant growth speed at a magnitude of million records per day. Moreover, these data are often related in temporal and spatial correlations. Typical examples include the wireless sensor data, RFID data and Web traffic data. These data often arrives unboundedly and rapidly, which forms a new class of data called "big stream data".

The focus on learning from big stream data is how to addressing the concept drifting challenge. Concept drift was first introduced by Wdimer and Kubat [1], where they noticed that the concept (the classification boundary or clustering centers) continuously changes with time elapsing. Based on the changing speed of concept, we formally divide the concept drifting into loose concept drift and rigorous concept drift [2]. In the former, concepts in adjacent data chunks are sufficiently close to each other; in the latter, genuine concepts in adjacent data chunks may randomly and rapidly changed.

Incremental learning [3] and ensemble learning [4] are two fundamental methods in learning from big stream data with concept drift. Incremental learning follows a machine learning paradigm where the learning process taking place whenever new examples emerge, and then adjusts to what has been learned from the new examples. While the ensemble learning employs multiple base learners and combines their predictions. The fundamental principle of dynamic ensemble learning is to dividing large data-stream into small data chunks and training classifiers on each data chunk independently. The most prominent difference of incremental learning from traditional machine learning is that incremental learning does not assume the availability of a sufficient training set before the learning process, but the training example appears over time. Moreover, the biggest difference between incremental learning and ensemble learning is that ensemble learning may discard training data outdated but incremental learning may not.

Although these two types of methods have their own strengths in data streams mining. However, the comparisons between them are rare. A.Tsymbal [5] described some types of concept drift and related works to handle it. Nevertheless, it not clearly categorizes the incremental and ensemble learning algorithms. In addition, they did no experiments on different learning framework.

In this paper we comparative study the incremental learning and ensemble learning algorithms. In addition, we compare performance between them in both accuracy and efficiency. Furthermore, some suggestions are given for choosing a better classifier.

This paper is organized as follows. In section Incremental learning, review and summarize the incremental learning algorithms. In section Ensemble learning, ensemble learning algorithms are learned and classified. In section Experiment results, incremental learning and ensemble learning algorithms are analysis and compare in a unified standard. The experiment results and discussions are given in section Conclusion and section 6.

Incremental learning

Generally, classification problem is defined as follows. A set of N training examples of the form (x, y) is given, where y is a discrete class label and x is a vector of d attributes (each of which may be symbolic or numeric). The goal is to produce from these examples a model $y = f(x)$ which will predict the classes y of future examples x with high accuracy.

To solve this problem, traditional statistic analysis method would load all training data into memory at once. However, compared to the explosive growth of today's information, the storage capacity is far from desirable. Moreover, when it comes to temporal series traditional data mining algorithms have showed limitations. Incremental learning algorithms are efficient method to these problems.

According to the differences of basic data learning method, incremental learning method can be sorted as there categories: incremental decision tree, incremental Bayesian and incremental SVM. According to the number of new instances to be added in a model at a time, it can be sorted as instance-by-instance learning and block-by-block learning.

Incremental decision tree

VFDT (very fast decision tree) [6] and CVFDT (concept-adapting very fast decision tree) [7] are two classical and impactive algorithms in incremental decision tree algorithms.

VFDT (very fast decision tree) Algorithm was first proposed by Domingos and Hulte in 2000. The author used hoeffding bounds verified that we can use a small sample of the available examples when choosing the split attribute at any given node and the output is asymptotically nearly identical to that of a conventional learner.

According to Hoeffding bounds, n independent observations of a real-valued random variable r with range R, with confidence $1 - \delta$, the true mean of r is at least $\bar{r} - \varepsilon$, where $\bar{r}$ is the observed mean of the samples and

$$\varepsilon = \sqrt{\frac{R^2 ln\left(\frac{1}{\delta}\right)}{2n}} \qquad (1)$$

Select $G(X_i)$ be the heuristic measure used to choose test attributes. Let X_a be the attribute with best heuristic measure and X_a be the second best attribute. Let $\triangle \overline{G} = G(X_a) - G(X_b)$. Applying the Hoeffding bound to $\triangle \overline{G}$, if $\triangle \overline{G} > \varepsilon$, we can confidently select X_a as the split attributes. So VFDT is a real-time system and able to learn from large amount of data within practical time and memory constraints.

But comes to rigorous concept drift, VFDT has its own limitations. In order to solve this problem, Hulten and Spencer proposed CVFDT (concept-adapting very fast decision tree) algorithm [7] in 2001 based on VFDT. In CVFDT, each internal node has a list of alternate sub-trees being considered as replacements for the sub-tree rooted at the node. It also supports a parameter which limits the total number of alternate trees being grown at any one time. Each node with a non-empty set of alternate sub-trees, l_{test}, enters a testing mode to determine if it should be replaced by one of its alternate sub-trees. l_{test} collects the next m training examples that arrives to compare the accuracy of the sub-tree it roots with the accuracies of all of its alternative sub-trees. If the most accurate alternate sub-tree is more accurate than the l_{test}, l_{test} is replaced by the alternate. CVFDT also prunes alternate sub-trees during the test phase. For each alternative sub-tree of l_{test}, l_{all}^i, CVFDT remembers the smallest accuracy difference ever achieved between the two, $\triangle min\left(l_{test}, l_{all}^i\right)$. CVFDT prunes any alternate whose current test phase accuracy difference is at least $\triangle min\left(l_{test}, l_{all}^i\right) + 1\%$. By this means of sub-tree, CVFDT can adapt itself to concept drift well than VFDT.

In summary these two algorithms are both real-time method for data-stream mining. CVFDT is faster than VFDT and also adapts better to concept drift. While VFDT cost less memory than CVFDT.

Incremental Bayesian algorithm

Besides the advantages such as feasible, accurate and fast shared by all incremental learning algorithms, Incremental Bayesian Algorithms [8-10] can handle training instances without labels. Generally speaking, Bayesian Algorithm implement incremental learning by constantly updating the priori probability according to incoming training instants. As it illustrates in Figures 1 and 2.

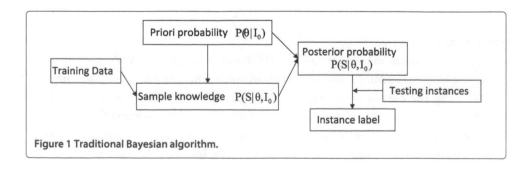

Figure 1 Traditional Bayesian algorithm.

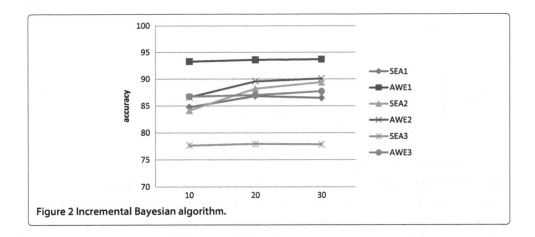

Figure 2 Incremental Bayesian algorithm.

In Bayesian algorithm priori probability $P(\theta|S, I_0)$ is a known quantity. While in the incremental Bayesian the priori probability change into $P(\theta|S, I_0)$ considering incoming new training instances. What we are concerning with is how to update a priori probability incrementally.

Firstly, make the following stipulation to some marks. The sample's space S is composed of attribute space I and class space C. Which is denote $S = \{S_1, S-2, \ldots, \S_n\} = < I, C >$. Each sample $S_i = \{a_1, a_2, \ldots, a_m, c_l\}$, the attribute is denoted by A_i, whose value is $\{a_{ik}\}$, and class attribute C is composed by I discrete values $(c_1, c_2, \ldots, c_l)$. The task of classifier is to learning the attribute space I and class space C, then finding out the mapping relation between them. Only one c_i in class attribute set $C = (c_1, c_2, \ldots, c_l)$ will be found to correspond given any one sample $s_i = \{a_1, a_2, \ldots, a_m\} \in I$. That is to say existing only one c_i for each instance $x = (a_1, a_2, \ldots, a_m) \in I$, let $P(c = c_i|x) \geq (j = 1, 2, \ldots, l)$.

For the training samples $D = \{x_1, x_2, \ldots, x_n\}$, assume that the priori probability follows dirichlet distribution. We can estimate the parameters as follows.

$$\theta_{ik|r} = P(A_{ik}|c_r; \theta) = \frac{1 + count(A_{ik} \wedge c_r)}{|A_i| + count(c_r)} \tag{2}$$

$$\theta_r = P(c_r|\theta) = \frac{1 + count(c_r)}{|C| + |D|} \tag{3}$$

Where A_{ik} is the k_{th} value of attribute A_i, $|A_i|$ is the number of values in attribute A_i. $|D|$ is the size of training samples.

According to incoming instances $T = \{x'_1, x'_2, \ldots, x'_m\}$, we consider two different situations: labeled instances and unlabeled instances. For labeled instances, we can update the parameters as follows:

$$\theta'_{ik|r} = P(A_{ik}|c_r; \theta')$$

$$= \frac{1 + count(A_{ik} \wedge c_r) + count'(A_{ik} \wedge c_r)}{|A_i| + count(c_r) + count'(c_r)} \tag{4}$$

$$\theta'_r = P(c_r|\theta') = \frac{1 + count(c_r) + count'(c_r)}{|C| + |D| + |D'|} \tag{5}$$

For the unlabeled instances, we can update the parameters as follows:

$$\theta'_r = \begin{cases} P(c_r|\theta') = \frac{\delta}{1+\delta}\theta_r & c_r \neq c'_p \\ P(c_r|\theta') = \frac{\delta}{1+\delta}\theta_r + \frac{\delta}{1+\delta} & c_r = c'_p \end{cases} \tag{6}$$

Where $\delta = |C| + |D|$

$$\theta'_{ik|r} = \begin{cases} P(A_{ik}|c_r;\theta') = \frac{\delta}{1+\delta}\theta_{ik|r} & c_r = c'_p \wedge A_{ik} \neq A'_{ip} \\ P(A_{ik}|c_r;\theta') = \frac{\delta}{1+\delta}\theta_{ik|r} + \frac{\delta}{1+\delta} & c_r \neq c'_p \wedge A_{ik} \neq A'_{ip} \\ \theta_{ik|r} & c_r \neq c'_p \end{cases} \qquad (7)$$

In summary, Bayesian Algorithm itself has incremental property. For the incoming training instances with labels, it is easy to complement an incremental algorithm. Otherwise, with instances without labels, we discusses the sampling policy and various classifying loss expressions to simplifies and improves the classifiers.

Incremental SVM

The two core concepts of SVM algorithm are mapping input vectors into a high dimensional feature space and structural risk minimization. There is a useful property in SVM algorithm: classification equivalence on SV set and the whole training set. Based on this property, Incremental SVM [11-18] can be trained by preserving only the SVs at each step, and add them to the training set for the next step. According to different situations, there are different ways to select training set at each step.

The problems discussed in Incremental SVM algorithm are how to discarding history samples optimally and how to selecting new training instances in successive learning procedure. But there is still some intrinsic difficulties. Firstly, Support vectors (SVs) is highly depended on kernel functions you selected. Secondly, when concept drift happens, previous support vectors could be useless.

Decision tree algorithms, Bayesian learning algorithms and SVM algorithms are three main algorithms in data mining. The problem we discussed in incremental algorithm is how to using old training result accelerating the successive learning procedure. Incremental decision tree (hoffding tree or VFDT) uses a statistic result (hoffding bounds) to guaranteeing that we can learn from abundant data within practical time and memory constraints. Incremental Bayesian algorithm updates the prior probability dynamically according to the incoming instances. Incremental SVM is based on the classification equivalence of SV set and the whole training set. So we can add only support vectors (SVs) to the incoming training set for incrementally training a new model. In these three algorithms, Incremental decision tree and Incremental Bayesian algorithms are based on experience risk minimization. While Incremental SVM is based on structural risk minimization. Incremental decision tree and Incremental Bayesian algorithm is faster and Incremental SVM algorithm has better a generalization ability.

All of these algorithms above update a classifier dynamically using the new coming data. On one hand, we need not to load all data into memory at once. On the other hand, we can real-time modify the classification model according to the new training instances. Moreover, the classifier can adapt to concept drift via real-time updating to new data. However, there are still shortcomings and limitations in incremental learning algorithms. For example, it can only unceasing absorb new data-streams, it cannot remove old instances in the classification model. Because of these shortcomings, incremental algorithms will be helpless when comes to rigorous concept drift.

Ensemble learning

The fundamental principle of dynamic ensemble learning is to dividing large data-stream into small data chunks. Then training classifiers on each data chunk independently. Finally, it develops heuristic rules to organize these classifiers into one super classifier.

This structure has many advantages. Firstly, each data chunk is relatively small so that the cost of training a classifier on it is not high. Secondly, we saved a well trained classifier instead of the whole instances in the data chunk which cost much less memory. Thirdly, it can adapt to various concept drifts via different weighing policies. So the dynamic ensemble learning models can cope with both unlimited increasing amounts of data and concept drift problems in data-stream mining.

There are many heuristic algorithms for ensemble learning. According to the ways of forming the base classifiers, it can be roughly divided into two classes: horizontal ensemble framework and vertical ensemble framework.

Horizontal ensemble framework

Horizontal ensemble framework tends to selecting the same type of classifiers and train them independently on different data-chunks, then using a heuristic algorithm to organize them together. It can be illustrated in Figure 3.

In this framework, almost all researches develop center on three issues: weighting policy, data selection and the choice of base classifiers. It can be formulized as:

$$f_{HE} = \Sigma_{i=1}^N \alpha_i f_i(x) \tag{8}$$

Where α_i is the weighting value assigned to the i_{th} data-chunk. $f_i(x)$ is the classifier trained on the i_{th} data-chunk. And the 1 to N is the data-chunks selected.

Weighting policy is the most important method in ensemble learning to guarantee accuracy. Street [19] proposed a SEA algorithm, which combined all the decision tree models using majority-voting. In this algorithm $\alpha_i = \frac{1}{N}$ $(i = 1, 2, \ldots, N)$. Kolter [20] also proposed a Dynamic Weighted Majority (DWM) algorithm. Yeon [21] proved majority-voting is the optimum solution in the case of no concept drift. In order to tracing the concept drift, Wang [22] proposed an accuracy-weighted ensemble algorithm, in which they assign each classifier a weight reversely proportional to the classifier's accuracy on the up-to-data chunk. In this algorithm $\alpha_i = -(MSE_i - MSE_r)$, where $MSE_i = \frac{1}{|S_n|} \Sigma_{(x,c) \in S_n} \left(1 - f_c^i(x)\right)^2$ is the mean square error of $f_i(x)$. S_n is the training set. $MSE_r = \Sigma_c p(c)(1 - p(c))^2$ is the mean square error of a random classifier. C is the labels

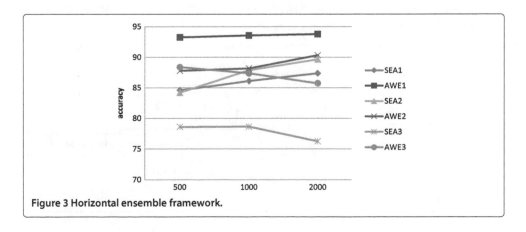

Figure 3 Horizontal ensemble framework.

of all instances. Tsymbal [5] proposed a dynamic integration of classifiers in which base classifier is given a weight proportional to its local accuracy. Zhang [23] develop a kernel mean matching (KMM) method to minimize the discrepancy of the data chunks in the kernel space for smooth concept drift and an Optimal Weight values for classifiers trained from the most recent data chunk for abrupt concept drift. Yeon [21] proposed an ensemble model has a form of a weighted average and ridge regression combiner. In this proposed algorithm a angle between the estimated weights and optimal weight is used to estimate concept drift, when concept drift is smooth $\alpha_i = \frac{1}{N}$ $(i = 1, 2, \ldots, N)$ otherwise $\alpha_i = arg_w min \Sigma_{i=1}^n \left(y_i - \Sigma_{j=1}^m \alpha_j f_j(x_i) \right)^2 + \lambda \Sigma_{j=1}^m \alpha_j^2$ subject to $\Sigma_{j=1}^m \alpha_j = 1, \alpha_j > 0$ where y_i is the label of instance. m is the number of classifiers and n is the number of instances. In this algorithm a penalty coefficient is employed to trace different level of concept drift.

As to instance selection, weighted instance and data discarded policy et al. are discussed. Fan [24] proposed a benefit-based greedy approach which can safely remove more than 90% of the base models and guarantee the acceptable accuracy. Fan [25] proposed a simple, efficient and accurate cross-validation decision tree ensemble method to discard old data and combine with new data to construct the optimal model for evolving concept. Zhao [26] proposed a pruning method (PMEP) to obtain the ensembles at a proper size. Lu [27] proposed a heuristic metric that considers the trade-off in accuracy and diversity to select the top p percent of ensemble members, depending on their resource availability and tolerable waiting time. Kuncheva [28] proposed a concept of "forgetting" by ageing at a variable rate.

Vertical ensemble framework

Vertical ensemble framework tends to selecting different type of classifiers and training it independently on the up-to-data data-chunk. Then it uses a heuristic algorithm to organizing them together. This algorithm often uses in a situation of rigorous concept drift, with little or no correlation of the decision concepts between data chunk. It can be illustrated in Figure 4.

In this frame work, we focus more on classifier diversity and a suited weighting policy. It can be formulized as:

$$f_{VE}^n(x) = \Sigma_{i=1}^m \beta_i f_{in}(x) \tag{9}$$

Where β_i is the weighting value assigned to the i_{th} classifier. And $f_{in}(x)$ is the i_{th} classifier trained on the n_{th} data-chunk.

In vertical ensemble framework, classifier diversity is a primary factor to guarantee accuracy. Zhang [29] proposed a semi-supervised ensemble method: $U_D EED$. It works by maximizing accuracies of base learners on labeled data while maximizing diversity among

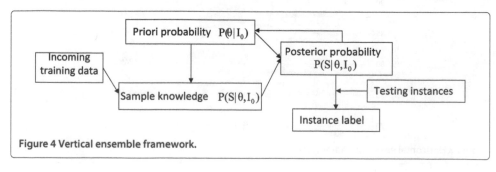

Figure 4 Vertical ensemble framework.

them on unlabeled data. Zhang [2] proposed an Optimal Weight values for classifiers in the case of abrupt concept drift, in this algorithm all classifiers using different learning algorithms, e.g., Decision Tree, SVM, LR, and then builds prediction models on and only on the up-to-data data chunk. Minku [30] show that low diverse ensemble obtain low error in the case of smooth concept drift while high diverse ensemble is better when abrupt concept drift happens.

The weighting policy in horizontal framework is almost commonly used in the vertical framework. It is also method like voting majority, weighted based on accuracy and weighted through a regression algorithm and so on.

Horizontal ensemble frame work building classifiers on different data-chunks, in this way it robust to noisy stream and concept drift because the final decisions are based on the classifiers trained from different chunks. Even if noisy data chunks and concept drift may deteriorate some base classifiers, the ensemble can still maintain relatively stable prediction accuracy. While vertical ensemble framework building classifiers using different learning algorithms on the same data-chunk, in this way it can decrease the expected bias error compared to any single classifiers. When we have no prior knowledge on the incoming data, it is difficult to determine which type of classifier is better, so combining multiple types of classifiers is likely to be a better solution than simply choosing either of them. We can also aggregate these two frameworks together. We can combine these base classifiers to form an aggregate ensemble through model defined in Eq. 10.

$$f_{AB} = \Sigma_{i=1}^{n} \Sigma_{j=1}^{m} \alpha_i \beta_j f_{ij}(x) \tag{10}$$

In a word, the core idea of ensemble learning is to organizing different weak classifiers into one strong classifier. The main method used in ensemble learning is divide-and-conquer. In ensemble learning large data-stream is divided into small data-chunks, and we train classifiers on each chunk independently. The difficult problems we discussed mostly in ensemble learning are as follows. First, what base classifier should we choose? Second, how to set the size of a data-chunk? Third, how to assign weighting values to different classifiers? Finally, how to discard previous data? As to setting the size of a data-chunk, large data-chunk is more robust while small data-chunk adapts better to concept drift. And the weighting policy direct influence on accuracy.

Experiment results

The aim of the experiments is to comparing the incremental learning with the ensemble learning algorithms. In incremental learning algorithms incremental decision tree (include VFDT and CVFDT), incremental Bayesian algorithm and incremental SVM were experimental verified. In ensemble learning algorithms horizontal framework and vertical ensemble framework were implemented. AWE was chosen to represent horizontal ensemble framework. In all the compared algorithms we compare basic characteristics on popular synthetic and real life data sets.

All of the tested algorithms were implemented in Java as part of the MOA and Weka framework. We implemented the AWE algorithms and implement incremental SVM in Libsvm, while all the other algorithms were already a part of MOA or Weka. The experiments were done on a machine equipped with an AMD Athlon (tm) II X3 435 @2.89 GHz Processor and 3.25 GB of RAM. To make the experimental more reliable, we experiment every algorithm on each data stream (from different starting point) for 10 times and calculated the mean and variance based on these values in the experimental. T-test was used for Significance Testing. Classification accuracy was calculated using the data block evaluation method, which works similarly to test-then-train paradigm. This method reads incoming examples without processing them, until they form a data block of size d. Each new data block is first used to test the existing classifier, and then it updates the classifier.

Synthetic and real data streams in experiment

In this part all five data-streams used in the experiment will be listed. There are four synthetic data-streams (Hyperplane 1, Hyperplane 2, Hyperplane 3 and KDDcup99) and one real data-streams (sensor data-stream).

In these data-streams Hyperplane 1, Hyperplane 2 and Hyperplane 3 are generated by Hyperplane generator in moa. They all have 9 attributes and one label with 2 classes, and there are 800,000 instances in each of the data-streams. The difference between these three synthetic data-streams is that they have different level of concept drifts. Hyperplane 1 has no concept drift. Hyperplane 2 has median level of concept drift and Hyper plane 3 has abrupt concept drift. Kddcup99 stream was collected from the KDD CUP challenge in 1999, and the task is to build predictive models capable of distinguishing between intrusions and normal connections. Clearly, the instances in the stream do not flow in similar way as the genuine stream data. In this data-stream each instance has 41 attributes and one label with 23 classes. Sensor stream contains information (temperature, humidity, light, and sensor voltage) collected from 54 sensors deployed in Intel Berkeley Research Lab. The whole stream contains consecutive information recorded over a 2 months period (1 reading per 1-3 minutes). sensor ID is used as the class label, so the learning task of the stream is to correctly identify the sensor ID (1 out of 54 sensors) purely based on the sensor data and the corresponding recording time. While the data stream flow over time, so does the concepts underlying the stream. For example, the lighting during the working hours is generally stronger than the night, and the temperature of specific sensors (conference room) may regularly rise during the meetings. So there are 5 attributes and a label of 54 classes in this data-stream.

In order to make a visual representation of the concept drift, we divided these data-streams into small data-chunks. And then, we train a C4.5 decision tree on the first data-chunk. Next, we use this classifier predict the labels of the following data-chunks and record the accuracy. If there is no concept drift, the accuracies will be stable. Otherwise the accuracies will changes dramatically.

As it show in Figure 5, we can see that KDDcup99 and HGstream1 data streams have no concept drift. The sensor data stream has the most rigorous concept drift. HGstream

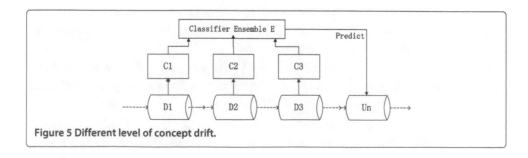

Figure 5 Different level of concept drift.

Table 1 The accuracy of four kinds of incremental learning algorithms

	Hyperplane 1	Hyperplane 2	Hyperplane 3	Sensor	KDDcup99
VFDT	$90.42_{\pm 0.13}$	$78.93_{\pm 1.7}$	$82.73_{\pm 3.08}$	$92.21_{\pm 2.19}$	$99.69_{\pm 0.01}$
CVFDT	$90.44_{\pm 0.14}$	$80.22_{\pm 1.55}$	$84.51_{\pm 2.68}$	$92.22_{\pm 2.12}$	
Incremental Bayesian	$93.8_{\pm 0.001}$	$73.54_{\pm 2.89}$	$81.65_{\pm 0.023}$	$93.29_{\pm 0.22}$	$98.50_{\pm 0.002}$
Incremental SVM	$90.8_{\pm 0.14}$	$70.5_{\pm 3.79}$	$80.12_{\pm 2.96}$	$91.89_{\pm 1.21}$	$97.96_{\pm 0.97}$

2 and HGstream 3 have median level of concept drift. While HGstream2 has a relatively rigorous concept drift and HGtream3 has a relatively loose concpet dirft.

Competitive study

Incremental learning and ensemble learning are two major solutions to large-scale data and concept drift in big stream data mining. Incremental learning is a style of learning where the learner updates its model of the environment where a new significant experience becomes available. And ensemble learning adopts a divide-and-conquer method to organize different base classifiers into one super classifier. They both can handle infinitely increasing amount of data and time series. Moreover, they both meet the real-time demands. Besides the above advantages they shared together each algorithm has its own relative merits. It will be discussed in detail in the followings.

Competitive study on accuracy and efficiency

Incremental learning and ensemble learning are two major solutions to large-scale data and concept drift in today's data stream mining. Incremental learning is a style of learning where the learner updates its model of the environment where a new significant experience becomes available. And ensemble learning adopts a divide-and-conquer method to organize different base classifiers into one super classifier. They both can handle infinitely increasing amount of data and time series. Moreover, they both meet the real-time demands. Besides the above advantages they shared together each algorithm has its own relative merits. It will be discussed in detail in the followings.

Competitive study on various concept drift

Incremental algorithm cannot adapt well to sudden concept drift. That is because almost of the incremental algorithms update its model according to incoming data-streams but it never discard history knowledge. For examples, in incremental Bayesian algorithms, priori probability is updated smoothly according to incoming instances. In incremental

Table 2 The mean of the accuracy on data stream Hyperplane1

	Data-chunk size	500	1000	2000
Classifier number	Algorithm			
10	SEA	$83.66_{\pm 2.49}$	$84.23_{\pm 2.01}$	$86.39_{\pm 0.35}$
	AWE	$92.88_{\pm 0.11}$	$93.34_{\pm 0.05}$	$93.61_{\pm 0.10}$
20	SEA	$85.82_{\pm 3.14}$	$87.06_{\pm 0.53}$	$87.49_{\pm 0.79}$
	AWE	$93.33_{\pm 0.12}$	$93.63_{\pm 0.06}$	$93.79_{\pm 0.09}$
30	SEA	$84.23_{\pm 2.01}$	$86.94_{\pm 1.62}$	$88.14_{\pm 0.27}$
	AWE	$93.49_{\pm 0.10}$	$93.70_{\pm 0.06}$	$93.85_{\pm 0.08}$

SEA get the optimal accuracy at a 2,000 data chunk size and 30 base classifiers, while AWE algorithm get optimal accuracy at a 2,000 data chunk size and 30 base classifiers.

Table 3 The mean of the accuracy on data stream Hyperplane2

Classifier number	Data-chunk size	500	1000	2000
	Algorithm			
10	SEA	$77.06_{\pm0.97}$	$87.91_{\pm1.97}$	$87.36_{\pm0.78}$
	AWE	$84.94_{\pm3.87}$	$85.72_{\pm0.53}$	$89.09_{\pm.012}$
20	SEA	$86.32_{\pm1.21}$	$87.17_{\pm0.99}$	$91.15_{\pm0.29}$
	AWE	$87.96_{\pm0.52}$	$89.27_{\pm0.96}$	$91.42_{\pm0.26}$
30	SEA	$89.22_{\pm1.56}$	$88.49_{\pm0.5}$	$90.44_{\pm0.08}$
	AWE	$90.36_{\pm0.43}$	$89.44_{\pm0.46}$	$90.39_{\pm0.04}$

SEA get the optimal accuracy at a 2,000 data chunk size and 20 base classifiers, while AWE algorithm get optimal accuracy at a 2,000 data chunk size and 20 base classifiers.

SVM algorithms, support vectors (SVs) are directly related to decision plane and kernel function. So it is very sensitive to concept drift. Only CVFDT an incremental decision algorithm can process time-changing concept by growing an alternative sub-tree. But it costs additional space to save alternative paths which decrease its efficiency dramatically.

In compared with incremental algorithms, ensemble learning algorithms is more flexible to concept drift. Firstly, it can set the size of data chunk to fit different level of concept drift: small data chunk for sudden concept drift and large data chunk for smooth concept drift. Secondly, it can assign different weighting values to different base classifiers to satisfy various concept drift. Thirdly different policy to select and discard base classifiers also helped.

As a result, ensemble learning algorithms adapt much better to concept drift than incremental learning algorithms.

Generally speaking, incremental algorithms is faster and has better anti-noise capacity than ensemble algorithms. While ensemble algorithms is more flexible and adapt itself better to concept drift. Moreover, incremental algorithms has more restrictions than ensemble algorithms. Not all classification algorithms can be used in incremental learning, but almost every classification algorithms can be used in an ensemble algorithms.

Therefore, when there is no concept drift or concept drift is smooth, an incremental algorithm is recommended. While huge concept drift or abrupt concept drift exist, ensemble algorithms are recommended to guarantee accuracy. Otherwise, in case of relatively simple data-stream or a high level of real-time processing is demanded incremental learning is a better choice. And in case of complicated or unknown distribution data-stream ensemble learning is a better choice.

Table 4 The mean of the accuracy on data stream Hyperplane3

Classifier number	Data-chunk size	500	1000	2000
	Algorithm			
10	SEA	$77.08_{\pm9.59}$	$78.44_{\pm11.07}$	$77.42_{\pm4.03}$
	AWE	$88.04_{\pm2.52}$	$86.99_{\pm2.97}$	$85.13_{\pm2.20}$
20	SEA	$79.4_{\pm18.41}$	$78.58_{\pm5.78}$	$75.8_{\pm4.98}$
	AWE	$88.26_{\pm2.61}$	$87.17_{\pm3.12}$	$85.53_{\pm2.04}$
30	SEA	$79.26_{\pm6.22}$	$78.82_{\pm8.45}$	$75.44_{\pm1.84}$
	AWE	$88.75_{\pm2.36}$	$87.86_{\pm2.70}$	$86.44_{\pm1.84}$

SEA get the optimal accuracy at a 500 data chunk size and 20 base classifiers, while AWE algorithm get optimal accuracy at a 500 data chunk size and 30 base classifiers.

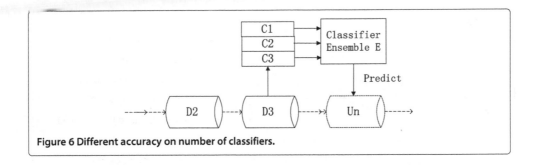

Figure 6 Different accuracy on number of classifiers.

Experiments on incremental algorithms

In this part we will experiment on different incremental algorithms.

Table 1 shows the accuracy of four kinds of incremental learning algorithms: VFDT (very fast decision tree), CVFDT (concept-adapting very fast decision tree), incremental bayesian algorithm and incremental SVM.We can see that the accuracy is decreased as the concept drift increase. CVFDT relatively adapts better to concept drift, but we can see in Table 1 when there is a large number of attributes in the data sets (KDDcup99) CVFDT can not work properly. In a word, majority of incremental algorithms can meet the requirement of real-time processing but not adapt well to abrupt concept drift.

Experiments on ensemble algorithms

In this section, horizontal ensemble framework is firstly discussed. And then we talked about vertical ensemble framework. In the end we compared these two ensemble frameworks.

Table 2, Table 3 and Table 4 show the relations between the size of data chunk, number of classifiers and classification accuracy on different concept drift. two kinds of most popular and most representative horizontal framework ensemble algorithms are tested. In all ensemble classifiers decision tree is selected as base classifier. We can point out that in a smooth concept drift we tend to select a relatively large data chunk and small size of classifiers while in the case of abrupt concept drift a small data chunk is better.

In these tables we can see that AWE algorithm is better than SEA algorithm, especially in case of concept drift (HGstream3). Moreover, we can see that different weighting policy directly lead to different accuracy on test instances. And many papers about ensemble algorithms are discussed on different weighting policies. Beside weighting policy, data

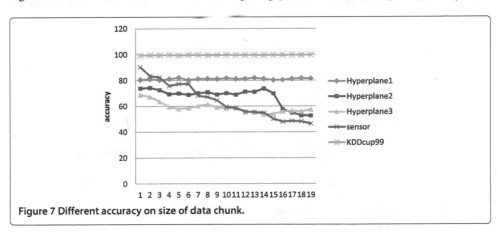

Figure 7 Different accuracy on size of data chunk.

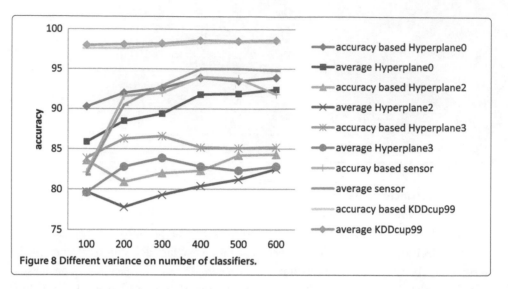

Figure 8 Different variance on number of classifiers.

chunk size and classifier number are other two influential factors on the performance of ensemble algorithms.

Figure 6 shows the algorithm accuracy on different number of classifiers. We can see that in a case of little or no concept drift more classifiers is better. While in a case of abrupt concept drift less classifiers is better. But the difference of this influential factor is not that obvious.

Figure 7 shows the algorithm accuracy on different size of data chunk. We can see that in a case of little or no concept drift a large data chunk is better and in a case of concept drift small data chunk is better. The influence of data chunk size is obvious. In both Figure 6 and Figure 7 we can see that data stream with less concept drift have better performance.

Figure 8 shows the algorithm variance on different number of classifiers. We can see that the influence of classifier numbers is not that obvious. Only in the case of high level concept drift, we can see that more base classifiers more stable.

Figure 9 shows the algorithm variance on different size of data chunk. We can see that the bigger the data chunk is the more table the algorithm performance is. And this tendency is very obvious. In both Figure 8 and Figure 9 we can see that AWE algorithm is more stable than SEA algorithm. And less concept drift directly lead to better performance. Meanwhile the influence on variance is more obvious than that on accuracy.

As show in Figure 10, we can see that besides in data stream KDDcup99, in data stream sensor vertical ensemble has better performance than in other data-streams. KDDcup99

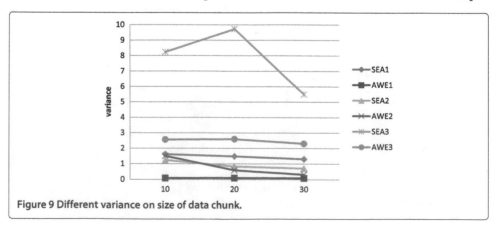

Figure 9 Different variance on size of data chunk.

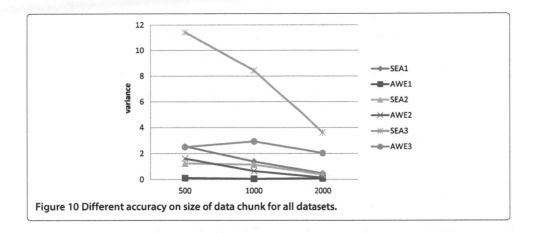

Figure 10 Different accuracy on size of data chunk for all datasets.

is a data-stream every classify algorithm will achieve a outstanding result and sensor is a data-stream with the highest level of concept drift. That is to say in a case of large concept drift vertical ensemble algorithm is a better choice. And generally in vertical ensemble algorithms we tend to selected a data chunk not larger than 1000 instances. Moreover a data chunk less than 500 instances is not stable and can not achieve a good performance.

As we show in Table 5 we can see that horizontal ensemble framework do a better job when concept drift is relatively smooth while the vertical do a better job in the case of abrupt concept drift. we also can regard the vertical ensemble framework as an extreme case of horizontal ensemble framework where only one base classifier is selected and trained on the latest data chunk.

Experiments on competitive learning

In this section, we will competitively discussed the advantages and disadvantages between incremental and ensemble algorithms. Consider the comparability, in each algorithm we selected decision tree as a base classifier. So we chose VFDT as representative of incremental algorithm and we used a accuracy based weighting algorithm in both horizontal ensemble and vertical ensemble algorithms.

Table 6 shows that ensemble algorithm is more accuracy than incremental algorithm. And in a case of high level concept drift, vertical ensemble algorithm has better performance while in smooth concept drift or no concept drift horizontal ensemble algorithm is better. But in a case when a single classifier also can perform very well in classification the ensemble learning algorithm is not as good as incremental learning algorithms.

Table 7 shows the cost time of different algorithms. In all these data-streams Hyperplane 1, Hyperplane 2 and Hyperplane 3 contains 300,000 instances and sensor contains 10,000 instances. KDDcup99 contains 100,000 instances. We can see that incremental algorithm is obvious faster than ensemble algorithms. While horizontal ensemble and vertical ensemble algorithms has a similar cost time.

Table 5 Competitive study on accuracy

	Hyperplane 1	Hyperplane 2	Hyperplane 3	Sensor	KDDcup99
Average vote horizontal ensemble	$88.14_{\pm0.27}$	$91.15_{\pm0.29}$	$78.82_{\pm8.45}$	$89.05_{\pm3.85}$	$99.44_{\pm0.01}$
Accuracy based horizontal ensemble	$93.85_{\pm0.08}$	$91.42_{\pm0.26}$	$88.75_{\pm2.36}$	$87.34_{\pm2.17}$	$99.31_{\pm0.04}$
Average vote vertical ensemble	$92.4_{\pm0.01}$	$82.5_{\pm0.07}$	$83.9_{\pm0.04}$	$95_{\pm0.02}$	$98.6_{\pm0.01}$
Accuracy based vertical ensemble	$93.6_{\pm0.01}$	$84.3_{\pm0.06}$	$86.6_{\pm0.04}$	$94_{\pm0.05}$	$98.4_{\pm0.01}$

Table 6 The accuracy of different algorithms

	Hyperplane 1	Hyperplane 2	Hyperplane 3	Sensor	KDDcup99
VFDT	$90.42_{\pm 0.13}$	$78.93_{\pm 0.17}$	$82.73_{\pm 3.08}$	$92.21_{\pm 2.19}$	$99.69_{\pm 0.01}$
Horizontal ensemble	$93.85_{\pm 0.08}$	$86.28_{\pm 0.74}$	$88.75_{\pm 2.63}$	$87.34_{\pm 2.17}$	$99.31_{\pm 0.043}$
Vertical ensemble	$93.9_{\pm 0.013}$	$84.3_{\pm 0.67}$	$86.6_{\pm 0.04}$	$95.1_{\pm 0.35}$	$98.4_{\pm 0.005}$

In a word, we can say that ensemble learning is more accuracy than incremental learning algorithms and incremental algorithm is more efficiency than ensemble algorithms.

Conclusion

Unlimited growth of big stream data and concept drift has been two most difficult problems in data-stream mining. There are two mainstream solutions to these problems: incremental learning and ensemble learning algorithms. Incremental learning algorithms employ a method of updating a single model by incorporating newly arrived data. While ensemble learning algorithms use the divide-and-conquer method to cutting up large data into small data chunks and training classifiers on each data chunk independently, then a heuristic algorithm is used to ensemble these classifiers together. In incremental algorithms, we talked mostly about how to recording previous knowledge and adapting to new knowledge. In ensemble learning algorithms, we discuss mostly about how to making a weighting policy for each base classifiers.

Both of these algorithms can handle big stream data and concept drift problems, and each of them has its own properties. Incremental learning algorithms have better performance on efficiency and ensemble learning adapts better to concept drift. Moreover, ensemble learning algorithms are more stable than incremental algorithms. The size of data chunk is another important factor in ensemble algorithms, which influences the algorithm performance. Generally, a better way to achieving high accuracy is that the higher levels a concept drift is the smaller a data chunk will be.

Therefore, in a case of loose concept drift or no concept drift an incremental algorithm is recommended and in a case of rigorous concept drift an ensemble algorithm is a better choice. Otherwise, when efficiency is first considering factor we tend to selecting incremental algorithm and when accuracy is the most important factor we choose an ensemble algorithm. We can employ different algorithms according to the real data-stream distributions.

Weighting policy, instances selection, classifier diversity and so on is the main rules discussed in previously researches. With the very fast development of information industry, we have to face the reality of information explosion. In that situation, more and more classifiers will be trained and real-time processing will become a challenge. Therefore, the next step is how to effectively managing large amount of classifiers. We can consider some pruning method or index technology on the classifiers. We can also consider some parallel algorithms to organizing the classifiers.

Table 7 Cost time of different algorithms

	Hyperplane 1	Hyperplane 2	Hyperplane 3	Sensor	KDDcup99
VFDT	3254.9	3310.6	3246.9	203.2	3479
Horizontal ensemble	67760	67913	64237	5426	348114
Vertical ensemble	63145	59876	62110	5897	30146

Authors' contributions

WZ and PZ have made substantial contributions to conception and design. WZ has been involved in drafting the manuscript. PZ and CZ revising it critically for important intellectual content; LG has given final approval of the version to be published. All authors read and approved the final manuscript.

Acknowledgments

This work was supported by the NSFC (No. 61370025), 863 projects (No.2011AA01A103 and 2012AA012502), 973 project (No. 2013CB329605 and 2013CB329606), and the Strategic Leading Science and Technology Projects of Chinese Academy of Sciences (No.XDA06030200).

References

1. Widmer G, Kubat M (1996) Learning in the presence of concept drift and hidden contexts. Mach Learn 23(1): 69–101
2. Zhang P, Zhu X, Shi Y (2008) Categorizing and mining concept drifting data streams. In: Proceedings of the 14th ACM SIGKDD international conference on knowledge discovery and data mining, pp 812–820
3. Giraud-Carrier C (2000) A note on the utility of incremental learning. AI Commun 13(4): 215–223
4. Polikar R (2006) Ensemble based systems in decision making. Circ Syst Mag 6(3): 21–45
5. Tsymbal A (2004) The problem of concept drift: definitions and related work. Computer Science Department, Trinity College Dublin
6. Domingos P, Hulten G (2000) Mining high-speed data streams, pp 71–80
7. Hulten G, Spencer L, Domingos P (2001) Mining time-changing data streams, pp 97–106
8. Hua C, Xiao-gang Z, Jing Z, Li-hua D (2009) A simplified learning algorithm of incremental Bayesian
9. Deng L, Droppo J, Acero A (2003) Incremental Bayes learning with prior evolution for tracking nonstationary noise statistics from noisy speech data
10. Alcobé JR (2004) Incremental augmented Naive Bayes classifiers 16: 539
11. Laskov P, Gehl C, Krüger S, Müller K-R (2006) Incremental support vector learning: analysis, implementation and applications. J Mach Learn Res 7: 1909–1936
12. Syed NA, Liu H, Huan S, Kah L, Sung K (1999) Handling concept drifts in incremental learning with support vector machines, pp 317–321
13. Fung G, Mangasarian OL (2002) Incremental support vector machine classification, pp 247–260
14. Zheng J, Yu H, Shen F, Zhao J (2010) An online incremental learning support vector machine for large-scale data. In: Artificial neural networks–ICANN, pp 76–81
15. Ruping S (2001) Incremental learning with support vector machines, pp 641–642
16. Xiao R, Wang J, Zhang F (2000) An approach to incremental SVM learning algorithm, pp 268–273
17. Tseng C-Y, Chen M-S (2009) Incremental SVM model for spam detection on dynamic email social networks 4: 128–135
18. Cauwenberghs G, Poggio T (2001) Incremental and decremental support vector machine learning. Advances in neural information processing systems: 409–415
19. Street WN, Kim Y A Streaming Ensemble Algorithm (SEA) for large-scale classification
20. Kolter JZ, Maloof MA (2003) Dynamic weighted majority: a new ensemble method for tracking concept drift, pp 123–130
21. Yeon K, Song MS, Kim Y, Choi H, Park C (2010) Model averaging via penalized regression for tracking concept drift. J Comput Graph Stat 19(2)
22. Wang H, Fan W, Yu PS, Han J (2003) Mining concept-drifting data streams using ensemble classifiers, pp 226–235
23. Zhang P, Zhu X, Shi Y (2008) Categorizing and mining concept drifting data streams, pp 812–820
24. Fan W, Chu F, Wang H, Yu PS (2002) Pruning and dynamic scheduling of cost-sensitive ensembles, pp 146–151. Menlo Park, CA; Cambridge, MA; London; AAAI Press; MIT Press, 1999
25. Fan W Systematic data selection to mine concept-drifting data streams
26. Zhao Q-L, Jiang Y-H, Xu M (2009) A fast ensemble pruning algorithm based on pattern mining process. Data Min Knowl Discov 19(2): 277–292
27. Lu Z, Wu X, Zhu X, Bongard J Ensemble pruning via individual contribution ordering
28. Kuncheva LI (2004) Classifier ensembles for changing environments. In: Multiple classifier systems, pp 1–15
29. Zhang P, Zhu X, Tan J, Guo L (2010) Classifier and cluster ensembles for mining concept drifting data streams, pp 1175–1180
30. Minku LL, White AP, Yao X (2010) The impact of diversity on online ensemble learning in the presence of concept drift. IEEE Trans Knowl Data Eng 5: 730–742

11

Paradigm Shift in Big Data SuperComputing: DataFlow vs. ControlFlow

Nemanja Trifunovic[1*], Veljko Milutinovic[1], Jakob Salom[2] and Anton Kos[3]

* Correspondence:
nemanja@maxeler.com
[1]School of Electrical Engineering,
University of Belgrade, Belgrade,
Serbia
Full list of author information is
available at the end of the article

Abstract

The paper discusses the shift in the computing paradigm and the programming model for Big Data problems and applications. We compare DataFlow and ControlFlow programming models through their quantity and quality aspects. Big Data problems and applications that are suitable for implementation on DataFlow computers should not be measured using the same measures as ControlFlow computers. We propose a new methodology for benchmarking, which takes into account not only the execution time, but also the power and space, needed to complete the task. Recent research shows that if the TOP500 ranking was based on the new performance measures, DataFlow machines would outperform ControlFlow machines. To support the above claims, we present eight recent implementations of various algorithms using the DataFlow paradigm, which show considerable speed-ups, power reductions and space savings over their implementation using the ControlFlow paradigm.

Introduction

Big Data is becoming a reality in more and more research areas every year. Also, Big Data applications are becoming more *visible* as they are slowly entering areas concerning the general public. In other words, Big Data applications that were up to now present mainly in the highly specialized areas of research, like geophysics [1,2] and financial engineering [3], are making its way into more general areas, like medicine and pharmacy [4], biology, aviation [5], politics, acoustics [6], etc.

In the last years the ratio of data volume increase is higher than the ratio of processing power increase. With the growing adoption of data-collecting technologies, like sensor networks, Internet of Things, and others, the data volume growth ratio is expected to continue to increase.

Among others, one important question arises: how do we process such quantities of data. One possible answer lies is in the shift of the computing paradigm and the programming model. With Big Data problems, it is many times more reasonable to concentrate on data rather than on the process. This can be achieved by employing DataFlow computing paradigm, programming model, and computers.

Background and literature review

The strength of DataFlow, compared to ControlFlow computers is in the fact that they accelerate the data flows and application loops from 10× to 1000×. How many orders of magnitude depends on the amount of data reusability within the loops. This feature is enabled by compiling down to levels much below the machine code, which brings important additional effects: much lower execution time, equipment size, and power dissipation.

The above strengths can prove especially important in Big Data applications that can benefit from one or more of the DataFlow advantages. For instance:

- A daily periodic Big Data application, which would not finish in time, if executed on a ControlFlow computer, executes in time on a DataFlow computer of the same equipment size and power dissipation,
- A Big Data application with limited space and/or power resources (remote locations such as ships, research stations, etc.) executes in a reasonable amount of time,
- With Big Data applications, where execution time is not a prime concern, DataFlow computers can save space and energy.

The previous paper [7] argues that time has come to redefine *TOP500* benchmarking. Concrete measurement data from real applications in geophysics [1,2], financial engineering [3], and some other research fields [8,9,10-12], shows that a DataFlow machine (for example, the Maxeler MAX series) rates better than a ControlFlow machine (for example, Cray Titan), if a different benchmark is used (e.g., a Big Data benchmark), as well as a different ranking methodology (e.g., the benchmark execution time multiplied by the number of 1U boxes needed to accomplish the given execution time - 1U box represents one rack unit or equivalent - it is assumed, no matter what technology is inside, the 1U box always has the same size and always uses the same power).

In reaction to the previous paper [7], scientific community insists that more light is shed on two issues: (a) Programming paradigm and (b) Benchmarking methodology. Consequently the stress of this viewpoint is on these two issues.

Discussion

What is the fastest, the least complex, and the least power consuming way to do (Big Data) computing?

Answer: Rather than writing one program to control the flow of data through the computer, one has to write a program to configure the hardware of the computer, so that input data, when it arrives, can flow through the computer hardware in only one way - the way how the computer hardware has been configured. This is best achieved if the serial part of the application (the transactions) continues to run on the ControlFlow host and the parallel part of the application is migrated into a DataFlow accelerator. A DataFlow part of the application does (parallel) Big Data crunching and execution of loops.

The early works of Dennis [13] and Arvind [14] could prove the concept, but could not result in commercial successes for three reasons: (a) Reconfigurable hardware technology was not yet ready. Contemporary ASIC was fast enough but not reconfigurable, while reconfigurable FPGA was nonexistent; (b) System software technology was not yet ready. Methodologies for fast creation of system software did exist, but effective tools for large scale efforts of this sort did not; and (c) Applications of those days were not of the Big Data type, so the streaming capabilities of the DataFlow computing model could not generate performance superiority. Recent measurements show, that, currently, Maxeler can move internally over 1 TB of data per second [15].

Programming model

Each programming model is characterized with its quantity and quality. The quantity and quality aspects of the Maxeler DataFlow model, as one of the currently best evaluated, are explained in the next two paragraphs, based on Figure 1. Other DataFlow programming initiatives exist [16] that follow similar approaches as Maxeler systems. To the best of our knowledge Maxeler is the leading player on the field and employs the most advanced and flexible model. For that reason we are using the Maxeler system platform for the presentation of the DataFlow programming model (one of many possible).

Quantitatively speaking, the complexity of DataFlow programming, in the case of Maxeler, is equal to $2n + 3$, where n refers to the number of loops migrated from the ControlFlow host to the DataFlow accelerator. This means, the following programs have to be written:

- One kernel program per loop, to map the loop onto the DataFlow hardware;
- One kernel test program per loop, to test the above;
- One manager program (no matter how many kernels there are) to move data:
  (1) Into the DataFlow accelerator,
  (2) In between the kernels (if more than one kernel exists), and

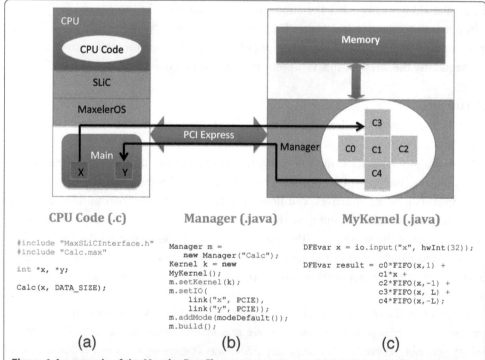

Figure 1 An example of the Maxeler DataFlow programming model: (a) Host code, (b) Manager code, and (c) Kernel code (a single kernel case): 2D convolution. Legend: SLiC = Compiler support for selected domain specific languages and customer applications. DFEvar = keyword used for defining the variables that internally flow through the configured hardware (in contrast to standard Java variables used to instruct the compiler). FIFO = First In First Out.

(3) Out of the DataFlow accelerator;
- One simulation builder program, to test code without the time consuming migration into the binary level;
- One hardware builder program, to exploit the code on the binary level.

In addition, in the host program (initially written in Fortran, Hadoop, MapReduce, MathLab, Matematika, C++, or C), instead of each migrated loop, one has to include a streaming construct (send data + receive results), represented by automatically generated C function Calc(x, DATA_SIZE, see Figure 1 (a).

Qualitatively speaking, the above quantity (2n + 3) is not any more difficult to realize because of the existence of a DSL (domain specific language) like MaxJ (an extension of standard Java with over 100 new functionalities). Figure 2 shows how a complex Big Data processing problem can be realized in MaxJ code. Note that the programming model implies the need for existence of two types of variables: (a) Standard Java variables, to control compile time activities, and (b) DFE (DataFlow Engine) variables, which actually flow through configured hardware (denoted with the DFE prefix in the examples of figures 1 and 2). The programming of the DataFlow part of the code is largely facilitated through the use of appropriate Java extensions.

Research design and methodology

Bare speed is definitely neither the only issue of importance nor the most crucial one [17]. Consequently, the TOP500 ranking should not concentrate on only one issue of importance, no matter if it is speed, power dissipation, or size (the size includes hardware complexity in the widest sense); it should concentrate on all three issues together, at the same time.

In this paper we argue that the best methodology for TOP500 benchmarking should be based on the holistic performance measure H ($T_{BigData}$, N_{1U}) defined as the number of 1U boxes (N_{1U} = one rack units or equivalent) needed to accomplish the desired execution time using a given Big Data benchmark. Instead of using theoretical measures of size and volume, we have opted in this paper for a more practical measure, which is related to international standardization efforts: The size of a 1U box. Issues like power dissipation (monthly electricity bill), and the physical size of the equipment

HostCode (.c)	FDKernel (.java)

```
for(t = 1; t < tmax; t++) {
  // Set-up timestep
  if(t < tsrc) {
    source = generate.soruce.wavelet(t);
    maxlib.stream.region_from_host(
              maxlib, "source", source
              srcx, srcy, srcz,
              srcx+1, srcy+1, srcz+1);
  }
  maxlib.stream_from_dram(maxlib, "curr",
curr_ptr);
  maxlib.stream_from_dram(maxlib, "prev",
prev_ptr);
  maxlib.stream_earthmodel_from_dram(maxlib,
dvv_array);

  maxlib.stream_to_dram(maxlib, "next", next_ptr);

  maxlib_run(maxlib); // Execute timestep

  swap_buffers(prev_ptr, curr_ptr, next_ptr);
}
```

```
public class IsotropicModelingKernel extends FDKernel {
  public IsotropicModelingKernel(FDKernelParameters p) {
    super(p);
    Stencil stencil =
      fixedStencil(-6, 6, coeffs, 1/8.0);
    DFEVar curr = io.wavefieldInput("curr", 1.0, 6);
    DFEVar prev = io.wavefieldInput("curr", 1.0, 0);
    DFEVar dvv = io.earthModelInput("dvv", 9.0, 0);
    DFEVar source = io.hostInput("source", 1.0n 0);

    DFEVar I =
      convolve(curr, ConvolveAxes.XYZ.stencil);

    DFEVar next = curr*2 - prev + dvv + I + source;

    io.wavefieldOutput("next", next);
  }
}
```

Figure 2 An example of the Host and Kernel code.

(the assumption here is that the equipment size is proportional to the hardware complexity, and to the hardware production cost) are implicitly covered by H ($T_{BigData}$, N_{1U}) (every 1U box has limited power dissipation and size). Selection of the performance measure H is coherent with the TPA concept introduced in [18] and described in Figure 3.

Note that the hardware design cost is not encompassed by the parameter A, which encompasses only the hardware production cost, and causes that the above defined H formula represents an upper bound for ControlFlow machines and a lower bound for DataFlow machines. This is due to the fact that ControlFlow machines are built using the Von Neumann logic, which is complex to design (execution control unit, cash control mechanism, prediction mechanisms, etc.), while the DataFlow machines are built using the FPGA logic, which is simple to design; mostly because the level of design repetitiveness is extremely high, etc. The latter is beneficiary for many Big Data problems, where a large amount of data is continuously processed through the use of relatively simple operations.

As indicated in the previous paper [7], the performance measure H puts PetaFlops out of date, and brings PetaData into the focus. Consequently, if the TOP500 ranking was based on the performance measure H, DataFlow machines would outperform ControlFlow machines. This statement is backed up with performance data presented in the next section.

Results

A survey of recent implementations of various algorithms using the DataFlow paradigm can be found in [19]. Future trends in the development of the DataFlow paradigm can be found in [20]. For comparison purposes, future trends in the ControlFlow paradigm can be found in [21].

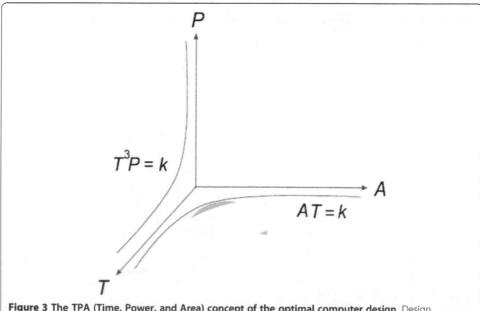

Figure 3 The TPA (Time, Power, and Area) concept of the optimal computer design. Design optimizations have to optimize the three essential issues jointly: T = Time, P = Power, and A = Area (complexity of a VLSI chip).

Some of recent implementations of various DataFlow algorithms interesting within the context of the performance measure H are summarized below.

(1) Lindtjorn et al. [1], proved: (T) That one DataFlow node has the performance equivalent to about 70 twin server Nehelem CPU machines and to 14 two card Tesla GPU machines (application: Schlumberger, GeoPhysics), (P) Using a 150 MHz FPGAs, and (A) Packaged as 1U.

The algorithm involved was Reverse Time Migration (RTM).

Starting from Acoustic wave equation:

$$\frac{\partial^2 u}{\partial t^2} = v^2 \left(\frac{\partial^2 u}{\partial x^2} + \frac{\partial^2 u}{\partial y^2} + \frac{\partial^2 u}{\partial z^2} \right)$$

where u is acoustic pressure and v is velocity.

(2) Oriato et al. [2], proved: (T) That two DataFlow nodes have the performance equivalent to more than 1,900 3 GHz X86 CPU cores (application: ENI, The velocity-stress form of the elastic wave equation), (P) Using sixteen 150 MHz FPGAs, and (A) Packaged as 2U.

The algorithm involved (3D Finite Difference) was:

$$\frac{\partial v\left(\vec{X}, t\right)}{\partial t} - b\left(\vec{X}\right) \frac{\partial \sigma ij\left(\vec{X}, t\right)}{\partial X_j} = b\left(\vec{X}\right) \left[f_i\left(\vec{X}, t\right) + \frac{\partial m_{ij}^a\left(\vec{X}, t\right)}{\partial X_j} \right],$$

$$\frac{\partial \sigma ij\left(\vec{X}, t\right)}{\partial t} - \lambda\left(\vec{X}\right) \frac{\partial v_k\left(\vec{X}, t\right)}{\partial X_k} \delta_{ij} - \mu\left(\vec{X}\right) \left[\frac{\partial vi\left(\vec{X}, t\right)}{\partial Xj} + \frac{\partial v_j\left(\vec{X}, t\right)}{\partial X_i} \right] = \frac{\partial m_{ij}^s\left(\vec{X}, t\right)}{\partial t}.$$

where λ and μ are the so-called Lamé parameters describing the elastic properties of the medium, σ is the stress and f is the source function (driving force).

(3) Mencer et al. [8] proved: (T) That one DataFlow node has the performance equivalent to more than 382 Intel Xeon 2.7 GHz CPU cores (application: ENI, CRS 4 Lab, Meteorological Modelling), (P) Using a 150 MHz FPGAs, and (A) Packaged as 1U.

The algorithm involved (Continuity (1) and (2) and thermal energy (3) equations) was:

$$\frac{\partial p_s}{\partial t} = \int_0^1 \nabla \cdot \left(\vec{V_h} \frac{\partial p}{\partial \sigma} \right) d\sigma \tag{1}$$

$$\frac{\partial q}{\partial t} = -\frac{u}{ah_x} \frac{\partial q}{\partial \lambda} \frac{v}{a} \frac{\partial q}{\partial \phi} - \sigma \frac{\partial q}{\partial \sigma} + F_q \tag{2}$$

$$\frac{\partial \theta}{\partial t} = -\frac{u}{ah_x} \frac{\partial \theta}{\partial \phi} - \sigma \frac{\partial \theta}{\partial \sigma} + F_\theta \tag{3}$$

Where $\vec{V_h}$ is the horizontal wind in vector form, for which Cartesian components are u and v, terms F_u, F_v, F_q and F_θ represent contributions to the tendencies from the parameterization of physical processes such as radiation, convection, dry adiabatic adjustments, surface friction, soil water and energy balance, large scale precipitation and evaporation. The PE describes the time evolution for the five prognostic variables u, v, p_s, q and θ.

(4) Stojanović et al. [9] proved: (T) That one DataFlow node has the performance of about 10 i7 CPU cores, (P) Power reduction of about 17, and (A) Packaged as 1U. The algorithm involved (Gross Pitaevskii equation) was:

$$ih\frac{\partial}{\partial t}\Phi(\mathrm{r},t) = \left(-\frac{h^2\nabla^2}{2m} + V\,ext(\mathrm{r}) + g|\Phi(\mathrm{r},t)|^2\right)\Phi(\mathrm{r},t)$$

where m is the mass of the boson, r is the coordinate of the boson, V_{ext} is the external potential, g is coupling constant and Φ is wave function.

(5) Chow et al. [3] proved: (T) That one DataFlow node has the performance of about 163 quad core CPUs, (P) Power reduction of about 170, and (A) Packaged as 1U. The algorithm involved (Monte Carlo simulation) was:

$$I\approx\langle f\,H\rangle N = \frac{1}{N}\sum_{i=1}^{N}\left(\overrightarrow{x_i}\right)$$

where $\rightarrow x_i$ is the input vector, N is the number of sample points, I is approximated expected value, and $\langle fH\rangle N$ is the sampled mean value of the quantity.

(6) Arram et al. [10] proved: (T) That one DataFlow node has the performance of about 13 Intel X5650 20 core CPUs and about 4 NVDIA GTX 580 GPU machine, (P) Using one 150 MHz FPGAs, and (A) Packaged as 1U.

The algorithm involved (Genetic Sequence Alignment) was based on FM-index. This index combines the properties of suffix array (SA) with the Burrows-Wheeler transform (BWT).

SA interval is updated for each character in pattern Q, moving from the last character to the first:

$$k_{new} = c(\chi) + s(\chi, k_{current}-1)$$

$$l_{new} = c(\chi) + s(\chi, l_{current}-1)$$

where pointers k and l are respectively the smallest and largest indices in the SA which starts with Q, $c(x)$ (frequency) is the number of symbols in the BWT sequence that are lexicographically smaller than x and $s(x, i)$ (occurrence) is the number of occurrences of the symbol x in the BWT sequence from the 0th position to the ith position.

(7) Guo et al. [11] proved: (T) That one DataFlow node has the performance of about 517 Intel i3 2.93 GHz CPU cores and of about 28 GPU machines, (P) Using one 150 MHz FPGA, and (A) Packaged as 1U. The algorithm involved (Gaussian Mixture Models) was:

$$p(\mathrm{X}|\lambda) = \sum_{i=1}^{M} w_i g\left(\mathrm{X}|\mu i, \sum_i\right)$$

where x is a d-dimensional continuous-valued data vector (i.e. measurement or features), w_i, i = 1, ..., M, are the mixture weights, and $g(x|\breve{e}_i, \acute{O}_i)$, i = 1, ..., M, are the component Gaussian densities.

(8) Kos et al. [12] proved: (T) That one DataFlow node has the performance of between 100 and 400 Intel Core2 Quad 2.66 GHz CPU cores, (P) using one 200 MHz FPGA, and (A) Packaged as 1U.

The algorithm involved was network sorting. An example of the simple sorting network is given in the Figure 4.

Size of the sorting network, the number of comparators needed, to sort N numbers is:

$$S = \frac{N \cdot \log_2 N \cdot (\log_2 N + 1)}{}$$

The achieved speed-up depended on N and the bit-size of numbers being sorted (between 8 and 64 bits).

Conclusion

The viewpoint presented in this paper sheds more light on the recent development of the DataFlow computing concept (more details can be found in [20-22]). The DataFlow computing paradigm requires new ways of thinking and new ways of programming. In general it redefines the subordination of program and data; instead of writing a program that controls how the data flows, the data flow defines the way a program is written.

DataFlow computing excells with applications which are having high repetettivenes of operation and some level of data reusability within the operations. The latter is particularly beneficiarry for many BigData problems, where a large amount of data is repetetively processed through the use of relatively simple operations.

The newly presented benchmarking methodology performance measure H (defined as the number of 1U boxes needed to accomplish the desired execution time using a given Big Data benchmark), would considerably reorder the TOP500 list. If the TOP500 ranking was based on the performance measure H, DataFlow machines would outperform ControlFlow machines. This statement is backed up with the presented performance results. The results show that when using DataFlow computers, instead od ControlFlow computers, time, energy, and/or space can be saved.

The above can be of great interest to those who have to make decisions about future developments of their Big Data centers. It also opens up a new important problem: The need for a development of a public cloud of ready-to-use Big Data applications.

The only remaining question is: can a Big Data application be broken in to a set of tasks and operations that are easily mappable into a DataFlow execution graph for a FPGA structure? We argue that for most Big Data applications the answer is positive!

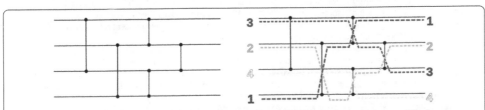

Figure 4 An example of a simple sorting network for sorting four input values with five comparators. Each comparator connects two wires and emits higher value to the bottom wire and lower value to the top wire. Two comparators on the left and two comparators in the middle can work in parallel. Parallel operation of this sorting network sorts the input numbers in three steps.

Comment

This paper was prepared in response to over 100 e-mail messages with questions from the CACM readership inspired by our previous CACM contribution [7].

Competing interests

The authors declare that they have no competing interests.

Authors' contributions

NT, VM, JS, and AK proposed a new methodology for benchmarking Big Data applications, which takes into account not only the execution time, but also the power and space, needed to complete the task. All authors read and approved the final manuscript.

Author details

[1]School of Electrical Engineering, University of Belgrade, Belgrade, Serbia. [2]Mathematical Institute of the Serbian Academy of Sciences and Arts, Belgrade, Serbia. [3]School of Electrical Engineering, University of Ljubljana, Ljubljana, Slovenia.

References

1. Flynn M, Mencer O, Milutinovic V, Rakocevic G, Stenstrom P, Trobec R, Valero M (2013) Moving from petaflops to petadata. In: Communications of the ACM, vol 5, 56th edn. ACM, New York, NY, USA, pp 39–42
2. Dennis J, Misunas D, 'A Preliminary Architecture for a Basic Data-Flow Processor', Proceedings of the ISCA '75 the 2nd Annual Symposium on Computer Architecture, ACM, New York, NY, USA, 1975, pp. 126–132
3. Agerwala T (1982) Arvind, –., "data flow systems: guest Editors' introduction", *IEEE*. Computer 15(2):10–13
4. Mencer O, "Multiscale Dataflow Computing", Proceedings of the Final Conference Supercomputacion y eCiencia, Barcelona Supercomputing Center, SyeC, Barcelona, Catalonia, Spain, May 27 - May 28, 2013
5. Resch M, "Future Strategies for Supercomputing", Proceedings of the Final Conference Supercomputacion y eCiencia, Barcelona Supercomputing Center, SyeC, Barcelona, Catalonia, Spain, May 27 - May 28, 2013
6. Flynn M, "Area - Time - Power and Design Effort: The Basic Tradeoffs in Application Specific Systems", Proceedings of the 2005 IEEE International Conference on Application-Specific Systems and Architecture Processors (ASAP'05), Samos, Greece, July 23-July 25, 2005
7. Salom J, Fujii H, "Overview of Acceleration Results of Maxeler FPGA Machines", IPSI Transactions on Internet Research, July 2013, Volume 5, Number 1, pp. 1–4
8. Maxeler Technologies FrontPage, http://www.maxeler.com/content/frontpage/, London, UK, October 20, 2011.
9. Patt Y (2009) Future microprocessors: what must We do differently if We Are to effectively utilize multi-core and many-core chips? IPSI Transactions on Internet Res 5(1):1–9
10. Lindtjorn O, Clapp G, Pell O, Mencer O, Flynn M, Fu H, "Beyond Traditional Microprocessors for Geoscience High-Performance Computing Applications,"IEEE Micro, Washington, USA, March/April 2011, Vol. 31, No. 2, pp. 1–9
11. Oriato D, Pell O, Andreoletti C, Bienati N, FD Modeling Beyond 70 Hz with FPGA Acceleration, "Maxeler Summary, http://www.maxeler.com/media/documents/MaxelerSummaryFDModelingBeyond70Hz.pdf, Summary of a talk presented at the SEG 2010 HPC Workshop, Denver, Colorado, USA, October 2010
12. Mencer O, "Acceleration of a Meteorological Limited Area Model with Dataflow Engines", Proceedings of the Final Conference Supercomputacion y eCiencia, Barcelona Supercomputing Center, SyeC, Barcelona, Catalonia, Spain, May 27 - May 28, 2013
13. Stojanovic S et al., "One Implementation of the Gross Pitaevskii Algorithm", Proceedings of Maxeler@SANU, MISANU, Belgrade, Serbia, April 8, 2013
14. Chow G C T, Tse A H T, Jin O, Luk W, Leong P H W, Thomas D B, "A Mixed Precision Monte Carlo Methodology for Reconfigurable Accelerator Systems", Proceedings of ACM/SIGDA International Symposium on Field Programmable Gate Arrays (FPGA), ACM, Monterey, CA, USA, February 2012, pp. 57–66
15. Arram J, Tsoi K H, Luk W, Jiang P, "Hardware Acceleration of Genetic Sequence Alignment", Proceedings of 9th International Symposium ARC 2013, ACM, Los Angeles, CA, USA, March 25–27, 2013. pp. 13–24
16. Guo C, Fu H, Luk W, "A Fully-Pipelined Expectation-Maximization Engine for Gaussian Mixture Models", Proceedings of 2012 International Conference on Field-Programmable Technology (FPT), Seoul, S. Korea, 10–12 Dec. 2012, pp. 182 – 189
17. Kos A, Ranković V, Tomažič S, "Sorting Networks on the Maxeler Data Flow Super Computing Systems", Advances in Computers, Elsevier, 225 Wyman Street, Waltham, MA 02451, USA, 2014
18. Flynn M, Mencer O, Greenspon I, Milutinovic V, Stojanovic S, Sustran Z, "The Current Challenges in DataFlow Supercomputer Programming", Proceedings of ISCA 2013, ACM, Tell Aviv, Israel, June 2013
19. Seebode C, Ort M, Regenbrecht C, Peuker M (2013) BIG DATA infrastructures for pharmaceutical research. IEEE International Conference on Big Data, California
20. Ayhan S, Pesce J, Comitz P, Sweet D, Bliesner S, Gerberick G, "Predictive analytics with aviation big data", Integrated Communications, Navigation and Surveillance ICNS Conference, 2013, Edinburgh, UK
21. Jinglan Zhang, Kai Huang, Cottman-Fields M, Truskinger A, Roe P, Shufei Duan, Xueyan Dong, Towsey M, Wimmer J, "Managing and Analysing Big Audio Data for Environmental Monitoring", IEEE 16th International Conference on Computational Science and Engineering CSE Conference, 2013, Sydney, Australia
22. Convey Computer Web Page: http://www.conveycomputer.com/technology/, October 31 2014

12

A review of data mining using big data in health informatics

Matthew Herland, Taghi M Khoshgoftaar and Randall Wald[*]

*Correspondence: rwald1@fau.edu
Florida Atlantic University, 777
Glades Road, Boca Raton, FL, USA

Abstract

The amount of data produced within Health Informatics has grown to be quite vast, and analysis of this Big Data grants potentially limitless possibilities for knowledge to be gained. In addition, this information can improve the quality of healthcare offered to patients. However, there are a number of issues that arise when dealing with these vast quantities of data, especially how to analyze this data in a reliable manner. The basic goal of Health Informatics is to take in real world medical data from all levels of human existence to help advance our understanding of medicine and medical practice. This paper will present recent research using Big Data tools and approaches for the analysis of Health Informatics data gathered at multiple levels, including the molecular, tissue, patient, and population levels. In addition to gathering data at multiple levels, multiple levels of questions are addressed: human-scale biology, clinical-scale, and epidemic-scale. We will also analyze and examine possible future work for each of these areas, as well as how combining data from each level may provide the most promising approach to gain the most knowledge in Health Informatics.

Keywords: Big data; Health informatics; Bioinformatics; Neuroinformatics; Clinical informatics; Public health informatics; Social media

Introduction

The field of Health Informatics is on the cusp of its most exciting period to date, entering a new era where technology is starting to handle Big Data, bringing about unlimited potential for information growth. Data mining and Big Data analytics are helping to realize the goals of diagnosing, treating, helping, and healing all patients in need of healthcare, with the end goal of this domain being improved Health Care Output (HCO), or the quality of care that healthcare can provide to end users (i.e. patients).

Health Informatics is a combination of information science and computer science within the realm of healthcare. There are numerous current areas of research within the field of Health Informatics, including Bioinformatics, Image Informatics (e.g. Neuroinformatics), Clinical Informatics, Public Health Informatics, and also Translational BioInformatics (TBI). Research done in Health Informatics (as in all its subfields) can range from data acquisition, retrieval, storage, analytics employing data mining techniques, and so on. However, the scope of this study will be research that uses data mining in order to answer questions throughout the various levels of health.

Each of the studies done in a particular subfield of Health Informatics utilizes data from a particular level of human existence [1]: Bioinformatics uses molecular level data,

Neuroinformatics employs tissue level data, Clinical Informatics applies patient level data, and Public Health Informatics utilizes population data (either from the population or on the population). These subfields do sometimes overlap (for example, a single study might consider data from two adjacent levels), but in the interest of minimizing confusion we in this work will classify a study based on the highest data level used (as this paper will be structured according to data usage). In addition, within a given data level we will break down studies based on the type (i.e., level) of question a study attempts to answer, where each question level is of a relatively comparable scope to one of the data levels. The tissue level is of analogous scope to the human-scale biology questions, the scope of patient data is related to clinical questions and the scope of the population data is comparable to the epidemic-level questions.

The scope of data used by the subfield TBI, on the other hand, exploits data from each of these levels, from the molecular level to entire populations [1]. In particular, TBI is specifically focused on integrating data from the Bioinformatics level with the higher levels, because traditionally this level has been isolated in the laboratory and separated from the more patient-facing levels (Neuroinformatics, Clinical Informatics, and Population Informatics). TBI and the idea of combining data from all levels of human existence is a popular new direction in Health Informatics. The main level of questions that TBI ultimately tries to answer are on the clinical level, as such answers can help improve HCO for patients. Research throughout all levels of accessible data, using various data mining and analytical techniques, can be used to help the healthcare system make decisions faster, more accurately, and more efficiently, all in a more cost-effective manner than without using such methods.

This paper is organized as follows: Section "Big data in health informatics" provides a general background on Big Data in Health Informatics. Section "Levels of health informatics data" delineates and discusses the subfields: Bioinformatics, Neuroinformatics, Clinical Informatics, and Public Health Informatics, as well as discussing their corresponding data and question levels (used to structure Sections "1" through 1). Section "Using micro level data – Molecules" looks at studies using data from the micro (molecular) level while the studies in Section "Using tissue level data" use data from the tissue level, Section "Using patient level data" covers research being done on the patient level, and the research efforts in Section "Using population level data – Social media" employ data gathered at the population level. The sub-field of TBI is discussed in Section "Translational bioinformatics". Section "Analysis and future works" analyzes the works shown and discusses both possible future work and the possible directions each line of research could take. Section "Conclusion" contains our conclusion.

Big data in health informatics

The term Big Data is a vague term with a definition that is not universally agreed upon. According to [2], a rough definition would be any data that is around a petabyte (10^{15} bytes) or more in size. In Health Informatics research though, Big Data of this size is quite rare; therefore, a more encompassing definition will be used here to incorporate more studies, specifically a definition by Demchenko et al. [3] who define Big Data by five V's: Volume, Velocity, Variety, Veracity, and Value. Volume pertains to vast amounts of data, Velocity applies to the high pace at which new data is generated, Variety pertains to the level of complexity of the data, Veracity measures the genuineness of the data, and Value evaluates how good the quality of the data is in reference to the intended results.

Data gathered for Health Informatics research does exhibit many of these qualities. Big Volume comes from large amounts of records stored for patients: for example, in some datasets each instance is quite large (e.g. datasets using MRI images or gene microarrays for each patient), while others have a large pool with which to gather data (such as social media data gathered from a population). Big Velocity occurs when new data is coming in at high speeds, which can be seen when trying to monitor real-time events whether that be monitoring a patient's current condition through medical sensors or attempting to track an epidemic through multitudes of incoming web posts (such as from Twitter). Big Variety pertains to datasets with a large amount of varying types of independent attributes, datasets that are gathered from many sources (e.g. search query data comes from many different age groups that use a search engine), or any dataset that is complex and thus needs to be seen at many levels of data throughout Health Informatics. High Veracity of data in Health Informatics, as in any field using analytics, is a concern when working with possibly noisy, incomplete, or erroneous data (as could be seen from faulty clinical sensors, gene microarrays, or from patient information stored in databases) where such data needs to be properly evaluated and dealt with. High Value of data is seen all throughout Health Informatics as the goal is to improve HCO. Although data gathered by traditional methods (such as in a clinical setting) is widely regarded as High Value, the value of data gathered by social media (data submitted by anyone) may be in question; however, as shown in Section "Using population level data – Social media", this can also have High Value.

It should be mentioned that not all the studies covered here or in the field of Health Informatics fit all 5 of the qualities in Demchenko et al.'s. definition of Big Data. Even so, many still impose significant computational constraints that need to be addressed in one way or another. Offline storage of datasets such as Electronic Health Records (EHR) can be difficult even if the data does not exhibit Big Velocity or Variety, and high-throughput processing seen in real-time continuous data requires capable and efficient techniques even when each individual data instance does not have Big Volume. Data that has Big Value without Big Veracity may need complex methods to find a consensus among various models, or which require time-consuming adjustments to the data which could expand the size of the dataset. Therefore, even datasets lacking Big Volume can still have Big Data problems, meaning that the Big Data definitions mainly focusing on Volume and Velocity may not be considering enough qualities of the dataset to fully characterize it.

It is noted in [4] and [5] that just in the United States, using data mining in Health Informatics can save the healthcare industry up to $450 billion each year. This is because the field of Health Informatics generates a large and growing amount of data. As of 2011, health care organizations had generated over 150 exabytes of data [4] (one exabyte is 1000 petabytes). This data needs to be sifted through and efficiently analyzed in order to be of any use to the health care system. As mentioned, health information can be stored in EHRs, which can store 44+ petabytes of patient data, which on top of this health data can come in many other forms. This explosion of data that is seen in Health Informatics has also been noticed in Bioinformatics as well, where genomic sequencing can generate many terabytes of data. With data coming from many different places and in many different forms, it is up to the Health Informatics community to find ways of dealing with all this data. It would seem that it is becoming more and more popular to integrate and combine different sources of data, even across different subfields (i.e. Translational Bioinformatics), and even across Health Informatics and Bioinformatics. Successful integration of this huge amount of data could lead to a huge improvement for the end users of the health care system, i.e. patients.

Levels of health informatics data

This section will be describing various subfields of Health Informatics: Bioinformatics, Neuroinformatics, Clinical Informatics, and Public Health Informatics. The lines between each subfield of Health Informatics can be blurred in terms of definition, confusing which subfield a study should fall under; therefore, this paper will be deciding subfield membership by the highest level of data used for research and will be the organizing factor for Sections "1" through 1 . The works from the subfield of Bioinformatics discussed in this study consist of research done with molecular data (Section "Using micro level data – Molecules"), Neuroinformatics is a form of Medical Image Informatics which uses image data of the brain, and thus it falls under tissue data (Section "Using tissue level data"), Clinical Informatics here uses patient data (Section "Using patient level data"), and Public Health Informatics makes use of data either about the population or from the population (Section "Using population level data – Social media").

In Health Informatics research, there are two sets of levels which must be considered: the level from which the data is collected, and the level at which the research question is being posed. The four subfields discussed in this study correspond to the data levels, but the question level in a given work may be different from its data level. These question levels are of similar scope to the data levels: the tissue level data is of similar scope to human-scale biology questions, the patient level data is of comparable scope to clinical questions, and the population level data is of proportionate scope to epidemic-scale questions. Each section will be further sub-sectioned by question level starting with the lowest to the highest. Table 1 summarizes the breakdown of Sections "1" through "Using population level data – Social media" including the sections (by data levels used), subsections (by question level used), and the questions the studies discussed are attempting to answer.

Bioinformatics

Research in Bioinformatics may not be considered as part of traditional Health Informatics, but the research done in Bioinformatics is an important source of health information at various levels. Bioinformatics focuses on analytical research in order to learn how the human body works using molecular level data in addition to developing methods of effectively handling said data. The increasing amount of data here has greatly increased the importance of developing data mining and analysis techniques which are efficient, sensitive, and better able to handle Big Data.

Data in Bioinformatics, such as gene expression data, is continually growing (due to technology being able to generate more molecular data per individual), and is certainly classifiable as Big Volume. The issue of Big Volume within molecular data leads to research such as McDonald et al. [24] who created a Bioinformatics suite of software tools they call khmer. This suite seeks to solve hardware computational problems through software. The tools in this suite pre-process Big Volume genomic sequence data by breaking

Table 1 Summary of Studies Covered

Sections	Data level(s) used	Subsections	Question level(s) answered	Questions to be answered
Using Micro Level Data – Molecules	Molecular	Using Gene Expression Data to Make Clinical Predictions	Clinical	What sub-type of cancer does a patient have? [6] Will a patient have a relapse of cancer? [7]
	Tissue	Creating a Connectivity Map of the Brain Using Brain Images	Human-Scale Biology	Can a full connectivity map of the brain be made [8,9]?
Using Tissue Level Data	Patient	Using MRI Data for Clinical Prediction	Clinical	Do particular areas of the brain correlate to clinical events? [10] What level of Alzheimer's disease does a patient have? [11]
		Prediction of ICU Readmission and Mortality Rate	Clinical	Should a patient be released from the ICU, or would they benefit from a longer stay? [12-14] What is the 5 year expectancy of a patient over the age of 50? [15]
Using Patient Level Data	Patient	Real-Time Predictions Using Data Streams	Clinical	What ailment does a patient have (real-time prediction) [16,17] Is an infant experiencing a cardiorespiratory spell (real-time)? [18]
		Using Message Board Data to Help Patients Obtain Medical Information	Clinical	Can message post data be used for dispersing clinically reliable information? [19,20]
Using Population Level Data – Social Media	Population	Tracking Epidemics Using Search Query Data	Epidemic-Scale	Can search query data be used to accurately track epidemics throughout a population? [5,21]
		Tracking Epidemics Using Twitter Post Data	Epidemic-Scale	Can Twitter post data be used to accurately track epidemics throughout a population? [22,23]

up long sequences into relatively short strings which can be stored in a Bloom filter-based hash table, helping both the ability and efficiency of analysis of Bioinformatics data.

Neuroinformatics

Neuroinformatics research is a young subfield, as each data instance (such as MRIs) is quite large leading to datasets with Big Volume. Only recently can computational power keep up with the demands of such research. Neuroinformatics concentrates its research on analysis of brain image data (tissue level) in order to: learn how the brain works, find correlations between information gathered from brain images to medical events, etc., all with the goal of furthering medical knowledge at various levels. We chose the field of Neuroinformatics to represent the broader domain of Medical Image Informatics because by limiting the scope to brain images, more in-depth research may be performed while still gathering enough information to constitute Big Data. From this point on Neuroinformatics research using tissue level data will be referenced by data level rather than the subfield.

Clinical informatics

Clinical Informatics research involves making predictions that can help physicians make better, faster, more accurate decisions about their patients through analysis of patient data. Clinical questions are the most important question level in Health Informatics as it works directly with the patient. This is where a confusion can arise with the term "clinical" when found in research, as all Health Informatics research is performed with the eventual goal of predicting "clinical" events (directly or indirectly). This confusion is the reason for defining Clinical Informatics as only research which directly uses patient data. With this, data used by Clinical Informatics research has Big Value.

Even with all research eventually helping answer clinical realm events, according to Bennett et al. [25] there is about a 15±2 year gap between clinical research and the actual clinical care used in practice. Decisions these days are made mostly on general information that has worked before, or based on what experts have found to work in the past. Through all the research presented here as well as with all the research being done in Health Informatics, the healthcare system can embrace new ways that can be more accurate, reliable, and efficient.

Public health informatics – Social media

Public Health Informatics applies data mining and analytics to population data, in order to gain medical insight. Data in Public Health Informatics is from the population, gathered either from "traditional" means (experts or hospitals) or gathered from the population (social media). In either event, population data has Big Volume, along with Big Velocity and Big Variety. Data gathered from the population through social media could possibly have low Veracity leading to low Value, but techniques for extracting the useful information from social media (such as Twitter posts), this line of data can also have Big Value. cdot

Using micro level data – Molecules

The studies covered in this section use data gathered from the molecular level, and answer the clinical question of using gene expression data for prediction of clinical outcome. Molecule-level data frequently experiences the problem of "high dimensionality," where the data has a large number of independent attributes; this is because molecule-level data tends to have thousands (or tens of thousands) of possible molecules, configurations of molecules, or molecule-molecule interactions, and these are represented in datasets as features. This high dimensionality can stymie approaches which do not consider feature selection to address this form of Big Data. Although we only focus on one form of clinical question in this paper, other applications of micro-level data exist, such as cheminformatics [26], high-throughput screening [27], and DNA sequence analysis [28].

Using gene expression data for prediction of clinical outcome

As stated, the studies in this subsection use gene expression data to answer clinical questions. Two research efforts are reviewed in this subsection, both of which focus on cancer: the first uses gene expression profiling to categorize leukemia into two different subclasses, while the second study uses gene expression data to predict relapse among patients in the early stages of colorectal cancer (CRC). Both of these studies (as well as similar studies) can help physicians guide, advise and treat their cancer patients.

Haferlach et al. [6] formulated a gene expression profiling classifier to place patients into 18 different subclasses of either myeloid or lymphoid leukemia. This study used 3,334 patients where about two-thirds were used for training (2,143 patients) and the rest one-third for testing (1,191 patients), and from each patient 54,630 gene probe set samples were taken ($3,334 \times 54,630 \approx 182$ million). The authors chose to use an all-pairwise classification design using the trimmed mean of the difference between perfect match and mismatch intensities with quantile normalization, all to handle the multiclass nature of this research. This technique, called Difference of Quantile Normalized values (DQN), is explained in greater detail in [29] by Liu et al. There are 153 class pairs created due to there being 18 distinct classes ($(18 \times 17)/2 = 153$) where for each pair there will be a linear binary classifier created using Support Vector Machines (SVM) [30]. They tested their method on the training pool using 30-fold cross-validation, where each of the 30 runs used the top 100 probe sets with the highest t-statistic for each class pair. The results of this testing yielded a mean specificity of 99.7% and an accuracy of 92.2%.

The second part of their study was to get the results for the testing pool of patients where Haferlach et al. achieve a median specificity of 99.8% and a median sensitivity of 95.6% for the classification of 14 subclasses of acute leukemia where 6 are lymphoid and 8 are myeloid. The authors also claim that using their methods with microarray data, on 57% of the discrepant instances they were able to achieve better results than with routine diagnostic methods. This research has shown promise that using microarray gene expression data patients can be reliably classified into different forms of leukemia, yet this study could have done more by exploiting any number of feature selection techniques (or in this case gene probe selection). Using feature selection techniques in this study could also lead to determining which gene probes have a strong correlation between different forms of leukemia.

Salazar et al. [7] construct a gene expression classifier seeking to predict, within a five-year period, whether or not a patient will relapse back into having CRC. The authors gathered a total of 394 patients where 188 were used for training and 206 were used for validation. The training pool was accumulated over a 19 year period (1983-2002) from three different institutions from different counties, and the validation pool was assembled over 8 years (1996-2004) from another institution from a different country. They decided on a set of 33,834 gene probes that were found to have variation within the patients from the test group ($33,834 \times 188 \approx 6.4$ million not counting the probes that showed no correlation). The authors decided for feature selection (gene probe selection) to use a leave-one-out cross-validation method to determine which gene probes were strongly correlated with the 5-year distant metastasis-free survival (DMFS) with a t-test as the deciding factor. After this selection method they ended up with an optimal set of 18 gene probes.

For classification, Salazar et al. used a Nearest Centroid-Base Classifier (NCBC) named ColoPrint. A basic explanation of a centroid based classification system would be: when a new instance is ready to be classified it is assigned to the class consisting of the training samples whose average centroid is closest to the new instance. ColoPrint also incorporates feature reduction to alleviate the problem of high dimensionality, by using a predefined set of 18 genes which were previously found to be useful in identifying CRC. With Colo-Print, a patient can be classified as either low or high risk. The authors note that in a similar study (for breast cancer prognostic tests [31]) that centroid-based classifiers have shown to give reliable results. The authors compared ColoPrint to an assortment of clinical factors through multivariate analysis to see which could best predict Relapse Free Survival, and ColoPrint was found to be one of the most significant factors with a hazard ratio of 2.69 at a confidence interval of 95% and a P value of 0.003. The hazard ratio shows the proportion of relapse rates of predicted-relapse and predicted-RFS patients). Through this study, they were able to find which patients were having a generally higher probability of being marked for high risk than other patients (e.g. males are more often marked as high risk than females).

The approach the authors took by gathering data from different sources for the training set (giving variation to the learning) and even another source for validation (giving variation to the testing) is a notably good strategy and is a strategy future research should employ. One place variation could have been added, though, is using more probe selection techniques: this would help test if the ColoPrint feature subset was indeed "optimal", especially since there were 33,834 probes to start with.

Both of the studies discussed in this subsection are showing the usefulness of microarray gene expression data as they can be used for determining both: if a patient will relapse back into cancer as well as which subtype of cancer a patient has. The results of these research efforts lead to the idea that microarray data could give similar results if these procedures were applied to other types of cancers in order to help physicians both diagnose and begin to treat their patients.

Using tissue level data

All the studies covered in this section will cover data at the tissue level and venture to answer human-scale biology questions including: creating a full connectivity map of the brain, and predicting clinical outcomes by using MRI data. This level, which incorporates imaging data, brings in a number of additional Big Data challenges, such as feature extraction and managing complex images. Studies which combine imaging data with other data sources also exemplify the Variety aspect of Big Data, by building models which incorporate diverse data sources.

Creating a connectivity map of the brain using brain images

This subsection will be covering two studies with the goal of answering human-scale biology questions attempting to develop a comprehensive connectivity diagram of the human brain. A diagram such as this can provide many opportunities for health information gain for physicians for prognosis, diagnosis, treatments, etc. through the execution of analysis and novel data mining.

There is a huge and ongoing project called the Human Connectome Project (HCP) led by the WU-Minn HCP consortium where the goal is to eventually map the human brain by making a comprehensive connectivity diagram. According to [9] HCP is looking to find a map of the neural pathways that make up the brain in order to advance current knowledge of how the brain functions and behaves region-to-region. The project is broken into two phases: 1.) in the first 2 years (Fall 2010- Spring 2012), methods for data acquisition and analysis were improved, 2.) in the last 3 years (summer 2012-Summer 2015), these methods will be applied to 1200 healthy adults (between the ages of 22 and 35 from varying ethnic groups) using top of the line methods of noninvasive neuroimaging. The subjects used are twins and non-twin siblings in order to also determine variability and heritability factors in brain structure and connectivity throughout such cases. This project is a five year long project that was started in fall 2010 and should be finished in 2015. The HCP data generated is being made freely accessible to the public, and the first and second quarterly data are now available at: http://www.humanconnectome.org/ containing the data generated from a total of 148 of the 1200 participants (about 12% of the total). The data available includes image data (T1w and T2w MRI, rfMRI, tfMRI, dMRI) as well as behavioral measures for a current total of about 4.5 TB. Data will be further released at a quarterly rate with each quarter including about 100 new participants.

According to Van Essen et al. [9], the project looks very promising because new and extremely important information can be gleaned from mining the HCP data coming out from the HCP consortium's research. Creating a full connectivity map of the brain could lead to information that could help in determining the reasons why people have certain brain disorders at a level previously unattainable, giving physician a possibility for easier diagnosis, early detection of future illnesses or maybe even prevention of mental or physical ailments. Considering this data is only recently released, the research applying this data is all in the future, but with the technology being so advanced there is endless possibility for studies employing this data for heath information gain. Once all the data for the 1200 patients have been generated, there could be similar data created on patients with various ailments and various ages to find the differences between such brains through data mining and analysis.

Annese [8] develops a system to link MRI (primarily diffusion tensor imaging (DTI)) measurements to that of an actual brain sample gathered from histological methods (physical studying of tissue) arguing that it is not enough to just depend on neuroimaging for making a comprehensive connectivity map of brain connectivity, but should also include histological methods of studying of actual brain tissue. The author mentions that the difficulties of matching up MRI measurements with that of anatomical measurements is a considerable issue interfering with making a comprehensive connectivity model of the human brain. MRIs are large and have high resolution, a higher resolution then histological methods which give results that are neither the same size nor quality. Annese also comments that it would be highly beneficial to validate MRIs with studies of actual brain tissue. The study was carried out on one patient that had died at the age of 88, and as the patient had a pacemaker (which prevented the acquisition of MRI images while the patient was alive), all images of the brain were taken after death and compared to the histological study of the brain tissue using the author's method.

To ensure that the histological images match the Big Volume found in typical MRI images, Annese takes stained histological slices of the brain at 20x magnification, with a resolution of around 0.4 μm/pixel. This creates 334,500 × 266,200 images. In addition, multiple MRI images were taken of the brain *in situ* prior to the histological imaging. The author was able to show that MRIs (and DTIs in particular) do show tissue properties that can be correlated to stained tissue (histological images), making comparison possible. The author argues that histological comparison to MRIs can help validate MRIs, localize neuropathlogical phenomena that show as MRI abnormalities, and create the full connectivity map of the human brain. Data mining and analysis of both types of images in parallel could offer more gains than simply using MRI data alone, offering a much more powerful set of data.

As technology only recently could handle the endeavor of creating a full connectivity map of the brain this line of research is very new. The HCP is creating and releasing Big Volumes of data with various amounts of different MRIs and behavioral measurements data, allowing for more analysis and novel data mining to be executed. Along with the HCP, there is discussion and testing being conducted for comparing MRIs to histological data to help validate MRI data, to help create the connectivity map of the brain and offer more power to the datasets being created for novel data mining. The HCP could benefit from employing a comparison to histological image data.

Using MRI data for clinical prediction

This subsection will be covering two studies with the goal of answering clinical level questions. The first study uses both MRI data and a list of clinical features with the goal to find correlations between physical ailments to that of different locations of the brain. The second looks to take MRI data and determine the amount a patient has Alzheimer's disease. Research using MRIs can be beneficial to clinical diagnosis and predictions giving physicians another option with which to make decisions.

Yoshida et al. [10] propose a novel method combining patients' clinical features with that of MRI image intensities consisting of millions of voxels (an element of volume representing a point on a grid in three dimensional space). The method the authors create is based on the algorithm of radial basis function-sparse partial least squares (RBF-sPLS) giving their method an advantage over similar methods granting the ability to select not only clinical characteristics but also determine effective brain regions. This is to say that by creating sparse, linear combinations of explanatory variables, the developed approach concurrently performs feature selection and dimensionality reduction (that is, creating new, more condensed features). Simultaneously doing both of these tasks is problematic for other techniques especially for vast amounts of data, but employing RBF-sPLS allows the authors to manage large amount of data efficiently. Yoshida et al. do a comparison of their RBF-sPLS to that of the original sPLS on a simulated dataset, and demonstrate that their technique outperforms the original in terms of sensitivity, specificity and c-index scores. The simulated dataset does appear to be the only testing of the RBF-sPLS and even with the results garnered being quite promising this method should be tested on real-world data so that their results can be considered clinically significant.

They do present an example of their prospective method using a dataset of 102 chronic kidney patients with the goal of attempting to identify if any locations of the brain are correlated to patients with chronic kidney disease. For each of these 102 patients they gathered 73 clinical features and around 2.1 million voxels from the MRI data. Through experiments Yoshida et al. found that there is a strong correlation between clinical variables related to chronic kidney disease and the bilateral temporal lobe area of the brain. They also determined that the bilateral temporal lobes are closely related to aging and arterial stiffness, while the occipital lobes correspond to clinical markers for anemia. As this is only a preliminary study, further testing will be needed to confirm the accuracy of these results.

Estella et al. [11] introduce a method with the goal of predicting to what degree a patient has Alzheimer's disease with three levels of classification: completely healthy, Mild Cognitive Impairment (MCI), and already has Alzheimer's. They gathered around 240GB of brain image data for 1200 patients stored by the Alzheimer's Disease Neuroimaging Initiative (ADNI). There are a number of steps to their devised method, which include spatial normalization, extraction of features, feature selection and patient classification. After the feature extraction step, the authors found two different subgroups of features: morphological and mathematical where 332 and 108 were respectively gathered. Examples of features from the morphological subgroup are Area Centroid, Major Axis Length, Whole Matter Volumes, etc. Examples of features from the mathematical subgroup are Mean, Cosine Transform Coefficients, Euclidean distance, etc. The authors also decided to have a third group that consists of features from both subgroups and deemed this group as "mixed". For the feature selection step they used a method based on Mutual Information (MI) along with some influence from the minimal Redundancy-Maximal-Relevance criterion (mRMR). MI will assist in determining the dependence between two given variables while the mRMR looks to acquire applicable features correlated to the final prediction while simultaneously removing redundancies from the model.

Fuzzy Decision Tree (FDT) classifiers work best with Estella et al.'s feature extraction and feature selection combination, getting better results than other classifiers tested in terms of classifying efficiency (able to make reliable diagnosis on a minimal set of features). FDT is an extension to the traditional decisions with the additional ability to handle fuzzy data. The authors found that by using their method they were able to get a classifying efficiency of 0.94 when using 75% of the mixed feature subset and when only using 10% of the mixed features could still get a reliable efficiency of 0.75. Estella et al. conclude that using their method while using only a minimal number of both morphological and mathematical variables they can efficiently and reliably classify patients into three levels of Alzheimer using only MRI data. Even though this study compared various classification techniques there was only one feature selection technique tested; there could be other feature selection methods that could have worked better with the FDT or one of the other classification techniques tested.

The studies shown in this section using MRI data have shown that they can be useful in answering clinical questions as well as making clinical predictions. More research (on real world data) will be needed before the brain regions, determined by Yoshida et al. [10] to have correlation with kidney disease, anemia and aging, can be determined as clinically significant. In Estella et al. [11], various features extracted from MRIs were shown here to have the ability to classify patients into varying degrees of dementia. This process could eventually be improved upon with the goal of adding more classification levels for Alzheimer patients leading to such patients being detected both earlier and more efficiently. This is an interesting line of research that could be very beneficial if a physician could one day have methods that can look at MRIs of the brain and be able to determine whether a patient has kidney disease, more likely to have kidney disease, determining how far along a patient is down the road to dementia, etc. With the promising results shown in these studies, further research should extend these research efforts to see what other correlations between MRIs and other diseases can be discovered, giving physicians one more tool to diagnose and treat a patient earlier and more accurately.

Using patient level data

All the studies presented in this section will cover data at the patient level and venture to answer clinical level questions including: Prediction of ICU readmission, prediction of patient mortality rate (after ICU discharge and 5 years) and making clinical predictions using data streams. Due to this use of streaming data, ICU data exemplifies the Velocity aspect of Big Data, as well as Variety, as clinical information can contain many different types of features. As with the molecular-level data, feature selection can help choose the most important features, which also helps in making quicker clinical decisions.

Prediction of ICU readmission and mortality rate

The focus of the research covered in this subsection will be on predicting Intensive Care Unit (ICU) readmission, mortality rate after ICU discharge as well as predicting a 5 year life expectancy rate. The five year life expectancy rate will be looking to see how likely a patient will survive within a 5 year period. This is a useful line of research in that it can potentially help physicians know what to look for in their patients, determine which patients should have their ICU stay extended, and better tell which patients should receive particular treatments.

The study done by Campbell et al. [12] focuses on ICU patients that were discharged and expected to both live and not return too early afterwards. Their research used 4376 ICU (out of 6208 total) admissions from a database containing admissions from one ICU from January 1995 to January 2005 (a 10 year period). There was a total of 16 attributes chosen for each ICU admission, where among these attributes there were a few well-known scores used for the prediction of ICU readmission and death after discharge including: Acute Physiology and Chronic Health Evaluation II (APAHACE II) score [32], Simplified Acute Physiology Score II (SAPS II) [33], and the updated Therapeutic Intervention Scoring System (TISS) [34] score. The APACHE II score is a popular and well tested score based severity of disease classification system (SoDCS), described in [32] by Knaus et al., which uses a simple set of 12 physiological variables for prediction. The SAPS II score is another popular and well tested SoDCS using 17 total features, including age, 12 physiology features, admission type, and 3 disease type features, which is discussed further by Gall et al. [33]. The TISS score is a third popular and well tested SoDCS where originally 57 therapeutic intervention measurements were used but was updated where some features were added and some removed, while test results stayed the same. The updated TISS score is covered by Keene et al. [34].

Campbell et al. decided upon three research directives for prediction: death after ICU discharge (but before hospital discharge), readmission to the ICU within 48 hours of ICU discharge (again, before hospital discharge), and readmission to the ICU at any point after ICU discharge (and before hospital discharge). It should be noted that each patient could potentially fall into more than one of these categories, but this is not an issue due to there being three separate binary models built. The importance these prediction models could potentially have would be to help physicians determine which of these patients fall into these three groups and most significantly why they fall into these groups. If physicians can know why then they can determine which patients need their ICU stay extended. The feature selection method decided upon was simple logistic regression for all three models to determine which of the 16 attributes had a strong correlation to each prediction ($P \leq 0.2$). Multiple Logistic regression was chosen for building the prediction models. All three of their models were tested using the Hosmer and Lemeshow goodness-of-fit (HLgof) test [35] and determined that the calibration was good and no more calibration was necessary. The HLgof is used to determine if logistic regression models have sufficient calibration (discussed by Hosmer et al. [35]).

The Area Under the (ROC) Curve (AUC) was used in this study to determine the classification and discrimination performance of the three models. According to Bradley [36], AUC is the best criteria for measuring the classification performance of a binary classifier such as logistic regression. AUC is a fitting metric to use on ICU admission data because the positive-class instances are a small percentage (i.e. only 3.3% of the patients were readmitted to the ICU within 48 hours). For determining the quality of the three models (using the chosen set of features) the AUC results for each model are compared to results obtained from the APACHE II score for each prediction. The first model, predicting death after ICU discharge (before hospital discharge) had an AUC value of 0.74 compared to AUC garnered from APACHE II of 0.69. The second model, for predicting readmission (before hospital discharge) obtained an AUC of 0.67 while APACHE II received an AUC of 0.63. The third model for predicting readmission within 48 hours of ICU discharge acquired an AUC value of 0.62 while APACHE II earned an AUC of 0.59.

The three models with the chosen set of features only achieved minimal improvement over APACHE II alone for the prediction of ICU readmission and mortality rate for ICU patients. Campbell et al. note that this minimal improvement could be because the APACHE II score already uses physiological variables, and it is these variables which are generally most useful for predicting ICU readmission and the mortality rate after ICU discharge. However, one non-physiological variable was shown to be highly correlated to both ICU readmission and death predictions: increasing age.

Only about 23.3% of patients used fall into one of these three model's positive class and should not have been released from the ICU where if their ICU stay was extended, maybe some of these patients could have been saved. One item to note is that Campbell et al. only used one feature selection method as well as only one prediction model for their research. There is a possibility if other methods were tested there could have been models built that were able to outperform APACHE II. Even though the data was gathered from a database containing a 10 year's worth of ICU patients, the data was still only from one ICU, and for the purpose of validation a larger variation (collecting from various ICUs) would have been beneficial.

Ouanes et al. [14] conducted their research with the goal of predicting whether a patient would die or return to the ICU within the first week after ICU discharge. Research was performed on 3462 patients (out of 5014) admitted to an ICU for a minimum of 24 hours, gathered from 4 different ICUs from the Outcomerea database. As Campbell et al. found in their data, the positive class is very small compared to the overall population with only about 3% (where 0.8% died and 2.1% were readmitted within 7 days). The feature selection method chosen was univariate analysis selecting variables with (P < 0.2) to add to the final model, and used the Akaike Information Criterion (AIC) [37] to identify the best model. AIC is a metric used to verify the overall quality of statistical models. The model created was then subjugated to a few validation and verification steps for testing (clinical relevancy, variable inter-correlation and co-linearity between variables) in order to end up with their final set of 6 variables from the original 41. The six variables chosen were age, SAPS II, the need for a central venous catheter, SIRS score during ICU stay, SOFA score, and discharge at night.

These variables were used to make the final prediction model using multivariate logistic regression, which will be used to develop their Minimizing ICU Readmission (MIR) score. The MIR score will be a quantitative measurement for determining whether a patient should be discharged from an ICU or not. The predictive results of MIR are compared to the results garnered from both SAPS II and Stability and Workload Index for Transfer (SWIFT) [38], another SoDCS using a small set of commonly available variables. Through MIR, Ouanes et al. were able to achieve good results with good calibration decided by the HLgof test and an AUC of 0.74 at a 95% confidence interval. The result SAPS II received for AUC was 0.64 and SWIFT getting an AUC score if 0.61, which shows that MIR performed considerably better. In this research only one feature selection method as well as only one classification method is used. The MIR score possibly could have yielded better results if more than one feature selection technique was used to determine which of the 41 variables would make the best model. In conjunction, MIR could possibly be further benefitted by testing out a number of other classifiers to develop the final model with the highest predictive power for this line of research. To fully test these results, one more comparison that should be made is their MIR score to that of either APACHE II or APACHE III scores, as shown in Campbell et al. [12] and Failho et al. [13].

Failho et al. [13] also seek to predict patients that will be readmitted to the ICU, but with the goal of only using a small amount of physiological variables, following the findings of Campbell et al. [12]. The prediction that this research is focusing on making is determining if patients will be readmitted within 3 days after discharge. The dataset they gathered was from the MIMIC II database [39] choosing only the patients over the age of 15 having an ICU stay of more than 24 hours giving a sample of 19,075 adults that were admitted to one of four ICUs. These 19,075 patients were further reduced by considering only patients for whom the researchers have all the variables available, leaving 3,034 patients. Further preprocessing reduced this to 1,267 patients. Finally, out of these 1,267 patients only 1,028 survived, giving a final dataset with 1,028 instances (and 13 members of the positive (readmittance) class).

Failho et al. decided upon two possible methods for feature selection: Sequential Forward Selection (SFS), or bottom-up approach, and Sequential Backwards Elimination (SBE), or top-down feature selection where both are discussed in [40]. SFS works on the original pool of features and starts with one feature then during each iteration one more feature will be added and the iterations will be stopped when the current model is deemed the best possible. SBE takes a different approach starting with the whole set of the original features and removing one feature at each iteration until the model is deemed the best possible. Failho et al. compared both of these methods in combination with their classifier, and found SFS to have better results than SBE in terms of AUC. Thus, it was chosen as their feature selection method. Using SFS, 6 out of the original 24 physiological variables were chosen: mean heart rate, mean temperature, mean platelets, mean blood pressure, mean SpO2, and mean lactic acid.

The classifier method used in this study was fuzzy modeling with sequential forward selection [40,41], specifically Takagi-Sugeno (TS) fuzzy modeling. Fuzzy models use linguistic interpretations to formulate rules and logical connectives in order to make connections between features and the final prediction. With the use of linguistic interpretation, fuzzy modeling is a good choice for this line of research as clinical data needs to be interpreted, as a physician would do in a clinical setting. The only worry would be that with the rule-based side of the models there could possibly be too much rigidity causing the absence of physician discernment in the final model.

Failho et al. compared the results they got from their set of 6 physiological variables (determined by SFS) in conjunction with TS to that of the sets determined by APACHE II and APACHE III [42] scores (also in conjunction with TS). APACHE III is another SoDCS, and was created with the goal of improving some of the problems in APACHE III as discussed in [42] by Knaus et al. The results show a significant advantage in favor of Failho et al.'s set securing an AUC score of 0.72 ± 0.04 while APACHE II and APACHE scored an AUC of 0.62 ± 0.03 and 0.64 ± 0.04 respectively. The SFS set also scored better in terms of specificity, sensitivity, and accuracy. This result shows that good prediction performance can be reached by using a small set of physiological variables. Even with the promising results there is more that could have been done in this research, one being that more variables, either physiological or not, could have been added to the original pool to see if results could have been improved. It might also have been beneficial to see if other feature selection techniques (tree-based or otherwise) may have improved upon the results achieved by SFS. Failho et al. do mention that fuzzy modeling has been shown to work comparably well to other classification methods for medical data yet there still could be benefit to this research if other classifier methods were tested to see if TS does yield the best results.

The research objective of Mathias et al. [15] is along a slightly different line where instead of trying to predict ICU readmission they look to predict a 5 year mortality rate through the construction of an Ensemble Index (EI). They used a group of 7463 patients taken from an Electronic Health Record (EHR) along with 980 attributes for each patient. There were two requirements for the patients to be used in this study: must be over the age of 50 (due to increasing age being a huge prediction factor for this line of study) and had at least 1 hospital visit within the year 2003. Due to the large amount of attributes in the original set of variables the feature selection method chosen was Correlation Feature Selection (CFS) [43] along with greedy stepwise search which will be used to create their EI. The CFS method finds variables that are both strongly correlated to the final prediction and that are weakly correlated between them. The CFS method with greedy stepwise search found a subset of 52 features which was broken down further by manual reduction followed by another round of CFS bringing the subset down to 23. This subset was then populated by one variable (gender) giving the final EI subset of 24 variables. The top 6 attributes in the EI (ranked by information gain) are age, comorbidity count, amount of hospitalization a year prior to admission, high blood urea nitrogen levels, low calcium, and mean albumin.

Rotation Forest Ensembling (RFE) [44] with Alternating Decision Tree (ADT) [45] was used to create their predictive model and was evaluated with tenfold cross-validation. Mathias et al. tested this technique with many other methods and found this technique to perform better (the reason it was used). The RFE algorithm is an ensemble of decision trees creating variation by assigning each tree a subset of features randomly chosen where Principle Component Analysis (PCA) is applied to each subset before each tree model is built. The ADT is a decision tree which instead of having a single class prediction located in its base leaf nodes, has a "probability of class membership" prior to each terminal node, and the sum of all these values are along an instance's whole path in order to predict its class value. RFE and ADT is a good combination as RFE brings accuracy and diversity to the model, and ADT allows for more information to be gained about an instance as it goes along the tree.

The Ensemble Index was able to achieve quite good results scoring better in recall, precision c-statistic, etc. than both the modified Walter Life Expectancy Index (WLEI) [46] and the modified Charlson Comorbidity Index (CCI) [47]. The modified WLE and CCI are two well-tested and better-known life expectancy indices that are used for prediction in similar research. Even though these good results were achieved for the EI, there was only one feature selection process used where if more techniques were used a better subset could have been created, which is possible with there being 980 attributes in the original set of features. Again more variation of data could be added to this research as all the data was gathered from one source.

The studies shown in this section have the potential to improve clinical discharge procedure, determining which patients should be released from the ICU and which patients should receive a particular line of treatment. The goal of these studies is to find which attributes are the most correlated to why patients return to ICUs early or do not survive after discharge. Looking at the research efforts of Campbell et al. [12], Failho et al. [13], and Ouanes et al. [14] that covered prediction of ICU readmission and death rate after discharge, the top variables of why are age, APACHE scores, various physiological variables (e.g. heart rate), amount of organ dysfunction, as well as a few others. If physicians can better predict which of their patients will return to the ICU or not survive then they would know which patients to keep in the ICU longer and to give more focused care potentially saving, if not, at least prolonging a life. According to Ouanes et al., between day one and day seven after discharge the readmission rate and death rate go down drastically, meaning that keeping a patient just a little longer could be beneficial, but could also take away an ICU bed from another patient that needs intensive care. These are the reasons that studies attempting to figure out why patients return early or die soon after ICU discharge are quite important as lives can potentially be saved. The target of this research of course is on those patients that have preventable death as not all death will be preventable.

The variables that were shown to be most telling for the 5 year survival rate (Mathias et al. [15]) happened to be similar with age and physiological variables being at the top of the list. One benefit of this research is by looking well into a patient's future can help physicians advise their patients better as far a treatment options. An example of this would be a physician could advise a patient whether or not to go through a particular rough line of treatment when they may not live long enough to reap the benefits of such treatment. This research is especially important for patients with increasing age as the older a patient is the less likely a harsh treatment would be beneficial.

Real-time predictions using data streams

The studies covered in this section are also on data gathered from the patient level and again have the intention of answering clinical level questions. Instead of predicting the patient's condition in the future (i.e. ICU readmission or 5 year survival), the research here will be using data streams in order to predict patient's conditions in real-time. Data streams are never ending torrents of data that requires continuous analysis giving the possibility for real-time results (a feature not available when using static data sets). This section will sample two different categories of data steam studies: making prognosis and diagnosis predictions for patients, and detecting if a new born is experiencing a cardiorespiratory spell both in a real time. The researchers here are attempting to develop methods that use these constant streams of data and make predictions in a continuous manner while keeping satisfactory accuracy and precision.

Zhang et al. [17] develop a clinical support system using data stream mining with the goal of analyzing patient data in order to make real-time prognosis and diagnosis. In order to handle the continuous stream of data an algorithm that can handle high-throughput data will be necessary leading the authors to choose Very Fast Decision Tree (VFDT). The VFDT algorithm is quite efficient as it was built to handle thousands of instances per second using basic hardware (discussed by Domingos et al. [48]). They discuss that VFDT has many advantages over other methods (e.g., rule based, neural networks, other decision trees, Bayesian networks) such as VFDT can make prediction both diagnostically and prognostically, can handle a changing non-static dataset, not using rigid rules (can be difficult for experts to put their knowledge into rules).

VFDT alone, though, is not able to give future predictions of a patient's status only the current status; therefore, Zhang et al. decided to modify VFDT. For the modified VFDT, one or more pointer(s) were added to each of the terminating leaf nodes, where each base node corresponds to a distinct medical condition and each pointer corresponds to one medical records of a previous patient. To connect each stored medical record to its corresponding pointer, the authors created a mapping table so when the VFDT runs through and ends up on a base node the map will connect the leaf to its pointer(s) (corresponding medical records). These medical records, through Natural Language Processing (sentence and semantic similarity [49,50]), will then be used to make a prediction about the patient's future and give physicians the ability to better treat and advise their patients based on previous similar situations. The VFDT and the mapping table are updated as necessary (i.e. when a physician makes a new diagnosis or when a new medical record is added to the map).

Zhang et al. compare their method to that of IBM's similar data stream mining technique covered by Sun et al. [51]. To test their method, IBM used 1500 ICU patients from the MIMIC II database along with various physiological waveforms (taken from an assortment of medical devices) and clinical data on each patient. IBM's method consists of three main parts: 1.) physiological stream processing, 2.) offline analysis, and 3.) online analysis. For the steam processing part, a correlation base technique was chosen as such techniques are able to correlate well among sensors and are able to efficiently handle missing data (estimating missing values by way of linear regression models using other sensors during that period of time). Better results could possibly have been attained if techniques other than linear regression models were used to estimate missing values. A correlation based technique was not the only technique tested, they also tried a window based technique which estimates missing values for a sensor by using an averaged value during a small window of time from that sensor and imputing that value for the missing time. The correlation based technique found better results and therefore was used in the final method.

During offline analysis, Sun et al. use a method they created called Locally Supervised Metric Learning (LSML), which learns an adjustable distance metric by using knowledge from the current domain (in this study, clinical knowledge). The last step of online analysis takes place when a new patient is ready for prediction of prognosis where the system will find the set of similar cases by way of temporal alignment, and this is followed by applying a regression model to account for the uniqueness of patients. Sun et al. ran a comparison of their LSML to that of PCA and Linear Discriminant Analysis (LDA) in terms of both precision and accuracy with LSML scoring considerably better in both.

Mentioned by Zhang et al., their system will use fewer computer resources to run compared to IBMs as offline analysis will not needed. This comes down to a comparison of the complexity between LSML and VFDT, where LSML is quite complex and does not allow the real-time nature that can be offered by VDFT (the most complex calculation of Zhang et al.'s. method). Zhang et al.'s. method is not tested on real world data and would need to be before its usefulness can be determined and can be legitimately compared to IBM's method. The real-time nature does offer the ability for making quick prognosis for patients, and if the results can be similar to the results found in IBM's method, then predictions could not just be made quickly but with good accuracy and precision.

Thommandram et al. [18] use data streams with a different goal attempting to detect and eventually classify neonatal cardiorespiratory spells (a condition that can be greatly helped by being detected and classified in real time). A cardiorespiratory spell is classified as some combination of a pause in breathing, drop in blood oxygen saturation, and a decrease in heart rate. The name of their system is called Artemis and is designed to use a steady stream of physiological data from the new born patient and both detect and ascertain which type of cardiorespiratory spell the patient is experiencing all in real-time. The real-time manner could potentially save the lives of these infants giving physicians more time to fix what is wrong as the need for human diagnosis will be less. The actual stream processing part of Artemis is handled by the middleware system developed by IBM called InfoSphere Streams [16], built to handle multiple high-throughput data streams. Middleware is software that works to connect two programs that are otherwise not connected. Three different data streams (from three different sensors) are used, which correspond to the three different conditions for a cardiorespiratory spell: a respiratory impedance wave, a decrease in blood oxygen saturation, and a decrease in heart rate.

The authors wanted to develop a system that will improve upon current machines used today that use the absolute change method (i.e. if a machine detects heart rate under or over a cutoff, then notify physicians). Artemis will use a relative change method, where instead of a cutoff; there will be a sliding baseline that will be continuously updated in real-time as the patients "normal" readings change over time. The sliding baseline method can give a more reliable reading as it adapts to the unique reading of each patient as well as allow for more accurate spell detection. For classification, the reading from the three streams will be analyzed through a hierarchal rule based temporal model to determine which of the many cardiorespiratory spells the infant is experiencing.

The detection part of Thommandram et al's. system was tested on one patient in a Neonatal ICU during a 24 hour period where the sliding baseline method was found to alert physicians as often as found in the cutoff method for both heart rate and SpO2 readings. From the results for this one tested patient, they showed that their sliding baseline method could achieve clinically significant results for heart rate detection, with a specificity of 98.9% and a sensitivity of 100%. They did not test their classification method as mentioned by the authors as their future work. The detection part of this method will need further testing on many more patients before this method can be considered as clinically acceptable. When the classification part is tested it could be beneficial if they were to compare other methods to their hierarchal rule based temporal model.

Data stream mining presented here has shown the potential to be beneficial for clinical practice as it can be extended to be used in real time by use of efficient algorithms and methods (that are not previously used in the clinic). By using these data stream diagnosis for prognosis and spell detection, physicians could make faster and more accurate decisions and start solving the problem without spending as much time developing a plan. This line of research is fairly young and more studies will be needed through the development and testing of various new methods for using data stream mining for medical data with the goal of outputting results in real-time.

Using population level data – Social media

All the studies covered in this section will use data at the population level, specifically social media data (data that can be from anyone) and venture to answer both clinical questions and epidemic-scale questions. Data in Health Informatics is "traditionally" gathered from the doctors, clinics, hospitals and such, but recently people all around the world are starting to document health information all over the internet. This data could be from Twitter, internet query data (e.g. Google search data), message boards, or anywhere else people put information on the internet. This form of Big Data, which brings additional challenges such as text mining and handling potentially malicious noise, could possibly lead to finding many new breakthroughs in the field of medicine.

The first line of research presented is determining whether message board data can be useful to help patients find information on a given ailment. The second line of study is testing if using search query data or Twitter post data can effectively track an epidemic across a given population (in real-time). As previously mentioned above, the challenge with social media data is that although it is clearly High Volume, Velocity, and Variety, it could have both low Veracity and Value (data coming in could be unreliable, as discussed by Hay et al. [52]). However, through analyzing and mining the data, the useful parts can be extracted and used to gain medical insight.

There is much that can be learned by employing research on social media data including but not limited to: spatiotemporal information of disease outbreaks, real-time tracking of a harmful and infectious diseases, increasing the knowledge of global distribution for various diseases, and creating an extremely accessible way of letting people get information about any medical questions they might have.

Using message board data to help patients

Research in this subsection concentrated on determining if message board entries could possibly be a useful source of data for helping people find health information that is beneficial in appropriating reliable medical knowledge (answering clinical questions). Even though this line of research does not appear to be all that popular, it could offer keys to unlocking boundless reliable health information (as 59% of US adults use look for health information on the internet [19]), where one in five use social media).

Ashish et al. [19] created a platform called Smart Health Informatics Program (SHIP) with the goal of helping patients connect to the medical experiences of other patients posted throughout the internet via message boards (i.e. forums, blogs etc.). This study used a pool of 50,000 discussions including over 400,000 posts from four different message board websites (inspire.com, medhelp.com, and 2 others). SHIP uses a pipeline structure taking in all the message board entries (discussions and posts) from these four websites and go through various steps to find the entries with useful medical information and store them in a database for patient retrieval.

The first step of SHIP's pipeline is Elementary Extraction, which will execute some basic text processing for each entry: parsing through the HTML and extracting information on each entry (number of replies, when discussion was last updated, etc.) and giving a unique ID to each discussion and post. This is followed by the Entity Extraction step looking to determine which of the entries have medical significance related to health (such as treatments, side-effects, hospitals, drugs, etc.). Ashish et al. decided to use the XAR system [53] (an information extraction system of free text), which they expanded by incorporating ontologies from UMLS (Unified Medical Language System) [54] as well as other vocabularies and ontologies. Then SHIP enters Expression Distillation which looks at each post and determines whether or not the post includes any number of many expression of interests broken into 5 categories: 1.) personal experience, 2.) advice, 3.) information, 4.) support, 5.) outcome. This step requires that 5 classifiers be built for each expression of interest and they decided upon the J48 decision tree algorithm using the WEKA tool [55]. The next step is Aggregation using the data from the previous steps (done at the post level) and aggregates them at the discussion level. After the entries have gone through this process the numerous facts and expressions (over 20 million) found in each entry are stored in a database.

For retrieval from the database the authors extended Lucene [56], an open-source Java-based text search engine library, by adding optimizations for indexing, dynamic score boosting, and local caching. They tested their system on a test case of a patient experiencing severe cough since starting Tarceva (a type of chemotherapy). This was chosen as a test case due to coughing not being listed as a possible side-effect on the Tarceva website [57] or on another website depicting a clinical trial for this drug. Through the authors system (website) a search of Tarceva shows that cough is actually the third most common side-effect. This system could also find advice (through search filters) on how to help with the cough due to Tarceva. As this system has been shown to be beneficial for patients there could also be benefits to physicians as they may be looking to clinical trials for answers they could use this system (employing message board data) to find other cases similar to their patients and find information helping to make diagnosis, treatment options, etc. The authors tested extraction accuracies for each of the 5 expression of interest categories in terms of precision and accuracy: personal experience (0.87 and 0.82), advise (0.91 and 0.62), Information (0.93 and 0.91), support (0.89 and 0.90), and outcome (0.80 and 0.58).

There will need to be more testing with more test cases to see if the data they are presenting through search is correct rather than just speculation as this data can be posted by anyone and even if it is predominantly posted by medical professionals, this does not automatically make the information correct. Martin [2] mentions that traditional health data should be used in the development of SHIP. This would help determine whether the data they gathered has medical importance or not, rather than relying on testing SHIP after it is constructed. From a data mining stand point the step of expression distillation could have been improved by using more classifiers other than J48 with which they could have improved the results they got for extraction accuracies.

Rolia et al. [20] devise a new system to use social health forums to help patients learn about their condition from posts by other patients with similar conditions. Their method consists of three steps: 1.) determining the patient's current medical condition from the personal health record (PHR), 2.) the system will ascertain which other users have a similar condition, 3.) a metric will be implemented evaluating and ranking the forum topics to determine the most relevant to present to the user. They describe their system implementation for a test case of type II diabetes mellitus (DM II). Due to privacy issues it was decided to use synthesized electronic medical health records (EMR) and PHRs with help from a medical professional. Also created is an aggregated clinical pathway that a patient can follow from the moment the patient is diagnosed onward where the path is determined by clinical factors (e.g. glucose levels) depicting a sequence of clinical events and was based on information found in medical research [58]. Using the aggregated clinical pathway they created 1000 synthetic patients (including their path and a few clinical variables) akin to ones that could be found in typically PHRs and EMRs as well as manually selecting 100 relevant posts from the websites: www.diabetesforum.com and www.diabetesdaily.com.

The system starts by creating and assigning the states to the synthesized patients and for DM II they decided upon 6 states (also described in medical research [58]). Assigning the patients into these six classes is done through rules (created by using NICE Pathways [59] and a medical expert who worked with Rolia et al.) guiding the patient along the pathway. The next step consists of appointing weights to forum topics (as for this example they only used the topic and not the content within). A medical expert will give the original set of weights to topics (for each of the six states) as percentages of likelihood that a patient with a given state would be benefitted by that topic, which will give the initial population model. This system will also offer the new user the ability to determine how relevant they want posts to be compared to their current state, which is implemented by calculating the cosine similarity between each state using the weights determined by each of the 100 posts. Now the system moves onto ranking the forum topics by correlation to the current user's state. The authors, in order to rank the topics used a metric deemed adjusted weights using the similarity between classes, patient preference (0 through 1), and the weights between post and clinical state; the higher the adjusted weight the higher the rank. The best feature about this system is its ability to learn as user feedback can adjust the weights of a post has to the given level of the current user (assuming using a similar method used by the expert). The user will also be able to change their current state as well as modify their patient preference.

The authors did build a prototype of this system and found that their system did behave as it was designed. One issue is that this system was not tested nor appears to be built with real data. A system such as this one is difficult to test outside letting real patients test this system in numerous field tests. As the authors mentioned they could possibly improve upon the cosine similarity by testing other such methods for defining weights. Another note, is that instead of a medical expert deciding the initial weights for posts through rules they could use a technique that would need to be tested and could then be approved by an expert, which could help with efficiency as well as the quality of the initial weights. This efficiency could help production of their classes as there are numerous diseases and ailments out there, and this research only discusses the construction for one.

Social media and the internet are becoming more and more popular for looking up and sharing medical data as mentioned in both [19] and [20]. The results found in these studies do show that there is a possibility that message board data could be used, but there is no real field testing to show that it works in the real world. If the research in these studies are found to be useful they could even be extended to help advise physician's diagnosis and treatments of their patients as other physicians and other patients with similar experiences to their current patients are located in these message board discussions.

Using search query data to track epidemics

The focus of the studies covered in this subsection will be discussing research done using search query data gathered from two popular search engines: Google (google.com) and Baidu (baidu.com) with the goal of predicting whether such data can be used to predict the occurrence and movement of Epidemics in a given population (all in real-time). The Center of Disease Control and Prevention (CDC) produces their results for influenza-like illness (ILI) epidemics, but there is generally a one to two week delay for this information. The research here is attempting to use search query data to get ILI epidemic information out to the public quicker than by the traditional method of the CDC reports. This research can help physicians and hospital to know both when and where an Epidemic is happening with real-time updates allowing them to act quicker in stopping the spread of the disease as well as help the patients already infected.

Ginsburg et al. [21] developed an automated method that can analyze a Big Volume of search queries from Google with the goal of tracking ILI within a given population. They conducted their research on Google search queries taken from historical logs during a 5 year period (between 2003 and 2008) using 50 million of the most popular searches as well as using data from the CDC historical data. These queries were taken directly, without combination, spelling correction, translation, or any other modification. They built and trained their model based on data from the years 2003-2007 and the validation was done on data from 2008. As a note, the CDC splits the US into 9 regions and this study looked to make predictions also using these regions of separation.

The model the authors built looks to find the probability that a patient visiting a physician is related to an ILI for a particular region using a single explanatory variable: the probability that a given search query is related to an ILI within the same region. To accomplish this the authors fit a linear model using both the log-odds for ILI physician visits and ILI related search queries giving: $logit(I(t)) = \alpha \times logit(Q(t)) + \epsilon$, where $I(t)$ is the percentage of ILI physician visits, α is a coefficient, $Q(t)$ stands for the fraction of queries related to ILI at time t, ϵ stands for the error in the formula (and $logit(p) = ln(p/1 - p)$).

The single explanatory variable $Q(t)$ is determined through an automated technique that does not need any prior knowledge of influenza. The authors tested each of the 50 million stored queries alone as $Q(t)$ to see which queries fit best with the CDC ILI visit percentage for each region (presumably univariate analysis). The top 45 search queries, sorted by Z-transformed correlation throughout the nine regions, were chosen to belong to $Q(t)$ as the top 45 scored the best after they tested (through cross-validation) the top 1 search query through the top 100 search queries. Examination of these top queries showed many connections to influenza symptoms, complications, and remedies, consistent with searches made by an individual affected by influenza. The model was trained using weekly ILI percentages from 2003 through part of 2007 for all nine regions jointly to end up with a coefficient α that is region independent. Ginsburg et al. were able to obtain good fit compared to that of the reported CDC ILI percentages scoring a mean correlation of 0.90 throughout all nine regions.

Validation was carried out on the data gathered for part of 2007 through 2008 on 42 points per region and was able to achieve a mean correlation of 0.97 compared to the reported CDC ILI percentages. This correlation is quite high and through the authors' method was able to be reported 1 to 2 weeks prior to the CDC reports; thus, showing that search query data can be used to determine an ILI epidemic in a more real-time manner. This study only used one feature selection method narrowing down the 50 million most popular search queries down to 45; the results achieved maybe could have been improved upon if other techniques were used to determine an optimal set other than the chosen 45.

Yuan et al. [5] developed a similar system using search query data, but this study uses search queries gathered from Baidu (baidu.com) with the goal of tracking ILI epidemics across China. The author gathered their data from Baidu's database (http://index.baidu.com/) which stores the online search query since June 2006. For this study they only gathered data from March 2009 to August 2012, which was during the H1N1 epidemic and compare their results to that of China's Ministry of Health (MOH). Similar to the United State's CDC the MOH also releases their data with a 1 to 2 week delay. Baidu releases their search query data on a daily basis allowing for methods exploiting this data the ability to give answers in near real-time.

Yuan et al.'s system is split into four main parts: 1.) choosing keywords, 2.) filtering these keywords, 3.) defining weights and composite search index, and 4.) fitting the regression model with the keyword index to that of the influenza case data. For choosing keywords they reference Ginsburg et al. mentioning the benefit of choosing an optimal set of keywords, but want a more efficient way of determining such a set. Yuan et al. determined the key words using a tool from a Chinese website (http://tool.chinaz.com/baidu/words.aspx) which determined keywords through recommendations from Baidu as well as from others mined using semantic correlation analysis from sources such as portal websites, online reports, and blogs. The source keyword put into the tool was the Chinese symbol for Flu giving a total of 94 related keywords (assuming a total of 95 including Flu is the current set). The current set of keywords is then taken into the filtering step where three conditions must be met: (i) the keyword must include aspects that could impact the influenza epidemic, (ii) the data for a keyword must be presented with a time series with a resolution (daily, weekly, or monthly), and finally, (iii) the time series data for the chosen keywords must have a maximum cross-correlation coefficient no less than 0.4 to that of the influenza case data.

The next step starts with defining the weights for the set of keywords that passed filtering. The authors tested two techniques for determining weights for the keywords: systematic assessment (SA) [60,61] and strength of the correlation coefficient (SCC) [21,62]. SA entails using the principal of prior evaluations to rate the keywords and assign these ratings as weights, while SCC compares the influenza epidemic curve to that of the keyword frequency curve determining the correlation coefficient between these and assigning the weights accordingly. Yuan et al. decide to determine the optimal set of keywords with the formula: $y = \alpha_0 + \alpha_1 \times index_j + \epsilon$, where α_0 is the intercept, α_1 is the coefficient, and ϵ is the error. The $index_j$ is equal to $\sum_{i=1}^{j} \omega_i x_i^l$, where ω_i is the weight for the ith keyword and x_i^l denotes the sequence after alignment (not used in this study, presumably set to 1). Each keyword will be brought into the model in a stepwise manner in an order determined by their correlation coefficient and then use a partial F test to evaluate goodness of fit after each keyword is brought into the model (this will be repeated until the goodness of fit stops improving). After all the keyword selection processes are concluded they are left with 8 keywords left for the optimal set.

The authors decided to use the following regression model: $ICD[t] = \beta_0 \times ICD[t - 1] + \beta_1 \times index[t] + \beta_2 \times index[t - 1] + \epsilon$, where ICD is the influenza case data, β_0, β_1, and β_2 are coefficients, $index$ represents the optimal set, and again ϵ represents the error. The variable t in this formula stands for time and can be broken into month time blocks. The formula therefore would be estimating ICD using the ICD from the previous month and on the optimal index for the current and previous months. The model was trained on the data from March 2009 to December 2011 and validated on the time period of January 2012 to August 2012. They achieved an R-squared of 0.95, an AIC of 18.50 and found that autocorrelation was not an issue due to the Durbin-Watson test results of 1.89. The validation of the model tested over the validation time period resulted in a mean absolute error of 10.6%, but in a more real-time manner of up to 1-2 weeks earlier. One area that could have improved in this study is the starting pool was very small compared to the study done by Ginsburg et al. [21], depending on other sources and not their techniques to determine the staring pool of keywords.

These studies have shown that search query data can be a useful tool for quickly and accurately detecting the occurrence of an ILI epidemic which could even be extended to tracking an epidemic. Additionally, it would be interesting to see if the formula created on this study could work as well for ILI epidemics that happen many years in the future from the time period used to train the model or in a different population that uses the same language. This line of research can help health officials, physicians, hospitals in reacting to epidemics faster and work to stop them better (faster) than with traditional methods used today such as the CDC or MOH reports.

Using twitter post data to track epidemics

The studies discussed in this subsection have a similar research goal to the previous subsection of attempting to detect and track ILI epidemics, but instead of using search query data the researchers use Twitter post data. One advantage to Twitter data over search query data is that Twitter posts come with context [23] (as opposed to not knowing why a person is searching for a topic). Twitter is a social networking site that allows its user to post any messages they like in 140 words or less (known as tweets), and currently has about 554 hundred million members worldwide with around 58 million tweets per day [63]. With this Big Volume of people (sensors) there is a high probability that there can be useful ILI epidemic information being posted, but, of course, there will be noisy sensors and only through data mining techniques and analysis can the useful information be found. Another issue that could make Twitter post data potentially not reliable is that it is difficult to directly ascertain the age of a given Twitter user, and in fact a user may be discussing a disease symptom from a family member who differs in age from the user anyway, but research shows [22] that this is not a deterrent to age-based prediction.

Signorini et al. [23], in their research, employ Twitter post data across the United States by searching through particular spatiotemporal areas and analyzing the data in order to predicate weekly ILI levels both across and within these regions (CDC's ILI regions). The focus of their efforts is on the time period when the H1N1 epidemic was happening in the US as they gathered a large amount of Tweets from October 1, 2009 - May 20, 2010 using Twitter's streaming application programmer's interface (API) [64]. The tweets were sifted through looking for posts containing a preset of key words correlation to H1N1 (*h1n1*, *flu*, *swine*, *influenza*). Twitter's posts stream does come with its own filters according to the API documentation; therefore, not all tweets in the United States were used, only the subset to come through Twitter's filtered stream.

Tweets containing the following attributes were not used for analysis: if located outside the United States, from a user with a time zone outside the US, containing less than five words, not in English, not containing ASCII characters, and those submitted through the "API". The tweets leftover are used to create a dictionary of English words, from which items such as (#hashtags, @user, and links) are not used and also words were brought to their root form through Porter's Stemming Algorithm [65] to make the dictionary as efficient to use as possible. Using this dictionary Signori et al. gathered daily and weekly statistics (such as amount of tweets a word is present within) for each word both in the dictionary throughout the US and within each of the CDC's 10 regions.

The authors use the weekly statistics in order to estimate the weekly ILI epidemic status through a more general class of SVM called Support Vector Regression [66]. This is a generalization of Support Vector Machines, a type of classifier which attempts to find a minimal-margin separator, which is a hyperplane in the space of instances such that one class is on one side of the hyperplane and the other class is on the other side, with the distance between each class's instances and the hyperplane being maximized. As data is rarely linearly separable in feature space, a kernel function is used to transform the data into a higher-dimensional space, which generally assures that such a hyperplane exists. Signorini et al. used a polynomial kernel function for this purpose. To extend SVMs to the problem of regression (as opposed to classification), the model disregards any training data points which are already within a threshold ϵ of the model prediction (just as a SVM classification model disregards points which lie outside such a margin, as those points cannot help in determining the optimal hyperplane), and then builds a nonlinear model to minimize a preselected linear-error-cost function. In this model, each point (or instance) is a tweet, and the features each represent dictionary terms which occur more than 10 times per week. The value of each feature is the fraction of total tweets within the given week which contain the corresponding dictionary word (after stemming).

Determining if Twitter data can indeed detect ILI epidemics by accurately estimating CDC ILI values was done on a weekly basis on a national level and a regional level (where region 2 is presented by the authors). For the national estimation they trained their method using 1 million of the tweets from October 1, 2009 - May 20, 2010 throughout the United States, with the objective being CDC's ILI values throughout the nation. Leave-one-out cross-validation was used to determine the accuracy of the model. The results found for the national level were quite accurate, scoring an average error of 0.28% with a standard deviation of 0.23%. In order to estimate the ILI levels in a particular region, with the goal being real-time prediction (as again, the CDC has a 1 to 2 week delay), they took the tweets that had geolocation information and fit these tweets to CDC region ILI readings from 9 of the 10 regions in order to construct the model to determine the results for last region (region 2). The authors argue that perhaps the smaller amount of tweets containing the geolocation information could have generated the slightly higher error rating of 0.37% with a standard deviation of 0.26%.

This study could have incorporated more words to include in their tweet searches rather than just the 4 they used as well as use methods to determine the most affective set. Also there was one prediction model applied, where as with more tested they could have found that a different model generated better results with less error across the US and within the tested region. As a note for this paper, Signorini et al. [23] also (and primarily) used the tweets to follow public concern for ILI epidemics throughout daily and monthly trends of tweets, but the scope of this survey does not look to cover such findings.

Achrekar et al. [22] devises a system deemed Social Network Enabled Flu Trends (SNEFT) that continuously monitors tweets with the goal of detecting and tracking the spread of ILI epidemics. This study uses a dataset of tweets and profile details of the Twitter users who have commented on flu keywords starting on October 18, 2009. The SNEFT network uses an OSN Crawler (bot that systematically searches online social networks) they developed to retrieve tweets from the internet using keywords *flu, H1N1*, and *swine flu* storing important information about the tweets (e.g. location, further determined by Google to determine geolocation), and relative keyword frequency in a spatio-temporal database. Also gathered are CDC ILI reports along with other influenza related data are downloaded from the internet.

The authors found that in one of their previous works using tweets from 2009–2010 (when influenza was a larger issue), the correlation coefficient was 0.98, but a huge drop was seen in this measure since for 2010-2011 at 0.47. Due to the H1N1 being less of an issue the noisy tweets are much more prominent resulting in a lower correlation coefficient, which leads to give something to think about: maybe this measure could be used to detect ILI in an area where the higher it is (without using methods to correct such noise) the more likely it is that an ILI epidemic is spreading through that region. The authors do try to alleviate the noise using text classification determining whether or not a tweet is correlated to a flu event or not.

For text classification they tested three different methods: decision tree, SVMs, and Naive Bayes, along with a few configurations for efficient learning. SVM was determined as the best classification method, beating the other two methods in both precision and recall. These classifiers were trained on a dataset of 25,000 tweets manually classified by the use of Amazon Mechanical Turk (an internet marketplace to perform such tasks by the coordinated use of human intelligence). The results of adding this text classifier caused the correlation coefficient to rise back up for the US as a whole and within each region. The authors also performed data cleansing from both retweets and multiple tweets posted by the same user during a single bout with the same illness (different time windows were tested for the length of a single bout). Results found that only retweets should be considered.

The prediction model they used is Logistic Autoregression with exogenous inputs (ARX), which has the goal of predicting the CDC ILI statistic during a given week using both the tweets details and the CDC data (percent of physician visits from preceding weeks). The autoregression part of the model is the prediction of current ILI activity employing ILI activity from past weeks, and the exogenous inputs come from the tweets from the previous weeks. As simple Linear ARX could not handle the fact that the number of Twitter users is only bounded below by 0 (rather than being completely bounded between 0% and 100%), and so the authors introduce a logit link function for the CDC data and use a logarithmic transformation of the Twitter data. The purpose of the model is to produce timely updates estimating the percentage of physician visits for the week. The model can optionally use two distinct variables to determine how many previous weeks of data are used for each data type, with m referring to CDC data and n referring to Twitter data. The authors used 10-fold cross-validation on 33 weeks of data (from October 3, 2010 - May 15, 2011) to determine the (m, n) model that gave the least root mean squared error, and the (2,1) model (using only the current twitter data and the two most recent instances of CDC data) gave the best results.

Using their methods they were able to achieve a higher correlation to the actual CDC percent of visits ILI-related compared to the Twitter data alone for the 33 week period in 2010-2011, yet the authors do mention that Twitter data alone would still predict higher toward the beginning and end of the annual flu season (and, of course, during an epidemic). Achrekar et al. also found that they could get good results for regions 1, 6, and 9 determining that Twitter data and percentage of visits ILI-related are correlated across regions. One issue with this research is that only one prediction method is used; it would have been beneficial to see if the jump in correlation could also be seen with other prediction models or that results could be better with other models.

Results shown here are impressive, showing that Twitter data can be used to detect and possibly track Influenza like epidemics in real time. Both research efforts have shown that they can get very little error for predicting ongoing ILI epidemics, and produce results up to 1-2 weeks faster than the CDC posts their results. One issue not looked at by either paper discussed here, but discussed by Doan et al. [67], is that results could be improved if the keywords used were more broad, using a more knowledge-based method with 37 symptom keywords under respiratory syndromes from the BioCaster Ontology (BCO) [79] plus the word *flu*. This leads to wondering what results could be found for ILI prediction if other keyword selection methods were chosen. It would be interesting if more areas across the globe were researched in order to see if the results shown here can be achieved worldwide. An example of such research could be to see if similar results can be garnered using a set of keywords used to achieve good prediction results in a given population could get the same results in another. This line of research, with the promising results shown, could possibly one day create a system that could continually be tracking twitter posts in order to create a worldwide ILI epidemic map in real time helping people and the health care systems stay one step ahead.

Translational bioinformatics

Many authors argue that although it is a young field, Translational BioInformatics (TBI) is the way of the future for Health Informatics. TBI is an interdisciplinary subfield that deals with High Volumes of biomedical data and genomic data, where current research areas include developing new techniques for integrating biological data and clinical data as well as improving clinical methodology by including findings from biological research [68]. According to Chen et al. [1], the scope of TBI encompasses all the same levels of Health Informatics in general: Micro Level (i.e. Molecules), Tissue Level, Patient Level, and Macro Level (i.e. Population). The main goal of TBI is answering various questions at the clinical level. However, TBI does not seem to have a universally accepted definition. Also confused is the dividing line between what is included as clinical information and overall Health Informatics (where both seem to be used interchangeably as biomedical). When clinical information is referenced, it does seem to include all Health Informatics' levels from the tissue, patient, and population levels (biomedical data), as they are all connected to health. TBI is the field to bridge the gap between these fields and the molecular level, by way of developing tools that can better link this disparate data as well as develop and test techniques that can efficiently and accurately analyze such data together with the end goal of improving HCO [69].

TBI looks to use the health information from the discussed levels, combine the aggregated information in order to provide the most health gains, and help in offering the best of modern health practices. It makes sense that any field of research containing numerous subfields (including Health Informatics) would eventually converge into "translation" between its subfields, and this is what appears to have happened in the construction of TBI. To fully or even partially encompass TBI, many discussions and research examples would need to be presented, but for the scope of this paper the essence of "translation" is what will be shown. Thus, this section will present a small sample of discussions (such as editorials, perspectives, and highlights) from JAMIA (the Journal of the American Medical Informatics Association) to give the overall feel of TBI.

Butte et al. [70], in their 2011 editorial, discuss several Translational Bioinformatics studies featured in JAMIA which combine biological data (e.g. microarray data) with medical records to achieve medical gains as more data angles are tested in tandem. The authors acknowledge that TBI started from research done by a small group who found how to bridge the gap between computational biology and medicine. They also comment that they expect TBI to exploit Big Data in the not-too-distant future, with the goal of answering various clinical level questions and leading to a number of clinically applicable decisions.

Sarkar et al. [69] in a perspective article (released in 2011) discuss three areas as being the primary research objectives of TBI: 1.) determining the molecular level (genotype) impacts on the evolution of diseases, 2.) learning the impact of therapeutic procedures as can be measured by molecular biomarkers, and 3.) understanding the overall consistency between the molecular, the phenotype, and environmental correlations across different populations. The authors believe that with the explosion of both the molecular level data and biomedical data, as well as with the technological advances, TBI is in a prime position to possibly determine many of the mysteries of complex diseases or any of the other primary research objectives mentioned.

Shah et al. [71], in their 2012 editorial, discuss JAMIA's focus of Big Data in TBI. The goal of their 2012 summit (as well as TBI in general) was bringing molecular level data into Health Informatics, which is now possible due to the explosion of computational power now available. With this new computational power, molecular level data can now be used to improve medical understanding, as the farther one deviates from the patient level, the more data will be generated. This editorial acknowledges many works that are implementing TBI methodologies with success, including Liu et al. [72], who combined chemical, biological, and phenotype properties of drugs to improve predictions of adverse drug reactions by 5%, compared to only using chemical properties of the drugs. The authors argue that data for TBI should include a Big Volume of molecular data and a small amount of patient measurements from a Big Volume of patients. This leads to us wondering why are the authors limiting the scope of TBI research to only these two levels, and why not (as shown in [1]) include all levels of accessible human existence. The authors also mention, in closing, that the TBI Summit and the Clinical Research Informatics Summit are increasing their synergy, which is a good start, but eventually study groups from all levels of accessible human existence should come together in the same way.

Analysis and future works

This section will cover analysis and future work that could be beneficial from the lines of research presented in this survey.

Covering molecule-level

For the subsection "Using Gene Expression Data to Make Clinical Predictions" (covering studies [6] and [7]), the main challenge is handling the Big Volume of the features (probes). A particular concern, with gene expression microarray data only getting larger, is developing and testing probe selection techniques. Future work will need to be put into making these probe selection techniques able to handle these vast amounts of gene probes and select the subset that has the best correlation to the final prediction in a way that is as fast, accurate, and efficient as possible.

Covering tissue-level

For the "Creating a Connectivity Map of the Brain Using Brain Images" subsection (presented by the studies [8,66], and [9]), actual data mining analysis of the connectivity map remains entirely in the scope of future work. With the Big Volume of data being created by the HCP and the study done by Anncsc [8] there is a lot of opportunity for novel data mining techniques to be employed, allowing for the possible discovery of previously-unattainable knowledge about the brain and how it connects to the health of the human body, leading to possibly giving physicians more accurate diagnosis methods, earlier detection of diseases, etc.

For the subsection "Using MRI Data for Clinical Prediction" (which covered research efforts [11] and [10]), the difficulty is handling the Big Volume of the high-resolution MRI data. As each instance in an MRI dataset is quite large, and numerous MRI samples are needed to perform acceptable research, attempting to analyze the whole brain MRI datasets can be of quite a Big Volume challenge; luckily, recent computational power has entered an era that can handle such data (meaning this line of research is fairly young). More testing will be needed here, and the way forward for using MRI data for clinical predictions is to create and test new machine learning methods that can accurately locate brain regions that best correlate to specific ailments to help physicians make more reliable predictions and diagnosis.

Covering patient-level

For the subsection "Prediction of ICU Readmission and Mortality Rate" (presented by the studies [12,13,15], and [14]), although all the studies had similar goals, none started with the same pool of variables; it could be beneficial in future work if all these variables and even variables from other data levels could be used in this area of research (as data from all 4 levels discussed here can be used to answer clinical questions). Also, data from the other studies presented previously could be used to expand the size of the starting pool (such as MRI data seen in [10], using the relative baseline method from [18], or even message board data from [19] and [20]). Another item to note is that throughout these studies only one feature selection technique was tested with minimal overlap; therefore, future work should look to test multiple feature selection techniques in order to find which one works the best with medical data. Classifiers that are employed for this line of research should be able to make decisions as a physician would do, that is, be able to look at a patient's medical attributes and make subjective decisions. Thus, there are three main concerns for making these predictions (starting variables, feature selection, and learning algorithms) and future research should be to test as many combinations of these three to find the best one that can make the most accurate and efficient predictions.

For the "Real-Time Predictions Using Data Streams" subsection (covered by the research efforts [16,18], and [17]), we see that this area of research is relatively new due to technology only very recently being able to handle the high-throughput processing necessary from the Big Velocity of data streams. As such, research is lacking testing and validation of developed methods as seen for Zhang et al. [17] and Thommandram et al. [18]. As sensors are not perfect (creating missing or erroneous data during a given time period), especially when being used for real-time analysis, future work will need to focus on developing and testing methods that can handle such data in the most reliable and efficient way. Another issue for future work in this line research is the need to devise and test numerous classification methods to find the best for both prognosis and acute problem detection (knowing that the best choices could be different for different ailments). It could also be beneficial if numerous sensors were checked to find the best set of sensors for each ailment prediction.

Covering population-level

For the "Using Message Board Data to Help Patients Obtain Medical Information" subsection (presented here by [19] and [20]), we find that the existing work does show that message board data does have the potential to supply patients with reliable medical information. More real world testing will be needed before this question can be fully answered, however. Message board data could be helpful if used in conjunction with studies such as Zhang et al.'s. [17] research on real-time diagnosis and prognosis, if it was found to give reliable medical data.

For the subsection "Tracking Epidemics Using Search Query Data" (shown by [21] and [5]), the results shown are promising as they could detect the occurrence of ILI epidemics in a given region in a relatively real-time manner with minimal error. Future work for this line of research will need to find ways of finding the optimal set of keywords/queries to use for predicting the occurrence of an ILI epidemic. Also work should be done to determine whether research done in one area of the world can be translated to another (e.g. could the results found from Ginsburg et al. [21] translate to China's region or visa-versa), or across different languages or different areas with the same language.

For the "Tracking Epidemics Using Twitter Post Data" subsection (covered by [22] and [23]), we see that Twitter data can be quite useful for detecting or even tracking ILI epidemics. In the future there should be more work on developing methods to best determine what keywords to use for study (filtering methods), as well as testing more text classification methods in order to reduce the noisy tweets in the collected datasets. More research should also be concentrated on determining the best model for using Twitter post data to predict the CDC's percentage of ILI related visits, as according to [22] this is one of the ways the CDC monitors ILI epidemics and Twitter is quite highly correlated to this statistic. This line of research, with the promising results shown, could be possibly one day help create a system that could continually track Twitter posts in order to create a worldwide ILI epidemic map in real time, helping people and the health care systems stay one step ahead. Also, this leads one to wonder what else Twitter data can be used to determine for the health care system.

Covering translational bioinformatics

As discussed by reviews and editorials by [1,69,70], and [71], the way forward for TBI and Health Informatics as a whole is for the translational approach to increasingly envelop the entire scope of Health Informatics and continue to combine data from all levels of human existence (as diseases and ailments handled by the healthcare system are very complex). Through this combination, questions throughout all levels can be more precisely answered and results can be validated both more quickly and more accurately. All future work in Health Informatics should look to take the translational approach shown by TBI, not just focusing on combining the molecular level with the other levels, but attempting to make connections across as many levels of data as possible. This combination of data would offer Big Volume, Velocity, Variety, Veracity, and, of course, Value, which could provide an unprecedented degree of medical knowledge gain.

Conclusion

This survey discussed a number of recent studies being done within the most popular sub branches of Health Informatics, using Big Data from all accessible levels of human existence to answer questions throughout all levels. Analyzing Big Data of this scope has only been possible extremely recently, due to the increasing capability of both computational resources and the algorithms which take advantage of these resources. Research on using these tools and techniques for Health Informatics is critical, because this domain requires a great deal of testing and confirmation before new techniques can be applied for making real world decisions across all levels. The fact that computational power has reached the ability to handle Big Data through efficient algorithms (as well as hardware advances, of course) lets data mining handle the Big Volume, Velocity, Variety, Veracity, and Value of the data generated by Health Informatics (traditional or otherwise). The use of Big Data provides advantages to Health Informatics by allowing for more tests cases or more features for research, leading to both quicker validation of studies and the ability to accrue enough instances for training when only a small fraction of instances exist within the positive class. The way forward for Health Informatics is definitely exploiting the Big Data created throughout all the various levels of medical data and finding ways to best analyze, mine and answer as many medical questions as possible.

As mentioned, the overall goal of answering any medical question, whether it be on the level of human-scale biology, clinical itself, or population, is to eventually improve healthcare for patients. The human body is a compound and complex system, containing many levels (not all of which may even be accessible as of now). Therefore, research needs to be done on data at all of these levels in order to answer the ever-growing list of medical questions on all of these levels. The studies covered here seek to answer questions on all four levels from data through analysis of data from the molecular, tissue, patient, and population levels.

TBI has the scope to use all these data levels with the goal of answering clinical questions, but this objective could benefit from not just attempting to answer clinical questions but questions on all levels. Perhaps future research in TBI and Health Informatics overall could focus on using data from all levels in order to find correlations and connections between them, possibly giving physicians more ways of diagnosing, treating, and helping their patients. All future work in Health Informatics should have a translational approach of using data from all levels of human existence.

All of the techniques discussed here show promise, provide inspiration for future work, and show the importance of using all accessible levels of data in Health Informatics. Each of the techniques presented in these studies can be both expanded and further tested using datasets with Big Volume and Variety (potentially on data from other levels) to see if their results are the same through different populations.

These studies are only a taste of the future possibilities that could be achieved through data mining and analysis of Big Data for Health Informatics. As computational power increases, more efficient and accurate methods will be developed. This could lead to possibly new levels of human existence becoming available for analysis, such as below the level of molecular data (e.g. the atomic scale) where the data gathered from each patient would be Really Big Data (RBD). Who knows, maybe a missing electron in a given chromosome could indicate a patient will be susceptible to cancer.

Even with the research discussed here and even with the promising results shown, it is up to future research to improve medical knowledge and create more advanced methods, as well as the readiness of the healthcare field to accept and apply these findings and techniques to improve HCO.

Competing interests

The authors declare that they have no competing interests.

Authors' contributions

MH performed the primary literature review and analysis for this work, and also drafted the manuscript. RW worked with MH to develop the article's framework and focus. TMK introduced this topic to MH and RW, and coordinated the other authors to complete and finalize this work. All authors read and approved the final manuscript.

References

1. Chen J, Qian F, Yan W, Shen B (2013) Translational biomedical informatics in the cloud: present and future. BioMed Res Int 2013: 8. [http://dx.doi.org/10.1155/2013/658925]
2. Martin M (2013) Big Cdata/social media combo poised to advance healthcare. HPC Source: 33–35. http://www.scientificcomputing.com/digital-editions/2013/04/hpc-source-big-data-beyond

3. Demchenko Y, Zhao Z, Grosso P, Wibisono A, de Laat C (2012) Addressing Big Data Challenges for Scientific Data Infrastructure In: IEEE 4th International Conference on Cloud Computing Technology and Science (CloudCom 2012). IEEE Computing Society, based in California, USA, Taipei, Taiwan, pp 614–617

4. Huan JL, Pai V, Teredesai AM, Yu S(Eds) (2013) IEEE Workshop on BigData In Bioinformatics and Health Care Informatics. http://www.ittc.ku.edu/~jhuan/BBH/

5. Yuan Q, Nsoesie EO, Lv B, Peng G, Chunara R, Brownstein JS (2013) Monitoring influenza epidemics in China with search query from Baidu. PLoS ONE 8(5): e64323. [doi: 10.1371/journal.pone.0064323]

6. Haferlach T, Kohlmann A, Wieczorek L, Basso G, Kronnie GT, Béné MC, De Vos J, Hernández JM, Hofmann WK, Mills KI, Gilkes A, Chiaretti S, Shurtleff SA, Kipps TJ, Rassenti LZ, Yeoh AE, Papenhausen PR, Wm Liu, Williams PM, Fo R (2010) Clinical utility of microarray-based gene expression profiling in the diagnosis and subclassification of leukemia: report from the international microarray innovations in leukemia study group. J Clin Oncol 28(15): 2529–2537. [http://jco.ascopubs.org/content/28/15/2529.abstract]

7. Salazar R, Roepman P, Capella G, Moreno V, Simon I, Dreezen C, Lopez-Doriga A, Santos C, Marijnen C, Westerga J, Bruin S, Kerr D, Kuppen P, van de Velde C, Morreau H, Van Velthuysen L, Glas AM, Van't Veer LJ, Tollenaar R (2011) Gene expression signature to improve prognosis prediction of stage II and III colorectal cancer. J Clin Oncol 29: 17–24. [http://jco.ascopubs.org/content/29/1/17.abstract]

8. Annese J (2012) The importance of combining MRI and large-scale digital histology in neuroimaging studies of brain connectivity and disease. Front Neuroinform 6: 13. [http://europepmc.org/abstract/MED/22536182]

9. Van Essen DC, Smith SM, Barch DM, Behrens TE, Yacoub E, Ugurbil K (2013) The WU-Minn human connectome project: an overview. NeuroImage 80(0): 62–79. [http://www.sciencedirect.com/science/article/pii/S1053811913005351]. [Mapping the Connectome]

10. Yoshida H, Kawaguchi A, Tsuruya K (2013) Radial basis function-sparse partial least squares for application to brain imaging data. Comput Math Methods Med 2013: 7. [http://dx.doi.org/10.1155/2013/591032]

11. Estella F, Delgado-Marquez BL, Rojas P, Valenzuela O, San Roman B, Rojas I (2012) Advanced system for automously classify brain MRI in neurodegenerative disease In: International Conference on Multimedia Computing and Systems (ICMCS 2012). IEEE, based in New York, USA, Tangiers, Morocco, pp 250–255

12. Campbell AJ, Cook JA, Adey G, Cuthbertson BH (2008) Predicting death and readmission after intensive care discharge. British J Anaesth 100(5): 656–662. [http://europepmc.org/abstract/MED/18385264]

13. Fialho AS, Cismondi F, Vieira SM, Reti SR, Sousa JMC, Finkelstein SN (2012) Data mining using clinical physiology at discharge to predict ICU readmissions. Expert Syst Appl 39(18): 13158–13165. [http://www.sciencedirect.com/science/article/pii/S0957417412008020]

14. Ouanes I, Schwebel C, Franais A, Bruel C, Philippart F, Vesin A, Soufir L, Adrie C, Garrouste-Orgeas M, Timsit JF, Misset B (2012) A model to predict short-term death or readmission after intensive care unit discharge. J Crit Care 27(4): 422.e1–422.e9. [http://www.sciencedirect.com/science/article/pii/S0883944111003790]

15. Mathias JS, Agrawal A, Feinglass J, Cooper AJ, Baker DW, Choudhary A (2013) Development of a 5 year life expectancy index in older adults using predictive mining of electronic health record data. J Am Med Inform Assoc 20(e1): e118–e124. [http://jamia.bmj.com/content/20/e1/e118.abstract]

16. Ballard C, Foster K, Frenkiel A, Gedik B, Koranda MP, Nathan S, Rajan D, Rea R, Spicer M, Williams B, Zoubov VN (2011) IBM Infosphere Streams: Assembling Continuous Insight in the Information Revolution. [http://www.redbooks.ibm.com/abstracts/sg.pages=247970html]

17. Zhang Y, Fong S, Fiaidhi J, Mohammed S (2012) Real-time clinical decision support system with data stream mining. J Biomed Biotechnol 2012: 8. [http://dx.doi.org/10.1155/2012/580186]

18. Thommandram A, Pugh JE, Eklund JM, McGregor C, James AG (2013) Classifying neonatal spells using real-time temporal analysis of physiological data streams: Algorithm development In: IEEE Point-of-Care Healthcare Technologies (PHT 2013). IEEE, based in New York, USA, Bangalore, India, pp 240–243

19. Ashish N, Biswas A, Das S, Nag S, Pratap R (2012) The Abzooba smart health informatics platform (SHIP)™– from patient experiences to big data to insights. CoRR abs/1203.3764: 1–3

20. Rolia J, Yao W, Basu S, Lee WN, Singhal S, Kumar A, Sabella S (2013) Tell me what i don't know - making the most of social health forums. Tech. Rep: HPL-2013–43. Hewlett Packard Labs [https://www.hpl.hp.com/techreports/2013/HPL-2013-43.pdf]

21. Ginsberg J, Mohebbi MH, Patel RS, Brammer L, Smolinski MS, Brilliant L (2009) Detecting influenza epidemics using search engine query data. Nature 457(7232): 1012–1014. [http://dx.doi.org/10.1038/nature07634]

22. Achrekar H, Gandhe A, Lazarus R, Yu SH, Liu B (2012) Twitter improves seasonal influenza prediction In: International Conference on Health Informatics (HEALTHINF'12). Nature Publishing Group, based in London, UK, Vilamoura, Portugal, pp 61–70

23. Signorini A, Segre AM, Polgreen PM (2011) The use of twitter to track levels of disease activity and public concern in the U.S. during the influenza A H1N1 pandemic. PLoS ONE 6(5): e19467. doi:10.1371/journal.pone.0019467

24. McDonald E, Brown CT (2013) khmer: Working with big data in Bioinformatics. CoRR abs/1303.2223: 1–18

25. Bennett C, Doub T (2011) Data mining and electronic health records: selecting optimal clinical treatments in practice. CoRR abs/1112: 1668

26. Ertl P (2003) Cheminformatics analysis of organic substituents: identification of the most common substituents, calculation of substituent properties, and automatic identification of drug-like bioisosteric groups. J Chem Inform Comput Sci 43(2): 374–38. [http://pubs.acs.org/doi/abs/10.1021/ci0255782]. [PMID: 12653499].

27. Zhang J, Chung TDY, Oldenburg KR (1999) Validation of high throughput screening assays. J Biomolecular Screening 4(2): 67–73

28. Tamura K, Dudley J, Nei M, Kumar S (2007) MEGA4: Molecular evolutionary genetics analysis (MEGA) Software version 4.0. Mol Biol Evol 24(8): 1596–1599. [http://mbe.oxfordjournals.org/content/24/8/1596.abstract]

29. Liu W, Li R, Sun JZ, Wang J, Tsai J, Wen W, Kohlmann A, Williams PM (2006) PQN and DQN: Algorithms for expression microarrays. J Theor Biol 243(2): 273–278. [http://www.sciencedirect.com/science/article/pii/S0022519306002530]

30. Bennett KP, Campbell C (2000) Support vector machines: hype or hallelujah SIGKDD Explor Newslett 2(2): 1–13. [http://doi.acm.org/10.1145/380995.380999]

31. Glas A, Floore A, Delahaye L, Witteveen A, Pover R, Bakx N, Lahti-Domenici J, Bruinsma T, Warmoes M, Bernards R, Wessels L, Van 't Veer L (2006) Converting a breast cancer microarray signature into a high-throughput diagnostic test. BMC Genomics 7: 278. [http://www.biomedcentral.com/1471-2164/7/278]

32. Knaus WA, Draper EA, Wagner DP, Zimmerman JE (1985) APACHE II: A severity of disease classification system. Crit Care Med 00003246-198510000-00009 13(10): 818–829. [http://journals.lww.com/ccmjournal/Fulltext/1985/10000/APACHE_II__A_severity_of_disease_classification.9.aspx]

33. Le Gall J, Lemeshow S, Saulnier F (1993) A new simplified acute physiology score (SAPS II) based on a European/North American multicenter study. JAMA 270(24): 2957–2963. [http://dx.doi.org/10.1001/jama.1993.03510240069035]

34. Keene AR, Cullen DJ (1983) Therapeutic intervention scoring system: Update 1983. Crit Care Med 00003246-198301000-00001 11: 1–3. [http://journals.lww.com/ccmjournal/Fulltext/1983/01000/Therapeutic_Intervention_Scoring_System__Update.1.aspx]

35. Hosmer DW, Lemesbow S (1980) Goodness of fit tests for the multiple logistic regression model. Commun Stat - Theory Methods 9(10): 1043–1069. [http://www.tandfonline.com/doi/abs/10.1080/03610928008827941]

36. Bradley AP (1997) The use of the area under the ROC curve in the evaluation of machine learning algorithms. Pattern Recognit 30(7): 1145–1159. [http://www.sciencedirect.com/science/article/pii/S0031320396001422]

37. Akaike H (1974) A new look at the statistical model identification. IEEE Trans Automatic Control 19(6): 716–723

38. Gajic O, Malinchoc M, Comfere TB, Harris MR, Achouiti A, Yilmaz M, Schultz MJ, Hubmayr RD, Afessa B, Farmer JC (2008) The stability and workload index for transfer score predicts unplanned intensive care unit patient readmission: initial development and validation *. Crit Care Med 36(3): 676–682. [http://journals.lww.com/ccmjournal/Fulltext/2008/03000/The_Stability_and_Workload_Index_for_Transfer.2.aspx]

39. Saeed M, Lieu C, Raber G, Mark R (2002) MIMIC II: a massive temporal ICU patient database to support research in intelligent patient monitoring In: Computers in Cardiology. IEEE Computer Society, based in California, USA, Memphis, Tennesee, USA, pp 641–644

40. Mendonça LF, Vieira SM, Sousa JMC (2007) Decision tree search methods in fuzzy modeling and classification. Int J Approximate Reason 44(2): 106–123. [http://www.sciencedirect.com/science/article/pii/S0888613X06000843]. [Fuzzy Decision-Making Applications]

41. Takagi T, Sugeno M (1985) Fuzzy identification of systems and its applications to modeling and control. IEEE Trans Syst Man Cybernet SMC-15: 116–132

42. Knaus WA, Wagner DP, Draper EA, Zimmerman JE, Bergner M, Bastos PG, Sirio CA, Murphy DJ, Lotring T, Damiano A (1991) The APACHE III prognostic system. risk prediction of hospital mortality for critically ill hospitalized adults. CHEST Journal 100(6): 1619–1636. [http://dx.doi.org/10.1378/chest.100.6.1619]

43. Hall M (1997) Correlation-based feature selection for machine learning. PhD thesis. The University of Waikato, Hamilton, New Zealand

44. Rodriguez JJ, Kuncheva LI, Alonso CJ (2006) Rotation forest: a new classifier ensemble method. IEEE Trans Pattern Anal Mach Intell 28(10): 1619–1630

45. Freund Y, Mason L (1999) The alternating decision tree learning algorithm In: Proceedings of the Sixteenth International Conference on Machine Learning, ICML '99. Morgan Kaufmann Publishers Inc, San Francisco, CA, USA, pp 124–133. [http://dl.acm.org/citation.cfm?id=.pages=645528657623]

46. Perkins AJ, Kroenke K, Unützer J, Katon W, Williams JW, Hope C, Callahan CM (2004) Common comorbidity scales were similar in their ability to predict health care costs and mortality. J Clin Epidemiol 57(10): 1040–1048. [http://www.sciencedirect.com/science/article/pii/S0895435604000812]

47. Walter LC, Covinsky KE (2001) Cancer screening in elderly patients: A framework for individualized decision making. JAMA 285(21): 2750–2756. [http://dx.doi.org/10.1001/jama.285.21.2750]

48. Domingos P, Hulten G (2000) Mining high-speed data streams In: Proceedings of the Sixth ACM SIGKDD International Conference on Knowledge Discovery and Data Mining, KDD '00. ACM, New York, NY, USA, pp 71–80. [http://doi.acm.org/10.1145/347090.347107]

49. Achananuparp P, Hu X, Shen X (2008) The evaluation of sentence similarity measures. In: Song IY, Eder J, Nguyen T (eds) Data Warehousing and, Knowledge Discovery, Volume 5182 of Lecture Notes in Computer Science. Springer Berlin, Heidelberg, pp 305–316. [http://dx.doi.org/10.1007/978-3-540-85836-2_29]

50. Thiagarajan R, Manjunath G, Stumptne M (2008) Computing semantic similarity using Ontologies. Tech. Rep.: HPL-2008-87. Hewlett Packard Labs [http://www.hpl.hp.com/techreports/2008/HPL-2008-87.pdf]

51. Sun J, Sow D, Hu J, Ebadollahi S (2010) A system for mining temporal physiological data streams for advanced prognostic decision support In: IEEE 10th International Conference on Data Mining (ICDM 2010), pp 1061–1066. doi:10.1109/ICDM.2010.102

52. Hay SI, George DB, Moyes CL, Brownstein JS (2013) Big data opportunities for global infectious disease surveillance. PLoS Med 10(4): e1001413. doi:10.1371/journal.pmed.1001413

53. Ashish N, Mehrotra S (2009) XAR An integrated framework for semantic extraction and annotation. In: Kalfoglou Y, IGI Global (eds) Cases on Semantic Interoperability for Information Systems Integration: Practices and Applications, Hershey, PA, USA, pp 235–254. [http://services.igi-global.com/resolvedoi/resolve.aspx?doi=10.4018/978-1-60566-894-9.ch011]

54. Bodenreider O (2004) The Unified Medical Language System (UMLS): integrating biomedical terminology. Nucleic Acids Res 32(suppl 1): D267–270. [http://nar.oxfordjournals.org/content/32/suppl_1/D267.abstract]

55. Hall MA, Frank E, Holmes G, Pfahringer B, Reutemann P, Witten IH (2009) The WEKA data mining software: An update. SIGKDD Explor Newslett 11: 10–18

56. The Apache Software Foundation (2013) Apache Lucene. [http://lucene.apache.org/]. [Accessed: 2013-9-18]

57. OSI Pharmaceuticals (2013) Tarceva®(erlotinib) tablets advanced-stage non-small cell lung cancer treatment possible risks and side effects. [http://www.tarceva.com/patient/considering/effects.jsp]. [Accessed: 2013-9-18]

58. Centers for Disease Control and Prevention (2012) Diabetes report card 2012. Tech. rep. Centers for Disease Control and Prevention, US Department of Health and Human Services, Atlanta, GA. [http://www.cdc.gov/diabetes/pubs/pdf/diabetesreportcard.pdf]

59. National Institute for HealthandCareExcellence (2013) NICE pathways. [http://pathways.nice.org.uk/]. [Accessed: 2013-9-18]

60. Boehm EA (2001) The contribution of economic indicator analysis to understanding and forecasting business cycles. Ind Econ Rev 36: 1–36. [http://www.jstor.org/stable/29794223]

61. Moore GH, Shiskin I (1967) Indicators of Business Expansions and Contractions. National Bureau of, Economic Research. [http://papers.nber.org/books/moor67-2]

62. Liu Y, Lv B, Peng G, Yuan Q (2012) A preprocessing method of internet search data for prediction improvement: application to Chinese stock market In: Proceedings of the Data Mining and Intelligent Knowledge Management Workshop, DM-IKM '12. ACM, New York, NY, USA, pp 3:1–3:7. [http://doi.acm.org/10.1145/2462130.2462133]

63. Statistic Brain ResearchInstitute publishing as Statistic Brain (2013) Twitter statistics – statistic brain. [http://www.statisticbrain.com/twitter-statistics/]. [Accessed: 2013-9-18]

64. Twitter Inc (2013) The streaming APIs. [https://dev.twitter.com/docs/streaming-apis]. [Accessed: 2013-9-18]

65. van Rijsbergen CJ, Robertson SE, Porter MF (1980) New Models in Probabilistic Information Retrieval. British Library research & development reports, Computer Laboratory, University of Cambridge. [http://books.google.com/books?id=WDZ3bwAACAAJ]

66. Drucker H, Burges CJC, Kaufman L, Smola A, Vapnik V (1997) Support vector regression machines. In: Mozer MC, Jordan MI, Petsche T (eds) Advances in neural information processing systems. MIT Press, Cambridge, MA, pp 155–161

67. Doan S, Ohno-Machado L, Collier N (2012) Enhancing twitter data analysis with simple semantic filtering: example in tracking influenza-like illnesses. IEEE Computing Society, based in California, USA, La Jolla, California, USA

68. American Medical Informatics Association (2013) Translational Bioinformatics. [http://www.amia.org/applications-informatics/translational-bioinformatics]. [Accessed: 2013-9-18]

69. Sarkar IN, Butte AJ, Lussier YA, Tarczy-Hornoch P, Ohno-Machado L (2011) Translational bioinformatics: linking knowledge across biological and clinical realms. J Am Med Inform Assoc 18(4): 354–357. [http://jamia.bmj.com/content/18/4/354.abstract]

70. Butte AJ, Shah NH (2011) Computationally translating molecular discoveries into tools for medicine: translational bioinformatics articles now featured in JAMIA. J Am Med Inform Assoc 18(4): 352–353. [http://jamia.bmj.com/content/18/4/352.short]

71. Shah NH, Tenenbaum JD (2012) The coming age of data-driven medicine: translational bioinformatics' next frontier. J Am Med Inform Assoc 19(e1): e2–e4. [http://jamia.bmj.com/content/19/e1/e2.short]

72. Liu M, Wu Y, Chen Y, Sun J, Zhao Z, Xw Chen, Matheny ME, Xu H (2012) Large-scale prediction of adverse drug reactions using chemical, biological, and phenotypic properties of drugs. J Am Med Inform Assoc 19(e1): e28–e35. [http://jamia.bmj.com/content/19/e1/e28.abstract]

Permissions

All chapters in this book were first published in JBD, by Springer; hereby published with permission under the Creative Commons Attribution License or equivalent. Every chapter published in this book has been scrutinized by our experts. Their significance has been extensively debated. The topics covered herein carry significant findings which will fuel the growth of the discipline. They may even be implemented as practical applications or may be referred to as a beginning point for another development.

The contributors of this book come from diverse backgrounds, making this book a truly international effort. This book will bring forth new frontiers with its revolutionizing research information and detailed analysis of the nascent developments around the world.

We would like to thank all the contributing authors for lending their expertise to make the book truly unique. They have played a crucial role in the development of this book. Without their invaluable contributions this book wouldn't have been possible. They have made vital efforts to compile up to date information on the varied aspects of this subject to make this book a valuable addition to the collection of many professionals and students.

This book was conceptualized with the vision of imparting up-to-date information and advanced data in this field. To ensure the same, a matchless editorial board was set up. Every individual on the board went through rigorous rounds of assessment to prove their worth. After which they invested a large part of their time researching and compiling the most relevant data for our readers.

The editorial board has been involved in producing this book since its inception. They have spent rigorous hours researching and exploring the diverse topics which have resulted in the successful publishing of this book. They have passed on their knowledge of decades through this book. To expedite this challenging task, the publisher supported the team at every step. A small team of assistant editors was also appointed to further simplify the editing procedure and attain best results for the readers.

Apart from the editorial board, the designing team has also invested a significant amount of their time in understanding the subject and creating the most relevant covers. They scrutinized every image to scout for the most suitable representation of the subject and create an appropriate cover for the book.

The publishing team has been an ardent support to the editorial, designing and production team. Their endless efforts to recruit the best for this project, has resulted in the accomplishment of this book. They are a veteran in the field of academics and their pool of knowledge is as vast as their experience in printing. Their expertise and guidance has proved useful at every step. Their uncompromising quality standards have made this book an exceptional effort. Their encouragement from time to time has been an inspiration for everyone.

The publisher and the editorial board hope that this book will prove to be a valuable piece of knowledge for researchers, students, practitioners and scholars across the globe.

List of Contributors

Arantxa Duque Barrachina
VMware, Inc, Cork, Ireland

Aisling O'Driscoll
Department of Computing, Cork Institute of Technology, Cork, Ireland

Chris A Mattmann
Jet Propulsion Laboratory, California Institute of Technology, 4800 Oak Grove Drive M/S 171-264, 91109 Pasadena, USA
Computer Science Department, University of Southern California, 941 W. 37th Place, 90089 Los Angeles, USA

Jose Berengueres
UAE University, 17551 Al Ain, Abu Dhabi, UAE

Dmitry Efimov
Moscow State University, Leninskie gori 1, 117234, Moscow

Richard Zuech
Florida Atlantic University, 777 Glades Road, Boca Raton, FL, USA

Taghi M Khoshgoftaar
Florida Atlantic University, 777 Glades Road, Boca Raton, FL, USA

Randall Wald
Florida Atlantic University, 777 Glades Road, Boca Raton, FL, USA

Dilpreet Singh
Department of Computer Science, Wayne State University, Detroit, MI 48202, USA

Chandan K Reddy
Department of Computer Science, Wayne State University, Detroit, MI 48202, USA

Michael A Hayes
Department of Electrical and Computer Engineering, Western University, London, Canada

Miriam AM Capretz
Department of Electrical and Computer Engineering, Western University, London, Canada

Yun Lu
School of Computing and Information Sciences, Florida International University, Miami, FL 33199, USA

Ming Zhao
School of Computing and Information Sciences, Florida International University, Miami, FL 33199, USA

Lixi Wang
School of Computing and Information Sciences, Florida International University, Miami, FL 33199, USA

Naphtali Rishe
School of Computing and Information Sciences, Florida International University, Miami, FL 33199, USA

Anand Kumar
Department of Computer Science and Engineering, University of South Florida, 4202 E. Fowler Ave., ENB118, 33620 Tampa, Florida, USA

Vladimir Grupcev
Department of Computer Science and Engineering, University of South Florida, 4202 E. Fowler Ave., ENB118, 33620 Tampa, Florida, USA

Meryem Berrada
Department of Computer Science and Engineering, University of South Florida, 4202 E. Fowler Ave., ENB118, 33620 Tampa, Florida, USA

Joseph C Fogarty
Department of Physics, University of South Florida, 4202 E. Fowler Ave., PHY114, 33620 Tampa, Florida, USA

Yi-Cheng Tu
Department of Computer Science and Engineering, University of South Florida, 4202 E. Fowler Ave., ENB118, 33620 Tampa, Florida, USA

Xingquan Zhu
Department of Electrical Engineering and Computer Science, Florida Atlantic University, 777 Glades Road, EE308, 33431 Boca Raton, Florida, USA

Sagar A Pandit
Department of Physics, University of South Florida, 4202 E. Fowler Ave., PHY114, 33620 Tampa, Florida, USA

Yuni Xia
Department of Computer Science, Indiana University - Purdue University Indianapolis, 723 W. Michigan St, SL280E, 46202 Indianapolis, Indiana, USA

Maryam M Najafabadi
Florida Atlantic University, 777 Glades Road, Boca Raton, FL, USA

Flavio Villanustre
LexisNexis Business Information Solutions, 245 Peachtree Center Avenue, Atlanta, GA, USA

Taghi M Khoshgoftaar
Florida Atlantic University, 777 Glades Road, Boca Raton, FL, USA

Naeem Seliya
Florida Atlantic University, 777 Glades Road, Boca Raton, FL, USA

Randall Wald
Florida Atlantic University, 777 Glades Road, Boca Raton, FL, USA

Edin Muharemagic
LexisNexis Business Information Solutions, 6601 Park of Commerce Blvd, Boca Raton, FL, USA

Wenyu Zang
Institute of Computing Technology, Chinese Academy of Science, South Road of Chinese Academy of Science, Beijing, China
Institute of Information Engineering, Chinese Academy of Science, MinZhuang Road, Beijing, China

Peng Zhang
Institute of Information Engineering, Chinese Academy of Science, MinZhuang Road, Beijing, China

Chuan Zhou
Institute of Information Engineering, Chinese Academy of Science, MinZhuang Road, Beijing, China

Li Guo
Institute of Information Engineering, Chinese Academy of Science, MinZhuang Road, Beijing, China

Nemanja Trifunovic
School of Electrical Engineering, University of Belgrade, Belgrade, Serbia

Veljko Milutinovic
School of Electrical Engineering, University of Belgrade, Belgrade, Serbia

Jakob Salom
Mathematical Institute of the Serbian Academy of Sciences and Arts, Belgrade, Serbia

Anton Kos
School of Electrical Engineering, University of Ljubljana, Ljubljana, Slovenia

Matthew Herland
Florida Atlantic University, 777 Glades Road, Boca Raton, FL, USA

Taghi M Khoshgoftaar
Florida Atlantic University, 777 Glades Road, Boca Raton, FL, USA

Randall Wald
Florida Atlantic University, 777 Glades Road, Boca Raton, FL, USA